"This book scores the highest marks for presentation and content. A well-written text is always a pleasure to have and study. I have always found Sybex study guides excellent when preparing for an exam and later as reference material. The *Network+ Study Guide* is ranked one of my top ten choices. After reading this text once, I was able to fill in all the areas that I needed to brush up on before writing this exam and achieved a 91% on the test. I am a Microsoft instructor and I will recommend this book to all my students that are seeking the certification."

A Reader From Fatbrain.com

"This book is all you will need for the Network+ test. I had no knowledge of networking when I read this book. I read the book from cover to cover 3 times within a 2 month time period and scored a 94% on the test. The author (David Groth) knows what he is talking about!"

A Reader From Amazon.com

"Excellent study and resource guide! Thank you for writing this excellent study guide. It was well written and will be a valuable resource guide to me in the future. I passed my Network+ certification exam with flying colors thanks to you."

Bob Davis, Walla Walla, Washington
A Reader From Fatbrain.com

"This is an essential study text for someone who wishes to understand what networking and network administration is all about. It covers a variety of requisite topics needed to understand and pass the exam, especially for those without network experience. Since certification is the bottom line, I strongly recommend that this text is good and be used along with Sybex's *TCP/IP 24seven*…an added tool and advantage to pass the exam first time with deep understanding."

Richard and Bola Opanuga, Maryland
Readers From Bookpool.com

OBJECTIVE	CHAPTER

Network Layer

Explain the following routing and Network layer concepts, including: 2

> The fact that routing occurs at the Network layer; The difference between a router and a brouter; The difference between routable and nonroutable protocols; The concept of default gateways and subnetworks; The reason for employing unique network IDs; The difference between static and dynamic routing

Transport Layer

Explain the following Transport layer concepts: 2

> The distinction between connectionless and connection transport; The purpose of name resolution, either to an IP/IPX address or a network protocol

TCP/IP Fundamentals

Demonstrate knowledge of the following TCP/IP fundamentals: 4

> The concept of IP default gateways; The purpose and use of DHCP, DNS, WINS, and host files; The identity of the main protocols that make up the TCP/IP suite, including TCP, UDP, POP3, SMTP, SNMP, FTP, HTTP, and IP; The idea that TCP/IP is supported by every operating system and millions of hosts worldwide; The purpose and function of Internet domain name server hierarchies (how e-mail arrives in another country)

Demonstrate knowledge of the fundamental concepts of TCP/IP addressing, including: 4

> The A, B, and C classes of IP addresses and their default subnet mask numbers; The use of port number (HTTP, FTP, SMTP) and port numbers commonly assigned to a given service

Demonstrate knowledge of TCP/IP configuration concepts, including: 4

> The definition of IP proxy and why it is used; The identity of the normal configuration parameters for a workstation, including IP address, DNS, default gateway, IP proxy configuration, WINS, DHCP, host name, and Internet domain name

TCP/IP Suite: Utilities

Explain how and when to use the following TCP/IP utilities to test, validate, and troubleshoot IP connectivity: 5

> ARP; Telnet; nbtstat; tracert; netstat; ipconfig/winipcfg; FTP; Ping

Remote Connectivity

Explain the following remote connectivity concepts: 7

> The distinction between PPP and SLIP; The purpose and function of PPTP and the conditions under which it is useful; The attributes, advantages, and disadvantages of ISDN and PSTN (POTS)

Specify the following elements of dial-up networking: 7

> The modem configuration parameters that must be set, including serial port IRQ, I/O address, and maximum port speed; The requirements for a remote connection

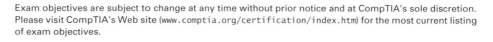
Exam objectives are subject to change at any time without prior notice and at CompTIA's sole discretion. Please visit CompTIA's Web site (www.comptia.org/certification/index.htm) for the most current listing of exam objectives.

SYBEX

OBJECTIVE	CHAPTER
Security	
Identify good practices to ensure network security, including:	8
Selection of a security model (user and share level); Standard password practices and procedures; The need to employ data encryption to protect network data; The use of a firewall	

Knowledge of Networking Practices

OBJECTIVE	CHAPTER
Implementing the Installation of the Network	
Demonstrate awareness that administrative and test accounts, passwords, IP addresses, IP configurations, relevant SOPs, and so on must be obtained prior to network implementation.	6
Explain the impact of environmental factors on computer networks. Given a network installation scenario, identify unexpected or atypical conditions that could either cause problems for the network or signify that a problem already exists, including:	6
Room conditions (for example, humidity, heat, and so on); The placement of building contents and personal effects (for example, space heaters, TVs, and radios); Computer equipment; Error messages	
Recognize visually or by description common peripheral ports, external SCSI (especially DB-25 connectors), and common network componentry, including:	6
Print servers; Peripherals; Hubs; Routers; Brouters; Bridges; Patch panels; UPSs, NICs, Token ring media filters	
Given an installation scenario, demonstrate awareness of the following compatibility and cabling issues:	6
The consequences of trying to install an analog modem in a digital jack; That the uses of RJ-45 connectors may differ greatly depending on the cabling; That patch cables contribute to the overall length of the cabling segment	
Maintaining and Supporting the Network	
Identify the kinds of test documentation that are usually available regarding a vendor's patches, fixes, upgrades, and so on.	6
Identify the kinds of test documentation that are usually available regarding a vendor's patches, fixes, upgrades, and so on.	9
Given a network maintenance scenario, demonstrate awareness of the following issues:	9
Standard backup procedures and backup media storage practices; The need for periodic applications of software patches and other fixes to the network; The need to install antivirus software on the server and workstations; The need to frequently update virus signatures	

SYBEX

Network+ Study Guide

Knowledge of Networking Technology

OBJECTIVE	CHAPTER
Basic Knowledge	
Demonstrate understanding of basic network structure, including:	1
The characteristics of star, bus, mesh, and ring topologies, their advantages and disadvantages; The characteristics of segments and backbones	
Identify the following:	3
The major network operating systems, including Microsoft Windows NT, Novell NetWare, and Unix; The clients that best serve specific network operating systems and their resources; The directory services of the major network operating systems	
Associate IPX, IP, and NetBEUI with their functions	4
Define the following terms and explain how each relates to fault tolerance or high availability:	9
Mirroring; Duplexing; Striping (with and without parity); Volumes; Tape backup	
Define the layers of the OSI model, and identify the protocols, services, and functions that pertain to each layer.	2
Recognize and describe the following characteristics of networking media and connectors:	1
The advantages and disadvantages of coax, Cat 3, Cat 5, fiber-optic, UTP, and STP and the conditions under which they are appropriate; The length and speed of 10Base2, 10BaseT, and 100BaseT; The length and speed of 10Base5, 100Base VGAnyLan, 100BaseTX; The visual appearance of RJ 45 and BNC and how they are crimped	
Identify the basic attributes, purpose, and function of the following network elements:	1
Full- and half-duplexing; WAN and LAN; Server, workstation, and host; Server-based networking and peer-to-peer networking; Cable, NIC, and router; Broadband and baseband; Gateway, as both a default IP router and as a method to connect dissimilar systems or protocols	
Physical Layer	
Given an installation, configuration, or troubleshooting scenario, select an appropriate course of action if a client workstation does not connect to the network after installing or replacing a network interface card. Explain why a given action is warranted. The following issues may be covered:	6
Knowledge of how the network card is usually configured, including EEPROM, jumpers, and Plug-and-Play software; Use of network card diagnostics, including the loopback test and vendor-supplied diagnostics; The ability to resolve hardware resource conflicts, including IRQ, DMA, and I/O base address	
Identify the use of the following network components and the differences between them:	2
Hubs; MAUs, Switching hubs; Repeaters; Transceivers	
Data Link Layer	
Describe the following Data Link layer concepts:	2
Bridges, what they are and why they are used; The 802 specs, including the topics covered in 802.2, 802.3, and 802.5; The function and characteristics of MAC addresses	

SYBEX

Troubleshooting the Network

Identify the following steps as a systematic approach to identifying the extent of a network problem, and given a problem scenario, select the appropriate next step based on this approach: 10

Determine whether the problem exists across the network; Determine whether the problem is workstation, workgroup, LAN, or WAN; Determine whether the problem is consistent and replicable; Use standard troubleshooting methods

Identify the following steps as a systematic approach for troubleshooting network problems, and, given a problem scenario, select the appropriate next step based on this approach: 10

Identify the exact issue; Re-create the problem; Isolate the cause; Formulate a correction; Implement the correction; Test; Document the problem and the solution; Give feedback

Identify the following steps as a systematic approach to determining whether a problem is attributable to the operator or the system, and, given a problem scenario, select the appropriate next step based on this approach: 10

Have a second operator perform the same task on an equivalent workstation; Have a second operator perform the same task on the original operator's workstation; See whether operators are following standard operating procedure

Given a network troubleshooting scenario, demonstrate awareness of the need to check for physical and logical indicators of trouble, including: 10

Link light; Power lights; Error displays; Error logs and displays; Performance monitors

Given a network problem scenario, including symptoms, determine the most likely cause or causes of the problem based on the available information. Select the most appropriate course of action based on this inference. Issues that may be covered include: 10

Recognizing abnormal physical conditions; Isolating and correcting problems in cases where there is a fault in the physical media (patch cable); Checking the status of servers; Checking for configuration problems with DNS, WINS, and HOST file; Checking for viruses; Checking the validity of the account name and password; Rechecking operator logon procedures; Selecting and running appropriate diagnostics

Specify the tools that are commonly used to resolve network equipment problems. Identify the purpose and function of common network tools, including: 10

Crossover cable; Hardware loopback; Tone generator; Tone locator (fox and hound)

SYBEX

Network+

Study Guide

Second Edition

Network+™
Study Guide
Second Edition

David Groth

San Francisco • Paris • Düsseldorf • Soest • London

Associate Publisher: Neil Edde
Contracts and Licensing Manager: Kristine O'Callaghan
Acquisitions and Developmental Editor: Elizabeth Hurley
Editors: Susan Hobbs, Pat Coleman
Production Editor: Shannon Murphy
Technical Editors: Robert Gradante, André Paree-Huff, Jutta VanStean
Contributors: Robert King, Jarret Buse
Book Designer: Bill Gibson
Graphic Illustrator: Tony Jonick
Electronic Publishing Specialist: Judy Fung
Proofreaders: Jennifer Campbell, Nanette Duffy, Laurie O'Connell
Indexer: Ted Laux
CD Coordinator: Kara Eve Schwartz
CD Technician: Kevin Ly
Cover Designer: Archer Design
Cover Photographer: Tony Stone Images

Library of Congress Card Number: 00-106426

ISBN: 0-7821-2863-7

SYBEX

To Our Valued Readers:

Over the past years, CompTIA's Network+ certification program has established itself as the premier general networking certification in the IT industry. Sybex is proud to have helped thousands of Network+ candidates prepare for their exam, and we are excited about the opportunity to continue to provide people with the skills they'll need to succeed in the highly competitive IT industry.

CompTIA recently made minor modifications to the exam objectives, expanded the question pool, and added drag-and-drop question formats, all in an effort to prevent the dreaded paper-certification syndrome, one in which individuals obtain a certification without a thorough understanding of the technology. Sybex supports this philosophy, as we have always advocated a comprehensive instructional approach to certification courseware. It has always been Sybex's mission to teach exam candidates how new technologies work in the real world, not to simply feed them answers to test questions. Sybex was founded on the premise of providing technical skills to IT professionals, and we have continued to build on that foundation, making significant improvements to our study guides based on feedback from readers, suggestions from instructors, and comments from industry leaders.

Our authors and editors have worked hard to ensure this new edition of the *Network+ Study Guide* is comprehensive, in-depth, and pedagogically sound. We're confident that this book will meet and exceed the demanding standards of the certification marketplace and help you, the Network+ exam candidate, succeed in your endeavors.

Good luck in pursuit of your Network+ certification!

Neil Edde
Associate Publisher—Certification
Sybex, Inc.

SYBEX Inc. 1151 Marina Village Parkway, Alameda, CA 94501
Tel: 510/523-8233   Fax: 510/523-2373   HTTP://www.sybex.com

To Linda and Alison.
Enjoy life. May you both be happy and healthy.

Acknowledgments

It takes many people to put a book together. First, I would like to thank my first edition coauthors, Ben Bergersen and Tim Catura-Houser (Tcat). We had fun at the Network+ exam writing sessions, and we had fun writing together. Ben is an MCSE, MCT, CNA, CTT, and A+ as well as being an IEE Computer Society member. He works at Monroe Community College in Rochester, New York.

Tim Catura-Houser, whom I also met at the Network+ exam writing session in Utah, is system engineer for Exam Cram Live. Some of you may have seen him on various chat groups as Tcat. He holds many certifications, including Microsoft's MCSE, MCT, and SP and IBM's PSE, as well as CTT, A+, and other certifications from Artisoft and Cisco. He and his wife live in the Puget Sound area and are fond of making their world-famous Seattle Super Salsa.

Thanks also to my technical editors—Jutta VanStean, Bob Gradante, and André Paree-Huff. Jutta VanStean, who tech edited the first edition of this book, is a CNE and MCNE. Jutta has been working in the IT industry for nine years in positions ranging from network administration to technical writing and curriculum design. During that time she earned the CNE 3, 4, and MCNE (Windows NT Integration track) certifications. She has authored and coauthored multiple networking training courses, and more recently has been working as a freelance writer. Bob Gradante and André Paree-Huff were the technical editors for this second edition of the *Network+ Study Guide*. Bob Gradante currently works as the technical training manager for New Horizons Computer Learning Center of Long Island. His certifications include MCSE+I (NT 4.0), MCSE (W2K), Network+, A+, CCNA, and MCT. He has been working in the IT industry since 1985. André Paree-Huff (CCNP, CCDA, MCSE+I, ASE, A+, Network+, I-Network+) has been working in the computer field for more than eight years. He is currently working for Compaq Computer Corporation as a Network Support Engineer level III for the North America Customer Support Center in Colorado Springs, Colorado. André handles troubleshooting of network hardware, specializing in Layers 2 and 3 of the OSI model. André has coauthored five network-related books and has been a technical editor on more than a dozen others. He is currently working toward his CCDE and CCIE.

This book would not exist if not for my developmental editor at Sybex, Elizabeth Hurley. Thank you for all the encouragement and support, as well as your hard work on this project. Additionally, thanks go out to Shannon Murphy for her work as production editor, Susan Hobbs for her work as editor, Judy Fung for her work as electronic publishing specialist, and Laurie O'Connell, Nanette Duffy, and Jennifer Campbell for their work as proofreaders.

I would also like to acknowledge my wife, family, and friends. My wife, Linda, tirelessly wrote and edited the appendices and kept me on the right track. She was a real trooper because she did it while watching our daughter, Alison, who can be a handful. Thank you to my family and friends who understood when I couldn't go out or help them with their projects because I had to work on the book. I really appreciate that.

Finally, thank you, the reader, for purchasing this book. I know that it has all the information in it to help you pass the test. If you have questions about Network+ or this book, feel free to e-mail me at dgroth@corpcomm.net. I can forward requests to the other authors. All three of us worked very hard on this book to make it the best Network+ study guide available. I hope you feel the same.

Contents at a Glance

Contents

Introduction

If you are like the rest of the networking community, you probably have many certifications. Certification is one of the best things you can do for your career in the computer or networking field. It proves that you know what you're talking about when it comes to the area in which you are certified.

In this book, you'll find out what the Network+ exam is all about. Each chapter covers a part of the exam. At the end of each chapter, there are review questions to help you prepare for the exam.

What Is the Network+ Certification?

Network+ is a certification developed by the Computing Technology Industry Association (CompTIA). This organization exists to provide resources and education for the computer and technology community. This is the same body that developed the A+ exam for computer technicians. In 1995, they convened to develop a new certification that tests skills for Information Technology (IT). It was sponsored by many IT industry leaders to ensure industry-wide support, including:

- Compaq Computers
- Digital Equipment Corporation (now a part of Compaq)
- IBM
- Lotus
- Microsoft
- Novell
- TSS
- U.S. Robotics
- US West
- Wave Technologies

The Network+ exam was designed to test the skills of network technicians with 18 to 24 months of experience in the field. It tests areas of networking technologies such as the definition of a protocol, the OSI (Open Systems

Interconnect) model and its layers, and the concepts of network design and implementation—such as which items are required for a network and the prerequisites for installation. In addition, it covers troubleshooting concepts and how-tos.

Why Become Network+ Certified?

The Network+ certification is a relatively new certification. But Network+ is the next certification in a line of CompTIA certifications, starting with the A+ Certification. Because CompTIA is a well-respected developer of industry vendor-neutral certifications, getting Network+ certified indicates that you are competent in the specific areas tested by Network+.

Three major benefits are associated with becoming Network+ certified:

- Proof of professional achievement
- Opportunity for advancement
- Fulfillment of training requirements

Proof of Professional Achievement

Networking professionals are competing these days to see who can get the most certifications. And technicians want the Network+ certification because it is broad, covering the entire field of networking, rather than only Microsoft or only Novell, for example. Thus, it can be a challenge to prepare for the Network+ exam. Passing the exam, however, certifies that you have achieved a certain level of knowledge about vendor-independent networking-related subjects.

Opportunity for Advancement

We all like to get ahead in our careers. With advancement comes more responsibility, to be sure, but usually it means more money and greater opportunities. In the information technology area, this usually can be accomplished by obtaining multiple technology certifications, including Network+.

Network+, because of its wide-reaching industry support, is recognized as a baseline of networking information. Some companies specify that Network+ certification will result in a pay raise at review time. And some companies specify that Network+ certification, in conjunction with A+

certification, is required before an employee's next review, or as a condition of employment.

Fulfillment of Training Requirements

A training requirement can be mandated by your employer, as we just mentioned, or it can be required as part of another certification. There has been talk of using the Network+ certification as a prerequisite to, or as part of, other vendors' certifications. It's a natural fit. For example, training for both the Novell and the Microsoft certification programs (CNE and MCSE) includes a course in the essential networking technologies. Because the Network+ exam covers network fundamentals and is vendor-neutral, it may be a good replacement for the Microsoft or the Novell exam.

How to Become Network+ Certified

The simplest way to find out how to become Network+ certified is to take the exam. It is administered by Prometric, with which most of you are familiar if you have taken any other computer certification exams. It is administered by computer. To register to take the exam, call Prometric (not the testing center) at 888-895-6116. You must pay for the exam at registration time with a major credit card (for example, VISA or Mastercard). The standard cost is $185; check CompTIA's Web site as prices may vary.

You can also register on the Internet through Prometric at www.prometric.com or www.2test.com.

The exam itself consists of approximately 65 questions. You have two and a half hours for the test. At the end of the exam, your score report will be displayed on the screen and printed so that you have a hard copy.

Who Should Buy This Book?

If you are one of the many people who want to pass the Network+ exam, and pass it confidently, then you should buy this book and use it to study for the exam. The Network+ exam is designed to measure the technical knowledge of networking professionals with 18–24 months experience in the IT industry. This book was written with one goal in mind: not to just prepare you for passing the Network+ exam, but to prepare to you for the challenges of the real IT world. This study guide will do that by describing in detail the concepts on which you'll be tested.

How to Use This Book and CD

This book includes several features that will make studying for the Network+ exam easier. At the beginning of the book (right after this introduction, in fact) is an assessment test that you can use to check your readiness for the actual exam. Take this exam before you start reading the book. It will help you to determine the areas you may need to "brush up" on. You can then focus on these areas while reading the book. The answers to this test appear on a separate page after the last question. Each answer also includes an explanation and a note telling you in which chapter this material appears.

In addition, there are review questions at the end of each chapter. As you finish each chapter, answer the questions and the check your answers, which will appear on the page after the last question. You can go back and reread the section in the chapter that deals with each question you got wrong to ensure that you know your stuff.

Appendix A includes a practice exam. Take this exam when you have finished reading all of the chapters and answering all of the review questions and you feel you are ready for the Network+ exam. Take the practice exam as if you were actually taking the Network+ exam (i.e. without any reference material). The answers to the practice exam can be found at the end of the test on the last page of the Appendix A. If you get more than 90 percent of the answers correct, you're ready to go ahead and take the real exam.

On the CD-ROM that is included with this book, there are several "extras" you can use to bolster your exam readiness:

Electronic "flashcards"   You can use these 150 flashcard-style questions to review your knowledge of Network+ concepts not only on your PC but also on your handheld devices. You can download the questions right into your Palm device for quick and convenient reviewing anytime, anywhere, without your PC!

Test engine   This portion of the CD-ROM includes all of the questions that appear in this book: the assessment questions at the end of this introduction, all of the chapter review questions, and the practice exam questions from Appendix A. Additionally, it includes a set of bonus questions that only appear on the CD-ROM. The book questions will appear similarly to the way they did in the book, and they will also be randomized. The randomized test will allow you to pick a certain number of questions and it will simulate the actual exam. Combined, these test engine elements will allow you to test your readiness for the real Network+ exam.

Full text of the book in PDF   If you are going to travel but still need to study for the Network+ exam and you have a laptop with a CD-ROM drive, you can take this entire book with you on the CD-ROM. This book is in PDF (Adobe Acrobat) format so it can be easily read on any computer.

Exam Objectives

In this section, we are going to look at the objectives that the Network+ exam is designed to test. These objectives were developed by a group of networking industry professionals through the use of an industry-wide job task analysis. CompTIA asked groups of IT professionals to fill out a survey, rating the skills they felt were important in their job. The results were grouped into objectives for the exam. These objectives are divided into two major areas, as follows (with the weighting percentages in parentheses):

- Knowledge of networking technologies (77%)

- Knowledge of networking practices (23%)

This section includes the outline of the exam objectives for the Network+ exam and the weighting of each objective category.

The objectives and weighting percentages given in this section can change at any time. Check CompTIA's Web site at www.comptia.org for a list of the most current objectives.

Knowledge of Networking Technology (77%)

I.1 Basic Knowledge (18%)

I.1.1 Demonstrate understanding of basic network structure, including:

- The characteristics of star, bus, mesh, and ring topologies, their advantages and disadvantages

- The characteristics of segments and backbones

I.1.2 Identify the following:

- The major network operating systems, including Microsoft Windows NT, Novell NetWare, and Unix

- The clients that best serve specific network operating systems and their resources

- The directory services of the major network operating systems

I.1.3 Associate IPX, IP, and NetBEUI with their functions.

I.1.4 Define the following terms and explain how each relates to fault tolerance or high availability:

- Mirroring

- Duplexing

- Striping

- Volumes

- Tape backup

I.1.5 Define the layers of the OSI model and identify the protocols, services, and functions that pertain to each layer.

I.1.6 Recognize and describe the following characteristics of networking media and connectors:

- The advantages and disadvantages of coax, Cat 3, Cat 5, fiber optic, UTP, and STP, and the conditions under which they are appropriate

- The length and speed of 10Base2, 10BaseT, and 100BaseT

- The length and speed of 10Base5, 100Base VGAnyLan, 100Base TX

- The visual appearance of RJ 45 and BNC and how they are crimped

I.1.7 Identify the basic attributes, purpose, and function of the following network elements:

- Full- and half-duplexing

- WAN and LAN

- Server, workstation, and host
- Server-based networking and peer-to-peer networking
- Cable, NIC, and router
- Broadband and baseband
- Gateway, as both a default IP router and as a method to connect dissimilar systems or protocols

I.2 Physical Layer (6%)

I.2.1 Given an installation, configuration, or troubleshooting scenario, select an appropriate course of action if a client workstation does not connect to the network after installing or replacing a network interface card. Explain why a given action is warranted. The following issues may be covered:

- Knowledge of how the network card is usually configured, including EPROM, jumpers, and plug-and-play software
- Use of network card diagnostics, including the loopback test and vendor-supplied diagnostics
- The ability to resolve hardware resource conflicts, including IRQ, DMA, and I/O base address

I.2.2 Identify the use of the following network components and the differences between them:

- Hubs
- MAUs
- Switching hubs
- Repeaters
- Transceivers

I.3 Data Link Layer (5%)

I.3.1 Describe the following Data Link layer concepts:

- Bridges, what they are and why they are used

- The 802 specs, including the topics covered in 802.2, 802.3, and 802.5

- The function and characteristics of MAC addresses

I.4 Network Layer (5%)

I.4.1 Explain the following routing and network layer concepts, including:

- The fact that routing occurs at the network layer

- The difference between a router and a brouter

- The difference between routable and nonroutable protocols

- The concept of default gateways and subnetworks

- The reason for employing unique network IDs

- The difference between static and dynamic routing

I.5 Transport Layer (5%)

I.5.1 Explain the following transport layer concepts:

- The distinction between connectionless and connection transport

- The purpose of name resolution, either to an IP/IPX address or a network protocol

I.6 TCP/IP Fundamentals (16%)

I.6.1 Demonstrate knowledge of the following TCP/IP fundamentals:

- The concept of IP default gateways

- The purpose and use of DHCP, DNS, WINS, and host files

- The identity of the main protocols that make up the TCP/IP suite, including TCP, UDP, POP3, SMTP, SNMP, FTP, HTTP, and IP

- The idea that TCP/IP is supported by every operating system and millions of hosts worldwide

- The purpose and function of Internet domain name server hierarchies (how e-mail arrives in another country)

I.6.2 Demonstrate knowledge of the fundamental concepts of TCP/IP addressing, including:

- The A, B, and C classes of IP addresses and their default subnet mask numbers

- The use of port number (HTTP, FTP, SMTP) and port numbers commonly assigned to a given service

I.6.3 Demonstrate knowledge of TCP/IP configuration concepts, including:

- The definition of IP proxy and why it is used

- The identity of the normal configuration parameters for a work-station, including IP address, DNS, default gateway, IP proxy configuration, WINS, DHCP, host name, and Internet domain name

I.7 TCP/IP Suite: Utilities (11%)

I.7.1 Explain how and when to use the following TCP/IP utilities to test, validate, and troubleshoot IP connectivity:

- ARP

- Telnet

- NBTSTAT

- TRACERT

- NETSTAT

- ipconfig/winipcfg

- FTP

- Ping

I.8 Remote Connectivity (5%)

I.8.1 Explain the following remote connectivity concepts:

- The distinction between PPP and SLIP

- The purpose and function of PPTP and the conditions under which it is useful

- The attributes, advantages, and disadvantages of ISDN and PSTN (POTS)

I.8.2 Specify the following elements of dial-up networking:

- The modem configuration parameters that must be set, including serial port IRQ, I/O address, and maximum port speed

- The requirements for a remote connection

I.9 Security (6%)

I.9.1 Identify good practices to ensure network security, including:

- Selection of a security model (user and share level)

- Standard password practices and procedures

- The need to employ data encryption to protect network data

- The use of a firewall

II. Knowledge of Networking Practices (23%)

II.1 Implementing the Installation of the Network (6%)

II.1.1 Demonstrate awareness that administrative and test accounts, passwords, IP addresses, IP configurations, relevant SOPs, and so on must be obtained prior to network implementation.

II.1.2 Explain the impact of environmental factors on computer networks. Given a network installation scenario, identify unexpected or atypical conditions that could either cause problems for the network or signify that a problem condition already exists, including:

- Room conditions (for example, humidity, heat, and so on)

- The placement of building contents and personal effects (for example, space heaters, TVs, radios, and so on)

- Computer equipment

- Error messages

II.1.3 Recognize visually, or by description, common peripheral ports, external SCSI (especially DB-25 connectors), and common network componentry, including:

- Print servers

- Peripherals

- Hubs
- Routers
- Brouters
- Bridges
- Patch panels
- UPSs
- NICs
- Token ring media filters

II.1.4 Given an installation scenario, demonstrate awareness of the following compatibility and cabling issues:

- The consequences of trying to install an analog modem in a digital jack
- That the uses of RJ-45 connectors may differ greatly depending on the cabling
- That patch cables contribute to the overall length of the cabling segment

II.2 Maintaining and Supporting the Network (6%)

II.2.1 Identify the kinds of test documentation that are usually available regarding a vendor's patches, fixes, upgrades, and so on.

II.2.2 Given a network maintenance scenario, demonstrate awareness of the following issues:

- standard backup procedures and backup media storage practices
- the need for periodic application of software patches and other fixes to the network
- the need to install anti-virus software on the server and workstations
- the need to frequently update virus signatures.

II.3 Troubleshooting the Network (11%)

II.3.1 Identify the following steps as a systematic approach to identifying the extent of a network problem, and given a problem scenario, select the appropriate next step based on this approach:

- Determine whether the problem exists across the network
- Determine whether the problem is workstation, workgroup, LAN, or WAN
- Determine whether the problem is consistent and replicable
- Use standard troubleshooting methods

II.3.2 Identify the following steps as a systematic approach for troubleshooting network problems, and, given a problem scenario, select the appropriate next step based on this approach:

- Identify the exact issue
- Re-create the problem
- Isolate the cause
- Formulate a correction
- Implement the correction
- Test
- Document the problem and the solution
- Give feedback

II.3.3 Identify the following steps as a systematic approach to determining whether a problem is attributable to the operator or the system, and, given a problem scenario, select the appropriate next step based on this approach:

- Have a second operator perform the same task on an equivalent workstation
- Have a second operator perform the same task on the original operator's workstation
- See whether operators are following standard operating procedure

II.3.4 Given a network troubleshooting scenario, demonstrate awareness of the need to check for physical and logical indicators of trouble, including:

- Link lights

- Power lights

- Error displays

- Error logs and displays

- Performance monitors

II.3.5 Given a network problem scenario, including symptoms, determine the most likely cause or causes of the problem based on the available information. Select the most appropriate course of action based on this inference. Issues that may be covered include:

- Recognizing abnormal physical conditions

- Isolating and correcting problems in cases where there is a fault in the physical media (patch cable)

- Checking the status of servers

- Checking for configuration problems with DNS, WINS, and HOST file

- Checking for viruses

- Checking the validity of the account name and password

- Rechecking operator logon procedures

- Selecting and running appropriate diagnostics

II.3.6 Specify the tools that are commonly used to resolve network equipment problems. Identify the purpose and function of common network tools, including:

- Crossover cable

- Hardware loopback

- Tone generator

- Tone locator (fox and hound)

Good Luck!

Here are a few things to remember when taking your test:

- Get a good night's sleep before the exam.

- Bring two forms of ID with you. One form must be a photo ID, such as a driver's license. The other can be a major credit card or a passport. Both forms must have a signature.

- Take your time on each question. Don't rush.

- Arrive at the testing center a few minutes early so that you can review your notes.

- Answer all questions, even if you don't know the answer. Unanswered or blank questions are considered wrong. On-screen "help" allows you to mark a question for answering later or review a previous question.

- There will be questions with multiple correct responses. When there are multiple correct answers, a message at the bottom of the screen will prompt you to "choose all that apply." Be sure to read the messages.

- Read the question twice and make sure you understand it.

Good luck on your Network+ exam and in your future in the IT industry.

Assessment Test

1. When trouble shooting a wiring problem in your office, you find that all of the computers attach to a single wire that snakes from computer to computer. This cable starts in your office and ends at the desk of Joe in Accounting. Which of the following wiring topologies does this describe?

   A. Bus

   B. Star

   C. Ring

   D. Mesh

2. When trouble shooting a wiring problem in your office, you find that each computer is directly wired into a box located at the back of your office. Which of the following wiring topologies does this describe?

   A. Bus

   B. Star

   C. Ring

   D. Mesh

3. When documenting a client's wide area network, you discover that every physical location has a dedicated link to every other physical location. Which of the following wiring topologies does this describe?

   A. Bus

   B. Star

   C. Ring

   D. Mesh

4. Which of the following cable types is traditionally used on Arcnet networks?

   A. RG-58 AU

   B. RG-58 U

   C. RG-8

   D. RG-62

5. Which of the following cables is used on 10Base2 networks?

   A. RG-58 AU

   B. RG-58 U

   C. RG-8

   D. RG-62

6. Which of the following OSI layers handles the function of formatting data for exchange?

   A. Session

   B. Transport

   C. Application

   D. Presentation

7. At which layer of the OSI model do most routing protocols function?

   A. Session

   B. Transport

   C. Network

   D. Presentation

8. What is the media access control mechanism in which stations first determine if another device is communicating on the wire and then resends its information in the event of a collision known as?

A. CSMA/CD

B. Token Passing

C. CSMA/CA

D. Arcnet

9. Which of the following devices work at the Network layer of the OSI model?

A. Router

B. Bridge

C. Gateway

D. Layer 3 switch

10. What is the server that holds a writable copy of the Security Accounts Manager database known as in a Microsoft Windows NT network?

A. Primary Domain Controller

B. Backup Domain Controller

C. Master Domain Controller

D. Delta Domain Controller

11. Which of the following TCP/IP protocols is responsible for ensuring that communication between hosts is reliable?

A. TCP

B. IP

C. ICMP

D. SMTP

12. Which of the following TPC/IP protocols is responsible for routing data to its destination?

    A. TCP

    B. IP

    C. ICMP

    D. SMTP

13. If IP does not have a route to the destination host for a packet, it will forward the packet to the host's:

    A. Primary server

    B. Default gateway

    C. DNS server

    D. WINS server

14. The IP address 190.0.40.10 is in which class of addresses?

    A. Class A

    B. Class B

    C. Class C

    D. Class D

15. The TCP/IP protocol that resolves IP addresses into MAC addresses is known as what?

    A. TCP

    B. IP

    C. ARP

    D. ICMP

16. The IP address 192.47.210.6 is in which class of IP address?

    A. Class A

    B. Class B

    C. Class C

    D. Class D

17. The TCP/IP configuration parameter that defines which bits represent the network portion of an address is known as the:

    A. Default Gateway

    B. IP address

    C. Subnet mask

    D. Network Identifier

18. The process of converting the user-friendly host name into its corresponding IP address is known as:

    A. Address conversion

    B. NAT

    C. Name resolution

    D. Address resolution

19. On a Windows 95/98-based computer, which of the following ARP command line switches will display the contents of the ARP cache?

    A. –a

    B. –d

    C. –s

    D. –g

20. Which of the following utilities can display a list of all outbound TCP/IP connections?

   A. ARP

   B. NETSTAT

   C. NBTSTAT

   D. IPCONFIG

21. Which of the following utilities will display a list of each router that a packet passes through on its path to a destination?

   A. NBTSTAT

   B. IPCONFIG

   C. TRACERT

   D. PING

22. What is it called when the electrical power to a computer drops for less than a second before returning to normal?

   A. Spike

   B. Surge

   C. Sag

   D. Brownout

23. Which of the following precautions would help to prevent ESD problems?

   A. Installing a dehumidifying system to keep the humidity levels between 5 and 10 percent

   B. Keeping the humidity levels between 40 and 60 percent

   C. Ensuring that all equipment is properly grounded

   D. Installing ESD preventative software on your computer

24. Which of the following protocols transmits passwords in clear text?

   A. PPP

   B. SLIP

   C. TCP

   D. IP

25. Which of the following would not make a good password?

   A. Your name

   B. Your birth date

   C. The name of your pet

   D. Your name spelled backwards

26. Your routers maintain a list of IP addresses that are allowed to utilize the services of servers on the private side of the firewall. Which type of firewall technology does this describe?

   A. ACL

   B. Demilitarized zone

   C. Proxy

   D. Protocol switching

27. What is the method of providing fault tolerance to disk subsystems which involves two disks, each containing the same data, controlled by separate disk controllers known as?

   A. Mirroring

   B. Duplexing

   C. RAID Level 5

   D. Data striping

28. You company backs up the entire server each Sunday. Monday through Saturday, only those files that have changed since Sunday are backed up. Which backup methodology are you using?

A. Normal backups

B. Incremental backups

C. Differential backups

D. Optimized backups

29. Your company backs up the entire server on Sunday. Monday through Saturday the files that have changed since the day before are backed up. Which backup methodology are you using?

A. Normal backups

B. Incremental backups

C. Differential backups

D. Optimized backups

30. In the Network+ troubleshooting model, which of the following steps would be earliest in the process?

A. Re-create the problem

B. Test the solution

C. Identify the exact issue

D. Give feedback

Answers to Assessment Test

1. **A.** In a bus topology, all computers are attached to a single continuous cable that terminates at both ends.

2. **B.** Each computer in a star topology is connected to a central point by a separate cable. The central point is a device known as a hub.

3. **D.** In a mesh topology, a path exists from each station or location to every other station or location in the network.

4. **D.** RG-62 coaxial cable is used on Arcnet networks.

5. **A.** 10Base2, or thinnet, networks use an RG-58 AU coaxial cable.

6. **D.** The Presentation layer is responsible for formatting data exchange. In this layer, character sets are converted, and data is encrypted. Data may also be compressed in this layer, and this layer usually handles the redirection of data streams.

7. **C.** The Network layer is responsible for logical addressing and translating logical names into physical address. In addition, the Network layer controls congestion, routes data from source to destination, and builds and tears down packets. Most routing protocols function at this layer.

8. **A.** Carrier Sense/Multiple Access with Collision Detection (CSMA/CD) controls network access through a simple attempt to avoid simultaneous communication and then a procedure for handling data collision on the wire.

9. **A, D.** Devices that function at the Network layer of the OSI model use network addressing information to route packets to the proper network segment.

10. **A.** The PDC holds the only copy of the SAM that can accept changes. These changes are then replicated to any BDCs.

11. **A.** Transmission Control Protocol (TCP) defines the *source port number* and the *destination port number that* allow the data to be sent back and forth to the correct process running on each computer, a series of *sequence numbers* that allows the datagrams to be rebuilt in the correct order in the receiving computer, and a *checksum* that allows the protocol to check whether the data sent is the same as the data received.

12. **B.** Internet Protocol (IP) is responsible for inserting routing information into the header of each packet. This information is used by network devices, such as routers, to determine the destination of the packet.

13. **B.** When IP does not know the path to the destination, it forwards the packet to the host's configured default gateway. The default gateway is then responsible for routing the packet to its destination. (The default gateway might, in turn, pass the packet to its own default gateway, if it also does not know the path to the destination.)

14. **B.** The first octet of valid class B IP addresses will be between 128 and 191.

15. **C.** Address Resolution Protocol (ARP) resolves IP addresses into MAC addresses of the corresponding host.

16. **C.** The first octet of valid class C IP addresses will be between 192 and 223.

17. **C.** The subnet mask works a bit like a template that, when superimposed on top of the IP address, indicates which bits in the IP address identify the network and which bits identify the host.

18. **C.** Name resolution is the process of resolving host names into IP addresses.

19. **A, D.** Both the –a and –g command line switches will display the contents of the ARP cache.

20. B. NETSTAT allows you to see the TCP/IP connections (both inbound and outbound) on your machine. You can also use it to view packet statistics (similar to the MONITOR.NLM utility on a NetWare server console), such as how many packets have been sent and received, the number of errors, and so on.

21. C. The TCP/IP Trace Route (TRACERT) command-line utility will show you every router interface a TCP/IP packet passes through on its way to a destination.

22. C. A sag is the opposite of a spike—power drops to unacceptable levels for a very short period of time before returning to normal.

23. B, C. Electrostatic Discharge (ESD) occurs when two items with dissimilar static electrical charges are brought together. Nature doesn't like things to be unequal, so static electrical charges will "jump" from the item with more electrons. Monitoring humidity levels and ensuring proper grounding can minimize the danger of ESD.

24. B. Serial Line Internet Protocol (SLIP) is a *remote access protocol* that manages the connection between a remote computer and a remote access server. It does not support the encryption of authentication traffic (and is therefore being replaced with more modern technology).

25. A, B, C, D. Generally speaking, a strong password is a combination of alphanumeric and special characters that is easy for you to remember and difficult for someone else to guess. Each of the choices listed above are based upon information that is easily accessed.

26. A. In an Access Control List-based (ACL) firewall, each router maintains a list of those IP addresses that are allowed to use services on the private side of the firewall—effectively limiting access from unauthorized devices.

27. B. Duplexing involves two disks with the exact same data on them, controlled by different controllers. If a disk, cable, or controller fails, the data on the other disk should still be available.

28. C.   In a differential backup strategy, a single, full backup is typically done once a week. Every night for the next six nights, the backup utility backs up all files that have changed since the last full backup.

29. B.   In an incremental backup, a full backup is used in conjunction with daily partial backups to back up the entire server, thus reducing the amount of time it takes for a daily backup.

30. C.   In the Network+ troubleshooting model, there are eight steps performed in the following order: (1) Identify the exact issue; (2) Re-create the problem; (3) Isolate the cause; (4) Formulate a correction; (5) Implement the correction; (6) Test the solution; (7) Document the problem and the solution; and (8) Give feedback.

Chapter 1

Network Fundamentals

NETWORK+ EXAM OBJECTIVES COVERED IN THIS CHAPTER:

✓ **Demonstrate understanding of basic network structure, including:**

- The characteristics of star, bus, mesh, and ring topologies, their advantages and disadvantages
- The characteristics of segments and backbones

✓ **Recognize and describe the following characteristics of networking media and connectors:**

- The advantages and disadvantages of coax, Cat 3, Cat 5, fiber-optic, UTP, and STP and the conditions under which they are appropriate
- The length and speed of 10Base2, 10BaseT, and 100BaseT
- The length and speed of 10Base5, 100Base VGAnyLan, 100BaseTX
- The visual appearance of RJ 45 and BNC and how they are crimped

✓ **Identify the basic attributes, purpose, and function of the following network elements:**

- Full- and half-duplexing
- WAN and LAN
- Server, workstation, and host
- Server-based networking and peer-to-peer networking
- Cable, NIC, and router
- Broadband and baseband
- Gateway, as both a default IP router and as a method to connect dissimilar systems or protocols

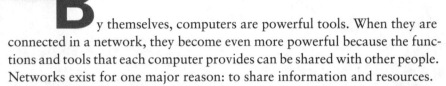

By themselves, computers are powerful tools. When they are connected in a network, they become even more powerful because the functions and tools that each computer provides can be shared with other people. Networks exist for one major reason: to share information and resources.

Networks can be very simple, such as a small group of computers that share information, or they can be very complex, spanning large geographical areas. Regardless of the type of network, a certain amount of maintenance is always required. Since each network is different and probably utilizes many diverse technologies, it is important to understand the fundamentals of networking and how networking components interact. This chapter will introduce the components of a network and help you establish a base of knowledge that you can use throughout your networking studies. This chapter will also help you prepare for the Network+ certification exam.

Network Elements

In the computer world, the term *network* describes two or more connected computers that can share a resource such as data, a printer, an Internet connection, applications, or a combination of these. Today, three types of networks are in common use:

- Local area network (LAN)

- Metropolitan area network (MAN)

- Wide area network (WAN)

The type used depends on the number of computers (and people) who need access, the geographical and physical layout of the enterprise, and, of course, financial resources. In this section, we'll discuss each type and describe the situation that is most appropriate for its use.

Local Area Network (LAN)

By definition, a LAN is limited to a specific area, usually an office, and cannot extend beyond the boundaries of a single building. The first LANs were limited to a range (from a central point to the most distant computer) of 185 meters (about 600 feet) and to no more than 30 computers. Today's technology allows a larger LAN, but practical administration limitations require dividing it into small, logical areas called *workgroups*. A workgroup is a collection of individuals who share the same files and databases over the LAN, for example, the sales department. Figure 1.1 shows an example of a small LAN and its workgroups.

FIGURE 1.1 A small LAN

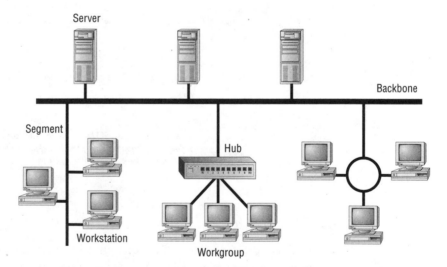

Metropolitan Area Network (MAN)

A MAN is a public, high-speed network that connects multiple LANs and can transmit voice and data over a maximum distance of about 80 kilometers (50 miles). It is larger than a LAN but smaller than a WAN. The term

MAN is rarely used anymore, but it is still found in reference material (and on the Network+ exam). Figure 1.2 shows an example of a MAN. Notice that each connection between LANs has a second, redundant connection.

FIGURE 1.2 A typical MAN

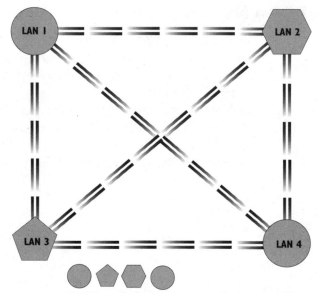

The LANs connected in such a network may be the same or different.

Because different types of LANs can be involved, connections to high-speed lines can take many forms. Bridges, routers, gateways, and switches are the most common connections.

Wide Area Network (WAN)

Chances are that you are an experienced WAN user and didn't know it. If you have ever connected to the Internet, you have used the largest WAN on the planet. A WAN is any network that crosses metropolitan, regional, or national boundaries. Most networking professionals define a WAN as any network that uses routers and public network links. The Internet fits both definitions.

WANs differ from LANs and MANs in the following ways:

- WANs cover greater distances.

- WAN speeds are slower.

- WANs can be connected on demand or be permanently connected. LANs have permanent connections between stations.

- WANs can use public or private network transports. LANs primarily use private network transports.

- WANs can use either full- or half-duplex communications. LANs typically use half-duplex communications (see the sidebar "Full-Duplex vs. Half-Duplex Communications").

The Internet is actually a specific type of WAN. The Internet is a collection of networks that are interconnected and is therefore technically an *internetwork*. (*Internet* is short for the word *internetwork*.)

A WAN can be centralized or distributed. A centralized WAN consists of a central computer (at a central site) to which other computers and dumb terminals connect. The Internet, on the other hand, consists of many interconnected computers in many locations. Thus, it is a *distributed* WAN.

Full-Duplex vs. Half-Duplex Communications

All network communications (including LAN and WAN communications) can be categorized as half-duplex or full-duplex. With half-duplex, communications happen in both directions, but only in one direction at a time. When two computers communicate using half-duplex, one computer sends a signal and the other receives; then they switch sending and receiving roles. Chances are that you are familiar with half-duplex communications. If you ever use a CB radio, you are communicating via half-duplex. One person talks, and then the other person talks.

Full-duplex, on the other hand, allows communication in both directions simultaneously. Both stations can send and receive signals at the same time. Full-duplex communications are similar to a telephone call, in which both people can talk simultaneously.

Host, Workstation, and Server

For the Network+ exam, you need a good understanding of the three primary components of a network: workstations, servers, and hosts.

Understanding Workstations

In the classic sense, a *workstation* is a powerful computer used for drafting or other math-intensive applications. The term is also applied to a computer that has multiple *central processing units (CPUs)* that are available to users. In the network environment, the term workstation normally refers to any computer connected to the network that is used by a user to do work. *Workstation* can also refer to software, as in Windows NT Workstation. It is important to distinguish between workstations and clients. A client is any network entity that can request resources of the network; a workstation is a computer that can request resources. Workstations can be clients, but not all clients are workstations. For example, a printer can request resources from the network, but it is a client, not a workstation.

Understanding Servers

In the truest sense, a *server* does exactly what the name implies: It provides resources to the clients on the network ("serves" them, in other words). Servers are typically powerful computers that run the software that controls and maintains the network. This software is known as the *network operating system*, and we'll discuss this topic in detail in Chapter 3.

Servers are often specialized for a single purpose. This is not to say that a single server can't do many jobs, but, more often than not, you'll get better performance if you dedicate a server to a single task. Here are some examples of servers that are dedicated to a single task:

File Server   Holds and distributes files.

Print Server   Controls and manages one or more printers for the network.

Proxy Server   Performs a function on behalf of other computers. Proxy means "on behalf of."

Application Server   Hosts a network application.

Web Server   Holds and delivers Web pages and other Web content using the Hypertext Transfer Protocol (HTTP).

Mail Server   Hosts and delivers e-mail. The electronic equivalent of a post office.

Fax Server   Sends and receives faxes (via a special fax board) for the entire network without the need for paper.

Remote Access Server   Hosts modems for inbound requests to connect to the network. Remote access servers provide remote users (working at home or on the road) with a connection to the network.

Telephony Server   Functions as a "smart" answering machine for the network. It can also perform call center and call routing functions.

Notice that each server type's name consists of the type of service the server provides (remote access, for example) followed by the word *server,* which, as you remember, means to serve.

Regardless of the specific role(s) these server(s) play, they all (should) have the following in common:

- Hardware and/or software for data integrity (such as backup hardware and software)

- The capability to support a large number of clients

Figure 1.1, earlier in this chapter, shows a sample network. Physical resources, such as hard drive space and memory, must be greater in a server than in a workstation because the server needs to provide services to many clients. Also, a server should be located in a physically secure area. Figure 1.3 shows a sample network that includes both workstations and servers. Note that there are more workstations than servers because a few servers can serve network resources to hundreds of users simultaneously.

FIGURE 1.3 A sample network including servers and workstations

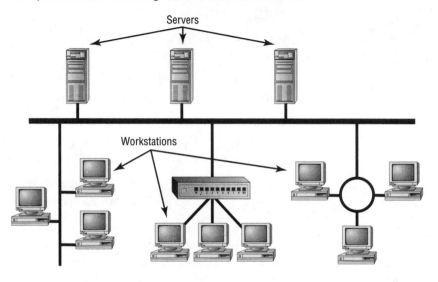

> If the physical access to a server is not controlled, you don't have security. Use this guideline: If anybody can touch it, it isn't secure. The value of the company data far exceeds the investment in computer hardware and software. We'll look at network security in detail in Chapter 9.

Understanding Hosts

The term *host* is most commonly used when discussing TCP/IP related services and functions. A *host*, in TCP/IP terms, is any network device that has a TCP/IP network address. Workstations, servers, and any other network device (as long as it has TCP/IP addresses) can all be considered hosts. In conversation, you may also hear the word *host* used to describe any minicomputer or server. For the Network+ exam, however, you should stick to the classic definition used here.

Peer-to-Peer vs. Client/Server Architecture

As we have mentioned, the purpose of networking is to share resources. How this is accomplished depends on the architecture of the network operating system software. The two most common network types are peer-to-peer and client/server.

If you were to look at an illustration of a group of computers in a LAN, it would be impossible to determine if the network was a peer-to-peer or a client/server environment. Even a videotape of this same LAN during a typical workday would reveal few clues as to whether it is peer-to-peer or client/server. Yet the differences are huge. Since you can't see the differences, you might guess correctly that they are not physical but logistical.

Peer-to-Peer Network

In *peer-to-peer networks*, the connected computers have no centralized authority. From an authority viewpoint, all computers are equal. In other words, they are peers. If a user of one computer wants access to a resource on another computer, the security check for access rights is the responsibility of the computer holding the resource.

Each computer in a peer-to-peer network can be both a client that requests resources and a server that provides resources. This is a great arrangement, provided the following conditions are met.

- Each user is responsible for local backup.

- Security considerations are minimal.

- A limited number of computers are involved.

Networks that run Windows 95/98 as their network operating system or networks using Windows NT Workgroup functionality are considered peer-to-peer networks. Figure 1.4 shows an example of a peer-to-peer network. Peer-to-peer networks present some challenges. For example, backing up company data becomes an iffy proposition. Also, it can be difficult to remember where you stored a file. Finally, because security is not centralized, users and passwords must be maintained separately on each machine, as you can see in Figure 1.4. Passwords may be different for the same users on different machines.

FIGURE 1.4 A peer-to-peer network

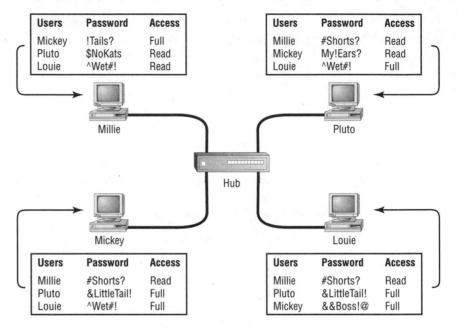

Users	Password	Access
Mickey	!Tails?	Full
Pluto	$NoKats	Read
Louie	^Wet#!	Read

Users	Password	Access
Millie	#Shorts?	Read
Mickey	My!Ears?	Read
Louie	^Wet#!	Full

Millie

Pluto

Hub

Mickey

Louie

Users	Password	Access
Millie	#Shorts?	Read
Pluto	&LittleTail!	Full
Louie	^Wet#!	Full

Users	Password	Access
Millie	#Shorts?	Read
Pluto	&LittleTail!	Full
Mickey	&&Boss!@	Full

Client/Server Network

In contrast to a peer-to-peer network, a *client/server* network uses a network operating system designed to manage the entire network from a centralized point, which is the server. Clients make requests of the server, and the server responds with the information or access to a resource.

Client/server networks have some definite advantages over peer-to-peer networks. For one thing, the network is much more organized. It is easier to find files and resources because they are stored on the server. Also, client/server networks generally have much tighter security. All usernames and passwords are stored in the same database (on the server), and individual users can't use the server as a workstation. Finally, client/server networks have better performance and can scale almost infinitely. It is not uncommon to see client/server networks with tens of thousands of workstations. Figure 1.5 shows a sample client/server network. Note that the server now holds the database of user accounts, passwords, and access rights.

FIGURE 1.5   A client/server network

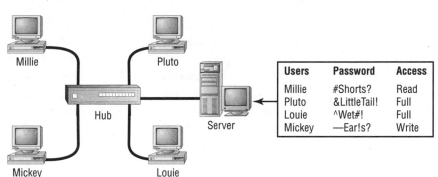

Physical Topologies

A *topology* is basically a map of a network. The *physical topology* of a network describes the layout of the cables and workstations and the location of all network components. Often, physical topologies are compared to *logical topologies,* which define how the information or data flows within the network. The topologies are usually similar. It is important to note, however, that a network can have one type of physical topology and a completely different logical topology. You'll learn more about this later in this chapter.

The cables or connections in a physical topology are often referred to as *network media* (or *physical media*). Choosing how computers will be connected in a company's network is critical. A wrong decision regarding physical topology and media is difficult to correct because it is costly and disruptive to change an entire installation once it is in place. The typical organization changes the physical layout and physical media of a network only once every 10 or 20 years, so it is important to choose a configuration that you can live with and that allows for growth.

In the next section, we'll look at physical media. In this section, we'll look at the four most common topologies:

- Bus

- Ring

- Star

- Mesh

The Bus Topology

In a bus topology, all computers are attached to a single continuous cable that is terminated at both ends, which is the simplest way to create a physical network. Originally, computers were attached to the cable with wire taps. This did not prove practical, so drop cables are now used to attach computers to the main cable. Figure 1.6 shows an example of a bus network. Notice how the cable runs from computer to computer with several bends and twists.

FIGURE 1.6 An example of a physical bus topology

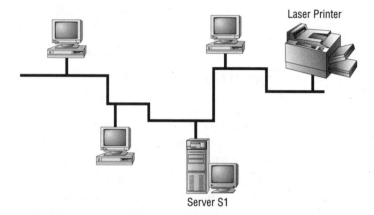

When communicating on a network that uses a bus topology, all computers see the data on the wire. This does not create chaos because the only computer that actually accepts the data is the one to which it is addressed. You can think of a bus network as a small party. David is already there, along with 10 other people. David would like to tell Tcat something. David yells out, "Tcat! Will you grab me a cup of coffee, please?" Everyone in the party can hear David, but only Tcat will respond. A star network with a hub, which we'll look at later in this chapter, also operates in this manner.

Despite the simplicity of the bus topology, there are some inherent disadvantages to this design. For example, what happens if the wire breaks or is disconnected? Neither side can communicate with the other, and signal bounce occurs on both sides. The result is that the entire network is down. For this reason, bus topologies are considered to have very little fault tolerance. Sometimes, because a cable is inside a wall, you cannot physically see a break. To determine if a break has occurred, you can use a tool known as a *Time Domain Reflectometer, or TDR* (also called a *cable tester*). This device sends out a signal and measures how much time it takes to return. Programmed with the specifications of the cable being tested, it determines where the fault lies with a high degree of accuracy. We'll discuss cable testers in Chapter 11.

As with most things, there are pros and cons to a bus topology. On the pro side, a bus topology:

- Is simple to install
- Is relatively inexpensive
- Uses less cable than other topologies

On the con side, a bus topology:

- Is difficult to move and change
- Has little fault tolerance (a single fault can bring down the entire network)
- Is difficult to troubleshoot

The Star Topology

Unlike in a bus topology, each computer in a star topology is connected to a central point by a separate cable. The central point is a device known as a *hub*. Although this setup uses more cable than a bus, if a failure occurs along one of the cables connecting to the hub, only that portion of the network is affected, not the entire network. This means that a star topology is much more fault tolerant than a bus topology. Figure 1.7 shows a typical star topology.

FIGURE 1.7 A typical star topology with a hub

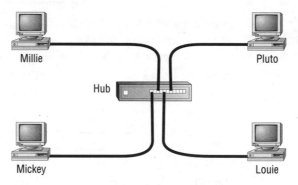

The design of a star topology resembles an old wagon wheel with the wooden spokes extending from the center point. The center point of the wagon wheel is also known as a hub. Like the wagon wheel, the network's most vulnerable point is the hub. If it goes awry, the whole system collapses. Fortunately, hub failures are extremely rare.

Just as with the bus topology, the star topology has advantages and disadvantages. The increasing popularity of the star topology is mainly due to the large number of advantages, which include the following:

- It can be reconfigured quickly.

- A single cable failure won't bring down the entire network.

- It is relatively easy to troubleshoot.

The disadvantages of a star topology include the following:

- Total installation cost can be higher because of the larger number of cables.

- It has a single point of failure, the hub.

The Ring Topology

In the ring topology, each computer is connected directly to two other computers in the network. Data moves down a one-way path from one computer to another, as shown in Figure 1.8. The good news about laying cable out in a ring is that the cable design is simple. The bad news is that, as with bus topology, any break, such as adding or removing a computer, disrupts the entire network. For this reason, the physical ring topology is seldom used.

FIGURE 1.8   A typical ring topology

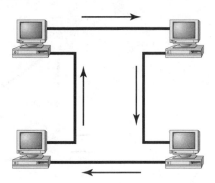

 Although its name suggests a relationship, Token Ring does not use a physical ring topology. It instead uses a physical star, logical ring topology. You will learn more about logical topologies later in this chapter and also in Chapter 2.

A few pros and many cons are associated with a ring topology, which is the reason that it is seldom used. On the pro side, the ring topology is relatively easy to troubleshoot. A station will know when a cable fault has occurred because it will stop receiving data from its upstream neighbor.

On the con side, a ring topology is:

- Expensive because multiple cables are needed for each workstation.

- Difficult to reconfigure.

- Not fault tolerant. A single cable fault can bring down the entire network.

The Mesh Topology

In a mesh topology (as shown in Figure 1.9), a path exists from each station to every other station in the network. While not usually seen in LANs, a variation on this type of topology, the hybrid mesh is used on the Internet and other WANs in a limited fashion. Hybrid mesh topology networks can have multiple connections between some locations, but this is done for redundancy. Also, there is not a true mesh because there is not a connection between each and every node; just a few for backup purposes. Notice (in Figure 1.9) how complex connections become with four connections, however.

FIGURE 1.9   A typical mesh topology

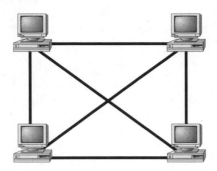

As you can see in Figure 1.9, a mesh topology can become quite complex as wiring and connections increase exponentially. For every n stations, you will have $n(n-1)/2$ connections. For example, in a network of four computers, you will have $4(4-1)/2$ connections, or six connections. If your network grows to only 10 computers, you will have 45 connections to manage! Given this impossible overhead, only small systems can be connected this way. The payoff for all this work is a more fail-safe, or fault-tolerant, network, at least as far as cabling is concerned.

Today, the mesh topology is rarely used, and then only in a WAN environment and only because the mesh topology is fault tolerant. Computers or network devices can switch between these multiple, redundant connections if the need arises. On the con side, the mesh topology is expensive and, as you have seen, quickly becomes too complex.

Backbones and Segments

With complex networks, we must have a way of intelligently identifying which part of the network we are discussing. For this reason, we commonly break networks into backbones and segments. Figure 1.10 shows a sample network and identifies the backbones and segments. You can refer to this figure as necessary as we discuss backbones and segments.

FIGURE 1.10   Backbone and segments on a sample network

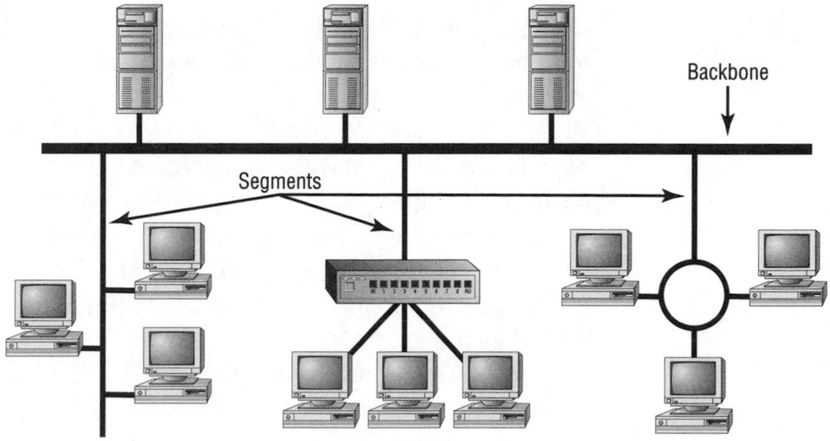

Understanding the Backbone

A *backbone* is the part of the network to which all segments and servers connect. A backbone provides the structure for a network and is considered the main part of any network. It usually uses a high-speed communications technology of some kind (such as FDDI [Fiber Distributed Data Interface] or 100 Megabit Ethernet [Fast Ethernet]). All servers and all network segments typically connect directly to the backbone so that any segment is only one segment away from any server on that backbone. Because all segments are close to the servers, the network is more efficient. Notice that the three servers and three segments connect to the backbone in Figure 1.10.

Understanding Segments

Segment is a general term for any short section of the network that is not part of the backbone. Just as servers connect to the backbone, workstations connect to segments. Segments are connected to the backbone to allow the workstations on them access to the rest of the network. Figure 1.10 shows three segments.

Selecting the Right Topology

Each topology has its advantages and drawbacks. The process of selecting a topology can be much like buying a pair of shoes. It's a matter of finding something that fits, feels right, and is within your budget. Instead of asking, What is your shoe size? ask questions such as, How much fault tolerance is necessary? How often will I need to reconfigure the network? Creating a simple network for a handful of computers in a single room is usually done most efficiently using a bus topology because it is simple and ease to install. Larger environments are usually wired in a star because moves, adds, and changes to the network are more efficient with a physical star than with any of the other topologies.

If you need uptime to the definition of *fault resistant*, (that is, 99 percent uptime, or less than 8 hours total downtime per year), you should seriously consider a mesh layout. While you are thinking about how fault tolerant a mesh network is, let the word maintenance enter your thoughts. Remember, you will have $n(n-1)/2$ connections to maintain, which will quickly become a nightmare and can exceed your maintenance budget.

Generally speaking, balance the following considerations when choosing a physical topology for your network:

- Cost

- Ease of installation

- Ease of maintenance

- Cable fault tolerance

Physical Media

Although it is possible to use several forms of wireless networking, such as radio and infrared, most networks communicate via some sort of cable. In this section, we'll look at three types of cables:

- Coaxial

- Twisted-pair

- Fiber-optic

Coaxial Cable

Coaxial cable (or coax) contains a center conductor, made of copper, surrounded by a plastic jacket, with a braided shield over the jacket. Either a plastic such as PVC or Teflon covers this metal shield. The Teflon-type covering is frequently referred to as a *plenum-rated* coating. That simply means that the coating does not produce toxic gas when burned (as PVC does) and is rated for use in air plenums that carry breathable air. This type of cable is more expensive but may be mandated by electrical code whenever cable is hidden in walls or ceilings. Plenum rating applies to all types of cabling.

Coaxial cable is available in different specifications that are rated according to the *RG* Type system. Different cables have different specifications and, therefore, different RG grading designations (according to the U.S. military specification MIL-C-17). Distance and cost are considerations when selecting coax cable. The thicker the copper, the farther a signal can travel—and with that comes higher costs and a less flexible cable.

Using Thick Ethernet

The original Ethernet cable is known as *Thick Ethernet* cable, or *Thicknet*. It is also called *10Base5* and is graded as RG 8. To the folks who installed the cable, it was more commonly called a "frozen garden hose" because of its 1/2" diameter.

With Thick Ethernet, a station attaches to the main cable via a vampire tap, which clamps onto the cable. A *vampire tap* is so-named because a metal tooth sinks into the cable, thus making the connection with the inner conductor. The tap is connected to an external transceiver that in turn has a 15-pin AUI connector (also called *DIX* or DB-15 connector) to which you attach a cable that connects to the station (shown in Figure 1.11). DIX got its name from the companies that worked on this format—Digital, Intel, and Xerox.

FIGURE 1.11 Thicknet and vampire taps

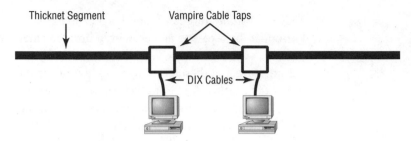

Not every Thick Ethernet cable connection type is a DIX. The other option that is found occasionally is the *N-Series connector*. The N connector comes in a male/female screw-and-barrel configuration. A CB radio uses the PL-259 connector, and the N connector looks similar (as shown in Figure 1.12).

FIGURE 1.12 An N-series connector

Using Thin Ethernet/10Base2

Thin Ethernet, also referred to as *Thinnet* or *10Base2*, is a thin coaxial cable. It is basically the same as thick coaxial cable, except the diameter of the cable is smaller (about 1/4" in diameter). Thin Ethernet coaxial cable is RG-58. Figure 1.13 shows an example of Thin Ethernet.

FIGURE 1.13 A stripped-back Thinnet

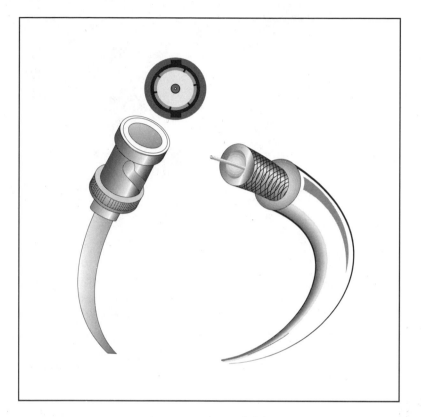

With Thinnet cable, you use *BNC* connectors (see Figure 1.14) to attach stations to the network. It is beyond our province to settle the long-standing argument over the meaning of the abbreviation BNC. We have heard BayoNet Connector, Bayonet Nut Connector, and British Navel Connector. What is relevant is that the BNC connector locks securely with a quarter-twist motion.

FIGURE 1.14 A male and female BNC connector

Male

Female

The BNC connector can be attached to a cable in two ways. The first is with a crimper, which looks like funny pliers and has a die to hold the connector. Pressing the levers crimps the connector to the cable. Choice number two is a screw-on connector, which is very unreliable. If at all possible, avoid the screw-on connector!

Table 1.1 shows some of the specifications for the different types of coaxial cable.

TABLE 1.1 Coaxial Cable Specifications

RG #	Popular Name	Ethernet Implementation	Type of Cable
RG-58 U	N/A	None	Solid copper
RG-58 AU	Thinnet	10Base2	Stranded copper
RG-8	Thicknet	10Base5	Solid copper
RG-62	ARCNet	N/A	Solid/stranded

Although some great advantages are associated with using coax cable, such as the braided shielding that provides fair resistance to electronic pollution like *electromagnetic interference (EMI)* and *radio frequency interference (RFI)*, all types of stray electronic signals can make their way onto a network cable and cause communications problems. Understanding EMI and RFI is critical to your networking success. For this reason, we'll go into detail in Chapter 6.

Signal Bounce

With coaxial cable, the signal travels up and down the entire length of the wire. When the signal reaches the end of the wire, the electrical change from copper to air prevents the conversation from simply falling out the end. So the signal bounces back down the wire it just traversed. This creates an echo, just as if you we're yelling into a canyon. These additional signals on the wire make communication impossible. To prevent this, you place a *terminator* on each end of the wire to absorb the unwanted echo.

Technically, proper termination also requires that one terminator be connected to a ground. Connecting both terminators to a ground can create a *ground loop*, which can produce all kinds of bizarre, ghostlike activity; for example, a network share that appears and disappears.

If you are not sure where to find a good ground point, connect one terminator to a screw holding a power supply inside a computer. This ensures that you are using the same ground as the PC. This does assume that the outlet into which the PC is plugged is properly grounded.

Twisted-Pair Cable

Twisted-pair cable consists of multiple, individually insulated wires that are twisted together in pairs. Sometimes a metallic shield is placed around the twisted pairs. Hence, the name *shielded twisted-pair (STP)*. (You might see this type of cabling in Token Ring installations.) More commonly, you see cable with no outer shielding, called unshielded twisted-pair (UTP). UTP is commonly used in 10BaseT, star-wired networks.

Let's take a look at why the wires in this cable type are twisted. When electromagnetic signals are conducted on copper wires that are in close proximity (such as inside a cable), some electromagnetic interference occurs.

In this scenario, this interference is called *crosstalk*. Twisting two wires together as a pair minimizes such interference and also provides some protection against interference from outside sources. This cable type is the most common today. It is popular for several reasons:

- It's cheaper than other types of cabling.

- It's easy to work with.

- It permits transmission rates considered impossible ten years ago.

UTP cable is rated in the following categories:

Category 1 Two twisted-pair (four wires). Voice grade (not rated for data communications). The oldest UTP. Frequently referred to as POTS, or Plain Old Telephone Service. Before 1983, this was the standard cable used throughout the North American telephone system. POTS cable still exists in parts of the Public Switched Telephone Network (PSTN).

Category 2 Four twisted-pair (eight wires). Suitable for up to 4Mbps.

Category 3 Four twisted-pair (eight wires), with three twists per foot. Acceptable for 10Mbps. A popular cable choice for a long time.

Category 4 Four twisted-pair (eight wires) and rated for 16Mbps.

Category 5 Four twisted-pair (eight wires) and rated for 100Mbps.

Category 6 Four twisted-pair (eight wires) and rated for 1000Mbps. (Became a standard in December 1998.)

Frequently, you will hear Category shorted to Cat. Today, any cable that you install should be a minimum of Cat 5. We say at a minimum because some cable is now certified to carry a bandwidth signal of 350MHz or beyond. This allows unshielded twisted-pair cables to reach a speed of 1Gbps, which is fast enough to carry broadcast-quality video over a network. The nomenclature of cabling is detailed shortly in the section "Cable Specifications." A common saying is that there are three ways to do things: the Right way, the Wrong way, and the IBM way. IBM uses types instead of categories when referring to TP (twisted-pair) cabling specifications. Even though a cabling type may seem to correspond to a cabling category (such as Type 1 and Category 1), the two are not the same; IBM defines its own specifications.

Category 5 Cabling Tips

If you expect data rates faster than 10Mbps over UTP, ensure that all components are rated to the category you want to achieve, and be very careful when handling all components. For example, pulling too hard on Cat 5 cable will stretch the number of twists inside the jacket, rendering the label on the outside of the cable, Cat 5, invalid. Also, be certain to connect and test all four pairs of wire. Although today's wiring usually uses only two pair, or four wires, at the time of this writing the proposed standard for Gigabit Ethernet over UTP requires that all four pairs, or eight wires, be in good condition.

And, beware. A true Cat 5 cabling system uses rated components from end to end, patch cables from workstation to wall panel, cable from wall panel to patch panel, and patch cables from patch panel to hub. If any components are missing or if the lengths do not match the Category 5 specification, you don't have a Category 5 cabling installation. Also, installers should certify that the installation is Category 5 compliant.

Connecting UTP

Clearly, a BNC connector won't fit easily on UTP cable, so you need to use an *RJ (Registered Jack)* connector. You are probably familiar with RJ connectors. Most telephones connect with an RJ-11 connector. The connector used with UTP cable is called RJ-45. The RJ-11 has four wires, or two pair, and the network connector RJ-45 has four pair, or eight wires.

In almost every case, UTP uses RJ connectors. Even the now-extinct ARCnet used RJ connectors. You use a crimper to attach an RJ connector to a cable, just as you use a crimper with the BNC connector. The only difference is that the die that holds the connector is a different shape. Higher quality crimping tools have interchangeable dies for both types of cables.

Signaling Methods

How much of a cable's available bandwidth (overall capacity, such as 10Mbps) is used by each signal depends on whether the signaling method is baseband or broadband. Baseband uses the entire bandwidth of the cable for each signal (using one channel). It is typically used with digital signaling.

In broadband, multiple signals can be transmitted on the same cable simultaneously by means of frequency division multiplexing (FDM). *Multiplexing* is dividing a single medium into multiple channels. With FDM, the cable's bandwidth is divided into separate channels (or frequencies), and multiple signals can traverse the cable on these frequencies simultaneously. FDM is typically used for analog transmissions. Another method, time division multiplexing (TDM), can also be used to further divide each individual FDM frequency into individual time slots. Additionally, TDM can be used on baseband systems.

Ethernet Cable Descriptions

Ethernet cable types are described using a code that follows this format:

$N<Signal>X$

Generally speaking, N is the signaling rate in megabits per second, and *<Signal>* is the signaling type, base or broad (baseband or broadband). X is a unique identifier for that Ethernet cabling scheme.

Let's use a generic example: 10BaseX. The two-digit number 10 indicates that the transmission speed is 10Mb, or 10 megabits. The value X can have different meanings. For example, the 5 in 10Base5 indicates the maximum distance that the signal can travel—500 meters. The 2 in 10Base2 is used the same way, but fudges the truth. The real limitation is 185 meters. Only the IEEE committee knows for sure what this was about. We can only guess that 10Base2 seems easier to say than 10Base1.85. Another 10Base standard is 10BaseT. The T is short for twisted-pair. This is the standard for running 10 Megabit Ethernet over two pairs (four wires) of Category 3, 4, or 5 UTP. The fourth and currently final 10Base is 10BaseF. The F is short for Fiber. 10BaseF is the standard for running 10 megabit Ethernet over fiber-optic cable. Table 1.2 a bit later in this section summarizes this data.

100BaseT

As network applications increased in complexity, so did their bandwidth requirements. Ten-megabit technologies were too slow. The 100BaseT standard is a general category of standards for Ethernet transmissions at a data rate of 100Mbps. This Ethernet standard is also known as *Fast Ethernet*. There are two major standards for 100BaseT.

100BaseTX   The implementation of 100BaseT that is simply a faster version of 10BaseT. It uses two UTP pairs (four wires) in a Category 5 UTP cable (or Type 1 STP).

100BaseT4   The implementation of 100BaseT that runs over four pair (eight wires) of Category 3, 4, or 5 UTP cable.

100BaseVG

This 100-megabit Ethernet replacement came from HP, and in the popularity race, it lost. Even the name wasn't settled upon, so you may find it referred to as VG LAN, VGAnyLAN, or AnyLAN. Although it used UTP cable, it didn't follow the popular Ethernet standard. It attempted to improve on Ethernet by using collision avoidance as a method of controlling network traffic You will see details on Ethernet and several methods of handling traffic in chapters throughout this book. The point here is that the 100BaseVG standard was not compatible with 10BaseX and Ethernet. Combining that with its actually less than 100Mbps throughput (due to its media access method, which is discussed elsewhere in this book) ultimately spelled its demise. However, it was basically 100Mb, and it was out the door early in the game. Because some companies implemented this standard, you need to know about it.

Fiber-Optic Cable

Because fiber-optic cable transmits digital signals using light pulses rather than electricity, it is immune to EMI and RFI. You will find a complete discussion of these terms in Chapter 6, but you should know at this point that they both could affect network performance. Anyone who has seen UTP cable for a network run down an elevator shaft would doubtless appreciate this feature of fiber. Light is carried on either a glass or a plastic core. Glass can carry the signal a greater distance, but plastic costs less. Regardless of which core is used, there is a shield wrapped around. The glass or plastic core is surrounded by cladding, which is more glass that refracts the light back into the core. This is then wrapped in an armor coating, typically Kevlar, and then sheathed in PVC or Plenum. Figure 1.15 shows the fiber-optic connectors of FDDI and SMA. SMA is the most popular connector in fiber optics today. The technical name is *Field-installable Subminiature Assembly (FSMA)*.

FIGURE 1.15 Fiber-optic connector examples of FDDI and SMA connectors. FDDI connectors are popular for connecting external hard disk systems to servers. SMA or FSMA is popular because it is field-installable.

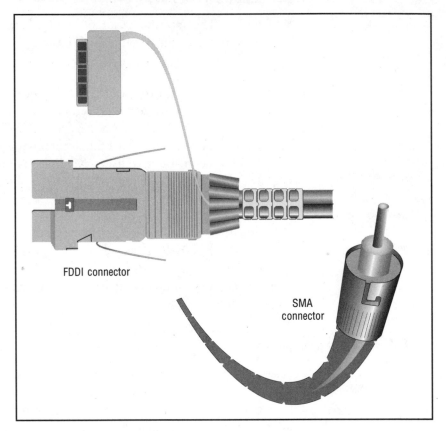

FDDI connector

SMA connector

 For more information about fiber-optic cabling, see *The Encyclopedia of Networking*, published by Sybex.

If data runs are measured in kilometers, fiber-optic is your cable of choice because copper cannot reach more than 500 meters (about 1500 feet) without electronics regenerating the signal. You may also want to opt for fiber-optic cable if an installation requires high security, because it does not create a readable magnetic field. Although fiber-optic technology was initially very expensive and difficult to work with, it is now being used in some interesting places, such as gigabit Internet backbones. Some companies plan to bring fiber-optic speeds to the desktop. Ethernet running at 10Mbps over fiber-optic cable is normally designated 10BaseF; the 100Mbps version of this implementation is 100BaseFX.

Although fiber-optic cable may sound like the solution to many problems, it has pros and cons, just as the other cable types. On the pro side, fiber-optic cable:

- Is completely immune to EMI or RFI
- Can transmit up to 4 kilometers (about 2 miles)

On the con side, fiber-optic cable:

- Is difficult to install
- Requires a bigger investment in installation and materials

Table 1.2 summarizes the cable types we have discussed in this section.

TABLE 1.2 Common Ethernet Cable Types

Ethernet Name	Cable Type	Maximum Speed	Maximum Transmission Distance	Notes
10Base5	Coax	10Mbps	500 meters per segment	Also called Thicknet, this uses vampire taps to connect devices to cable

TABLE 1.2 Common Ethernet Cable Types *(continued)*

Ethernet Name	Cable Type	Maximum Speed	Maximum Transmission Distance	Notes
10Base2	Coax	10Mbps	185 meters per segment	Also called Thinnet, a very popular implementation of Ethernet over coax
10BaseT	UTP	10Mbps	100 meters per segment	One of the most popular network cabling schemes
100BaseT	UTP	100Mpbs	100 meters per segment	One of the most popular network cabling schemes
100BaseVG	UTP	100Mpbs	213 meters (Cat 5) 100 meters (Cat 3)	
100BaseT4	UTP	100Mpbs	100 meters per segment	Requires 4 pairs of Cat 3, 4, or 5 UTP cable
100BaseTX	UTP, STP	100Mpbs	100 meters per segment	2 pairs of Category 5 UTP or Type 1 STP
10BaseF	Fiber	10Mbps	Varies (ranges from 500 meters to 2000 meters)	Ethernet over fiber-optic implementation
100BaseFX	Fiber	100Mbps	2000 meters	100Mbps Ethernet over fiber-optic implementation

Common Network Connectivity Devices

Now that we have discussed the various types of network media and connections, let's look at some devices commonly found on today's networks. Because these devices connect network entities, they are known as connectivity devices. The three most popular are:

- The network interface card (NIC)
- The router
- The gateway

The Network Interface Card (NIC)

The *network interface card (NIC)*, as its name suggests, is the expansion card you install in your computer to connect (interface) your computer to the network. This device provides the physical, electrical, and electronic connections to the network media. NICs are either an expansion card (the most popular implementation) or built in to the motherboard of the computer. In most cases, a NIC connects to the computer through *expansion slots*. An expansion slot connects expansion cards that are plugged in to a slot to the main computer assembly through a deceptively simple looking connector, which is known as a *bus*. In some notebook computers, NIC adapters can be connected to the printer port or through a PC card slot.

The Router

A *router* is a network device that connects multiple, often dissimilar, network segments into an internetwork. The router, once connected, can make intelligent decisions about how best to get network data to its destination based on network performance data that it gathers from the network itself.

The Gateway

A gateway is any hardware and software combination that connects dissimilar network environments. Gateways are the most complex of network devices because they perform translations at multiple layers of the OSI model.

For example, a gateway is the device that connects a LAN environment to a mainframe environment. The two environments are completely different. LAN environments use distributed processing, baseband communications, and the ASCII character set. Mainframe environments use centralized processing, broadband and baseband communications, and the EBCDIC character set. Each of the LAN protocols is translated to its mainframe counterpart by the gateway software.

Another popular example is the e-mail gateway. Most LAN-based e-mail software, such as Novell's GroupWise and Microsoft's Exchange, can't communicate directly with Internet mail servers without the use of a gateway. This gateway translates LAN-based mail messages into the SMTP format that Internet mail uses.

Key Terms

Before you take the exam, be certain you are familiar with the following terms:

backbone

BNC

bus

client/server

coaxial cable

crosstalk

expansion slot

fault resistant

ground loop

logical topology

multiplexing

network media (or physical media)

N-Series connector

physical topology

plenum-rated

router

segment

shielded twisted-pair (STP)

terminator

Thick Ethernet

topology

uptime

workgroup

Review Questions

1. Which of the following are characteristic of a peer-to-peer network?

   A. Centralized security and administration.

   B. A computer can be both a client and a server.

   C. A limited number of computers are involved.

   D. Does not require a hub.

2. The best cable choice for linking a few computers in a small office using a bus Ethernet network is cable with an _____ designation.

   A. RG/47

   B. RG/58

   C. RG/59

   D. RG/62

3. Which of the following are characteristic of a true client/server environment?

   A. Does not require a hub.

   B. A computer can be both a client and a server.

   C. Centralized security and administration.

   D. Centralized backup.

4. Proper termination in a coaxial cable requires _____ terminators.

   A. 0

   B. 1

   C. 2

   D. 3

5. Which of the following is characteristic of a mesh network?

    A. Controls cable costs

    B. Improved reliability

    C. Required by fire code

    D. Needs a token to operate

6. Which type of network topology uses terminators?

    A. Star

    B. Bus

    C. Ring

    D. Mesh

7. Which of the following best describes a star topology?

    A. Centralized management.

    B. Any cable fault halts all network traffic.

    C. Uses less cable than a bus or ring.

    D. All the above.

8. A client/server approach uses what type of security model?

    A. Centralized

    B. Decentralized

    C. Server

    D. Distributed

9. In a Thicknet Ethernet network, _____ typically connect the NIC's transceiver to the backbone cable.

    A. Screws

    B. Radio Frequency Transmitters

    C. Vampire Taps

    D. Bolts

10. Plenum cable has which of the following characteristics?

    A. Lower cost than PVC

    B. Meets fire codes

    C. Transmits data faster

    D. All the above

11. Which of the following is the most widely used LAN wiring system for connections between desktop and server?

    A. STP

    B. UTP

    C. Coax

    D. Fiber-optic

12. Which of the following has the highest possible throughput?

    A. STP

    B. UTP

    C. Coax

    D. Fiber-optic

13. Which 100-megabit Ethernet standard is designed to use two pairs of wires in a UTP cable?

    A. 100BaseVG

    B. 10BaseF

    C. 100BaseT4

    D. 100BaseTX

14. A transmission technology that divides that transmission medium into discrete channels so that multiple signals can share the same cable is known as _____.

    A. Duplex

    B. Baseband

    C. Sideband

    D. Broadband

15. Windows NT is primarily based on the _____ protocol.

    A. IPX

    B. NetBEUI

    C. TCP

    D. All the above

16. An RJ-45 connector should be wired with _____ pairs when used on a Category 5 UTP cable.

    A. 1

    B. 2

    C. 3

    D. 4

17. Thicknet (10Base5) can be extended to _____ meters per segment.

    A. 100

    B. 200

    C. 500

    D. 1000

18. IPX was designed for use with which network operating system?

    A. Windows NT

    B. Unix

    C. NetWare

    D. All the above

19. Failure to terminate a bus topology properly will result in _____.

    A. Electrical shock hazard

    B. Unwanted signal echo

    C. Fire hazard

    D. All the above

20. What device must you install in a computer to provide it with a physical, an electrical, and an electronic connection to a network?

    A. Router

    B. NIC

    C. Gateway

    D. BNC Connector

Answers to Review Questions

1. B, C. Computers participating in a peer-to-peer network can be either client or server or both. Additionally, the peer-to-peer model has some practical limitations, including the number of computers involved. Answer A is incorrect, because the administration is NOT centralized. Answer D is incorrect because some peer-to-peer networks use hubs.

2. B. The only coax cable designation that should be used with Ethernet is RG/58.

3. C, D. Answers C and D are correct because in a true client/server environment, the server contains all the data and administration information. But it is just a server. It cannot run client applications (like word processing). Answer A is also incorrect as a true client/server environment can use a hub, but it can also use a bus topology.

4. C. Coaxial cable requires two terminators: one at the beginning, and one at the end.

5. B. The major advantage to mesh networks is their increased reliability. There are multiple redundant connections between all nodes in the network. Answer A is incorrect because the cable costs are much, much more. Answer C is simply a distracter because mesh is NOT required by fire codes. Answer D is incorrect because most Token-based networks could not operate in a mesh environment.

6. B. The only type of network topology that uses terminators is the bus topology.

7. A. The main advantage to star topology is the fact that there is a central device (the hub) that controls and manages the physical aspects of the network. It doesn't use less cable than a physical bus or physical ring. In fact, it uses more. Additionally, if there's a cable fault, the hub will shut down traffic to that port, thus allowing the network to continue operating.

8. A. In a centralized security model, one center entity (usually the server) maintains and controls the security information for the entire network.

9. C. Vampire taps are used in Thicknet Ethernet to connect transceivers directly to the thicknet cable.

10. B. Answer B is the only correct answer. Plenum cable actually has a higher cost than PVC. Additionally, because the conductors are also made of copper, it doesn't conduct data any faster than PVC-coated cable.

11. B. Although fiber-optic, STP, and coax are all good choices for this application, UTP is currently the most popular for its versatility, low cost, and ease of installation. Fiber-optic is quickly replacing UTP, but the cost is still somewhat prohibitive.

12. D. Although all methods have megabit performance, fiber-optic has the greatest throughput potential.

13. D. Answer D is the 100-megabit standard that uses only two pairs of wires (four wires total). Answers A & C use all four pairs of a standard UTP. 10BaseF is a 10-megabit standard and it uses fiber- optic cable instead of UTP.

14. D. In broadband communications (like television communications, for example), the communications medium is divided into discrete channels. Each channel can carry its own signal. In baseband communications, the transmission takes up the whole communications channel. Duplex communications are where a sender and receiver can each send and receive signals simultaneously. Sideband is a distracter.

15. B. Although Windows NT can use all of the protocols listed, it is primarily based on NetBEUI.

16. D. Although you can wire any combination of pairs in an RJ-45 connector, you should wire all four pairs in a Category 5 UTP into an RJ-45 connector to support those network technologies that may need all four pairs (such as. 100BaseT), even if you aren't currently using them.

17. C. The maximum segment length for 10Base5 is 500 meters.

18. C. Novell, Inc. designed IPX for use with their NetWare product, although it can be used with any of the listed NOSes.

19. B. If one or both of the ends of a bus cable are not terminated, the network signal will reflect off the end of the cable and interfere with the signal already present, causing problems. The terminator absorbs this "echo," preventing the problem. Shock or fire hazard are not problems relating to not installing the terminator(s).

20. B. The Network Interface Card (NIC) is responsible for providing the physical, electrical, and electronic connections to the network. Routers and Gateways are devices on the network. BNC connectors are a type of physical connector on a bus network.

Chapter

2

The OSI Model

NETWORK+ EXAM OBJECTIVES COVERED IN THIS CHAPTER:

✓ **Define the layers of the OSI model, and identify the protocols, services, and functions that pertain to each layer.**

✓ **Identify the use of the following network components and the differences between them:**

- Hubs
- MAUs
- Switching hubs
- Repeaters
- Transceivers

✓ **Describe the following Data Link layer concepts:**

- Bridges, what they are and why they are used
- The 802 specs, including the topics covered in 802.2, 802.3, and 802.5
- The function and characteristics of MAC addresses

✓ **Explain the following routing and Network layer concepts, including:**

- The fact that routing occurs at the Network layer
- The difference between a router and a brouter
- The difference between routable and nonroutable protocols
- The concept of default gateways and subnetworks
- The reason for employing unique network IDs
- The difference between static and dynamic routing

✓ **Explain the following Transport layer concepts:**

- The distinction between connectionless and connection transport

- The purpose of name resolution, either to an IP/IPX address or a network protocol

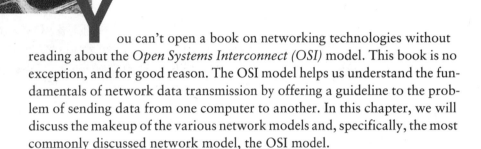

You can't open a book on networking technologies without reading about the *Open Systems Interconnect (OSI)* model. This book is no exception, and for good reason. The OSI model helps us understand the fundamentals of network data transmission by offering a guideline to the problem of sending data from one computer to another. In this chapter, we will discuss the makeup of the various network models and, specifically, the most commonly discussed network model, the OSI model.

Introducing the Open Systems Interconnect (OSI) Model

The OSI model was designed to promote interoperability by creating a guideline for network data transmission between computers that have different hardware vendors, software, operating systems, and protocols. Let's look at the simple process of transferring a file. From a user's perspective, just a single operation has been performed to transfer the file. However, many different procedures had to take place behind the scenes to accomplish this seemly simple task. Network data-transmission (like the file transfer) is performed through the use of a protocol suite, also known as a protocol stack.

A protocol suite is most easily defined as a set of rules used to determine how computers communicate with each other. This is similar to language. If I speak English and you speak English, then we can communicate. But, if I speak Spanish and you speak English, we won't be able to communicate. The

OSI model is used to describe what tasks a protocol suite performs as we explore how data moves across a network. Keep in mind that not all protocols map directly to the guideline provided for us through the OSI model, but there are enough similarities to use the OSI model to examine how these protocols function. There are a myriad of protocol suites in use today, including IPX/SPX, NetBIOS, and TCP/IP. Each performs a specific function. Many of these functions provided through the use of a protocol stack and its components are standard functions performed by other components in other protocol stacks.

The most commonly referenced protocol model, the OSI model, was developed in 1977 by the International Organization for Standardization (ISO) to provide "common ground" when describing any network protocol (see Figure 2.1).

FIGURE 2.1 The Open Systems Interconnect (OSI) model

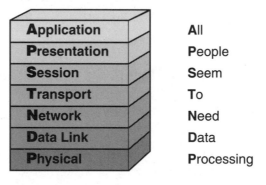

Application	**A**ll
Presentation	**P**eople
Session	**S**eem
Transport	**T**o
Network	**N**eed
Data Link	**D**ata
Physical	**P**rocessing

ISO is not an abbreviation for International Organization for Standardization but is derived from the Greek word *isos*, which means equal and was adopted by the organization. For more information, go to www.iso.ch/.

Some people use mnemonic devices to help them remember the order of the OSI model layers: APSTNDP (from top to bottom). The most popular mnemonic for this arrangement is **A**ll **P**eople **S**eem **T**o **N**eed **D**ata **P**rocessing. A reverse mnemonic (from Physical to Application, bottom to top) is **P**lease **D**o **N**ot **T**hrow **S**ausage **P**izza **A**way. (Good advice, don't you think?)

As you can see in Figure 2.1, the OSI model consists of seven layers. Each layer performs a specific function and then passes the result on to another layer. When a sending station has data to send, it formats a network request and then passes that request to the network protocol at the top layer, the Application layer. The protocol that runs at the Application layer performs an operation on the request and then passes it to the next lower layer. Each protocol at each layer underneath the Application layer performs its own calculations and appends its own information to the data sent from the layer above it. At the receiving station, the process happens in reverse. Figure 2.2 illustrates this basic process.

FIGURE 2.2   How data travels through the layers of the OSI model

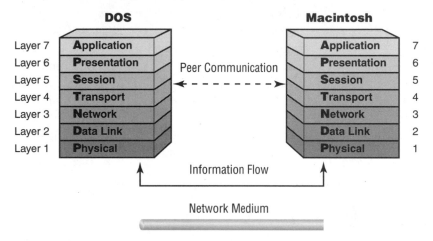

The OSI model is only a model; it is not a protocol. Nobody is running the "OSI protocol" (at least no one had developed one at the time of this writing). Let's take a brief look at the layers of the OSI model and the basic protocol functions they describe. We'll start at the top with the Application layer and work our way down to the Physical layer.

The Application Layer

The top layer of the OSI model does not refer to applications such as word processors, but rather refers to a set of tools that an application can use to accomplish a task, such as a word processor application requesting a file transfer. This layer is responsible for defining how interaction occurs between network services (applications) and the network. Services that function at the Application layer include, but are not limited to, file, print, and messaging services. The Application layer may also support error recovery.

The Presentation Layer

This layer is responsible for formatting data exchange. In this layer, character sets are converted, and data is encrypted. Data may also be compressed in this layer, and this layer usually handles the redirection of data streams.

The Session Layer

This layer defines how two computers establish, synchronize, maintain, and end a session. Practical functions, such as security authentication, connection ID establishment, data transfer, acknowledgments, and connection release, take place here. This list is not all-inclusive. Any communications that require milestones or, put another way, require "Have you got that data I sent?" answers are performed here. Typically these are called *checkpoints*. Once a checkpoint has been crossed, any data not received only need retransmission from the last good checkpoint. Adjusting checkpoints to account for very reliable or unreliable connections can greatly improve the actual throughput of data transmission.

The Transport Layer

This layer is responsible for checking that data was delivered error free. It is also used to divide a message that is too long into smaller segments and, in the reverse, take a series of short messages and combine them into one longer segment. These smaller or combined segments must later be correctly reassembled. This is accomplished through segment sequencing (usually by appending a number to each of the segments). This layer also handles logical address/name resolution. Additionally, this layer can send an acknowledgment that it got the data packet. Frequently you will see this referred to as an ACK, which is short for acknowledgment. This layer is responsible for the majority of error and flow control in network communications.

The Network Layer

This layer is responsible for logical addressing and translating logical names into physical address. A little-known function of the Network layer is prioritizing data. Not all data is of equal importance. Nobody is hurt if an e-mail message is delayed a fraction of a second. Delaying audio or video data a fraction of a second could be disastrous to the message. This prioritization is known as *Quality of Service,* or *QoS.*

In addition, the Network layer controls congestion, routes data from source to destination, and builds and tears down packets. Most routing protocols function at this layer.

The Data Link Layer

This layer takes raw data from the Physical layer and gives it a logical structure. This logic includes information about where the data is meant to go, which computer sent the data, and the overall validity of the bytes sent. In most situations, after a data frame is sent, the Data Link layer then waits for a positive ACK. If one is not received or if the frame is damaged, another frame is sent.

The Data Link layer also controls functions of logical network topologies and physical addressing as well as data transmission synchronization and connection.

The Physical Layer

This layer is responsible for controlling the functional interface, such as transmission technique, pin layout, and connector type.

Now that you have a broad overview of the OSI model, let's examine the functions of each layer in a little more detail, starting with the lower layers.

The OSI Model Lower Layers

In the last section, we took a brief look at the functions of the layers of the OSI model. In the following sections, we will discuss the lower layers in detail. In addition to the concepts, we will discuss some of the devices that operate at those layers and some of their installation concepts.

The Physical Layer

The easiest way to think about the Physical layer is that it deals with measurable, physical entities. Any protocol or device that operates at the Physical layer deals with the physical concepts of a network.

Physical Layer Concepts

Generally speaking, Physical layer concepts deal with a network component you can touch. When a protocol at the Physical layer receives information from the upper layers, it translates all the data into signals that can be transmitted on a transmission medium. This process is known as *signal encoding* (or *encoding*, for short). With cable media (also called *bounded media*), the protocols that operate at the Physical layer translate the ones and zeros of the data into electrical ons and offs.

Additionally, the Physical layer specifies how much of the media will be used (in other words, its *signaling method*) during data transmission. If a network signal uses all available signal frequencies (or put differently, the entire bandwidth), the technology is said to use *baseband* signaling. Most LAN technologies, such as Ethernet, use baseband signaling. On the other hand, if a signal only uses one frequency (or only part of the bandwidth), the technology is said to use *broadband* signaling. This means multiple signals can be transmitted on the media simultaneously. Television signals use broadband signaling.

Finally, the Physical layer specifies the layout of the transmission media (its *topology*, in other words). A physical topology describes the way the cabling is physically laid out (as opposed to a logical topology, discussed later in "The Data Link Layer" section). The physical topologies include the following:

- Bus
- Star
- Ring
- Mesh

The Bus Topology

In a physical bus topology, every computer is directly connected to a common medium. A physical bus network uses one network cable that runs from one end of the network to the other. Workstations connect at various points along this cable. The main advantage to this topology is simplicity. Only one cable is used. However, a cable fault can bring down the entire network, thus making a physical bus topology the least fault-tolerant of all the physical topologies. A physical bus topology typically requires less cable than other physical topologies. Figure 2.3 shows a sample physical bus network.

FIGURE 2.3   A sample physical bus topology

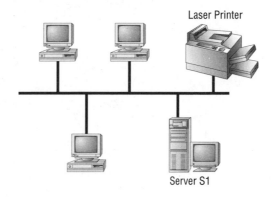

The Star Topology

In a physical star topology, a cable runs from each network entity to a central device. This central device (called a *hub*) allows all devices to communicate as if they were all directly connected. The main advantage to a physical star topology is its fault tolerance. If one node or cable malfunctions, the rest of the network is not affected. The hub simply won't be able to communicate with the station attached to that port. An Ethernet 10BaseT network is one example of a network type that requires a physical star topology. Figure 2.4 shows a sample network that uses a physical star topology.

FIGURE 2.4   A physical star topology

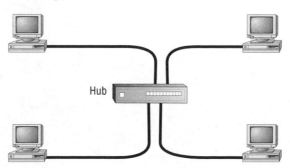

The Ring Topology

A physical ring topology isn't seen much in the computer networking world. If you do see it, it's usually in a WAN environment. In a physical ring topology, every network entity connects directly to only two other network entities (the one immediately preceding and the one immediately following). The complexity of the ring topology makes it a poor choice in most network environments. Figure 2.5 shows a physical ring network.

FIGURE 2.5   A physical ring topology

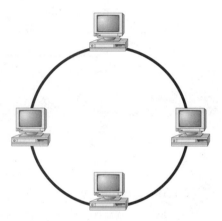

The Mesh Topology

A physical mesh topology is another physical topology that isn't widely used in computer networks (except in special WAN cases). In a physical mesh topology, every computer is directly connected to every other computer in the network. The more computers there are on a mesh network, the more cables that make up the network. If a mesh network has n computers, there will be $n(n-1)/2$ cables. With ten computers, there would be $10(10-1)/2$, or 45 cables. As you can see, this topology quickly becomes unmanageable with only a few computers. Figure 2.6 shows a sample mesh network.

FIGURE 2.6   A physical mesh topology

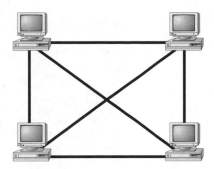

Physical Layer Devices

Several devices operate primarily at the Physical layer of the OSI model. These devices mainly manipulate the physical aspects of a network data stream (such as the voltages, signal direction, and signal strength). Let's take a quick look at some of the most popular:

- Network Interface Card (NIC)
- Transceivers
- Repeaters
- Hubs
- MAUs

The Network Interface Card (NIC)

Probably the most common component on any network is the *network interface card (NIC)*. A NIC is the component that provides the connection between a computer's internal bus and the network media. NICs come in many shapes and sizes. They vary by the type of bus connection they employ and their network media connection ports. Figure 2.7 shows an example of a network interface card.

FIGURE 2.7 A sample network interface card

The Transceiver

In the strictest definition, a *transceiver* is the part of any network interface that transmits and receives network signals (transmitter/receiver). Every network interface has a transceiver. The appearance and function of the transceiver vary with the type of network cable and topology in use.

Some network interface cards have an *Attachment Unit Interface (AUI)* port · (typically a 15-pin DIN connector) that allows a different, external transceiver type to be used, thus changing the media types to which the NIC can connect. For example, if you are using an Ethernet 10Base2 network interface card with an AUI port, you can connect to an Ethernet 10BaseT network by using an external transceiver attached to the AUI port. A DIN connector meets the specification of the German national standards body, *Deutsche Industrie Norm*, or *DIN*.

The Repeater

The simplest of all the Physical layer devices is the *repeater*, which simply amplifies the signals it receives on one port and resends (or "repeats") them on another. Repeaters are used to extend the maximum length of a network segment. They are often used if a few network stations are located far from the rest of the network. Figure 2.8 shows a network that uses a repeater.

FIGURE 2.8   A repeater installed on a network

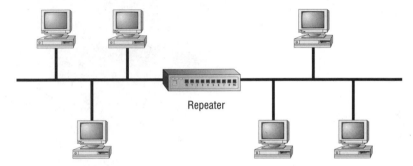

The main downfall of a repeater is that it repeats *everything* it receives on one port, including noise, to its other ports. This has the ultimate effect of limiting the number of repeaters that can be practically used on a network. The 5-4-3 Rule dictates how many repeaters can be used on a network and where they can be placed. According to this rule, a single network can have five network segments connected by four repeaters, with three of the segments populated. If this rule is violated, one station may not be able to see the rest of the network. Figure 2.9 illustrates the 5-4-3 Rule.

FIGURE 2.9   The 5-4-3 Rule for network repeaters

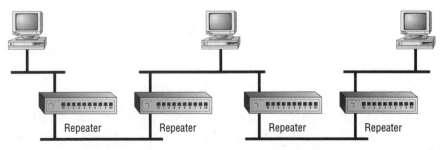

The Hub

Besides the NIC, a hub is probably the next most common Physical layer device found on networks today. A *hub* (also called a *concentrator*) serves as a central connection point for several network devices. At its basic level, a hub is nothing more than a multiport repeater. A hub repeats what it receives on one port to all other ports. It is, therefore, also subject to the 5-4-3 Rule. Figure 2.10 shows an example of a hub.

FIGURE 2.10 A standard hub

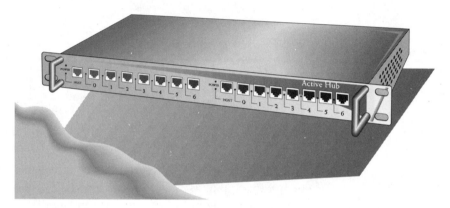

There are many classifications of hubs, but two of the most important are active and passive:

- An active hub is usually powered and actually amplifies and cleans up the signal it receives, thus doubling the effective segment distance limitation for the specific topology (for example, extending an Ethernet segment another 100 meters).

- A passive hub typically is unpowered and makes only physical, electrical connections. Typically, the maximum segment distance of a particular topology is shortened because the hub takes some power away from the signal strength in order to do its job.

The Multistation Access Unit (MAU)

This Physical layer device is unique to Token Ring networks. Token Ring networks use a physical star topology, yet they use a logical ring topology (discussed later). The central device on an Ethernet star topology network is a hub, but on a Token Ring network, the central device is a Multistation

Access Unit (MAU, sometimes called MSAU). The functionality of the MAU is similar to that of a hub, but the MAU provides the data path that creates the logical "ring" in a Token Ring network. The data can travel in an endless loop between stations. In a Token Ring network, you can have up to 33 MAUs chained together. MAUs are shown in Figure 2.11.

FIGURE 2.11   MAUs in a Token Ring network

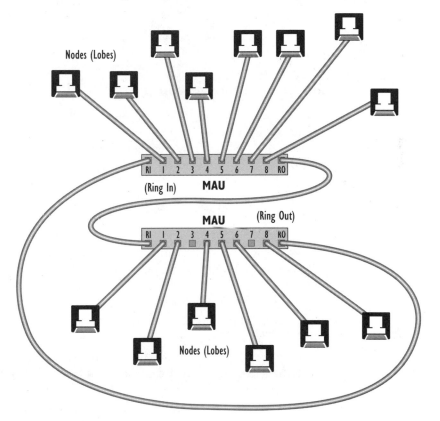

The Data Link Layer

The Data Link layer is actually made up of two sublayers:

- The Media Access Control (MAC)
- The Logical Link Control (LLC)

Figure 2.12 illustrates this arrangement.

FIGURE 2.12 Sublayers of the Data Link layer

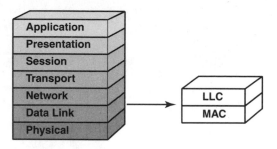

Data Link Layer Concepts

Protocols that operate at the Data Link layer have several responsibilities, including creating, transmitting, and receiving packets. Additionally, the Data Link layer is responsible for physical (MAC) addressing and logical link control processing, creating logical topologies, and controlling media access.

Packets

At the Data Link layer, data coming from upper layer protocols are divided into logical chunks called *packets*. A packet is a unit of data transmission. The size and format of these packets depend on the transmission technology.

The Hardware (MAC) Address

Every network interface card has an address, typically assigned at the factory. This address is protocol-independent and is often called the hardware address. But its technically accurate name is *MAC address* because it exists at the MAC sublayer of the Data Link layer. This address is also called the *Ethernet address* or the *physical address*.

The MAC address itself is a 12-digit hexadecimal number. If you'll remember, hexadecimal uses all digits from 0 through 9 and A through F. Each two digits are separated by colons, like so:

07:57:AC:1F:B2:76

Normally, the MAC address of a network interface card is set at the factory and cannot be changed. For this purpose, all NIC manufacturers keep track of the MAC addresses they use and don't duplicate addresses between vendors. As of late, however, some manufacturers have started reusing their blocks of MAC addresses. This made it necessary for administrators to be able to change the MAC addresses of the cards they received (using a factory-supplied program). If they discovered a duplicated MAC address, they could resolve the conflict.

Logical Topology

In addition to these responsibilities, the Data Link layer can also dictate the *logical topology* of a network; in other words, the way the packets move through a network. A logical topology differs from a physical topology in that the physical topology dictates the way the cables are laid out; the logical topology dictates the way the information flows. The types of logical topologies are the same as the physical topologies, except that the information flow specifies the type of topology to use.

Finally, the Data Link layer can describe the method of media access. The three main methods of media access are:

- Contention, in which every station "competes" with other stations for the opportunity to transmit, and each has an equal chance at transmitting. If two stations transmit at the same time, an error, referred to as a *collision,* occurs, and the stations try again.

- Polling, in which a central device, called a *controller*, polls each device, in turn, and asks if it has data to transmit. This type of media access virtually eliminates collisions.

- Token passing, which uses a special data packet called a *token.* When a station has the token, it can transmit. If it doesn't have the token, it can't transmit. This media access technology also eliminates collision problems.

Media Access

With many stations on the same piece of network media, there has to be a way of vying for time on the cable. This process is called media access, and there are three main methods:

Carrier Sense/Multiple Access with Collision Detection (CSMA/CD)
This media access technology with the extremely long acronym is probably the most common. When a protocol that uses CSMA/CD has data to transmit, it first senses if a signal is already on the wire (a *carrier*), indicating that someone is transmitting currently. That's the "Carrier Sense"

part. If no one else is transmitting, it attempts a transmission and then listens to hear if someone else tried to transmit at the same time. If someone else transmits at the exact same time, a condition known as a *collision* occurs. Both senders "back off" and don't transmit until some random period of time has passed. They then both retry. That's the "Collision Detection" part. The final part that we didn't mention (Multiple Access) just means that more than one station can be on the network at the same time. CSMA/CD is the access method used in Ethernet networks.

Token Passing   This media access method uses a special packet called a token. The first computer turned on creates the token. It then passes the token on to the next computer. The token passes around the network until a computer that has data to send takes the token off the network, modifies it, and puts it back on the network along with the data it has to send. Each station between the sender and the receiver along the network reads the destination address in the token. If the destination address doesn't match its own, the station simply sends the package on its way. When the destination station recognizes its address in the destination address of the token, the NIC copies the data into the station's memory and modifies the token, indicating it has received the data. The token continues around the network until the original sender receives the token back again. If the original sender has more data to send, the process repeats itself. If not, the sender modifies the token to indicate that the token is "free" for anyone else to use. With this method, there are no collisions (as in CSMA/CD networks) because everyone has to have "permission" to transmit (via the token).

Carrier Sense/Multiple Access with Collision Avoidance (CSMA/CA) This technology works almost identically to CSMA/CD, but instead of sending the whole data chunk and then listening to hear if it was transmitted, the sender transmits a request to send (RTS) packet and waits for a clear to send (CTS) before sending. When it receives the CTS, the sender sends the chunk. AppleTalk networks use this method of media access. The difference between CSMA/CD and CSMA/CA has been described like this: Say you want to cross a busy street and you want to use one of these protocols to cross it. If you are using CSMA/CD, you just cross the street. If you get hit, you go back to the curb and try again. If you're using CSMA/CA, you send your little brother across. If he makes it, it's probably OK for you to go.

Project 802

One of the major components of the Data Link layer is the result of the Institute of Electrical and Electronics Engineers (IEEE) 802 subcommittees and their work on standards for Local Area and Metropolitan Area Networks (LANs/MANs). The committee met in February 1980, so we have 1980, the second month, and thus the name Project 802. The designation for an 802 standard always includes a dot (.) followed by either a single or a double digit. These numeric digits specify particular categories within the 802 standard. Currently, there are 12 standards. These are listed in Table 2.1 and shown in Figure 2.13.

TABLE 2.1   IEEE 802 Networking Standards

Standard	Topic
802.1	LAN/MAN Management (and Media Access Control Bridges)
802.2	Logical Link Control
802.3	CSMA/CD
802.4	Token Bus
802.5	Token Ring
802.6	Distributed Queue Dual Bus (DQDB) Metropolitan Area Network (MAN)
802.7	Broadband Local Area Networks
802.8	Fiber-Optic LANs and MANs
802.9	Integrated Services (IS) LAN Interface
802.10	LAN/MAN Security
802.11	Wireless LAN
802.12	Demand Priority Access Method

FIGURE 2.13   The IEEE standards' relationship to the OSI model

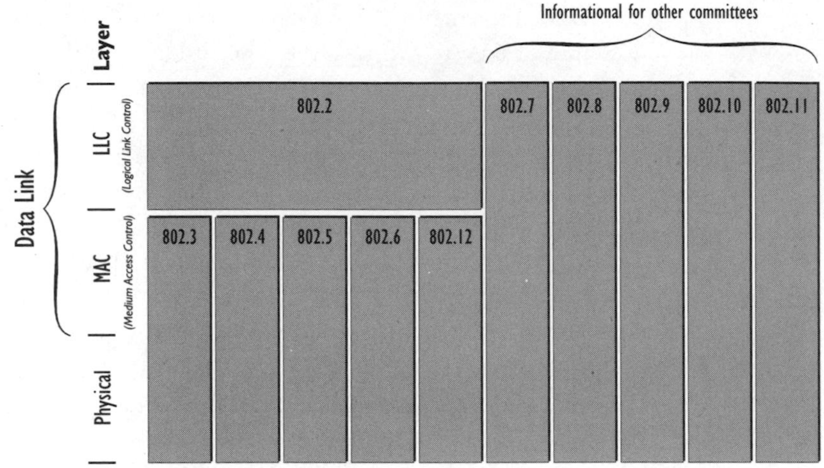

The 802.1 LAN/MAN Management (and Media Access Control Bridges)

IEEE 802.1 discusses standards for LAN and MAN management, as well as MAC bridges. One of the derivatives of 802.1 is the spanning tree algorithm for network bridges (discussed later in this chapter). The spanning tree algorithm helps to prevent bridge loops in a multibridge network.

The 802.2 Logical Link Control

This standard specifies the operation of the logical link control (LLC) sublayer of the Data Link layer of the OSI model. The LLC sublayer provides an interface between the MAC sublayer and the Network layer. The 802.2 standard is used by the IEEE 802.3 Ethernet specification (discussed next), but not by the earlier Ethernet 2 specifications (used in early implementations of Ethernet).

The 802.3 CSMA/CD

This standard specifies a network that uses a bus topology, baseband signaling, and a CSMA/CD network access method. This standard was developed to match the Digital, Intel, and Xerox (DIX) Ethernet networking technology. So many people implemented the 802.3 standard, which resembles the DIX Ethernet, that people just started calling it Ethernet. It is the most widely implemented of all the 802 standards because of its simplicity and low cost.

Recently the 802.3u working group updated 802.3 to include Ethernet 100BaseT implementations.

The 802.4 Token Bus

This standard specifies a physical and a logical bus topology that uses coaxial or fiber-optic cable and a token-passing media access method. It is mainly used for factory automation and is seldom used in computer networking. It most closely resembles the Manufacturing Automation Protocol (MAP), developed by General Motors and used by many manufacturing companies. Some people think that the IEEE 802.4 standard is for a technology known as the Attached Resource Computer Network (ARCNet). That is an incorrect assumption. Although the technologies are similar, the IEEE 802.4 standard more closely resembles MAP, not ARCNet.

The 802.5 Token Ring

This standard is one example of a commonly used product becoming a documented standard. Typically, a standard is developed and then products are written to conform to the standard. Token Ring was developed by IBM in 1984, and the 802.5 standard soon followed. And 802.5 and Token Ring are almost identical.

Like Ethernet, Token Ring can use several cable types. Most often, it is installed using *twisted-pair* cabling, which can be either *shielded* or *unshielded*. Shielding adds to the cable investment but offers the advantage of resistance to unwanted electrical signals, which could impair the network signal.

Token Ring uses a physical star, logical ring topology with token-passing media access. Possible transmission rates for Token Ring increased with time. After 4Mbps Token Ring came 16Mbps Token Ring. If you install 4Mbps NICs on a network that otherwise uses 16Mbps NICs, your entire ring speed is reduced to 4Mbps. Unlike Ethernet, a computer cannot talk unless it has a token. This can cause some grief if a token gets "stuck." Unlike ARCNet, Token Ring is still used in a number of locations for two reasons:

- IBM made sure that Token Ring did a fine job of talking to IBM mainframes, which are still commonly used.

- Token Ring network performance "degrades with grace."

The latter means that as network traffic increases, the network slowly gets slower, because the single token, which can only travel in one direction, gets busy carrying all that traffic. Ethernet, on the other hand, can become so flooded as network traffic increases that the entire network fails. Now, suppose you were wiring a computerized fire alarm system for a large building. Which would you rather use, Ethernet or Token Ring? To increase performance, some Token Ring technologies implement early token release, whereby the token isn't hogged by the sending station. It simply grabs the token, sends its data, and frees the token.

In Token Ring, just as in all ARCNet and most Ethernet schemes, there is a central device to which stations connect. It isn't, however, called a hub. IBM calls it an *MAU*, or *Multistation Access Unit*. IBM always seems to have a different name for things. Even their name for Token Ring cabling is different. In telephone and computer networks, twisted cable is rated by *categories*. IBM rates Token Ring cable by *type*. One final difference between Token Ring and the others is the *regeneration process*. Data signals are read, amplified, and repeated by every device on the network, to reduce degradation. This includes MAUs and NICs and is one reason that Token Ring is fairly expensive. An average Token Ring NIC is upward of $200, whereas a similar Ethernet card can be less than $100.

The 802.6 Distributed Queue Dual Bus (DQDB) Metropolitan Area Network

In some ways, asking what defines *a Metropolitan Area Network (MAN)* is like asking how long is a rope. We can safely say that a MAN reaches beyond the area of a Local Area Network (LAN). The interesting question is, When does a MAN become a Wide Area Network (WAN)? Sorry to say, there is no easy answer. Like a WAN, a MAN can support many computers. How many miles a MAN can cover has more to do with regulations than with geography. For example, from a geographical standpoint, Portland, Oregon, and Vancouver, Washington, are separated by nothing more than several hundred feet of water. From a political standpoint, they are in different states, and, therefore, different telecommunication regulations apply to each city. This could mean that no MANs can connect Portland and Vancouver. For our purposes, we need to know only that a MAN generally encompasses a city-sized area and can support many-to-many connections. Transmission speeds vary with the size of an enterprise's bank account. The standard recommends the use of Distributed Queue Dual Bus (DQDB) technologies for MANs.

The 802.7 Broadband Local Area Networks

Don't let the fancy phrasing fool you. You have used broadband if you have seen cable TV. When one cable carries multiple signals, that is broadband. The most common method for separating signals is to have them on different frequencies. This is called *Frequency Division Multiplexing (FDM)*. Each channel on TV uses a different frequency. It is as simple as that. Maybe you can win a beer from some friends by seeing if they can explain Frequency Division Multiplexing. If they can't, collect your reward, and tell them that is how all those TV channels get into their TV from one cable. The alternative to sending a set of signals this way is to use the entire cable for one signal. This is known as *baseband* and is used by standards such as Ethernet.

The 802.8 Fiber-Optic LANs and MANs

As the name implies, this working group handed down guidelines for fiber-optic usage on networks defined by 802.3 through 802.6, which includes *Fiber Distributed Data Interface (FDDI)* as well as *10BaseFL*. 10BaseFL defines Ethernet over fiber-optic cable. As you can see, some of the 802 definitions have more to do with our day-to-day work than others.

The 802.9 Integrated Services (IS) LAN Interface

For a while, it seemed that this definition would have a profound effect on daily networking, as it laid out how *Integrated Switched Digital Network (ISDN)* behaves. Late in 1998, many industry watchers began to call for the slow death of ISDN, because both cable modems and *Asymmetrical Digital Subscriber Line (ADSL)* have overtaken ISDN with less-complicated setup, higher performance, and lower cost.

The 802.10 LAN/MAN Security

This standard provides a secure pathway for data across a shared path. An implementation of this is using the public Internet as a backbone for a private interconnection between locations. The term for this form of connecting is known as *Virtual Private Networking (VPN)*. Because VPN costs are less than the cost for direct private connections, VPN is likely to become popular in the near future.

The 802.11 Wireless LAN

Wireless networking usually requires a higher up-front investment than a cable-based network. Still, the cost can be justified if an office is rearranged with any regularity or must be moved from location to location to satisfy business requirements. A famous example is the Red Cross. This agency would not be effective if it had to wire computers together every time before assisting a disaster area.

As of this writing, an update to 802.11 is expected, the 802.11ab standard, which specifies higher wireless speeds. This demonstrates that the 802 standards are not static from almost 20 years ago, but a dynamic set of rules that are updated as technology moves forward.

The 802.12 Demand Priority Access Method

First developed by Hewlett-Packard, this standard combines the concepts of Ethernet and ATM. The communication scheme used is called Demand Priority (thus, the name of the standard). It uses "intelligent" hubs that allocate more bandwidth to frames that have been assigned a higher priority by the sending computer. The hub scans its ports and then allocates bandwidth according to each frame's priority. This is extremely valuable for real-time audio and video transmissions. The 802.12 standard is also known as *100VG (Voice Grade), 100VG-AnyLAN, 100Base VG,* and *AnyLAN.* The 100 is short for 100Mbps, or 10 times faster than the original Ethernet speeds. Other manufacturers didn't buy into the ideas of 100VG, perhaps in part because of the higher overhead of demand priority due to port scanning. Instead, they updated the original Ethernet to *Fast Ethernet,* which also supports 100Mbps while maintaining the 802.3 standards.

Data Link Layer Devices

Two main devices manipulate data at the Data Link layer:

- Bridges

- Switches

Both are more complex than their Physical layer counterparts and thus are more expensive and more difficult to implement. But they each bring unique advantages to the network.

The Bridge

A *bridge* is a network device, operating at the Data Link layer, that logically separates a single network into two segments, but lets the two segments appear to be one network to higher layer protocols. The primary use for a bridge is to keep traffic meant for stations on one side of the bridge and not let it pass to the other side. For example, if you have a group of workstations that constantly exchange data on the same network segment as a group of workstations that don't use the network much, the busy group will slow down the performance of the network for the other users. If you put in a bridge to separate the two groups, only traffic destined for a workstation on the other side of the bridge will pass to the other side. All other traffic stays local. Figure 2.14 shows a network before and after bridging.

FIGURE 2.14 A sample network before and after bridging

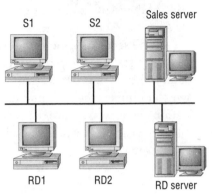

Before Bridging

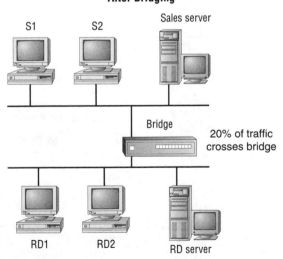

After Bridging

Bridges can connect dissimilar network types (for example, Token Ring and Ethernet) as long as the bridge operates at the LLC sublayer of the Data Link layer. If the bridge operates at the lower sublayer (the MAC sublayer) only, the bridge can connect only similar network types (Token Ring to Token Ring and Ethernet to Ethernet).

The Switching Hub

In the past few years, the switching hub has received a lot of attention as a replacement for the standard hub. The switching hub is more intelligent than a standard hub in that it can actually understand some of the traffic that passes through it. A switching hub (or switch for short) operates at the Data Link layer and is also known as a Layer 2 Switch. Layer 2 switches build a table of the MAC addresses of all the connected stations (see Figure 2.15).

When two stations attached to the switch want to communicate, the sending station sends its data to the switch. This part of the process is similar to the way a standard hub functions. However, when the switch receives the data, rather than broadcasting it out all its other ports as a hub would, the switch examines the data link header for the MAC address of the receiving station and forwards it to the correct port. This opens a virtual pipe between ports that can use the full bandwidth of the topology. Switches have received a lot of attention because of this ability. If a server and several workstations were connected to the same 100Mbps Ethernet switch, each workstation would need a dedicated 100Mbps channel to the server, and there would never be any collisions.

FIGURE 2.15   A switch builds a table of all MAC addresses of all connected stations

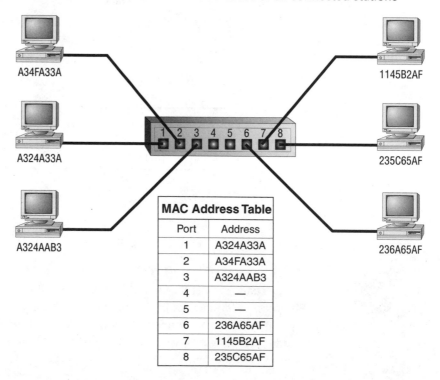

MAC Address Table	
Port	Address
1	A324A33A
2	A34FA33A
3	A324AAB3
4	—
5	—
6	236A65AF
7	1145B2AF
8	235C65AF

The OSI Model Middle Layers

As we move up the OSI model, the protocols at each successive layer get more complex and have more responsibilities. At the middle are the Network and Transport layers, which perform the bulk of the work for a protocol stack. We'll see why in the sections to follow. Let's begin with the Network layer.

The Network Layer

The Network layer of the OSI model defines protocols that ensure that the data arrive at the correct destination. This is probably the most commonly discussed layer of the OSI model.

Network Layer Concepts

The most important Network layer concepts are:

- Logical network addressing
- Routing

Logical Network Addressing

In the last section, we mentioned that every network device has an address (the MAC address) assigned at the factory and that it is protocol-independent. But, as you know, most networks communicate using protocols that must have their own addressing scheme. If the MAC address is the Data Link layer physical address, the protocol addressing scheme at the Network layer defines the logical address.

Each logical network address is protocol-dependent. For example, a TCP/IP address is not the same as an IPX address. Additionally, the two protocols can coexist on the same computer without conflict. However, two different stations using the same protocol cannot have the same logical network address on the same network. If that happens, neither station can be seen on the network (see Figure 2.16).

FIGURE 2.16 Address conflicts on a network

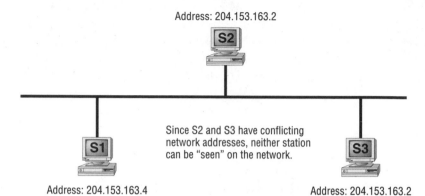

Address: 204.153.163.2

Since S2 and S3 have conflicting network addresses, neither station can be "seen" on the network.

Address: 204.153.163.4

Address: 204.153.163.2

If IP addresses are duplicated on Windows 95/98 workstations, the first station that is assigned an address gets to use it. Any other station that has that address receives error messages about duplicated IP addresses. The address is then unassigned. The first station receives error messages as well, but it can continue to function.

Address conflicts can be common with TCP/IP because an administrator often needs to assign IP addresses. IPX addresses don't suffer from conflict nearly as often because they use the MAC address as part of the IPX address. The MAC address is unique and can't be changed. For more information on network addresses, see Chapter 4.

Network Address Formats

Every network address in either TCP/IP or IPX has both a network portion and a node portion. The network portion is the number that is assigned to the network segment to which the station is connected. The node portion is the unique number that identifies that station on the segment. Together, the network portion and the node portion of an address ensure that a network address will be unique across the entire network.

IPX addresses use an eight-digit hexadecimal number for the network portion. This number, called the *IPX network address,* can be assigned randomly by the installation program or manually by the network administrator. The node portion is the 12-digit hexadecimal MAC address assigned by the manufacturer. A colon separates the two portions. Here is a sample IPX address:

Network Address   Node Address

00004567:006A7C11FB56

TCP/IP addresses, on the other hand, use a dotted decimal notation in the format xxx.xxx.xxx.xxx as shown in the following:

199.217.67.34   IP Address

255.255.255.0   Subnet Mask

The address consists of four collections of eight-digit binary numbers (or up to three decimal digits) called *octets,* separated by periods. Each decimal number in an IP address is typically a number in the range 1 through 254. Which portion is the network and which portion is the node depends on the class of the address and the *subnet mask* assigned with the address. A subnet mask is also a dotted-decimal number with numbers in the range 0 through 255. If a subnet mask contains 255 in a position (corresponding to a binary number of all ones), the corresponding part of the IP address is the network address. For example, if you have the mask 255.255.255.0, the first three octets are the network portion, and the last portion is the node.

Routing

Routing is the process of moving data throughout a network, passing through several network segments using devices called routers that can select the path the data takes. Placing routers on a network to connect several smaller routers turns a network into an entity known as an *internetwork.* Routers get information about which paths to take from files on the routers called *routing tables.* These tables contain information about which router network interface (or port) to place information on in order to send it to a particular network segment. Routers will not pass unknown or broadcast packets. A router will only route a packet if it has a specific destination. Figure 2.17 illustrates these components and their participation in the routing process.

FIGURE 2.17 Routing components

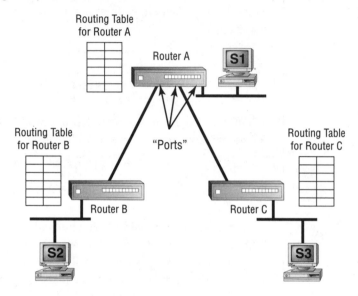

Information gets into routing tables in two ways:

- Through static routing
- Through dynamic routing

In *static routing,* the network administrator manually updates the router's routing table. The administrator enters every network into the routing table and selects the port that the router should place data on when the router intercepts data destined for that network. Unfortunately, on networks with more than a few segments, manually updating routing tables is time-intensive and prohibitive. When using a Windows NT server as a router, use the ROUTE command to add, change, or remove static routes.

Dynamic routing, on the other hand, uses route discovery protocols (or routing protocols, for short) to talk to other routers and find out what networks they are attached to. Routers that use dynamic routing send out special packets to request updates of the other routers on the network as well as to send their own updates. Dynamic routing is the most popular routing technology.

With dynamic routing, the two categories of route discovery protocols are distance vector and link state. Older route discovery protocols, such as Routing Information Protocol (RIP) for TCP/IP and RIP for IPX, use the distance vector method. In distance vector routing, a router sends out its routing table when it is brought online and the contents of its routing tables every 60 seconds thereafter. When another router receives it, it adds 1 to the hop count of each route in the list of routes and then rebroadcasts the list. A *hop* is one pass through a router. This process typically takes place every 60 seconds.

The main downside to distance vector route discovery is the overhead required in broadcasting the entire routing table every 60 seconds. Link state route discovery is more efficient. Routers using link state route discovery routers send out their routing table via a multicast, not broadcast packet, every five minutes or so. If there is an update, only the update is sent. NetWare Link Services Protocol (NLSP) for IPX and Open Shortest Path First (OSPF) for TCP/IP are two link state route discovery protocols.

Several protocols can be routed, but a few protocols can't be routed. It is important to know which protocols are routable and which aren't so that you can choose the appropriate protocol when it comes time to design an internetwork. Table 2.2 shows a few of the most common routable and nonroutable protocols and the routing protocols they use, if any.

TABLE 2.2 Routable and Nonroutable Protocols

Protocol	Route Discovery Protocol	Routable?
IPX	RIP	Yes
IPX	NLSP	Yes
NetBEUI	None	No
TCP/IP	RIP	Yes
TCP/IP	OSPF	Yes
XNS	RIP	Yes

When setting up routing on your network, you may have to configure a default gateway. A *default gateway,* when configured on a workstation, is the router that all packets are sent to when the workstation doesn't know where the station is or can't find it on the local segment. TCP/IP networks sometimes have multiple routers as well and must use this parameter to specify which router is the default. Other protocols don't have very good routing functions at the workstation, so they must use this feature to "find" the router.

Network Layer Devices

Three devices operate at the Network layer:

- Routers
- Brouters
- Layer 3 Switches

The Router

The router is the device that connects multiple networks or segments to form a larger internetwork. It is also the device that facilitates communication within this internetwork. It makes the choices about how best to send packets within the network so that they arrive at their destination.

Several companies manufacture routers, but probably the two biggest names in the business are Bay Networks and Cisco. Bay Networks is a conglomeration of smaller networking companies bought out by networking giant Synoptics. Cisco has always been a built-from-the-ground-up router company. Both companies make other products, to be sure, but their bread and butter is routing technologies.

Routers have many functions other than simply routing packets. Routers can connect many small segments into a network, as well as connect networks to a much larger network, such as a corporate WAN or the Internet. Routers can also connect dissimilar lower layer topologies. For example, you can connect an Ethernet and a Token Ring network using a router. Additionally, with added software, routers can perform firewall functions and packet filtering.

Routers are probably the most complex devices on a network today. Consequently, they are also probably the most expensive. But simple, low-end routers have been introduced by Bay Networks, Cisco, and other companies in the sub-$1000 range that make Internet connectivity more affordable. Hub vendors have begun to introduce basic, intranetwork routing functionality into their products as well. But we will discuss that later.

The Brouter

The *brouter* is a unique device that combines the functionality of a bridge and a router. It routes most packets, but if it can't route a particular packet, it will try and bridge it. It is not seen much any more and was mainly used to connect different network topologies and to bridge them. Unfortunately, if you try to use a brouter as either a bridge or a router, it will fall short in functionality of either.

Layer 3 Switches

A fairly new Network layer device that has received much media attention of late is the Layer 3 Switch. The Layer 3 part of the name corresponds to the Network layer of the OSI model. It performs the multiport, virtual LAN, data pipelining functions of a standard Layer 2 Switch, but it can perform basic routing functions between virtual LANs. In some workgroups, a Layer 3 Switch can replace a workgroup router.

The Transport Layer

The Transport layer defines the protocols for structuring messages and checks the validity of transmissions.

Transport Layer Concepts

The Transport layer reminds us of what our old Net Tech instructors used to pound into our heads: "Reliable end-to-end error and flow control." (Thanks, Doug and Al!) The Transport layer does other things as well, but the protocols that operate at the Transport layer mainly ensure reliable communications between upper peer layers.

The Connection Type

To provide error and flow control services, protocols at the Transport layer use connection services. The two types of connection services are:

- Connection-oriented
- Connectionless

Connection-oriented connection services use acknowledgments and responses to establish a virtual connection between sending and receiving stations. The acknowledgments are also used to ensure that the connection is maintained. Connection-oriented connections are similar to phone calls. You dial the intended recipient, and the recipient picks up and says hello. You then identify yourself and say that you'd like to talk about something, and the conversation begins. If you hear silence for a while, you might ask, "Are you still there?" to make sure the recipient is still on the line. When finished, you both agree to end the connection by hanging up. Connection-oriented services work in the same way, except that instead of mouths, phones, and words, they use computers, NICs, and special packets. Figure 2.18 shows an example of the beginning of communications between two computers using connection-oriented services.

FIGURE 2.18 Initiating communications using a connection-oriented service

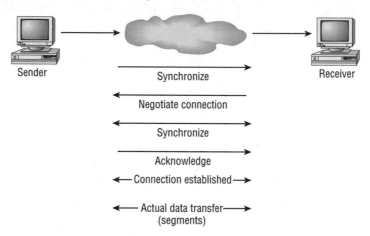

Connectionless services, on the other hand, don't have error and flow control. They do have one simple advantage—speed. Because connectionless services don't have the overhead of maintaining the connection, the sacrifice in error control is more than made up for in speed. To make another analogy, connectionless services are similar to a postcard. Each message is considered singular and not related to any other. So, if one part of the message is lost, it can simply be resent.

Name Resolution

The Transport layer also handles logical address to logical name resolution. In some protocols, a node address such as 185.45.2.23 isn't the best way to reference a host. Some protocol stacks (TCP/IP and IPX/SPX, for example) can use Transport layer logical names for hosts in addition to their Network layer logical addresses. These logical names make it easier for human beings to find hosts on the network.

At the Transport layer, various protocol stacks implement a protocol to translate Network layer addresses into Transport layer logical names.

Transport Layer Implementations

Before we discuss the other layers of the OSI model, let's take a look at the IPX/SPX, TCP/IP, and NetBEUI implementations of the Transport layer.

The IPX/SPX Protocol

As far as the connection services of IPX/SPX are concerned, there are two transport protocols: IPX and SPX. IPX is connectionless and thus enjoys the benefits of connectionless transports, including increased speed. SPX, on the other hand, uses connection-oriented services.

IPX/SPX has no name resolution system by default. That functionality is employed when a NetWare server is running Novell Directory Services (NDS) and the NDS directory requester (which runs at the Session, Presentation, and Application layers) can make requests of an NDS database.

The TCP/IP Protocol

Like the IPX/SPX protocol stack, the TCP/IP protocol stack has two transport protocols:

- Transmission Control Protocol (TCP)

- User Datagram Protocol (UDP)

TCP is connection-oriented, and UDP is connectionless. Some upper-layer protocols such as FTP and HTTP require reliable connection-oriented service and, therefore, use TCP. Other upper-layer protocols such as Trivial File Transfer Protocol (TFTP) and Network File System (NFS) require increased speed and will trade reliability for that speed. They, therefore, use UDP.

For network address to name resolution, TCP/IP uses Domain Name Services (DNS). We think that DNS is what the OSI model Transport layer name resolution was designed for. Many operating systems use DNS for name resolution, but Unix (whose networking is based on TCP/IP) uses DNS almost exclusively. DNS is probably the most cross-platform name resolution method available. Chapter 4 discusses the function and operation of DNS.

The NetBEUI Implementation

Because it is based on the NetBIOS protocol, NetBEUI has datagram support and thus support for connectionless transmission. It doesn't, however, have support for connection-oriented services. NetBIOS does allow hosts to have logical names (using WINS), but the naming service, as with NDS, functions at the upper layers of the OSI model.

The OSI Model Upper Layers

The upper layers of the OSI model deal with less esoteric concepts. Even though we're still discussing computer networking, the top three layers (Session, Presentation, and Application) seem easier to understand. Because the Network+ exam doesn't cover the upper layers (and since many times these top three layers are grouped together), we're only going to give a brief overview.

The Session Layer

Protocols that operate at the Session layer of the OSI model are responsible for establishing, maintaining, and breaking sessions, or *dialogs*. This is different from the connection services provided at the Transport layer because the Session layer operates at a higher level and looks at the bigger picture—the entire conversation, not just one sentence. Many gateways operate at the Session layer.

The Presentation Layer

The Presentation layer does what you think it does: It changes the look, or *presentation*, of the data from the lower layers into a format that the upper layer processes can work with. Among other things, the Presentation layer deals with encryption, data compression, and network redirectors.

In addition, the Presentation layer deals with character set translation. Not all computer systems use the same table to convert binary numbers into text. Most standard computer systems use the American Standard Code for Information Interchange (ASCII). Mainframe computers (and some IBM networking systems) use the Extended Binary Coded Decimal Interchange Code (EBCDIC). The two are totally different. Protocols at the Presentation layer can translate between the two.

The Application Layer

Now I know what you're thinking, "This layer is for my programs, right?" Wrong. The Application layer defines several standard network services that fall into categories such as file transfer, print access, and e-mail relay. The applications that access these network services are located above the Application layer (although some people say that applications are an extension of the Application layer).

Upper Layer Devices

There are only a few upper layer devices, none of which operate at any specific layer. Because they perform a range of functions for the network, they fall into the class of devices known as *gateways*. A gateway translates one type of network data into another. There are many, many types of gateways, but the one most people think of is an e-mail gateway. E-mail gateways translate e-mail messages from one type of e-mail system so that they can be transmitted on another (for example, from GroupWise e-mail to SMTP mail for the Internet).

Gateways can be either hardware or software. But the most popular way to run a gateway is as a software program on a dedicated computer.

Key Terms

Before you take the exam, be certain you are familiar with the following terms:

100BaseVG

100VG (Voice Grade)

100VG-AnyLAN

10BaseFL

AnyLAN

Asymmetrical Digital Subscriber Line (ADSL)

baseband

bounded media

broadband

brouter

carrier

category

checkpoint

collision

concentrator

connectionless services

connection-oriented

controller

default gateway

dialogs

dynamic routing

encoding

Ethernet address

Fast Ethernet

Fiber Distributed Data Interface (FDDI)

Frequency Division Multiplexing (FDM)

gateway

hop

hub

Integrated Switched Digital Network (ISDN)

internetwork

IPX network address

MAC address

packet

physical address

presentation

QoS

Quality of Service

regeneration process

routing

routing table

shielded

signal encoding

signaling method

static routing

subnet mask

token

transceiver

twisted-pair

type

unshielded

Virtual Private Networking (VPN)

Review Questions

1. Which layer of the OSI model ensures reliable, end-to-end communications?

   A. Network

   B. Transport

   C. Session

   D. Presentation

2. Which layer of the OSI model provides routing functionality?

   A. Transport

   B. Data Link

   C. Physical

   D. Network

3. Which layer of the OSI model translates the data from upper layer protocols into electrical signals and places them on the network media?

   A. Physical

   B. Transport

   C. Data Link

   D. Network

4. You are a consultant designing a network for a company with more than 1000 users. Which 802 standard would you implement to ensure that bandwidth would be sufficient and equal without bridging or additional segments?

   A. 802.1

   B. 802.2

   C. 802.3

   D. 802.5

5. You have a limited budget and need to design a network for 50 users. Which 802 standard would you implement?

   A. 802.1

   B. 802.3

   C. 802.5

   D. 802.9

6. You are installing a Windows 95/98–based TCP/IP network. You accidentally set workstation B to the same IP address as workstation A. Which workstation(s) will receive an error message?

   A. A

   B. B

   C. Neither

   D. Both

7. You are installing a Windows 95/98–based TCP/IP network. You accidentally set workstation B to the same IP address as workstation A. Which workstation(s) will have a valid IP address?

   A. A

   B. B

   C. Neither

   D. Both

8. Unix uses which method to resolve Transport layer names into logical network addresses?

   A. WINS

   B. NDS

   C. DNS

   D. TRS

9. Which of these protocols use a connectionless transport?

   A. HTTP

   B. TCP

   C. TFTP

   D. IP

   E. NetBIOS

10. Which protocols use a connection-oriented transport?

    A. UDP

    B. NetBIOS

    C. HTTP

    D. NLSP

11. Which name resolution system is implemented with TCP/IP by default?

    A. DNS

    B. NDS

    C. SND

    D. WINS

12. Which OSI model layer has both a MAC sublayer and an LLC sublayer?

    A. Physical

    B. Transport

    C. Network

    D. Data Link

13. Which OSI model layer is responsible for establishing, maintaining, and breaking down dialog?

 A. Application

 B. Gateway

 C. Session

 D. Network

14. Which OSI layer is responsible for network services such as messaging and file transfer?

 A. Transport

 B. Network

 C. Application

 D. Session

15. Which OSI layer is responsible for building and tearing down packets?

 A. Network

 B. Transport

 C. Data Link

 D. Physical

16. On an Ethernet network, every station must have a _____.

 A. Hub

 B. NIC

 C. Switch

 D. Transceiver

17. Which type of hub doesn't require power?

    A. Active

    B. Passive

    C. Intelligent

    D. Switched

18. You are the administrator of a 100-station Ethernet network. Your users are complaining of slow network speeds. What could you replace your hub with to increase your network throughput?

    A. Router

    B. Bridge

    C. Switch

    D. NIC

19. At which OSI model layer do routers operate?

    A. Physical

    B. Data Link

    C. Transport

    D. Network

20. Which of the following is a MAC address?

    A. 199.165.217.45

    B. 00076A: 01A5BBA7FF60

    C. 01:A5:BB:A7:FF:60

    D. 311 S. Park St.

Answers to Review Questions

1. B. Of the layers listed, the only OSI layer that is responsible for reliable, end-to-end communications is the Transport layer. The Network layer is responsible for logical network addresses, the Session layer is responsible for opening and maintaining session information, and the Presentation layer is responsible for how data "looks" to the upper layer(s).

2. D. Of the OSI model layers listed, the Network layer is the only one that is responsible for routing information since it contains information for logical network addressing.

3. A. The Physical layer, as its name suggests, is the layer responsible for placing electrical transitions on the physical media. The other layers are all upper layers.

4. D. The 802.5 standard is similar to the Token Ring technology developed by IBM. That technology scales well and could handle more than 1000 users without bridging or additional segments. The performance would be better than any of the other technologies listed.

5. B. The 802.3 standard (similar to Ethernet) would work best in this situation because it is flexible, simple to implement, and most importantly, cheaper than the other technologies listed.

6. D. Through broadcasts, both workstations will detect if there is a duplicate IP address on the network and will display error messages to that effect.

7. A. Since workstation A had a valid IP address to begin with, Windows takes a "first come, first served" attitude with the IP addresses and lets "A" keep its IP address. Workstation B detects that "A" already has it and just deactivates that address.

8. C. Domain Name Services (DNS) is the primary method most UNIX implementations use to map logical names to network (IP) addresses. Although some versions of UNIX can use WINS and NDS, DNS is the preferred method.

9. C, E. Answers C and E both use a connectionless transport. Answer B is, in fact, a connection-oriented transport protocol. HTTP uses TCP, so therefore it is connection-oriented. And IP is a network-layer protocol.

10. C. Of all the protocols listed, HTTP is the only one that uses a connection-oriented transport protocol (TCP). The others use connectionless transport.

11. A. Although WINS is a name resolution that does use TCP/IP, it only works on Windows-based networks. The only true name resolution system that almost every TCP/IP networks uses is DNS.

12. D. The Data Link layer is divided into two sublayers: the MAC sublayer and an LLC sublayer. The other layers aren't normally subdivided.

13. C. The Session layer is responsible for establishing, maintaining, and breaking down dialog.

14. C. The services listed are all network applications, and the only layer that provides network application services is the Application layer.

15. A. The network layer is responsible for packaging data into packets. The other layers use different terms for data packages, such as frames.

16. B. All devices, except the NIC, are external devices. Additionally, there is usually only one of each of the other devices on a network, but there has to be at least one NIC per station.

17. B. Passive hubs simply make physical connections, and thus are usually unpowered. All the other types require power.

18. C. A switch would increase performance by making virtual, direct connections between sender and receiver. A bridge and router would actually decrease performance because these devices introduce latency into the communication. Replacing the hub with a NIC just can't be done.

19. D. Routers operate at the network layer because they deal with logical network addresses.

20. C. MAC addresses use a 12-digit hexadecimal number that is separated into six pairs of hex numbers. The only one that corresponds to that format is Answer C.

Chapter 3

Major Network Operating Systems

NETWORK+ EXAM OBJECTIVES COVERED IN THIS CHAPTER:

✓ Identify the following:

- The major network operating systems, including Microsoft Windows NT, Novell NetWare, and Unix

- The clients that best serve specific network operating systems and their resources

- The directory services of the major network operating systems

Every network today uses some form of software to manage its resources. This software runs on a special, high-powered computer and is called *a network operating system* (or *NOS*, for short). The NOS is one of the most important components of the network. In this chapter, we will look at three of the most popular network operating systems:

- Novell NetWare

- Microsoft Windows NT

- Unix

NetWare, developed by Novell, Inc., was the first network operating system to gain wide acceptance in the PC market. Windows NT, introduced by Microsoft in 1993, is gaining market share as of late because of its ease of use. Unix, while being the oldest network operating system, is only starting to gain popularity with PC users through PC-based flavors of Unix, such as Linux. This rise in popularity is due in part to the Internet, which is based on Unix standards and protocols. The fourth network operating system in use today—though used in a much smaller part of the networking market—is IBM's network and desktop operating system, Operating System/2 (OS/2), which we will look at briefly.

Novell NetWare

NetWare is one of the more powerful network operating systems on the market today. It is almost infinitely scalable and has support for multiple client platforms. Although most companies larger than a few hundred stations are running NetWare, this NOS enjoys success in many different types of networks.

Currently, NetWare is at version 5 and includes workstation management support, Internet connectivity, Web proxy, native TCP/IP (Transmission Control Protocol/Internet Protocol) protocol support, as well as continued support for its award-winning directory service, NDS.

For more information on NetWare, check out Novell, Inc.'s Web site at www.novell.com.

Features of NetWare

NetWare is popular in large networks (more than 20 servers) because of features such as centralized administration of all users and their properties. The most important features of NetWare 4.*x* and later are the following:

- The directory service (NDS)
- The simple user interface
- Fairly minimal hardware requirements
- Scalable hardware support
- Third-party support
- Interoperability with many types of computer systems

NetWare has always been an excellent directory, file, and print server, but with its acquisition of many Java technologies, it is starting to encroach on the application server market. These features make NetWare an excellent choice in the directory, file, and print environments.

The NetWare Server User Interface

With NetWare 5 servers, you can choose from three interfaces:

- The command-line console (see Figure 3.1)
- The menu-based utilities (such as the MONITOR utility shown in Figure 3.2)
- The new Java-based graphical interface

The new graphical interface is based on the Unix X Window standard and has been a long time coming. You can interact with a NetWare 5 server using the mouse to issue commands in this graphical environment, an option previously unavailable.

Even though the NetWare graphical interface looks like X Window, it is a Java-based approximation, not the real thing. You can't run X Window programs on a NetWare server. You can, however, run programs written in Java.

Java, Anyone?

Java is a programming language similar to BASIC, Pascal, COBOL, C+, and C++, but with one major distinguishing feature: Programs written in Java run on any platform that has a Java Virtual Machine (JVM) installed.

JVM is software that creates a virtual Java computer. Most (if not all) operating systems have a JVM. This means that a programmer writes a program once, without having to recompile or rewrite the same program for all platforms. One of Java's slogans is "Write Once, Run Anywhere." Java was developed by Sun Microsystems and is beginning to be widely used on corporate networks.

FIGURE 3.1 The NetWare command-line console

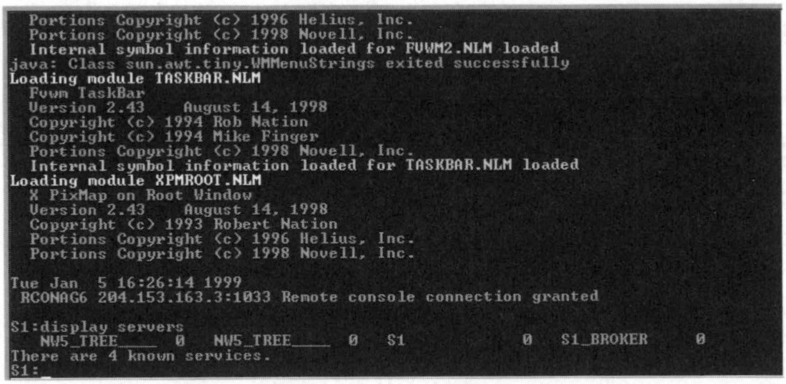

FIGURE 3.2 The MONITOR menu-based utility

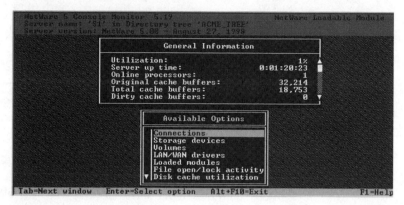

Scalable Hardware Requirements

In the days of NetWare 3.*x*, you could run NetWare on a server that had as little as 4MB of RAM; other network operating systems of the time required a minimum of 24MB. This made NetWare popular among hardware buyers, but not with those who made the hardware.

Other hardware support also makes NetWare a popular choice. For example, out of the box, the NetWare 5 kernel supports as many as 32 processors, as long as the hardware configuration complies with the Intel Multiprocessor Specification 1.1 or 1.4. In addition, NetWare 5 supports hot-pluggable PCI cards. Many other operating systems must be specially modified to include this support; NetWare comes with it.

A hot-pluggable PCI card enables you to install or remove a device while the server is powered up and functioning.

Table 3.1 lists the hardware requirements and recommendations for a NetWare 5 server. Each requirement is actually fairly minimal compared with today's typical server running another network operating system.

TABLE 3.1   NetWare 5 Hardware Requirements and Recommendations

Hardware	Minimum	Recommended
Processor	Pentium	Pentium 90MHz or faster.
Display	VGA	SVGA.
Hard disk space	600MB	1GB or more.
Memory	64MB	128MB or more.
Network card	At least one	As many as required.
CD-ROM	One	One
Mouse	Not required	Recommended if using the graphical interface. The PS/2 style is the best choice.

Always try to exceed the manufacturer's recommendations when selecting hardware for an operating system. You will be happier with the performance.

Third-Party Support

If you want to write your own operating system, you can. Other people have done it, such as the developers of Linux (discussed later in this chapter). However, you won't sell many copies without third-party software support. This means making your source code available to other developers so that they can write software for it. If source code isn't made available, no one can write programs to run on it, and if there aren't any programs available to run on the operating system, how much sense does it make for anyone to buy it? The same holds true for network operating systems. Without support for popular network services (such as backup programs), the platform will not be widely used.

Fortunately, servers are big business. It is in the interests of many third parties to write server-based software for new network operating systems. Server-based software includes, but is not limited to, the following:

- Backup programs

- E-mail

- Internet access

Until recently being surpassed by Windows NT, NetWare had the largest base of third-party programs. However, NetWare use and support are climbing again now that Novell is embracing Java technologies.

NetWare Interoperability

NetWare can communicate with just about any computing environment, including:

- Windows 95/98

- Windows NT

- Mac OS

- VMS

- OS/400

- Unix

- OS/2

When each of these operating systems tries to communicate with a NetWare server, the server appears as though it were a member of that network type.

For example, on a Mac OS network, a NetWare server can appear to be just another Macintosh server, but in reality it's a Pentium-class box running NetWare. We have found that a NetWare server makes a better server for Macs than Apple's own servers running the AppleShare network operating system.

NetWare Architecture

NetWare, like most other network operating systems, is modular. It consists of a core component and other pieces that can be loaded into memory as necessary. In NetWare parlance, the core component is called the *Core OS (or Kernel)*, and the other modules are called *NetWare Loadable Modules (NLMs)*. This design makes efficient use of the hardware resources (memory and hard disk space, for example) of the computer on which it is running. Unneeded services or components can be unloaded, thus conserving memory. Figure 3.3 shows the NetWare architecture.

FIGURE 3.3 The NetWare architecture

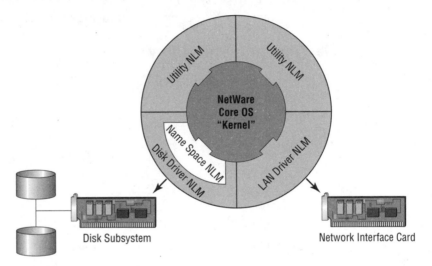

NLMs fall into four categories:

- Disk drivers
- LAN drivers
- Name space modules
- Utilities

Disk Drivers

These NLMs give NetWare access to the disk channel. Older disk driver NLM files have a .DSK extension, whereas newer disk drivers (those that conform to the NetWare Peripheral Architecture, or NPA) have the extension .HAM or .CDM. For NetWare 5, a combination of IDEATA.HAM and IDEHD.CDM provides access to local IDE (Integrated Drive Electronics) drives. NetWare versions 4.1 and later can use this technology, which is the only type of disk driver technology available for NetWare 5. For example, the IDE.DSK file is the disk driver that allows NetWare 3.x to access local IDE drives. This file won't work on NetWare 5 servers. You would have to use the IDEATA.HAM and IDEHD.CDM combination.

LAN Drivers

Every network board installed in a NetWare server must have a corresponding LAN driver, which is the interface between the NetWare kernel and the network interface card. These files typically have the file extension .LAN. For example, the 3C5X9.LAN file is the driver that allows NetWare to access a 3COM EtherLink III NIC.

Name Space Modules

As we mentioned, NetWare can "look" like another type of server. Part of that functionality is configured by the protocols in use. A name space module controls how files "look" or how they are stored on a disk. By default, NetWare stores files using the DOS naming convention (eight alphanumeric characters, a period, and then a three-letter extension; also called 8.3). Different operating systems use different naming conventions for files, and the name space modules make it possible to store those files on volumes on a NetWare server. The extension of these name space modules is .NAM. For example, the NFS.NAM name space module enables NetWare to store files on a disk using the Unix NFS (Network File System) naming convention. Additionally, if you want to store files that use the Windows long filename naming convention, you load the LONG.NAM names.

Be careful when loading multiple name space modules. Loading multiple modules not only requires more memory, but also reduces the total number of files that can be stored on that volume.

Utility NLMs

This category includes any kind of NLM that doesn't fall into the other three categories. More than 70 percent of NLMs on a NetWare server are of this type. These NLMs typically have the file extension .NLM. Examples include:

- MONITOR.NLM, which monitors the server

- NWCONFIG.NLM, which is a NetWare configuration NLM

- NDPSMGR.NLM, which is the NDPS (Novell Distributed Print Services) manager that loads the NetWare printing manager

As we mentioned, a great deal of third-party support is available for NetWare. Manufacturers write software for NetWare servers in the form of NLMs. Most hardware manufacturers write LAN and disk driver NLMs so that NetWare will run on their server platforms. Additionally, some companies write special utility NLMs, such as backup and management utilities, for NetWare servers. But, with the advent of NetWare 5 and the inclusion of server-based JVM (see the earlier sidebar "Java, Anyone?"), several hundred more server applications will soon become available.

One type of utility NLM that deserves special mention is new with NetWare 5. The *Platform Support Module (PSM)* enables NetWare 5 to communicate with a multiprocessor architecture. Each PSM is characterized by the extension .PSM. For example, the MPS14.PSM file provides NetWare with support for the Intel Multiprocessor Specification version 1.4. Once loaded, this file enables NetWare to use the multiprocessor functions of any server that follows the MPS 1.4 specification.

Major Versions of NetWare in Use

Three major versions of NetWare are in use today:

- NetWare 3.*x*

- NetWare 4.x

- NetWare 5

Each version has unique characteristics. Let's take a brief look at each one.

NetWare 3.*x*

NetWare 3.*x* includes NetWare 3.11 and 3.12. Based on the Novell product known as NetWare 386 (introduced about the same time as the Intel 80386 processor), NetWare 3.*x* made NetWare the de facto standard for business networks.

NetWare 3.*x* supports multiple, cross-platform clients and has minimal hardware requirements (4MB of RAM, 75MB of hard disk space). It uses a database called the bindery, which will be discussed later, to keep track of users and groups, and it is administered with a DOS, menu-based utility known as SYSCON. The design of NetWare 3.*x* included one utility for every function:

- SYSCON, for user administration

- PCONSOLE, for printing setup

- FILER, for file operations

This was nice for basic operations, but complete network administration was difficult because you had to switch between utilities to perform any network administration function (for example, add the user in SYSCON, assign the user rights in FILER). This drawback was resolved in NetWare 4 with the introduction of NetWare Administrator.

From its introduction in the early '90s until the mid-'90s when newer versions were released, NetWare 3.*x* was the most popular NOS. Because of this popularity and a loyal installed user base, Novell released an upgrade for NetWare 3.*x* in 1998, NetWare 3.2. It keeps the same architecture and basic kernel, but applies some patches and adds some new features (such as a Windows administration utility) to keep it up-to-date without changing the basic operating system features that users and administrators love.

NetWare 4.*x*

Introduced in 1993, NetWare 4 was the first version to include a new, centralized administration service, Novell Directory Services (NDS). This new feature simplified the administration of multiple servers. With NetWare 3.*x* and previous versions, if a server wanted access to multiple servers, you made a user on each server and then assigned that user rights on all servers. With the introduction of NDS, all administration was centralized. You could make a user once, instead of 10 times for 10 servers. Version 4 was a radical departure from the way network administrators were using to thinking about administering a NetWare network. Unfortunately, NetWare 4 was also fairly buggy. Novell quickly made and released patches until the version number was up to 4.02—the first version considered stable.

Many versions have come and gone since 4.02. Versions 4.1 and 4.11 are the most popular versions of NetWare 4.x in use in corporate networks today. At the time of this writing, there has been a new release of NetWare 4.*x*, NetWare 4.2. A stepping-stone upgrade toward NetWare 5, it gives a Novell network administrator some features of NetWare 5 (such as the Z.E.N.works starter pack that provides workstation management) in order to prepare for a full migration from NetWare 4.*x* to 5.

What Is IntranetWare?

Novell released NetWare 4.11 as a package called *IntranetWare*. The name change capitalized on the popularity of the intranet craze. IntranetWare included a Web server and an FTP (File Transfer Protocol) server, as well as an IPX/IP (Internet Packet eXchange/Internet Protocol) gateway to facilitate connection to the Internet and a corporate intranet.

Industry analysts were skeptical, to say the least. Novell threw away several years' worth of brand recognition by changing the product name. The actual operating system was still NetWare, but the package that included all the products was called IntranetWare. With the release of NetWare 5, the package name was changed back to NetWare.

NetWare 5

At the time of this writing, the most current version of NetWare is Net-Ware 5. Probably the most talked-about feature of NetWare 5 is its capability to use TCP/IP in its pure form. Other companies tout "native" IP, but that usually means encapsulating some other protocol inside TCP/IP. In the NetWare 5 TCP/IP implementation, only TCP/IP RFC (Request for Comment) protocols are used to communicate between clients and servers as well as between servers. Using the NetWare 5 TCP/IP implementation is becoming popular because an administrator can use the same protocol on a local LAN and a WAN.

As with any major version change, NetWare 5 includes a few important function changes. As previously mentioned, NetWare 5 includes a multi-processing kernel. Although earlier versions supported multiple processors, you had to load several additional NLMs (including SMP.NLM). Also, NetWare 5 includes a five-user version of Oracle8, the leading relational database software for NetWare. Finally, NetWare 5 includes many expansions to the NDS database, for example, the Z.E.N.works workstation management software.

TCP/IP is covered in more detail in Chapter 4.

Directory Services

A *directory service* is a feature of a network operating system that enables users to find network resources. There are two main types of directory services for NetWare:

- The bindery (pronounced with a long *i*), which is a simple, flat database of users, groups, and security information that resides on a server (available in versions of NetWare prior to version 4).

- NDS, which provides access to a global, hierarchical database of network entities (called *objects*), available in version 4 and later. Based on the X.500 Internet directory standard (a standard way of naming network entities), this database (called the Directory with a capital *D*— not to be confused with a DOS directory) is distributed and replicated to all NetWare servers on the network. Each server contains a part of the directory database. Additionally, all servers know about one another and the directory information that each contains.

A major advantage of NDS over the bindery is that with NDS the entire network is organized into a hierarchical structure, called an NDS Tree. This tree is a logical representation of a network. It includes objects that represent the network's users, servers, printers, and other resources (see Figure 3.4). On the other hand, the bindery contains user information for that server only. NDS is described as a *network-centric* directory service, whereas the bindery is *server-centric*.

To contrast these two directory services, let's look at an example. If a user on a NetWare 3.*x* network wants to log in to multiple servers, the administrator must create users on every server. If there are 20 servers on the network, the administrator must create that user 20 times, once on each server.

With NDS, however, the administrator simply creates a single user object in the Directory. The user can then log in to the network on any server. The administrator simply assigns rights to the resources that the user needs to access.

FIGURE 3.4   A sample NDS Tree

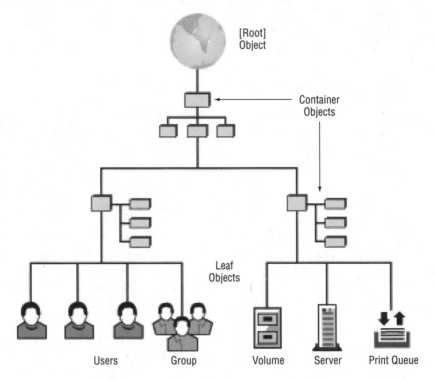

To change the Directory database, a NetWare network administrator uses a program called NetWare Administrator. Although this graphical Windows utility has gone through several iterations in the past six years since its introduction, it is the only administrative utility you need to modify NDS objects and their properties. Many utilities are available for specific functions, but NetWare Administrator is the one utility that can do it all. Figure 3.5 shows a sample NetWare Administrator screen. From this one screen, an administrator can modify any object's properties, including security settings, object names, and network parameters. You can manage your entire network from this one program.

FIGURE 3.5   A NetWare Administrator screen

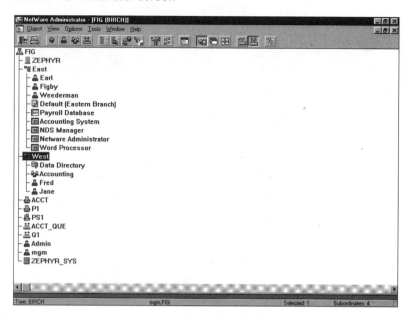

Each iteration of NetWare Administrator included new features and a new filename. Table 3.2 lists the myriad versions and their associated filenames.

TABLE 3.2   NetWare Administrator Filenames

Version	Filename
NetWare Administrator (original version)	NWADMIN.EXE
NetWare Administrator for Windows 3.*x*	NWADMN3X.EXE
NetWare Administrator for Windows 95	NWADMN95.EXE
NetWare Administrator for Windows NT	NWADMNNT.EXE
NetWare Administrator for Windows (32-bit)	NWADMN32.EXE

At the time of this writing, NDS runs only on NetWare servers and some Unix servers. Novell has announced its intention to port NDS to all platforms, enabling them to use the features and benefits of NDS.

Design Issues

When designing a NetWare network, you must consider a couple of issues:

- The number of servers you will need
- Your NDS tree design

Because NetWare is infinitely scalable, you are limited only by the amount and performance of the server's hardware. Single NetWare servers that support hundreds (sometimes thousands) of users are not uncommon. It is possible to load a single server with all the services (including file, print, Internet, and e-mail functionality) you need for your small business network. Assuming you have enough RAM, the server will run fine. A typical design guideline is approximately one server for every 100 to 200 users, a ratio that is more flexible than that for other network operating systems.

If you are running a version of NetWare that uses NDS, your NDS tree should mimic your network. Figure 3.6 shows a sample network and its associated NDS tree design.

There are no "wrong" NDS tree designs. Some are just better for a particular network than others.

FIGURE 3.6   Sample network and a sample NDS tree

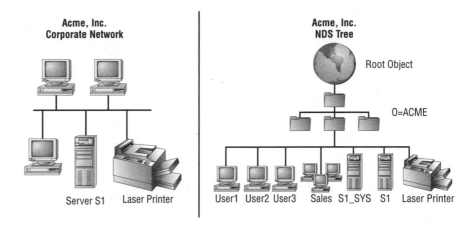

There are other, more detailed NDS design concepts. For more information on NDS design, see *The Complete Guide to Novell Directory Services* by David Kearns and Brian Iverson, Sybex, 1998.

Available Client Software

Diverse clients can talk to a NetWare server. To facilitate this, Novell developed client software that allows many client operating systems to take advantage of all NetWare features. Specifically, Novell's clients (sometimes called NDS clients) enable access to the NDS database. Even though some clients are included with various operating systems and the vendors themselves design them, you should implement Novell's client on the client operating systems you are running to get the most functionality out of NetWare—including being able to administer NetWare. The NetWare client written by Novell for the particular operating system provides full NDS functionality and is therefore the best choice for connecting that operating system to a NetWare network.

Table 3.3 lists the Novell clients that are available for NetWare and the special feature(s) of each.

TABLE 3.3   Available Novell Clients

Operating System	Client	Special Features
DOS and Windows 3.x	Novell Client for Windows 3.1x	Uses only 4KB of conventional memory. Full 32-bit implementation. No longer included with NetWare.
Windows 95/98	Novell Client for Windows 95/98	Fully integrated with the Windows 95/98 Explorer. Included with NetWare versions after 4.11.
Windows NT	Novell Client for Windows NT	Replaces graphical login screen with an interface that allows you to simultaneously log in to both NetWare and Windows NT.
OS/2	NetWare Client for OS/2	Not included with NetWare 5. Allows login from either a DOS or Windows session under OS/2.
Mac OS	NetWare Client for Mac OS	Not included with NetWare 5. Design and support for this client transferred to ProSoft Engineering (www.prosofteng.com/NW4MAC/index.htm).

There are NDS clients for Unix, but the Unix vendor usually develops them. One rare exception is UnixWare, a product Novell developed several years ago. This rather cool version of Unix has been completely integrated with NetWare.

Microsoft Windows NT

There has been a buzz in the computer industry as of late about Windows NT. Everyone's asking, "Should I be installing it?" With the same graphical interface as other versions of Windows and simple administration possible from the server console, it is a force to be reckoned with. Microsoft introduced Windows NT in 1993 with version 3.1 (about the same time Windows 3.1 was taking off as a desktop graphical interface for DOS). No one paid it much heed because it was fairly buggy, and a mountain of hardware was required to run it. This NOS went pretty much unnoticed until version 3.51 was introduced about a year later. Windows NT 3.51 was quite stable, and, by this time, hardware vendors had met the challenge with the 486 and Pentium processors. Because of its similarity to Windows 3.1 and powerful networking features, Windows NT gained popularity. Microsoft began to put its significant marketing muscle behind it, and Windows NT started to become a viable alternative in the network operating system market, previously dominated by Novell NetWare and the various flavors of Unix.

For more information on Windows NT, check out Microsoft's Web site at www.microsoft.com.

Windows NT Features

Windows NT is the first choice of developers because of the similarity in programming for Windows 95/98 and Windows NT. Additionally, the installation CD includes a complete Internet server suite (including WWW, FTP, and DNS [Domain Name Service] server programs). Finally, because the look and feel of Windows NT is almost identical to that of Microsoft's desktop operating systems, Windows 3.x and Windows 95/98, training administrators requires much less time. These features along with many others have skyrocketed Windows NT use in the corporate network infrastructure. It is important to note that "Windows NT" actually refers to two separate products: Window NT Server (the NOS) and Windows NT Workstation (the client OS, designed to be a high-security desktop OS). Let's take a look at a few of the more popular features of Windows NT.

The Windows NT User Interface

The Windows NT interface is the same as the Windows interface we've come to love (or hate, depending on your view). Windows NT 3.1 and 3.5x use the same basic look and feel as Windows 3.1. Windows NT 4 uses the interface from Windows 95. And the newly-released Windows 2000 will have the same basic interface as Windows 98.

Although there might be subtle differences between the desktop operating systems and their Windows NT counterparts, the basic look and feel is the same. Because of this, a novice administrator can easily learn to use Windows NT. Analysts refer to this as a shallow learning curve.

Third-Party Support

Because of its ease of use and relatively inexpensive cost, Windows NT is selling well. Third-party vendors are writing thousands of software titles for Windows NT. Currently the number of third-party network programs for Windows NT surpasses the number for NetWare.

One reason for the range of software available for Windows NT is that developers can create them using many of the development tools they use to write Windows programs. Additionally, Microsoft makes much of the code available to developers for little or no charge. Other vendors often charge to download their development tools, although that trend is rapidly changing. Finally, a program that is certified as Windows Compatible must work on both Windows 95/98 and Windows NT. Because it's so easy to develop programs for both versions and because Microsoft requires it for Windows certification, the number of programs available for NT is constantly growing. That isn't to say that all NT programs are network enabled, but when given the choice, developers usually choose to create programs for NT rather than for other network operating system platforms.

Windows NT Interoperability

With the vast diversity of client operating systems out there, any network operating system must be able to provide services to multiple clients. For this reason, Windows NT Server includes file and print services for Apple Macintosh. The Windows NT server appears as if it were a Macintosh server.

Additionally, Windows NT can run text-mode native OS/2 programs without modification. For example, administrators with multiple OS/2 computers running OS/2 text mode e-mail gateways can consolidate them into a single Windows NT server and run each gateway in a separate window.

NetWare Integration

When Windows NT Server was released in 1993, NetWare was the primary network operating system available. As a matter of fact, it had more than 75 percent of the installed network operating system base. For this reason, Microsoft has software for Windows NT that allows it to coexist in a NetWare environment. Three main programs facilitate the integration of Windows NT and NetWare:

- Gateway Services for NetWare (GSNW)

- Client Services for NetWare (CSNW)

- File and Print Services for NetWare (FPNW)

Gateway Services for NetWare installs as a service on a Windows NT server and translates requests for Windows NT resources into NetWare requests. At a lower level, GSNW is translating SMB (Server Message Block) protocol requests into NCP (NetWare Core Protocol) requests. GSNW allows multiple Windows NT clients to connect through a Windows NT server to NetWare servers using only Windows NT client software and protocols. Figure 3.7 illustrates this arrangement.

FIGURE 3.7   Gateway Services for NetWare (GSNW) operation

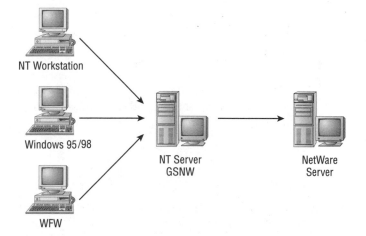

Gateway Services for NetWare has a relatively undocumented feature: any number of Windows NT clients can connect to NetWare resources through GSNW and use only one license on the NetWare server being accessed. With this capability, it is theoretically possible to build a network of mostly NetWare servers, but license all of them for five users or fewer. Novell is understandably peeved. However, GSNW performance is very poor in this application. Microsoft doesn't recommend GSNW for high NetWare traffic environments.

Client Services for NetWare (CSNW) is probably the simplest of all the software, but it requires the most overhead to implement. You must install CSNW on every Windows NT Workstation computer that needs access to NetWare resources.

Additionally, all users who want to access NetWare resources need user accounts and rights on the NetWare servers they access.

File and Print Services for NetWare (FPNW) is really a method for providing files and printers hosted by Windows NT Server to Novell clients. When installed and configured on a Windows NT Server, this service makes a Windows NT Server look like a NetWare server to Novell clients. This service is good when you have a small number of NT servers and a large number of NetWare servers.

Windows NT Architecture

Windows NT sports a fairly complex architecture that's hidden behind a nice, graphical front end. This powerful operating system is available in two packages:

- Windows NT Server
- Windows NT Workstation

The two share the same basic underlying architecture, but there are several key differences. Table 3.4 details these differences.

TABLE 3.4   Windows NT 4 Server vs. Windows NT 4 Workstation

Feature	Windows NT Server	Windows NT Workstation
Maximum number of processors supported	4 (a maximum of 32 with additional software components)	2
Maximum number of connections	Unlimited	10 inbound, unlimited outbound
Support for Macintosh services	Yes	No
Remote Access Service	A maximum of 256 sessions	1 session
RAID (Redundant Array of Inexpensive Disks) support	Yes	No
Can perform NT domain authentication	Yes (if the server is a domain controller)	No

Application Support Subsystems

Windows NT is designed as a modular system. With this in mind, examine Figure 3.8. Components fall into either the *user* mode or the *kernel* mode. This simply indicates which entity uses those components.

FIGURE 3.8 Windows NT architecture

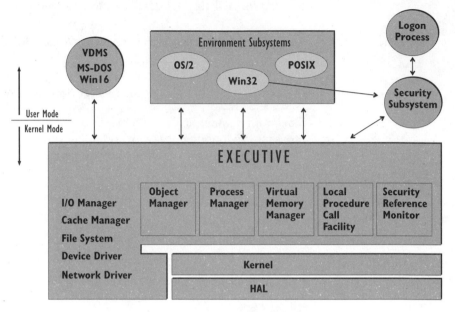

The two components to note in this diagram are the Hardware Abstraction Layer (HAL) and the many subsystems that can run applications. These two components enable NT to run many types of applications on many hardware types.

Win16 Applications (Win16 Subsystem)

Windows NT can run just about any 16-bit Windows application, providing it conforms to the Microsoft standards for writing Windows 3.*x* applications. Each application can run in a separate Virtual DOS Machine (VDM) with its own memory protection.

Win32 Applications (Win32 Subsystem)

Windows NT can run applications designed for both Windows 95/98 and Windows NT.

OS/2 Applications (OS/2 Subsystem)

Windows NT can run OS/2 applications in character mode if these applications use only the pure OS/2 development tools. Windows NT cannot run OS/2 graphical applications.

Unix Applications (POSIX Subsystem)

One the most talked-about features when Windows NT was introduced was its support for a standard Unix programming environment known as POSIX (Portable Operating System Interface for Computer Environments). Programs written to the POSIX standard can run on any POSIX implementation (including that of Windows NT). Windows NT can run any application that adheres strictly to the Institute of Electrical and Electronics Engineers (IEEE) POSIX standards.

Processor Options for Windows NT

In addition to the application support subsystems, Windows NT can run on many processor types. Before NT, most network operating systems ran only on the Intel platform. But the Hardware Abstraction Layer of the Windows NT architecture allows NT to run on different hardware platforms by simply using a different HAL. Currently, Windows NT supports the following CPU types:

Intel 386 (I386) Architecture   Arguably the most popular platform for NT. This type includes the 80386, 80486, Pentium, Pentium Pro, Pentium II, and Pentium III as well as any newer processors in that line. A rule of thumb: If an I386 architecture runs DOS, it will run NT.

Digital Equipment Corporation (DEC) Alpha AXP Architecture   Second only to the Intel architecture, this architecture has become popular because of the sheer speed of the DEC Alpha processor (now called Compaq Alpha). This is due, in part, to its Reduced Instruction Set Computing, or RISC, design.

MIPS R4x00 Architecture   Another RISC processor that is gaining popularity. Windows NT and Unix are among the operating systems that run on the MIPS architecture.

Motorola PowerPC Architecture   A RISC processor developed jointly by IBM, Motorola, and Apple. The Apple Macintosh Power Mac and a version of the IBM PC use this processor. The Power Mac is now so popular among Macintosh users that Apple's current line of Macintosh computers all contain PowerPC-based units. The only operating system that the IBM PC implementation runs is Windows NT. And, unfortunately, Microsoft has announced plans to discontinue support for this architecture.

NT loads network applications as services. A service is a Windows program (a file with either an .EXE or a .DLL extension) that is loaded automatically by the server or manually by the administrator. Network applications that are written specifically for Windows NT are written as Windows NT services.

The Major Versions of Windows NT

In 1993, amid the increased popularity of networking PCs, Microsoft released Windows NT 3.1 as a high-end server platform for Windows networks. It was a powerful operating system that could take advantage of the 32-bit features of the Intel 386 processor, including support for as much as 4GB of memory and preemptive multitasking. However, its greater memory requirements and lack of stability with some programs made people nervous about adopting it as their only network operating system, and it was not widely adopted.

The release of Windows NT 3.51 in 1994 didn't elicit an enthusiastic response. People quickly realized, however, that it was a stable, robust server platform that could be easily implemented in small- to medium-sized networks. Popularity and support for Windows NT grew in the computing community.

Windows NT 4, which was released in 1996, has the look and feel of Windows 95/98 and includes Internet Information Server (IIS), a Web server, and the Internet Explorer Web browser. This, in addition to simple server administration and RAID support, made Windows NT 4 the choice for many small- to medium-sized networks. It is becoming more widely used as an enterprise network, but has not been accepted as the backbone NOS for many large networks.

Microsoft hopes to change that with Windows 2000 (formerly known as Windows NT 5), which was released in early 2000. The major difference between Windows 2000 and NT 4 is the replacement of the NT Directory Service (NTDS) with Microsoft Active Directory (MAD or AD). MAD is supposedly a true X.500-based Directory, similar to Novell's NDS. In reality, it is a hierarchy of DNS names for domains (discussed in the next section).

Directory Services

As we mentioned, a *directory service* provides access to a central database of information that contains details about the resources available on a network. In Windows NT, the Security Accounts Manager (SAM) database (also called the domain database) contains information about all the users and groups within a domain. A *domain* is a group of computers that share a single SAM database. There can be more than one domain on a network. For the users in one domain to use resources that reside in a different domain, a relationship known as a *trust* must exist. This system of domains and trusts for a Windows NT Server network is known as *Windows NT Directory Service (NTDS)*. Figure 3.9 illustrates a simple NTDS network.

FIGURE 3.9   An NTDS network

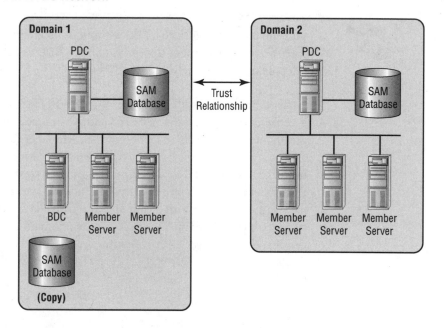

In an NTDS network, any computer that has Windows NT Server installed can have a copy of the domain database on it. However, only one copy of the database can be considered the master copy. This master copy is the only database responsible for initiating changes on the network. The computer that contains this master copy of the SAM is called the *Primary Domain Controller*, or *PDC*. Any other Windows NT server can have a copy of the SAM for backup purposes, in case something happens to the PDC. These computers are called *Backup Domain Controllers (BDCs)*. Further, any computer that has NT Server installed, but doesn't have a copy of the SAM, is called a *Member Server*. All these server types are shown in Figure 3.9.

The importance of these distinctions is that all network administration for a domain happens at a PDC. BDCs can authenticate users, but if the PDC is down, you can't make administrative changes (add users, for example) until the PDC comes back up. Member servers typically offer services to the network, but don't take part in authentication (other than to indicate on which server the SAM database resides).

You can promote a BDC to a PDC without reinstalling, but, unfortunately, you can't promote a Member Server to either a BDC or PDC without completely reinstalling NT server.

In contrast to Novell NetWare, Windows NT has no one utility that you can use to manage all the network entities and resources. Instead, user and group information is managed with User Manager for Domains. Figure 3.10 shows a sample screen from the User Manager for Domains. You use this utility to manage all users, groups, and policies for the domain. All users for this domain are shown in the top half, and all groups are shown in the bottom half. To select another domain, you must have previously established a trust with that domain. To select another domain and view its users and groups, choose User Select Domain.

FIGURE 3.10   User Manager for Domains

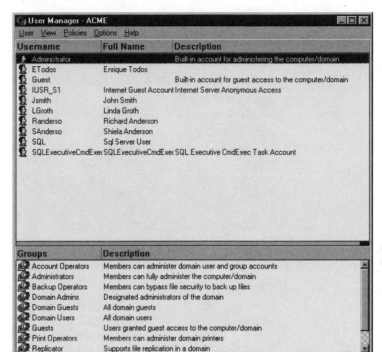

Even though Windows NT has its own directory service, Novell has been hard at work to implement its NDS on the Windows NT platform. NDS for NT completely replaces the Windows NT directory service while maintaining compatibility with Windows NT programs that rely on the NTDS.

Many people have tried to compare User Manager for Domains to NetWare Administrator. Their functionality is not the same. User Manager can deal with only one domain at a time, and then only with the users, groups, and policies of that domain. NetWare Administrator can manage the entire NDS tree and all network entities.

Minimum Requirements for Windows NT

Because of its graphical nature and complexity, Windows NT has greater hardware requirements than other network operating systems. With each successive version, the hardware requirements seem to at least double, if not triple. The minimum hardware requirements and recommended hardware configuration for Windows NT 4 are listed in Table 3.5. (Microsoft had not released the requirements for Windows 2000 at the time of this writing, but expect them to double, if not triple.)

TABLE 3.5 Windows NT 4 Hardware Requirements

Hardware	Minimum	Recommended
Processor	Intel 80486 or higher (I386 Architecture) or a supported RISC processor (MIPS R4x00, Alpha AXP, or PowerPC)	Pentium 90Mhz or higher (the faster the better)
Display	VGA	SVGA
Hard disk space	125MB free	300MB free
Memory	16MB	32MB or greater
Network card	At least one that matches the topology of your network	At least one that matches the topology of your network
CD-ROM	Required	4x or greater
Mouse	Required	Required

In addition to the hardware listed in Table 3.5, Microsoft recommends running NT 7 Server on only the hardware in its Hardware Compatibility List (HCL). You'll find the HCL at www.microsoft.com/hwtest/hcl/. If the hardware you are trying to use with Windows NT Server or Workstation isn't on the HCL and you call Microsoft with a problem, you may have support difficulties.

Available Client Software

The nicest feature of Windows NT is less a feature than a fact of the state of networking today. If you implement Windows NT Server on your network, chances are you have Windows 95/98 as your client. All Windows 95/98 and

Windows NT workstations install the Microsoft Client for Microsoft Networks by default whenever a network card is installed in a client workstation. This client enables the workstation to access any machine running a Microsoft operating system with networking components (for example, Windows NT Server or Workstation or Windows 95/98). This client must be installed to access the resources of a Windows NT network. Really the only client operating systems that can access a Windows NT network without additional gateway software on the server (such as the products for NetWare that we mentioned earlier) are Windows 95/98 and Windows NT versions of the Microsoft Client for Microsoft Networks.

Macintoshes can also access a Windows NT server, but Services for Macintosh (SFM) must be installed and configured. There is no Microsoft Client for a Macintosh, per se. But there is an authentication module for the Macintosh that makes logons easier and provides a secure logon session for the Mac user.

In addition to the Microsoft Client for Microsoft Networks, Windows 95/98 and Windows NT include the Microsoft Client for NetWare Networks, which allows users to log in to NetWare servers. This client supports an NDS login, but doesn't allow administration of an NDS tree using NetWare Administrator. When used in conjunction with the Microsoft Client for Microsoft Networks, this solution provides the most interoperability for clients in a network that has mostly NT servers and only a few NetWare servers, since they can log in to both Microsoft and Novell networks. The only caveat is that a user may not be able to access all the features on a NetWare server (including NDS, since this client performs bindery logins only).

Unix Flavors

Of the other network operating systems available, the various forms of Unix are probably the most popular. It is probably also the oldest of the network operating systems. Bell Labs developed Unix, in part, in 1969. We say *in part* because there are now so many iterations, commonly called flavors, of Unix that it is almost a completely different operating system.

Although the basic architecture of all flavors is the same (32-bit kernel, command-line based, capable of having a graphical interface, as in X Window), the subtle details of each make one flavor better in a particular situation than another.

Unix flavors incorporate a kernel, which constitutes the core of the operating system. The kernel can access hardware and communicate with various types of user interfaces. The two most popular user interfaces are the command-line interface (called a *shell*) and the graphical interface (X Window). The Unix kernel is similar to the core operating system components of Windows NT and NetWare. In Unix, the kernel is typically simple and, therefore, powerful. Additionally, the kernel can be recompiled to include support for more devices. As a matter of fact, some flavors include the source code so that you can create your own flavor of Unix.

Let's look at a few of the more popular flavors and their subtleties.

Only a very few questions on the Network+ exam have to do with Unix. We're providing this information mainly for comparison purposes.

Linux

The Unix flavor that has been receiving the most attention lately is Linux. Linux is a fairly easy-to-use (as Unix goes, anyway) flavor developed by Linus Torvalds at the University of Helsinki, Finland. He started his work in 1991 and released version 1 of the Linux kernel in 1994. At the time of this writing, the current Linux kernel is version 2.2. Since Torvalds adds features daily, it's only a matter of time before a new release.

Linux runs mainly on the Intel platform, although some distributions run on RISC processors such as the MIPS and Alpha. Attempts have been made, successfully, to run the RISC version on other platforms, such as the Macintosh. Linux is easy to install, and most distributions are free and include the source code. Hardware requirements can vary widely with each distribution.

And there are various flavors of Linux. People acquire Linux, come up with a new feature, recompile Linux with the new feature, and then redistribute Linux. According to Linux's distribution agreement (called the GNU public license), any sale or distribution must include the source code so that others can also develop custom Linux applications.

Most Linux distributions include a full suite of applications, such as a word processor, the X Window graphical interface, and source code compilers. Additionally, most Unix applications that comply with the POSIX standard should run on Linux with little or no modification.

Because Linux is a flavor of Unix, it comes with network support for TCP/IP. In particular, Caldera's OpenLinux is making its mark in the networking world. OpenLinux was developed for corporate networking, so it supports multiple protocols (including PPP [Point-to-Point Protocol], AppleTalk, IPX, and SMB). It also includes support for integration with other network operating systems.

For more detailed information on Linux, as well as locations to download Linux, check out www.linux.org.

Two other distributions of Linux should be noted: Red Hat and Slackware. Red Hat Linux is the most portable version of Linux, with code that runs natively on the Intel, Alpha, and SPARC processors. The Slackware distribution was specifically designed for the Intel platform and, as such, supports many PC hardware devices, including Ethernet and multiple (up to 16) processors.

For a list of the various English Linux distributions, check out www.linux.org/dist/english.html.

SCO Unix

The Santa Cruz Operation (SCO), in California, makes two main flavors of Unix: OpenServer and UnixWare. OpenServer is considered the Intel Unix flavor of choice since it is robust and scalable. Corporate networks are favorably inclined toward OpenServer because SCO provides excellent support for its product.

In 1997, Novell sold its Unix product, UnixWare, to SCO. The distinguishing feature of this product is its interoperability with Novell-based networks. Additionally, it is easy to install and administer.

For more information on OpenServer and other SCO products, check out SCO's home page at www.sco.com.

Solaris Unix

Of the non-Intel Unix flavors, the most popular is probably Solaris, made by Sun Microsystems. This flavor was designed to run primarily on the SPARC family, a RISC platform developed by Sun. Sun sells both the Solaris operating system and the hardware to run it on, which includes both the logic boards and the systems. These computers running Solaris are widely used as Internet servers.

Not to be outdone by Linux and the SCO flavors, Sun released a version of Solaris for the Intel architecture called Solaris for *x86* in 1995. It is designed for use on low-end application and Internet servers.

Solaris is based on the original version of Unix that came out of Bell Labs and, as such, is widely compatible with a number of Unix server applications.

For more information on Solaris, check out Sun Microsystem's Web site at www.sun.com.

OS/2

No discussion of network operating systems would be complete without at least a mention of IBM's desktop and server product, OS/2. OS/2 was the result of a joint venture that started in 1990 between IBM and Microsoft when IBM was looking for a new operating system for its IBM PC product line. The result was Operating System/2 (or more commonly, OS/2).

OS/2 was the first operating system to take full advantage of the Intel 80386 multitasking features. IBM attempted to develop an operating system that could be installed on its PCs without relying on Microsoft's MS-DOS. Over time, OS/2 developed into a powerful desktop and server operating system with many networking capabilities. It is similar to Windows NT in many ways.

This operating system had many benefits, including preemptive multitasking and support for 16-bit Windows programs, each running in its own memory area. OS/2 was supposedly less prone to crashes than Windows 3.*x*, even though it had greater memory and hardware requirements.

OS/2 holds only a minority of the market share for network operating systems and is most often used as an application server or gateway platform. Windows NT and OS/2 have similar features, but Windows NT is less expensive, and, therefore, OS/2 usually loses in the battle for this unique NOS niche.

IBM still develops OS/2, and the current desktop product is called OS/2 Warp 4. The current server product is OS/2 Warp Server 4. A new version code-named Aurora was due out in the first quarter of 1999, but is still under development at the time of the writing of this book.

For more information on OS/2, check out IBM's OS/2 Web site at www .software.ibm.com/os/warp/index.html.

Key Terms

Before you take the exam, be certain you are familiar with the following terms:

Backup Domain Controllers

directory service

domain

kernel

Member Server

network-centric

object

Primary Domain Controller

server-centric

shell

user

Review Questions

1. Which directory service is based mainly on the Internet directory standard X.500?

   A. NTDS

   B. NDS

   C. X.25

   D. IETF

2. Which network operating system(s) have a graphical interface?

   A. Unix

   B. NetWare 5

   C. NetWare 4

   D. Windows NT Server

3. Which client would you install on a Windows 95 machine to allow access to all features and services of a NetWare server?

   A. Microsoft Client for NetWare Networks

   B. Novell Client for Windows 95

   C. Microsoft Client for Microsoft Networks

   D. Novell Client for NetWare Networks

4. On a Windows NT network with a few NetWare 4 servers, which Windows 95 clients would you install on a workstation to allow a user to access the greatest number of network services?

   A. Microsoft Client for NetWare Networks

   B. Novell Client for Windows 95

   C. Microsoft Client for Microsoft Networks

   D. Novell Client for NetWare Networks

5. What is the name of the domain user and group administration program for Windows NT Server?

   A. NTADMIN

   B. User Manager for Domains

   C. Domain Administrator

   D. NT Domain Manager (NTDM)

6. What utility allows an administrator to modify NDS objects and their properties?

   A. User Manager

   B. SYSCON

   C. NetWare Administrator

   D. NWCONFIG

7. Which component of the NetWare server architecture can be loaded and unloaded as required, thus conserving memory?

   A. NLM

   B. VLM

   C. OSI

   D. ISO

   E. SCO

8. By default, on which directory service does Windows NT Server 4 rely?

   A. NDS

   B. AD

   C. SCO

   D. NTDS

9. By default, which directory service is used by NetWare 4 and later?

    A. NDS

    B. AD

    C. SCO

    D. NTDS

10. Which network operating systems can run on an Intel Pentium?

    A. NetWare

    B. Windows NT Server

    C. Linux

    D. Solaris

11. Which processor types does Windows NT support?

    A. Intel 386

    B. SPARC

    C. DEC Alpha

    D. PowerPC

12. The many flavors of Unix can use which types of interfaces?

    A. Biometric

    B. Command line

    C. Graphical

    D. Psychic

13. You are the network administrator for a network that includes two NT servers and 5 NetWare 4.1 servers. Your network has only Windows 95/98 clients. Which client(s) should you install so that all clients can access all the resources and functions of all servers?

    A. Microsoft Client for Microsoft Networks

    B. Microsoft Client for NetWare Networks

    C. Novell Client for Windows 95/98

    D. Novell Client for Microsoft Networks

14. Which platforms does NDS run on natively?

    A. NetWare 3.*x*

    B. NetWare 4.*x*

    C. NetWare 5.*x*

    D. Windows NT

    E. Solaris

15. What is the most current released version of Windows NT?

    A. 3.1

    B. 3.51

    C. 4

    D. 4.1

16. Which category of NetWare Loadable Modules (NLMs) is used to interface between the NetWare core operating system and the disk subsystem?

    A. LAN drivers

    B. Disk drivers

    C. Utility NLMs

    D. Maintenance NLMs

17. Which category of NetWare Loadable Modules (NLMs) is used to interface between the NetWare core operating system and the Network Interface Card (NIC)?

    A. LAN drivers

    B. Disk drivers

    C. Name space modules

    D. Maintenance NLMs

18. Which category of NetWare Loadable Modules (NLMs) is used to make NetWare capable of storing files with different naming conventions?

    A. LAN drivers

    B. Disk drivers

    C. Name space modules

    D. Maintenance NLMs

19. Which distribution of Linux was designed specifically for the Intel platform and supports many of its features, including multiple (up to 16) processors?

    A. Red Hat

    B. Slackware

    C. OpenLinux

    D. Yggdrasil

20. The command-line interface to Unix is known as a _____.

    A. Linux

    B. Shell

    C. Window

    D. NIC

Answers to Review Questions

1. B. The only two answers listed that are directory services are NTDS and NDS. Of those two, the only one that is a X.500 compliant directory service is NDS.

2. A, B, D. All the NOSes listed, except NetWare 4, have a graphical interface. Unix has X Windows, NetWare 5 has the Graphical Java Console, and Windows NT Server uses a Windows-based interface.

3. B. The Novell Client for Windows 95 is Novell's NetWare client for the Windows 95 platform. It enables a Windows 95 machine to access the full range of NetWare (and NDS) services.

4. B, C. The Novell Client for Windows 95 (as previously mentioned) and the Microsoft Client for Microsoft Networks will allow the station to access Windows NT Servers.

5. B. Because Windows NT Server manages users and groups in domains, the name of the administration program is User Manager for Domains.

6. C. Although all of the listed utilities are administration utilities of some type, the name of the administration program for modifying NDS objects in NetWare 4 and above is NetWare Administrator.

7. A. The NetWare Loadable Module (NLM) component of a NetWare server is the modular component of a NetWare server that can help conserve memory by being loaded and unloaded as necessary.

8. D. The NT Directory Service (NTDS) is the directory service used by default by Windows NT.

9. A. Novell Directory Services (NDS) is the default directory service used by NetWare 4 and later.

10. A, B, C, D. All the operating systems listed are available in one form or another for the Intel platform.

11. A, C, D. For the Network+ exam, you should know that Windows NT supports, Intel 386, DEC Alpha, and the PowerPC platform (even though some of these platforms have been dropped since Network+ came out).

12. B, C. Unix has two main methods of interacting with users: through a text-based command line and through a graphical interface.

13. A, C. The Microsoft Client for Microsoft Networks will allow the clients to access the Windows NT Server, and the Novell Client for Windows 95/98 will allow the clients to access the NetWare servers.

14. B, C, E. The only platforms that NDS runs on natively are NetWare 4.x and 5.x and Solaris. NDS will NOT run natively on NetWare 3.x. Native NDS support for Windows NT is planned, but its not on the exam at the time of this writing.

15. C. The most current version of Windows NT for the Network+ exam is version 4.

16. B. Disk driver NLMs provide the interface between the core operating system and the disk subsystem hardware (including disk drives and controllers).

17. A. LAN drivers are the NLMs that provide the interface between the Network Interface Card (NIC) and the NetWare core OS.

18. C. Name Space Modules make it possible to store different types of files on the NetWare file system.

19. B. Although all the listed distributions have ports to the Intel platform, the Slackware distribution was specifically developed for the Intel platform.

20. B. The main command line interface in Unix is known as a shell.

Chapter 4

TCP/IP Fundamentals

NETWORK+ EXAM OBJECTIVES COVERED IN THIS CHAPTER:

✓ **Associate IPX, IP, and NetBEUI with their functions**

✓ **Demonstrate knowledge of the following TCP/IP fundamentals:**

- The concept of IP default gateways
- The purpose and use of DHCP, DNS, WINS, and host files
- The identity of the main protocols that make up the TCP/IP suite, including TCP, UDP, POP3, SMTP, SNMP, FTP, HTTP, and IP
- The idea that TCP/IP is supported by every operating system and millions of hosts worldwide
- The purpose and function of Internet domain name server hierarchies (how e-mail arrives in another country)

✓ **Demonstrate knowledge of the fundamental concepts of TCP/IP addressing, including:**

- The A, B, and C classes of IP addresses and their default subnet mask numbers
- The use of port number (HTTP, FTP, SMTP) and port numbers commonly assigned to a given service

✓ **Demonstrate knowledge of TCP/IP configuration concepts, including:**

- The definition of IP proxy and why it is used
- The identity of the normal configuration parameters for a workstation, including IP address, DNS, default gateway, IP proxy configuration, WINS, DHCP, host name, and Internet domain name

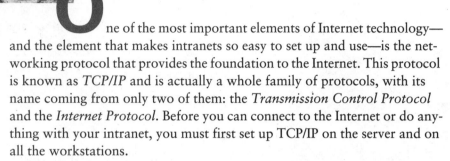

One of the most important elements of Internet technology—
and the element that makes intranets so easy to set up and use—is the networking protocol that provides the foundation to the Internet. This protocol
is known as *TCP/IP* and is actually a whole family of protocols, with its
name coming from only two of them: the *Transmission Control Protocol*
and the *Internet Protocol*. Before you can connect to the Internet or do anything with your intranet, you must first set up TCP/IP on the server and on
all the workstations.

This chapter starts by describing the TCP/IP family of protocols, continues with a description of IP addressing and address classifications, and goes
on to describe several of the name-resolution services available. We'll con-
clude with a detailed discussion of how to set up and configure TCP/IP on
Windows NT Workstation and Windows 98.

Introducing TCP/IP

Because TCP/IP is so central to working with the Internet and with
intranets, we are going to look at it in detail. We'll start with some background on TCP/IP and how it came about and describe the technical goals
defined by the original designers, and then we'll look at how TCP/IP compares against a theoretical model, the Open Systems Interconnect (OSI)
model.

A Brief History of TCP/IP

The TCP/IP protocol was first proposed in 1973, but it was not until 1983 that a standardized version was developed and adopted for wide area use. In that same year, TCP/IP became the official transport mechanism for all connections to ARPAnet, a forerunner of the Internet.

Much of the original work on TCP/IP was done at the University of California at Berkeley, where computer scientists were also working on the Berkeley version of Unix (which eventually grew into the Berkeley Software Distribution [BSD] series of Unix releases). TCP/IP was added to the BSD releases, which in turn was made available to universities and other institutions for the cost of a distribution tape. Thus, TCP/IP began to spread in the academic world, laying the foundation for today's explosive growth of the Internet and of intranets as well.

During this time, the TCP/IP family continued to evolve and add new members. One of the most important aspects of this growth was the continuing development of the certification and testing program carried out by the U.S. government to ensure that the published standards, which were free, were met. Publication ensured that the developers did not change anything, or add any features specific to their own needs. This open approach has continued to the present day; use of the TCP/IP family of protocols virtually guarantees a trouble-free connection between many hardware and software platforms.

TCP/IP Design Goals

When the U.S. Department of Defense began to define the TCP/IP network protocols, their design goals included the following:

- It had to be independent of all hardware and software manufacturers. Even today, this is fundamentally why TCP/IP makes such good sense in the corporate world: it is not tied to IBM, Novell, Microsoft, DEC, or any other specific company.

- It had to have good built-in failure recovery. Because TCP/IP was originally a military proposal, the protocol had to be able to continue operating even if large parts of the network suddenly disappeared from view, say after an enemy attack.

- It had to handle high error rates and still provide completely reliable end-to-end service.

- It had to be efficient with a low data overhead. The majority of data packets using the IP protocol have a simple, 20-byte header, which means better performance in comparison with other networks. A simple protocol translates directly into faster transmissions, giving more efficient service.

- It had to allow the addition of new networks without any service disruptions.

As a result, TCP/IP was developed with each component performing unique and vital functions that allowed all the problems involved in moving data between machines over networks to be solved in an elegant and efficient way. Before looking at both TCP and IP individually, let's see where TCP/IP fits into the broader world of network protocols and particularly how it compares to the theoretical reference model published by the International Organization for Standardization (ISO) as the *Open Systems Interconnect (OSI)* model.

Benefits of Using TCP/IP Rather Than Other Networking Protocols

- TCP/IP is a widely published open standard and is completely independent of any hardware or software manufacturer.

- TCP/IP can send data between different computer systems running completely different operating systems, from small PCs all the way to mainframes and everything in between.

- TCP/IP is separated from the underlying hardware and will run over Ethernet, Token Ring, or X.25 networks and even over dial-up telephone lines.

- TCP/IP is a routable protocol, which means it can send datagrams over a specific route, thus reducing traffic on other parts of the network.

- TCP/IP has reliable and efficient data-delivery mechanisms.

- TCP/IP uses a common addressing scheme. Therefore, any system can address any other system, even in a network as large as the Internet. (We will look at this addressing scheme in the "Understanding IP Addressing" section later in this chapter.)

The popularity that the TCP/IP family of protocols enjoys today did not arise just because the protocols were there, or even because the U.S. government mandated their use. They are popular because they are robust, solid protocols that solve many of the most difficult networking problems, and do so in an elegant and efficient way.

TCP/IP and the OSI Model

As we discussed in Chapter 2, the OSI model divides computer-to-computer communications into seven connected layers; TCP/IP uses the Department of Defense (DoD) model, which describes communications in only four layers , as Figure 4.1 shows. Each successively higher layer builds on the functions provided by the layers below.

FIGURE 4.1   A comparison of the seven-layer OSI model, the four-layer DoD model, and how TCP/IP maps to each model

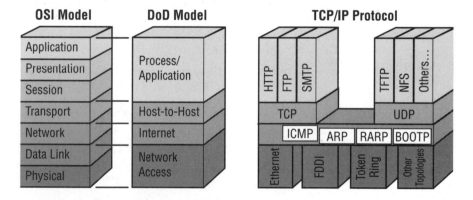

As you may remember from the OSI model, these layers are as follows:

Application Layer   The highest layer; defines the manner in which applications interact with the network—including databases, e-mail, and terminal-emulation programs.

Presentation Layer   Defines the way in which data is formatted, presented, converted, and encoded.

Session Layer   Coordinates communications and maintains the session for as long as it is needed—performing security, logging, and administrative functions.

Transport Layer   Defines protocols for structuring messages and super-vises the validity of the transmission by doing some error checking.

Network Layer   Defines data-routing protocols to ensure that the infor-mation arrives at the correct destination node.

Data Link Layer   Validates the integrity of the flow of the data from one node to another by synchronizing blocks of data and controlling the flow.

Physical Layer   Defines the mechanism for communicating with the transmission medium and the interface hardware.

Although no commercially available networking protocol follows the OSI model exactly, most perform all the same functions.

In the DoD model, the four layers are as follows:

Process/Application Layer   The highest layer; applications such as FTP, Telnet, and others interact through this layer.

Host-to-Host Layer   TCP and other protocols add transport data to the data packet.

Internet Layer   Adds IP information to the packet.

Network Access Layer   Defines the mechanism for communicating with the transmission medium and the interface hardware.

Each layer adds its own header and trailer data to the basic data packet and encapsulates the data from the layer above. On the receiving end, this header information is stripped, one layer at a time, until the data arrives at its final destination.

Now let's look at how TCP and IP work together.

The Transmission Control Protocol

*T*ransmission Control Protocol (TCP) is the transmission layer of the protocol and serves to ensure reliable, verifiable data exchange between hosts on a network. TCP breaks data into pieces, wrapping it with the infor-mation needed to route it to its destination, and reassembling the pieces at the receiving end of the communications link. The wrapped and bundled pieces are called *datagrams*. TCP puts a header on the datagram that pro-vides the information needed to get the data to its destination. The most important information in the header includes the source and destination port numbers, a sequence number for the datagram, and a checksum.

The *source port number* and the *destination port number* allow the data to be sent back and forth to the correct process running on each computer. The *sequence number* allows the datagrams to be rebuilt in the correct order in the receiving computer, and the *checksum* allows the protocol to check whether the data sent is the same as the data received. It does this by first totaling the contents of a datagram and inserting that number in the header. This is when IP enters the picture. Once the header is in the datagram, TCP passes the datagram to IP to be routed to its destination. The receiving computer then performs the same calculation, and if the two calculations do not match, an error occurred somewhere along the line, and the datagram is re-sent.

Figure 4.2 shows the layout of the datagram with the TCP header in place.

FIGURE 4.2 A datagram with its TCP header

Source Port	Destination Port	
Sequence Number		
Acknowledgment Number		
Offset / Reserved / Flags	Window	TCP Header
Checksum	Urgent Pointer	
Options	Padding	
Start of Data		

In addition to the source and destination port numbers, the sequence number, and the checksum, a TCP header contains the following information:

Acknowledgment number Indicates that the data was received successfully. If the datagram is damaged in transit, the receiver throws the data away and does not send an acknowledgment back to the sender. After a predefined time-out expires, the sender retransmits the data for which no acknowledgment was received.

Offset Specifies the length of the header.

Reserved Variables set aside for future use.

Flags Indicates that this packet is the end of the data or that the data is urgent.

Window   Provides a way to increase packet size, which improves efficiency in data transfers.

Urgent pointer   Gives the location of urgent data.

Options   A set of variables reserved for future use or for special options as defined by the user of the protocol.

Padding   Ensures that the header ends on a 32-bit boundary.

The data in the packet immediately follows this header information.

A Summary of TCP Communications

- Flow control allows two systems to cooperate in datagram transmission to prevent overflows and lost packets.

- Acknowledgment lets the sender know that the recipient has received the information.

- Sequencing ensures that packets arrive in the proper order.

- Checksums allow easy detection of lost or corrupted packets.

- Retransmission of lost or corrupted packets is managed in a timely way.

The Internet Protocol

The network layer portion of TCP/IP is called Internet Protocol. This is what actually moves the data from Point A to Point B, a process that is called *routing*.

IP is referred to as *connectionless*; that is, it does not swap control information (or handshaking information) before establishing an end-to-end connection and starting a transmission. The Internet Protocol must rely on TCP to determine that the data arrived successfully at its destination and to retransmit the data if it did not. IP's only job is to route the data to its destination. In this effort, IP inserts its own header in the datagram once it is received from TCP. The main contents of the IP header are the source and destination addresses, the protocol number, and a checksum.

You may sometimes hear IP described as unreliable because it contains no error detection or recovery code.

Without the header provided by IP, intermediate routers between the source and destination, commonly called *gateways*, would not be able to determine where to route the datagram. Figure 4.3 shows the layout of the datagram with the TCP and IP headers in place.

FIGURE 4.3 A datagram with TCP and IP headers

Version	IHL	TOS	Total Length	
Identification		Flags	Fragmentation Offset	IP Header
Time to Live	Protocol	Header Checksum	
TCP Header				
Start of Data				

Let's take a look at the fields in the IP header.

Version   Defines the IP version number. Version 4 is the current standard, and values of 5 or 6 indicate that special protocols are being used. IP version 6 is currently supported by the newest equipment and is quickly becoming the new standard.

IHL (Internet Header Length)   Defines the length of the header information The header length can vary; the default header is five 32-bit words, and the sixth word is optional.

TOS (Type of Service)   Indicates the kind or priority of the required service.

Total Length   Specifies the total length of the datagram, which can be a minimum of 576 bytes and a maximum of 65,536 bytes.

Identification   Provides information that the receiving system can use to reassemble fragmented datagrams.

Flags   The first flag bit specifies that the datagram should not be fragmented and must therefore travel over subnetworks that can handle the size without fragmenting it; the second flag bit indicates that the datagram is the last of a fragmented packet.

Fragmentation Offset   Indicates the original position of the data and is used during reassembly.

Time to Live   Originally, the time in seconds that the datagram could be in transit; if this time was exceeded, the datagram was considered lost. Now interpreted as a *hop* count and usually set to the default value 32 (for 32 hops), this number is decremented by each router through which the packet passes.

Protocol   Identifies the protocol type, allowing the use of non-TCP/IP protocols. A value of 6 indicates TCP, and a value of 17 indicates User Datagram Protocol (UDP).

Header Checksum   An error-checking value that is recalculated at each stopover point; necessary because certain fields change.

TCP Header   The header added by the TCP part of the protocol suite.

The data in the packet immediately follows this header information.

Gateways and Routing

As we mentioned, routing is the process of getting your data from point A to point B. Routing datagrams is similar to driving a car. Before you drive off to your destination, you determine which roads you will take to get there. And sometimes along the way, you have to change your mind and alter your route.

The IP portion of the TCP/IP protocol inserts its header in the datagram, but before the datagram can begin its journey, IP determines whether it knows the destination. If it does know it, IP sends the datagram on its way. If it doesn't know and can't find out, IP sends the datagram to the host's default gateway.

Each host on a TCP/IP network has a default gateway, an off-ramp for datagrams not destined for the local network. They're going somewhere else, and the gateway's job is to forward them to that destination if it knows where it is. Each gateway has a defined set of routing tables that tell the gateway the route to specific destinations.

Because gateways don't know the location of every IP address, they have their own gateways that act just like any TCP/IP host. In the event the first gateway doesn't know the way to the destination, it forwards the datagram to its own gateway. This forwarding, or routing, continues until the datagram reaches its destination. The entire path to the destination is known as the *route*.

Datagrams intended for the same destination may actually take different routes to get there. Many variables determine the route. For example, overloaded gateways may not respond in a timely manner or may simply refuse to route traffic and so time out. That timeout causes the sending gateway to seek an alternate route for the datagram.

Routes can be predefined and made static, and alternate routes can be predefined, providing a maximum probability that your datagrams travel via the shortest and fastest route.

The Application Protocols

The following applications were built on top of the TCP/IP protocol suite and are available on most implementations.

Simple Network Management Protocol (SNMP)   Allows network administrators to collect information about the network. SNMP is a communications protocol for collecting information about devices on the network, including hubs, routers, and bridges. Each piece of information to be collected about a device is defined in a Management Information Base (MIB). SNMP uses UDP (User Datagram Protocol) to send and receive messages on the network.

File Transfer Protocol (FTP)   Provides a mechanism for single or multiple file transfers between computer systems; when written in lowercase, ftp is also the name of the client software used to access the FTP server running on the remote host. The FTP package provides all the tools needed to look at files and directories, change to other directories, and transfer text and binary files from one system to another. File Transfer Protocol uses TCP to actually move the files. We'll look at how to transfer files using FTP in detail in the next chapter.

Simple Mail Transfer Protocol (SMTP)   Allows a simple e-mail service and is responsible for moving messages from one e-mail server to another. The e-mail servers run either Post Office Protocol (POP) or Internet Mail Access Protocol (IMAP) to distribute e-mail messages to users.

Post Office Protocol (POP)   Provides a storage mechanism for incoming mail; the latest version of the standard is known as POP3. When a client connects to a POP3 server, all the messages addressed to that client are downloaded; there is no ability to download messages selectively. Once the messages are downloaded, the user can delete or modify messages without further interaction with the server. In some locations, POP3 is being replaced by another standard, Internet Mail Access Protocol (IMAP).

Internet Mail Access Protocol (IMAP)   Allows users to download mail selectively, to look at the message header, to download just a part of a message, to store messages on the e-mail server in a hierarchical structure, and to link to documents and Usenet newsgroups. Search commands are also available so that users can locate messages based on their subject or header, or based on the content they contain. IMAP has strong authentication features and supports the Kerberos authentication scheme originally developed at MIT.

Telnet   A terminal emulation package that provides a remote logon to another host over the network.

Internet Control Message Protocol (ICMP)   Works at the IP network layer level and provides the functions used for network-layer management and control. Routers send ICMP messages to respond to undeliverable datagrams by placing an ICMP message in an IP datagram and then sending the datagram back to the original source. The Ping command, used in network troubleshooting and described in Chapter 5, uses ICMP.

Hypertext Transfer Protocol (HTTP)   The command and control protocol used to manage communications between a Web browser and a Web server. When you access a Web page on the Internet or on a corporate intranet, you see a mixture of text, graphics, and links to other documents or other Internet resources. HTTP is the mechanism that opens the related document when you select a link, no matter where that document is actually located.

Secure Hypertext Transfer Protocol (which you will see abbreviated as SHTTP, S-HTTP, or even HTTP/S) is a secure version of HTTP that provides a variety of security mechanisms to the transactions between a Web browser and the server. S-HTTP allows browsers and servers to sign, authenticate, and encrypt an HTTP network packet.

Address Resolution Protocol (ARP)   Helps to reference the physical hardware address of a network node to its IP address. Under ARP, a network interface card (NIC) contains a table (known as the address resolution cache) that maps logical addresses to the hardware addresses of nodes on the network. When a node needs to send a packet, it first checks the address resolution cache to see if the physical address information is already present. If so, that address is used, and network traffic is reduced; otherwise, a normal ARP request is made to determine the address. See Chapter 5 for more on ARP.

User Datagram Protocol (UDP)   A transport-layer connectionless protocol that does not provide the reliability services available with TCP. UDP gives applications a direct interface with IP and the ability to address a specific application process running on a host via a port number without setting up a connection session. UDP also uses IP to deliver its packets.

Figure 4.4 shows how some of these components fit together.

FIGURE 4.4   The components in a TCP/IP block diagram

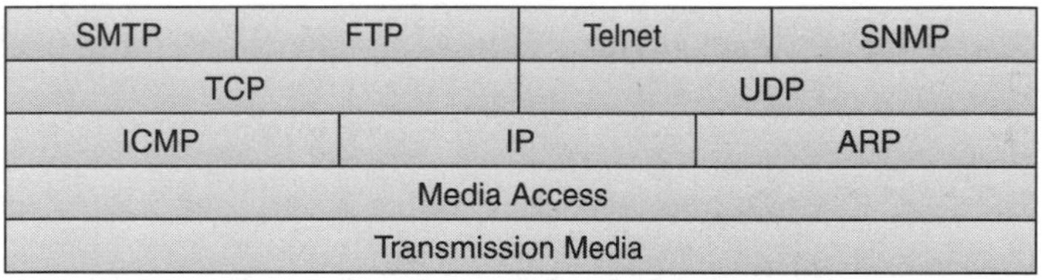

SMTP	FTP	Telnet	SNMP
TCP		UDP	
ICMP	IP	ARP	
Media Access			
Transmission Media			

The Novell NetWare IPX/SPX Protocol Suite

The Novell NetWare proprietary protocol suite consists of two main parts:

- Internetwork Packet eXchange (IPX)

- Sequenced Packet eXchange (SPX)

IPX is based on the *Xerox Network System (XNS)* protocol developed in the 1970s and is an internetworking protocol that provides datagram services in the network layer and also provides routing services. IPX is very efficient and uses a simple addressing scheme that is based on a 4-byte network number, a 6-byte node number, and a 2-byte socket number. A network number is assigned to each segment in the network. The node number or hardware address identifies a specific network interface card or device, and the socket number identifies a particular process in the computer.

IPX packets consist of a 30-byte header that includes the network, node, and socket addresses for the source and the destination, followed by the data area, which can be from 30 bytes (just the header) to 65,535 bytes in length. Most networks impose a more realistic maximum packet size of about 1500 bytes.

The IPX packet header contains the following fields:

Checksum   For data integrity checking.

Packet length   Length of the packet in bytes.

Transport control   Number of routers a packet can cross before being discarded.

Packet type   The service that created the packet.

Destination network   Network address of the destination network.

Destination node   Media access control (MAC) address of the destination node.

Destination socket   Address of the process running on the destination node.

Source network   Network address of the source network.

Source node   MAC address of the source node.

Source socket   Address of the process running on the source node.

The other part of the protocol suite, *SPX*, works at the transport layer and guarantees packet delivery by making the destination node verify that the data was received correctly. If no response is received within a specified time, SPX retransmits the packet. If several retransmissions fail to return an acknowledgment, SPX assumes the connection has failed and informs the outside world of the error condition. All packets in the transmission are sent in sequence, and they all take the same path to their destination.

If we compare the IPX/SPX protocol suite to the TCP/IP family, IP and IPX are connectionless datagram protocols, and SPX and TCP are connection-oriented protocols. IPX provides routing and internetwork services similar to IP, and SPX provides transport layer services similar to TCP.

> Novell NetWare uses two routing protocols:
>
> - Routing Information Protocol (RIP)
>
> - NetWare Link Services Protocol (NLSP)
>
> *NLSP* is more efficient at maintaining routing information and adapting to changes in the network configuration and allows large or small networks to be connected without causing routing inefficiencies.
>
> *NetWare Core Protocol (NCP)* is the main protocol used to manage service requests between a client and a server. It includes routines for logon requests, for manipulating files and directories, for opening semaphores, for printing, and for creating and destroying service connections. NCP was designed with the assumption that client and server would be physically close; once a router is added to the system, and connections are made over a wide area link, NCP creates network traffic congestion.

Ports and Sockets Explained

On a TCP/IP network, data travels from a port on the sending computer to a port on the receiving computer. A *port* is an address that identifies the application associated with the data. The *source port number* identifies the application that sent the data, and the *destination port number* identifies the application that receives the data. All ports are assigned unique 16-bit numbers in the range 0 through 32,767.

Today, the very existence of ports and their numbers is more or less transparent to the users of the network, as many ports are standardized. Thus, a remote computer can know which port it should connect to for a specific service. For example, all servers that offer Telnet services do so on port 23, and Web servers normally run on port 80. This means that when you dial up the Internet to connect to a Web server via the Internet, you automatically connect to port 80, and when you use Telnet, you automatically connect to port 23. The TCP/IP protocol uses a modifiable lookup table to determine the correct port for the data type. Table 4.1 lists some of the well-known port numbers for common protocols.

TABLE 4.1 Well-known Port Numbers for Common Protocols

Number	Protocol
21	File Transfer Protocol (FTP)
23	Telnet
25	Simple Mail Transfer Protocol (SMTP)
70	Gopher
79	Finger
80	Hypertext Transfer Protocol (HTTP)
110	Post Office Protocol 3 (POP3)
119	Network News Transfer Protocol (NNTP)

In multiuser systems, a program can define a port on the fly if more than one user requires access to the same service at the same time. Such a port is known as a *dynamically allocated port* and is assigned only when needed, for example, when two remote computers dial into a third computer and simultaneously request Telnet services on that system.

The combination of an IP address (more on IP addresses in a moment) and a port number is known as a *socket*. A socket identifies a single network process in terms of the entire Internet. You may hear or see the words socket and port used as if they were interchangeable terms, but they are not. Two sockets, one on the sending system and one on the receiving host, are needed to define a connection for connection-oriented protocols, such as TCP.

In the Novell NetWare world, a socket is part of an IPX internetwork address and acts as a destination for the IPX data packet. Most socket numbers are allocated dynamically, but a few are associated with specific functions.

Sockets were first developed as a part of the BSD Unix system kernel, in which they allow processes that are not running at the same time or on the same system to exchange information. You can read data from or write data to a socket just as you can do with a file. Socket pairs are bidirectional so that either process can send data to the other.

Understanding IP Addressing

As you saw in "The Internet Protocol" section earlier in this chapter, IP moves data between computer systems in the form of a datagram, and each datagram is delivered to the destination port number that is contained in the datagram header. This destination port number, or address, is a standard 16-bit number that contains enough information to identify the receiving network as well as the specific host on that network for which the datagram is intended.

In this section, we'll go over what IP addresses are, why they are so necessary, and how they are used in TCP/IP networking. But first, let's clear up a possible source of confusion—Ethernet addresses and IP addresses.

Ethernet Addresses Explained

You may remember that in an earlier section we mentioned that TCP/IP is independent of the underlying network hardware. If you are running on an Ethernet-based network, be careful not to confuse the Ethernet hardware address and the IP address required by TCP/IP.

Each Ethernet network card (and any other NIC, for that matter) has its own unique hardware address, known as the media access control (MAC) address. This hardware address is predefined and preprogrammed on the NIC by the manufacturer of the board as a unique 48-bit number.

The first three parts of this address are called the *OUI (Organizationally Unique Identifier)* and are assigned by the Institute of Electrical and Electronics Engineers (IEEE). Manufacturers purchase OUIs in blocks and then assign the last three parts of the MAC address, making each assignment unique. Remember, the Ethernet address is predetermined and is hard-coded onto the NIC. IP addresses are very different; let's take a look.

IP Addresses Explained

TCP/IP requires that each computer on a TCP/IP network have its own unique IP address. An *IP address* is a 32-bit number, usually represented as a four-part number, with each of the four parts separated by a period or decimal point. You may also hear this method of representation called *dotted decimal* or *quad decimal*. In the IP address, each individual byte, or octet as it is sometimes called, can have a usable value in the range 0 through 255.

The term *octet* is the Internet community's own term for an 8-bit byte and came into common use because some of the early computers attached to the Internet had bytes of more than 8 bits; DEC's systems have blocks of 18-bits.

The way these addresses are used varies according to the class of the network, so all you can say with certainty is that the 32-bit IP address is divided in some way to create an address for the network and an address for each host. In general, though, the higher-order bits of the address make up the network part of the address, and the rest constitutes the host part of the address. In addition, the host part of the address can be divided further to allow for a *subnetwork* address. We'll be looking at all this in more detail in the "IP Address Classification" and "Understanding IP Subnets" sections later in this discussion.

Some host addresses are reserved for special use. For example, in all network addresses, host numbers 0 and 255 are reserved. An IP host address with all host bits set to zero identifies the network itself; so 52.0.0.0 refers to network 52. An IP address with all host bits set to 255 is known as a *broadcast address*. The broadcast address for network 204.176 is 204.176.255.255. A datagram sent to this address is automatically sent to every individual host on the 204.176 network.

InterNIC (Internet Network Information Center) assigns and regulates IP addresses on the Internet; you can get one directly from InterNIC, or you can ask your Internet Service Provider (ISP) to secure an IP address on your behalf. Another strategy is to obtain your address from InterNIC and only use it internally until you are ready to connect to the Internet.

If you are setting up an intranet and you don't want to connect to the outside world through the Internet, you don't need to register with InterNIC the IP addresses you use on your intranet. Registering your addresses with InterNIC simply ensures that the addresses you propose to use are unique over the entire Internet. If you never connect to the Internet, there's no reason to worry about whether those addresses are redundant with a computer that *isn't on your network.*

IP Address Classifications

In the 32-bit IP address, the number of bits used to identify the network and the host vary according to the network class of the address. If you never connect your intranet to the outside world and the Internet, you have no need to concern yourself with this information. If you do plan to connect to the Internet, you'll need to know that the several classes are as follows:

- Class A is used for very large networks only. The high-order bit in a Class A network is always zero, which leaves 7 bits available to define 127 networks. The remaining 24 bits of the address allow each Class A network to hold as many as 16,777,214 hosts. Examples of Class A networks include General Electric, IBM, Hewlett-Packard, Apple, Xerox, DEC, Columbia University, and MIT. All the possible Class A networks are in use, and no more are available.

- Class B is used for medium-sized networks. The 2 high-order bits are always 10, and the remaining bits are used to define 16,384 networks, each with as many as 65,534 hosts attached. Examples of Class B networks include Microsoft and Exxon. All the Class B networks are in use, and no more of them are available.

- Class C is for smaller networks. The 3 high-order bits are always 110, and the remaining bits are used to define 2,097,152 networks, but each network can have a maximum of only 254 hosts. Class C networks are still available.

- Class D is a special multicast address and cannot be used for networks. The 4 high-order bits are always 1110, and the remaining 28 bits allow access to more than 268 million possible addresses.

- Class E is reserved for experimental purposes. The first 4 bits in the address are always 1111.

Figure 4.5 illustrates the relationships among these classes and shows how the bits are allocated by InterNIC.

FIGURE 4.5 The IP address structure

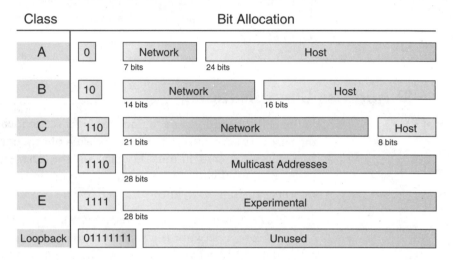

Because the bits used to identify the class are combined with the bits that define the network address, we can draw the following conclusions from the size of the first octet, or byte, of the address:

- A value of 126 or less indicates a Class A address. The first octet is the network number; the next three, the host address.

- A value of exactly 127 is reserved as a loopback test address. If you send a message to 127.0.0.1, the ping doesn't actually generate any network traffic. However, it does test that TCP/IP is installed correctly. Using this number as a special test address has the unfortunate effect of wasting more than 24 million possible IP addresses.

- A value of 128 through 191 is a Class B address. The first two octets are the network number, and the last two are the host address.

- A value of 192 through 223 is a Class C address. The first three octets are the network address, and the last octet is the host address.

- A value greater than 223 indicates a reserved address

Another special address is 192.168.*xxx.xxx*, an address specified in RFC 1918 as being available for anyone who wants to use IP addressing on a private network, but does not want to connect to the Internet. If you fall into this category, you can use this address without the risk of compromising someone else's registered network address.

Understanding Subnets

The IP addressing scheme provides a flexible solution to the task of addressing thousands of networks, but it is not without problems. The original designers did not envision the Internet growing as large as it has; at that time, a 32-bit address seemed so large that they quickly divided it into different classes of networks to facilitate routing rather than reserving more bits to manage the growth in network addresses. (Who ever thought we would need a PC with more than 640KB of memory?) To solve this problem, and to create a large number of new network addresses, another way of dividing the 32-bit address was developed, called *subnetting*.

An IP subnet modifies the IP address by using host address bits as additional network address bits. In other words, the dividing line between the network address and the host address is moved to the right, creating additional networks, but reducing the number of hosts that can belong to each network.

When IP networks are subnetted, they can be routed independently, which allows a much better use of address space and available bandwidth. To subnet an IP network, you define a bit mask known as a *subnet mask*, in which a bit pattern cancels out unwanted bits so that only the bits of interest remain.

Working out subnet masks is one of the most complex tasks in network administration and is not for the faint of heart. If your network consists of a single segment (in other words, there are no routers on your network), you will not have to use this type of subnetting, but if you have two or more segments (or subnets), you will have to make some sort of provision for distributing IP addresses appropriately. Using a subnet mask is the way to do just that.

The subnet mask is similar in structure to an IP address in that it has four parts, or octets, but now it defines three elements (network, subnet, and host) rather than two (network and host). It works a bit like a template that, when superimposed on top of the IP address, indicates which bits in the IP address identify the network and which bits identify the host. If a bit is on (such as a "1") in the mask, that equivalent bit in the address is interpreted as a network bit. If a bit is off (such as a "0") in the mask, the bit is part of the host address. The 32-bit value is then converted to dotted-decimal notation. In general, you will only use one subnet mask on your network.

A subnet is only known and understood locally; to the rest of the Internet, the address is still interpreted as a standard IP address. Table 4.2 shows how all this works for the standard IP address classes.

TABLE 4.2 Default Subnet Masks for Standard IP Address Classes

Class	Subnet Mask Bit Pattern	Subnet Mask
A	11111111 00000000 00000000 00000000	255.0.0.0
B	11111111 11111111 00000000 00000000	255.255.0.0
C	11111111 11111111 11111111 00000000	255.255.255.0

Routers then use the subnet mask to extract the network portion of the address so that they can sent the data packets along the proper route on the network.

Because all the Class A and Class B networks are taken, you are most likely to encounter subnet-related issues when working with a Class C network. In the next section, we'll take a detailed look at how to subnet a Class C network.

The Advantages of Subnetting

- It reduces the size of routing tables.

- It minimizes network traffic.

- It isolates networks from others.

- It maximizes performance.

- It optimizes IP address space.

- It enhances the ability to secure a network.

How to Subnet a Class C Network

How do you find out the values you can use for a Class C network subnet mask? Remember from the previous discussion that InterNIC defines the leftmost three octets in the address, leaving you with the rightmost octet for your own network addresses. If your network consists of a single segment, you have the following subnet mask:

11111111 11111111 11111111 00000000

which, when expressed as a decimal number, is:

255.255.255.0

Because all of your addresses must match these leftmost 24 bits, you can do what you like with the last 8 bits, given a couple of exceptions that we'll look at in a moment.

You might decide to divide your network into two equally sized segments, say with the numbers 1 through 127 as the first subnet (00000001 through 01111111 in binary), and the numbers 128 through 255 as the second subnet (10000000 through 11111111 in binary). Now the number inside the subnets can vary only in the last seven places, and the subnet mask becomes:

255.255.255.128

In binary this is:

11111111.11111111.11111111.10000000

Use the Windows Calculator in scientific mode (choose View Scientific) to look at binary-to-decimal and decimal-to-binary conversions. Click on the Bin (binary) button, and then type the bit pattern that you want to convert. Click on the Dec (decimal) button to display its decimal value; you can also go the other way and display a decimal number in binary form.

Now let's get back to the exceptions we mentioned earlier. The network number is the first number in each range, so the first subnet's network number is X.Y.Z.0, and the second is X.Y.Z.128 (X, Y, and Z are the octets assigned by InterNIC.) The default router address is the second number in each range, X.Y.Z.1 and X.Y.Z.129, and the broadcast address is the last address, or X.Y.Z.127 and X.Y.Z.255. You can use all the other addresses within the range, as you see fit, on your network.

Table 4.3 describes how you can divide a Class C network into four equally sized subnets with a subnet mask of 255.255.255.192. This gives you 61 IP addresses on each subnet once you have accounted for the network, router, and broadcast default addresses.

TABLE 4.3   Class C Network Divided into Four Subnets

Network Number	First Address	Broadcast Address
X.Y.Z.0	X.Y.Z.1	X.Y.Z.63
X.Y.Z.64	X.Y.Z.65	X.Y.Z.127
X.Y.Z.128	X.Y.Z.129	X.Y.Z.191
X.Y.Z.192	X.Y.Z.193	X.Y.Z.255

Table 4.4 describes how you can divide a Class C network into eight equally sized subnets with a subnet mask of 255.255.255.224. This gives you 29 IP addresses on each subnet once you have accounted for the network, router, and broadcast default addresses.

TABLE 4.4   Class C Network Divided into Eight Subnets

Network Number	First Address	Broadcast Address
X.Y.Z.0	X.Y.Z.1	X.Y.Z.31
X.Y.Z.32	X.Y.Z.33	X.Y.Z.63
X.Y.Z.64	X.Y.Z.65	X.Y.Z.95

TABLE 4.4 Class C Network Divided into Eight Subnets *(continued)*

Network Number	First Address	Broadcast Address
X.Y.Z.96	X.Y.Z.97	X.Y.Z.127
X.Y.Z.128	X.Y.Z.129	X.Y.Z.159
X.Y.Z.160	X.Y.Z.161	X.Y.Z.191
X.Y.Z.192	X.Y.Z.193	X.Y.Z.223
X.Y.Z.224	X.Y.Z.225	X.Y.Z.255

Classless Internetwork Domain Routing (CIDR)

InterNIC no longer gives out addresses under the Class A, B, or C designations. Instead, it uses a method called *Classless Internetwork Domain Routing (CIDR)*, usually pronounced "cider." CIDR networks are described as "slash *x*" networks; the *x* represents the number of bits in the IP address range that InterNIC controls. This allows InterNIC to define networks that fall between the old classifications, and means that you can get a range of addresses much better suited to your needs than in times past. In CIDR terms, a network classified as a Class C network under the old scheme becomes a slash 24 network, because InterNIC controls the leftmost 24 bits and you control the rightmost 8 bits. Table 4.5 shows some example slash *x* network types.

You can also combine multiple Class C networks into a single network using this same designation system. This process is known as *supernetting*.

TABLE 4.5 Example CIDR Network Types

InterNIC Network Type	Subnet Mask	Approximate Number of IP Addresses
slash 8	255.0.0.0	16,000,000

TABLE 4.5   Example CIDR Network Types *(continued)*

InterNIC Network Type	Subnet Mask	Approximate Number of IP Addresses
slash 12	255.240.0.0	1,000,000
slash 16	255.255.0.0	65,536
slash 20	255.255.240.0	4,096
slash 21	255.255.248.0	2,048
slash 22	255.255.252.0	1,024
slash 23	255.255.254.0	512
slash 24	255.255.255.0	256
slash 25	255.255.255.128	128
slash 26	255.255.255.192	64
slash 27	255.255.255.224	32
slash 28	255.255.255.248	16
slash 29	255.255.255.248	8
slash 30	255.255.255.254	4

IP Proxy Servers Explained

A *proxy server* is one of several solutions to the problems associated with connecting your intranet or corporate network to the Internet. A proxy server is a program that handles traffic to external host systems on behalf of the client software running on the protected network; this means that clients access the Internet through the proxy server. It's a bit like those one-way mirrors—you can see out of it, but a potential intruder cannot see in.

Another mechanism used to monitor and control traffic between the Internet and an internal network is a *firewall*. Although the functions performed by proxy servers and firewalls are related and are starting to appear in combination products, we'll talk about the proxy server functions here, and you will find more information on firewalls in Chapter 9.

A proxy server sits between a user on your network and a server out on the Internet. Instead of communicating with each other directly, each talks to the proxy (in other words to a "stand-in"). From the user's point of view, the proxy server presents the illusion that the user is dealing with a genuine Internet server. To the real server on the Internet, the proxy server gives the illusion that the real server is dealing directly with the user on the internal network. So it depends on which way you are facing; a proxy server can be both a client and a server. The point to remember here is that the user is never in direct contact with the Internet server, as Figure 4.6 illustrates.

FIGURE 4.6   How a proxy server works

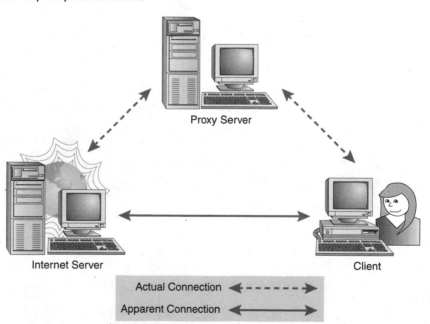

However, the proxy server doesn't just forward requests from your users to the Internet and back. Because it examines and makes decisions about the requests that it processes, it can control what your users can do. Depending on the details of your security policy, client requests can be approved and forwarded, or they can be denied. Rather than requiring that the same restrictions be enforced for all users, many advanced proxy server packages can offer different capabilities to different users.

A proxy server can be effective only if it is the only connection between an internal network and the Internet. As soon as you allow another connection that does not go through a proxy server, your network is at risk.

Proxy Server Caching

Many proxy servers can cache documents, which is particularly useful if a number of clients request the same document independently; the client request is filled more quickly, and Internet traffic is reduced. Caching can be of the following types:

Active caching   The proxy server uses periods of low activity to go out and retrieve documents it thinks will be requested by clients in the near future.

Passive caching   The proxy server waits for a client to make a request, retrieves the document, and then decides whether to cache the document.

Some documents, such as those from a paid subscription service or those requiring specific authentication, cannot be cached.

Large companies may have multiple proxy servers, and two caching standards have emerged: Internet Cache Protocol and Cache Array Routing Protocol.

Internet Cache Protocol (ICP)

Internet Cache Protocol (ICP) specifies a message format used for communications between proxy servers; these messages are used to exchange information about the presence or absence of a specific Web page in the proxy server cache. Unfortunately, ICP is not scalable, and the number of ICP messages exchanged between proxy servers climbs rapidly as the number of proxy servers increases.

Cache Array Routing Protocol (CARP)

Cache Array Routing Protocol (CARP) offers a solution to this problem by using multiple proxy servers with a single large cache. CARP removes the need for proxy-server-to-proxy-server communications and also prevents the information in the cache from becoming redundant over time. CARP is also referred to as queryless distributed caching and is supported in Netscape and Microsoft proxy-server products.

Name Resolution Methods

Internet host names are used because they are easier to remember than long dotted-decimal IP addresses. Host names are typically the name of a device that has a specific IP address, and on the Internet are part of what is known as a *fully qualified domain name.* A fully qualified domain name consists of a host name and a domain name.

Although we have Social Security numbers and can remember them when we need to do so, life would be difficult if we had to remember the Social Security numbers of all our friends and associates. We might be able to remember the Social Security numbers of as many as 10 friends and relatives, but after that things would get a bit difficult. Likewise, it's easier to remember `www.microsoft.com` than it is to remember 198.105.232.6.

The process of finding the host name for any given IP address is known as *name resolution*, which can be performed in several ways, and we'll look at all of them in the next few sections. But first we need to take a look at Internet domains and how they are organized.

Internet Domain Organization

On the Internet, domains are arranged in a hierarchical tree structure. The seven top-level domains currently in use are:

`com`: A commercial organization. Most companies will end up as part of this domain.

edu: An educational establishment, such as a university.

gov: A branch of the U.S. government.

int: An international organization, such as NATO or the United Nations.

mil: A branch of the U.S. military.

net: A network organization.

org: A nonprofit organization.

Unfortunately, the word *domain* is used in several ways, depending on the context. In talking about the Internet, a domain refers to a collection of network host computers; see Chapter 3 for a discussion of how Microsoft Windows NT Server defines a domain.

Your local ISP is probably a member of the .net domain, and your company is probably part of the .com domain. The .gov and .mil domains are reserved strictly for use by the government and the military within the United States. In other parts of the world, the final part of a domain name represents the country in which the server is located—.ca for Canada, .jp for Japan, .uk for Great Britain, and .ru for Russia, for example. The .com domain is by far the largest, followed by the .edu domain, and well over 130 countries are represented on the Internet.

If you want to contact someone within one of these domains by e-mail, you just add that person's e-mail name to their domain name, separated by an at (@) sign. For example, if you want to e-mail the president of the United States, send your e-mail to this address:

President@whitehouse.gov

To increase the number of domain names available for use—after all, there is only one mcdonalds.com domain name available—several alternative top-level domains have been suggested, including .firm for businesses and companies, .store for businesses selling good rather than services, .arts for cultural and entertainment organizations, and .info for informational services.

InterNIC assigns all Internet domain names and makes sure no names are duplicated. Names are assigned on a first-come, first-serve basis, but if you try to register a name that infringes on someone else's registered trademark, your use of that name will be rescinded if the trademark holder objects.

Now that we have detailed how Internet domain names work and where they came from, we can return to our discussion of name-resolution methods.

Using HOSTS

Several automatic conversion systems are available to translate an IP address into a host name, and HOSTS is one of the simplest. You create a file called HOSTS and enter a line into it for every system, like this:

```
198.34.56.25 myserver.com #My server's information
198.34.57.03 yourserver.com
```

Now comes the nasty part. You must store this ASCII file on *every single workstation on your network*; when you make a change, you must change the contents of the HOSTS file on *every single workstation on your network*. Simple but painful inside a network, but what happens if you want to go out to other networks or to the Internet? The file size would be simply enormous. Fortunately, there are better solutions, as you will see in the next two sections.

Any information entered to the right of a pound sign in a HOSTS file is ignored, so you can use it for comments.

Using DNS

The abbreviation DNS stands for *Domain Name Service*. You use DNS to translate host names and domain names to IP addresses, and vice versa, by means of a standardized lookup table that the network administrator defines and configures. The system works just like a giant telephone directory.

Suppose you are using your browser to surf the Web, and you enter the URL http://www.microsoft.com to go to the Microsoft home page. Your Web browser then asks the TCP/IP protocol to ask the DNS server for the IP address of www.microsoft.com. When your Web browser receives this address, it connects to the Microsoft Web server and downloads the home page. DNS is an essential part of any TCP/IP network, simplifying the task of remembering addresses; all you have to do is simply remember the host name and domain name.

DNS tables are composed of records. Each record is composed of a host name, a record type, and an address. There are several record types, including the address record, the mail exchange record, and the CNAME record.

The *address record*, commonly known as the A record, maps a host name to an IP address. The example below shows the address record for a host called `mail` in the `company.com` domain:

```
mail.company.com.       IN      A       204.176.47.9
```

The *mail exchange (MX) record* points to the mail exchanger for a particular host. DNS is structured so that you can actually specify several mail exchangers for one host. This feature provides a higher probability that e-mail will actually arrive at its intended destination. The mail exchangers are listed in order in the record, with a priority code that indicates the order in which the mail exchangers should be accessed by other mail delivery systems.

If the first priority doesn't respond in a given amount of time, the mail delivery system tries the second one, and so on. Here are some sample mail exchange records:

```
hostname.company.com.   IN      MX      10 mail.company.com.
hostname.company.com.   IN      MX      20 mail2.company.com.
hostname.company.com.   IN      MX      30 mail3.company.com
```

In this example, if the first mail exchanger, `mail.company.com`, does not respond, the second one, `mail2.company.com` is tried, and so on.

The *CNAME record*, or *canonical name record*, is also commonly known as the *alias record* and allows hosts to have more than one name. For example, your Web server has the host name www, and you want that machine also to have the name ftp so that users can easily FTP in to manage Web pages. You can accomplish this with a CNAME record. Assuming you already have an address record established for the host name www, a CNAME record adding ftp as a host name would look something like this:

```
www.company.com.        IN      A       204.176.47.2
ftp.company.com.        IN      CNAME   www.company.com
```

When you put all these record types together in a file, it's called a *DNS table*, and it might look like this:

```
mail.company.com.       IN      A       204.176.47.9
mail2.company.com.      IN      A       204.176.47.21
```

```
mail3.company.com.        IN    A       204.176.47.89
yourhost.company.com.     IN    MX      10 mail.company.com.
yourhost.company.com.     IN    MX      20 mail2.company.com.
yourhost.company.com.     IN    MX      30 mail3.company.com.
www.company.com.          IN    A       204.176.47.2
ftp.company.com.          IN    CNAME   www.company.com.
```

You can establish other types of records for specific purposes, but we won't go into those in this book. DNS can become very complex very quickly, and entire books are dedicated to the DNS system.

Using WINS

WINS, or *Windows Internet Naming Service*, is an essential part of the Microsoft networking topology. But before we get into a discussion of WINS, we must define a few terms, including these two horrors—NetBIOS and NetBEUI.

NetBIOS (pronounced net-bye-os) is an acronym formed from *network basic input/output system*, a session-layer network protocol originally developed by IBM and Sytek to manage data exchange and network access. NetBIOS provides an API with a consistent set of commands for requesting lower-level network services to transmit information from node to node, thus separating the applications from the underlying network operating system. Many vendors provide either their own version of NetBIOS or an emulation of its communications services in their products.

NetBEUI (pronounced net-boo-ee) is an acronym formed from *NetBIOS Extended User Interface*, an implementation and extension of IBM's NetBIOS transport protocol from Microsoft. NetBEUI communicates with the network through Microsoft's NDIS (Network Driver Interface Specification). NetBEUI is shipped with all versions of Microsoft's operating systems today and is generally considered to have a lot of overhead. NetBEUI also has no networking layer and therefore no routing capability, which means it is only suitable for small networks; you cannot build internetworks with NetBEUI, and so it is often replaced with TCP/IP. Microsoft has added extensions to NetBEUI in Windows NT to remove the limitation of 254 sessions per node; this extended version of NetBEUI is called the NetBIOS Frame (NBF).

WINS is used in conjunction with TCP/IP and maps NetBIOS names to IP addresses. For example, you have a print server on your LAN that you have come to know as PrintServer1. In the past, to print to that server you needed only to remember its name and to select that name from a list. However, TCP/IP is a completely different protocol and doesn't understand NetBIOS names; it therefore has no way of knowing the location of those servers or their addresses. That's where WINS comes in.

Each time you access a network resource on a Windows NT network using TCP/IP, your system needs to know the host name or IP address. If WINS is installed, you can continue using the NetBIOS names that you have previously used to access the resources because WINS provides the cross-reference from name to address for you.

A NetBIOS name doesn't always just refer to a machine. Several services on a machine can have their own NetBIOS names.

When you install and configure TCP/IP, as described later in this chapter, you'll see a place to specify the WINS server addresses. These addresses are stored with the configuration, and TCP/IP uses them to query for host names and addresses when necessary. WINS is similar to DNS in that it cross-references host names to addresses; however, as we mentioned earlier, WINS references NetBIOS names to IP addresses, and DNS references TCP/IP host names to IP addresses.

Another major difference between WINS and DNS is that WINS builds its own reference tables dynamically, and you have to configure DNS manually. When a workstation running TCP/IP is booted and attached to the network, it uses the WINS address settings in the TCP/IP configuration to communicate with the WINS server. The workstation gives the WINS server various pieces of information about itself, such as the NetBIOS host name, the actual username logged on to the workstation, and the workstation's IP address. WINS stores this information for use on the network and periodically refreshes it to maintain accuracy.

Microsoft, however, has developed a new DNS record that allows the DNS server to work in perfect harmony with a WINS server. The Microsoft DNS Server software currently ships with Windows NT. Here's how it works. When a DNS query returns a WINS record, the DNS server then asks the WINS server for the host name address. Thus, you need not build complex DNS tables to establish and configure name resolution on your server; Microsoft DNS relies entirely on WINS to tell it the addresses it needs to resolve. And because WINS builds its tables automatically, you don't have to edit the DNS tables when addresses change; WINS takes care of this for you.

Network Address Translation (NAT) is the process of converting between the IP addresses used on a corporate intranet or other private network and Internet IP addresses. This makes it possible to use a large number of addresses within the private network without depleting the limited number of available numeric IP addresses. NAT is usually performed within a router.

You can use both WINS and DNS on your network, or you can use one without the other. Your choice is determined by whether your network is connected to the Internet and whether your host addresses are dynamically assigned. When you are connected to the Internet, you must use DNS to resolve host names and addresses because TCP/IP depends on DNS service for address resolution.

Configuring TCP/IP on Windows Workstations

Now that the discussion on TCP, IP, and IP addressing is out of the way, we can take a look at how you can configure a Windows client to use TCP/IP. We'll assume that you already have Windows 98 or Windows NT Workstation running on the client.

If you are using Plug-and-Play network interface cards, Microsoft Windows may already have recognized your TCP/IP network; in which case, you can skip ahead to the discussion in Chapter 5 on how to use the TCP/IP utilities to confirm that your system is up and running properly.

There is very little difference between installing TCP/IP on a Windows 98 client and installing TCP/IP on a Windows NT Workstation client; the dialog boxes you use are virtually identical. We'll use Windows 98 for the discussion that follows.

If Windows has not automatically recognized your TCP/IP connection or if you want to look at or change some of the configuration settings, stay with this chapter.

To begin installing TCP/IP, follow these steps:

1. Choose Start ➤ Settings ➤ Control Panel ➤ Network to open the Network dialog box, which lists all the currently installed network components.

You can also right-click the Network Neighborhood icon on the Windows desktop and select Properties from the shortcut menu to open the Network dialog box.

2. Click Add to open the Select Network Component Type dialog box:

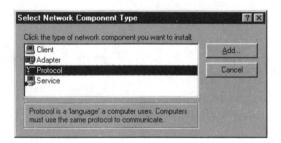

3. Select Protocol from the list of network components, and click Add to open the Select Network Protocol dialog box. This dialog box lists the various software manufacturers and their respective networking protocols.

4. Select Microsoft from the list of manufacturers, and select TCP/IP from the Network Protocols list.

5. Click OK to continue.

When you click OK, Windows installs the Microsoft TCP/IP protocol and displays it in the list of networking components in the Network dialog box. Clicking OK completes the installation, and the system prompts you to restart the computer so the changes can take effect.

TCP/IP Properties

Many configuration settings are associated with TCP/IP, and to look at or change them, follow these steps:

1. Choose Start ➢ Settings ➢ Control Panel ➢ Network to open the Network dialog box.

2. Select TCP/IP, and click the Properties button to open the TCP/IP Properties dialog box.

   Across the top of the TCP/IP Properties dialog box you will see several tabs, including:

   - IP Address
   - Bindings
   - Gateway
   - Advanced
   - WINS Configuration
   - DNS Configuration
   - NetBIOS (if used)

Each tab controls the settings associated with a specific aspect of using TCP/IP under Windows, and in the sections that follow, we'll look at all the settings you can configure on all these tabs. The settings that you use on your system will obviously depend on the configuration of that system and exactly how you intend to use it. And in certain circumstances, you may see other tabs in the TCP/IP Properties dialog box. For example, if you are using Net-BIOS, you will see a tab that lets you use NetBIOS over TCP/IP.

The IP Address Tab

You use the IP Address tab, shown in Figure 4.7, to specify an IP address for this client. If you accept the default option, Obtain an IP Address Automatically, your computer obtains this address from the Dynamic Host

Configuration Protocol (DHCP) server on your network or from an ISP if you are connecting directly to the Internet. We'll talk more about DHCP in a moment.

FIGURE 4.7 The IP Address tab of the TCP/IP Properties dialog box

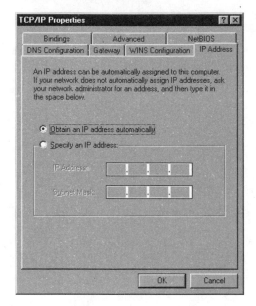

If you select Specify an IP Address, you can enter the appropriate IP address and subnet mask for use on this computer.

Dynamic Host Configuration Protocol

The primary reason for using DHCP is to centralize the management of IP addresses. When the DHCP service is used, pools of IP addresses are assigned for automatic distribution to client computers on an as-needed basis. The address pools are centralized on the DHCP server, allowing all IP addresses on your network to be administered from a single server. It should be apparent that this saves loads of time when changing the IP addresses on your network. Instead of running around to every workstation and server and resetting the IP address to a new address, you simply reset the IP address pool on the DHCP server. The next time the client machines are rebooted, they are assigned new addresses.

However, Dynamic Host Configuration Protocol can manage much more than the IP addresses of client computers. It can also assign DNS servers, gateway addresses, subnet masks, and many other tasks.

If the client workstation cannot locate the DHCP server on the network automatically, you will see an error message to that effect when you restart the client workstation.

In the Windows family of operating systems, only computers running Windows NT Server 3.51 or later can act as a DHCP server; a computer running Windows 98 cannot be a DHCP server. In the Novell world, NetWare 4.11 comes with DCHP as a standard service, and in NetWare 5, this service is administered using a Java-based snap-in module for the administrator utility called the DNS/DHCP Management Console.

The Bindings Tab

The Bindings tab of the TCP/IP Properties dialog box, shown in Figure 4.8, displays the bindings available on the computer and also lets you select the ones you want to use. When you install a new protocol, Windows binds the new protocol to all possible client and service components. In some cases, certain network components may not work if you have the wrong protocol bindings selected, so make sure that the bindings shown here reflect the appropriate protocol.

The Network Driver Interface Specification

The *Network Driver Interface Specification (NDIS)*, originally developed by Microsoft and 3Com in 1990, is a device driver specification that is independent of both the underlying network hardware and of the networking protocol in use.

NDIS also provides protocol multiplexing so that multiple protocol stacks can be used at the same time on the same computer.

FIGURE 4.8 The Bindings tab of the TCP/IP Properties dialog box

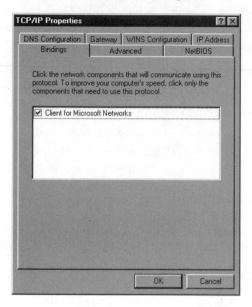

The Gateway Tab

You use the Gateway tab, shown in Figure 4.9, to specify the IP address of one or more gateway routers installed on your network. To enter the information for a new gateway, type the IP address in the New Gateway box, and click the Add button. The IP address will appear in the Installed Gateways box lower down in this dialog box.

FIGURE 4.9   The Gateway tab of the TCP/IP Properties dialog box

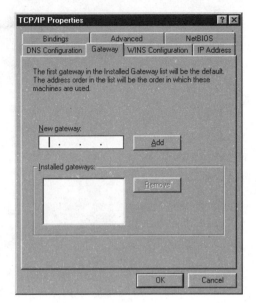

 Windows uses the first gateway listed in the Installed Gateways box as the default gateway.

To remove an installed gateway, select it from the list in the Installed Gateways box and click Remove.

The Advanced Tab

You use the Advanced tab to specify that Windows should use this protocol as the default if no protocol has been selected. No other configurable properties are available in this tab.

WINS Configuration Tab

Selecting Disable WINS Resolution in the WINS Configuration tab, shown in Figure 4.10, turns off the use of WINS; this is the default setting.

FIGURE 4.10 The WINS Configuration tab of the TCP/IP Properties dialog box

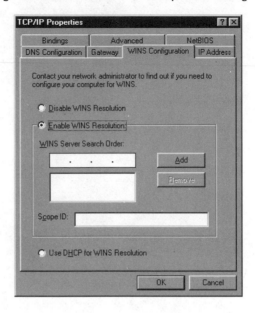

If you select Enable WINS Resolution, you can enter IP address values for the primary WINS server and a secondary WINS server on your network if one is available. The system first tries to use the primary WINS server for name resolution, but if it can't find the primary WINS server, it will try to locate a secondary WINS server.

The Scope ID field may contain a set of text characters if you have an internetwork connection that uses NetBIOS over TCP/IP. All the computers in a group that share the same Scope ID are able to communicate with each other, but not with computers outside the group. In most cases, the Scope ID field is left blank.

At the bottom of this dialog box, you will see the option button Use DHCP for WINS Resolution. Click this button if you want to enable DHCP to set up the WINS configuration.

The DNS Configuration Tab

You use the DNS Configuration tab of the TCP/IP Properties dialog box, shown in Figure 4.11, to enable or disable DNS. When DNS is enabled, you can enter information into the Host, Domain, DNS Server Search Order, and Domain Suffix Search Order fields.

FIGURE 4.11   The DNS Configuration tab of the TCP/IP Properties dialog box

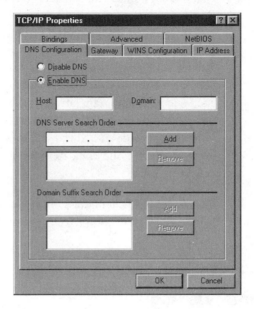

The Host field contains the name of the local computer, usually the name used to configure networking services, but it can be different. The name can be a set of alphanumeric characters and the hyphen; use a period as a separator.

A *Fully Qualified Domain Name (FQDN)* consists of the name of the host followed by the domain name. For example, if the name of the local computer is `wallaby`, and the domain is `sybex.com`, the FQDN is `wallaby.sybex.com`.

The Domain field is optional and, if used, contains the name of the DNS domain to which this computer belongs.

The term *domain* is used in different ways in different contexts. The domain specified here for DNS is not the same domain as a Windows NT domain, an OS/2 LAN Server domain, or a LAN Manager domain.

The DNS Server Search Order field can contain the IP addresses of as many as three DNS servers that can be used for name resolution services. To add the IP address of a DNS server, type the IP address in the entry field, and click Add. To delete an IP address from the list, select an IP address, and click Remove.

The Domain Suffix Search Order field contains a list of domain suffixes that the system can use when creating an FQDN from a short name. The system adds the local domain name to the short name and queries the DNS server for name resolution. If the FQDN is not resolved, the system appends each successive domain suffix in this list to the short name and retries for name resolution. To add a domain suffix to the list, type the domain name you want to add, and click Add. If you want to delete a domain name from the list, select it and click Remove.

 If a Windows 98 client does not respond to the network as you expect, run the Windows 98 Networking Troubleshooter as a first step in tracking down the problem.

The Windows Registry

All this TCP/IP configuration information is stored in the *Windows Registry* database, along with lots of other hardware and software configuration information. You can change most of the TCP/IP parameters by using the Network applet in Control Panel as we have just seen. Certain parameters, however, such as Time to Live and the default Type of Service, can only be changed using the Registry Editor (regedit.exe on Windows 98 or regedit32 on Windows NT). If you change some of these Registry parameters without detailed knowledge of TCP/IP configuration parameters, you may affect the performance of TCP/IP on your system in an adverse and unexpected way.

If you are configuring TCP/IP on a Windows NT Workstation client, and you want to know more, check out the Microsoft KnowledgeBase article Q120642 on the Microsoft Web site at www.microsoft.com. This article covers all the standard, optional, and nonconfigurable TCP/IP parameters and describes which parameters are updates by the Network applet in Control Panel and which are changed using the Registry Editor.

In the next chapter, we'll look at some of the utilities in the TCP/IP toolkit that you can use to view and troubleshoot your TCP/IP network. These tools are all based on the original Unix tools, but these days they are available in one form or another for all operating systems, including all versions of Unix, Novell NetWare, and Microsoft Windows 98 and NT.

Key Terms

Before you take the exam, be certain you are familiar with the following terms:

address

alias record

broadcast address

checksum

CNAME record

connectionless

Control Protocol

datagram

destination port number

domain

Domain Name Service

dotted decimal

dynamically allocated port

firewall

fully qualified domain name

gateway

hop

Internet Protocol

IP address

mail exchange

name resolution

NetBIOS Extended User Interface

network basic input/output system

octet

port

proxy server

quad decimal

route

routing

sequence number

socket

source port number

subnet mask

subnetting

subnetwork

supernetting

TCP/IP

Transmission

Review Questions

1. The main advantage of the TCP/IP protocol is _____.

   A. Ease of setup

   B. Interfaces without regard to operating system

   C. Not routable

   D. Can be exported to other countries

2. Which feature listed below is not available in NetBEUI/NetBIOS?

   A. Self-tuning

   B. Fast in small networks

   C. Little configuration

   D. Routable

3. The Class B address range for the first octet is _____.

   A. 1–127

   B. 128–191

   C. 192–223

   D. 224–255

4. A subnet mask separates _____.

   A. Network ID and Host ID

   B. Workgroups from each other

   C. Host ID

   D. All the above

5. HTTP usually connects to a Web server on port number _____.

   A. 21

   B. 25

   C. 80

   D. 147

6. The port number for POP3 mail is _____.

   A. 25

   B. 80

   C. 100

   D. 110

7. FTP usually connects to the server on port number _____.

   A. 21

   B. 25

   C. 80

   D. 110

8. Internet mail is sent between mail servers via which protocol?

   A. SNMP

   B. SMTP

   C. POP

   D. Telnet

9. A default subnet mask for a Class C address is _____.

   A. 255.0.0.0

   B. 255.255.0.0

   C. 255.255.255.0

   D. 255.255.255.255

10. Network Address Translation is found in _____.

   A. Windows 3.*x*

   B. Windows 98

   C. NIC Protocol Drivers

   D. Routers

11. DHCP is an acronym for _____.

   A. Dynamic Host Carrier Protocol

   B. Dynamic Host Configuration Protocol

   C. Dynamic Host Client Protocol

   D. Dynamic Host Control Protocol

12. Which protocol is considered connection-oriented?

   A. DDP

   B. TCP

   C. NetBEUI

   D. UDP

13. Features of IPX include _____ (choose all that apply).

   A. Connection-oriented

   B. Very efficient

   C. No addressing problems

   D. Excellent scaling without performance issues

14. SMTP normally operates through port number _____.

   A. 21

   B. 25

   C. 80

   D. 110

15. FQDN is an acronym for _____.

    A. Fully Qualified Division Name

    B. Fully Qualified DNS Name

    C. Fully Qualified Dynamic Name

    D. Fully Qualified Domain Name

16. What delimiter separates domain spaces?

    A. : (colon)

    B. # (pound)

    C. ~ (tilde)

    D. . (period)

17. Which is used to begin a comment in a HOSTS file?

    A. : (colon)

    B. # (pound)

    C. ~ (tilde)

    D. . (period)

18. FTP is the abbreviation for _____.

    A. Formal Transfer Protocol

    B. Full Transfer Protocol

    C. Final Transfer Protocol

    D. File Transfer Protocol

19. Which of the following is not a feature of a proxy server?

    A. Can reduce Internet traffic requests

    B. Can assist with security

    C. Can reduce user wait time for request

    D. Can convert a non-routable protocol to a routable protocol

20. HTTP is short for _____.

    A. Hypertext Transport Protocol

    B. Half Track Transport Protocol

    C. Hyper Transport Tally Protocol

    D. Hickson-Trollwood Transport Protocol

Answers to Review Questions

1. B. The main advantage is that the TCP/IP protocol stack is available for just about every operating system. Although TCP/IP is easy to set up and can be exported, these are not the primary reasons the TCP/IP enjoys such popularity.

2. D. The NetBEUI/NetBIOS protocol stack contains no Network layer routing protocol and, as such, cannot be routed.

3. B. 128-191 is the range of the numbers for the first octet in a Class B IP addressing scheme. 1-127 is for Class A, 192-223 is for Class C, and 224-255 is reserved for other classes and purposes.

4. A. The purpose of a subnet mask is to separate the Network portion and the Host portion of an IP address.

5. C. Port 80 is the TCP port number used to initiate HTTP connections between web client (browser) and web server.

6. D. The TCP port number used to initiate connections between POP3 clients and servers is 110.

7. A. FTP clients connect to FTP servers using TCP port 21.

8. B. Internet e-mail servers send mail between themselves using the SMTP protocol. The SNMP protocol is used for management and monitoring of various network devices. The POP protocol is used to download e-mail from mail servers. Telnet is used for remote terminal emulation.

9. C. 255.255.255.0 is the default subnet mask for a Class C address. 255.0.0.0 is the default for a Class A, 255.255.0.0 is the default for Class B, and 255.255.255.255 is the universal broadcast address.

10. D. Most often, NAT is used in routers and Internet gateways to translate between two different IP addresses.

11. B. The only correct acronym expansion is Dynamic Host Configuration Protocol

12. B. Of those listed, the only one that maintains a virtual "connection" is TCP. UDP and NetBEUI are both connectionless, and DDP is a fictitious protocol.

13. B, C, D. IPX is an efficient, self-addressing, scalable protocol. It is not, however, connection-oriented. IPX is, in fact, a connectionless protocol.

14. B. SMTP initiates connections between servers using TCP port number 25.

15. D. The correct acronym expansion for FQDN is Fully Qualified Domain Name.

16. D. Domain names are normally separated by periods (.). An example of this syntax would be `www.sybex.com`.

17. B. When inserting comments into a HOSTS file, you must use a pound sign (#) to begin each comment line.

18. D. The proper expansion of FTP is File Transfer Protocol.

19. D. Proxy servers act on behalf of clients to provide Internet access and other Internet services. However, generally speaking, a proxy server does not convert a non-routable protocol to a routable protocol.

20. A. The abbreviation HTTP is short for Hypertext Transport Protocol. This is the primary protocol used to deliver web content over the Internet.

TCP/IP Utilities

NETWORK+ EXAM OBJECTIVES COVERED IN THIS CHAPTER:

✓ **Explain how and when to use the following TCP/IP utilities to test, validate, and troubleshoot IP connectivity**

- ARP
- Telnet
- nbtstat
- tracert
- netstat
- ipconfig/winipcfg
- FTP
- Ping

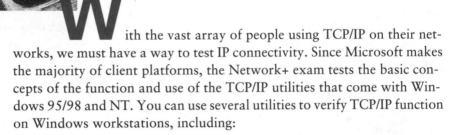

With the vast array of people using TCP/IP on their networks, we must have a way to test IP connectivity. Since Microsoft makes the majority of client platforms, the Network+ exam tests the basic concepts of the function and use of the TCP/IP utilities that come with Windows 95/98 and NT. You can use several utilities to verify TCP/IP function on Windows workstations, including:

- ARP
- netstat
- nbtstat
- FTP
- Ping
- ipconfig/winipcfg
- tracert
- Telnet

Using the Address Resolution Protocol (ARP)

The ARP protocol is part of the TCP/IP (Transmission Control Protocol/Internet Protocol) protocol stack, and it translates TCP/IP addresses to MAC (media access control) addresses using broadcasts. When a machine running TCP/IP wants to know which machine on an Ethernet network uses a particular IP address, it will send an ARP broadcast that says, in effect,

"Hey! Who is the IP address xxx.xxx.xxx.xxx?" The machine that owns the specific address will respond with its own MAC address. The machine that made the inquiry then adds that information to its own ARP table.

In addition to the normal usage, the ARP designation refers to a utility in Windows 95/98 and NT that you can use to manipulate and view the local workstation's ARP address resolution table.

The Windows ARP Table

The *ARP table* in Windows 95/98 and NT is a list of TCP/IP addresses and their associated physical (MAC) addresses. This table is cached in memory so that Windows doesn't have to perform ARP lookups for frequently accessed TCP/IP addresses (for example, servers and default gateways). Each entry contains not only an IP address and a MAC address, but a value for Time to Live (TTL), which indicates how long each entry stays in the ARP table.

The ARP table contains two kinds of entries:

- Dynamic

- Static

Dynamic ARP table entries are created whenever the Windows TCP/IP stack makes an ARP request and the MAC address is not found in the ARP table. The ARP request is broadcast on the local segment. When the MAC address of the requested IP address is found, that information is added to the ARP table.

Periodically the ARP table is cleared of dynamic entries whose Time to Live has expired to ensure that the entries are current.

Static ARP table entries serve the same function as dynamic entries, but are made manually using the ARP utility.

The ARP Utility

To start the ARP utility in Windows 95/98, follow these steps:

1. Choose Start ➢ Programs ➢ MS-DOS Prompt to open the MS-DOS prompt window.

2. At the command prompt, type ARP and any switches you need.

To start the ARP utility in Windows NT, follow these steps:

1. Choose Start ➢ Programs ➢ Command Prompt to open the Command Prompt window.

2. At the command prompt, type ARP and any switches you need.

Entered by itself, the ARP command lists only the switches you must use in order to use the ARP utility correctly.

The ARP utility is primarily useful for resolving duplicate IP addresses. For example, a workstation receives its IP address from a DHCP (Dynamic Host Configuration Protocol) server, and it accidentally receives the same address as another workstation. When you try to ping it, you get no response. Your workstation is trying to determine the MAC address, and it can't do so because two machines are reporting that they have the same IP address. To solve this problem, you can use the ARP utility to view your local ARP table and see which TCP/IP address is resolved to which MAC address. To display the entire, current ARP table, use the ARP command with the –a switch, like this:

```
ARP —a
```
You'll see something similar to the following:

```
Interface: 204.153.163.3 on Interface 2
Internet Address        Physical Address        Type
204.153.163.2           00-a0-c9-d4-bc-dc       dynamic
204.153.163.4           00-a0-c0-aa-b1-45       dynamic
```

The -g switch will accomplish the same result.

From this output, you can tell which MAC address is assigned to which IP address. Then, by examining your network documentation (you do have it, don't you?), you can tell which workstation has the IP address and if it is indeed supposed to have it.

If the machine has more than one network card (as may happen in Windows NT machines), each interface will be listed separately.

In addition to displaying the ARP table, you can use the ARP utility to manipulate it. To add static entries to the ARP table, use the ARP command with the –s switch. These entries stay in the ARP table until the machine is rebooted. A static entry hard-wires a specific IP address to a specific MAC address so that when a packet needs to be sent to that IP address, it is sent automatically to that MAC address. Here's the syntax:

`ARP —s [IP Address] [MAC Address]`

Simply replace the `[IP Address]` and `[MAC Address]` sections with the appropriate entries, like so:

`ARP —s 204.153.163.5 00-a0-c0-ab-c3-11`

You can now take a look at your new ARP table by using the ARP –a command. You should see something like this:

```
Interface: 204.153.163.3 on Interface 2
Internet Address          Physical Address          Type
204.153.163.2             00-a0-c9-d4-bc-dc         dynamic
204.153.163.4             00-a0-c0-aa-b1-45         dynamic
204.153.163.5             00-a0-c0-ab-c3-11         static
```

Finally, if you want to delete entries from the ARP table, you can either wait until the dynamic entries time out, or you can use the –d switch with the IP address of the static entry you'd like to delete, like so:

`ARP —d 204.153.163.5`

This deletes the entry from the ARP table in memory.

The ARP utility doesn't confirm successful additions or deletions, but it will give you an error message if you use incorrect syntax.

Using netstat

Using *netstat* is a great way to see the TCP/IP connections (both inbound and outbound) on your machine. You can also use it to view packet statistics (similar to the MONITOR.NLM utility on a NetWare server console), such as how many packets have been sent and received, the number of errors, and so on.

When used without any options, netstat produces output similar to that in Figure 5.1, which shows all the outbound TCP/IP connections (in the case of Figure 5.1, a Web connection). The netstat utility, used without any options, is particularly useful in determining the status of outbound Web connections.

The Proto column lists the protocol being used. Since this is a Web connection, the protocol is TCP. The Local Address column lists the source address and the source port. In this case, default indicates that the local IP address and the source ports are four separate TCP ports used to open four separate TCP connections. The Foreign Address for all four connections is 204.153.163.2:80, indicating that the address of the destination machine is 204.153.163.2 and that the destination port is TCP port 80 (in other words HTTP [Hypertext Transport Protocol] for the Web). The State column indicates the status of each connection. This column only shows statistics for TCP connections. Usually, this column indicates ESTABLISHED once a connection between your computer and the destination computer is established.

FIGURE 5.1 Output of the netstat command without any switches

```
C:\NETSTAT
Active Connections

Proto     Local Address      Foreign Address        State
TCP       default:1026       204.153.163.2:80       ESTABLISHED
TCP       default:1027       204.153.163.2:80       ESTABLISHED
TCP       default:1028       204.153.163.2:80       ESTABLISHED
TCP       default:1029       204.153.163.2:80       ESTABLISHED
```

If the address of your computer or the destination computer can be found in the HOSTS file on your computer, the destination computer's name, rather than the IP address, will show up in either the Local Address or Foreign Address column.

The output of the netstat utility depends on the switch. You can use the following switches:

    -a
    -e
    -r
    -s
    -n
    -p

Simply type **netstat,** followed by a space, and then the switch. Some switches have options, but the syntax is basically the same.

The –a Switch

When you use the –a switch, netstat displays all TCP/IP connections and all UDP (User Datagram Protocol) connections. Figure 5.2 shows sample output produced by the nestat –a command.

FIGURE 5.2   Sample output of the netstat –a command

C:\ NETSTAT -a

Active Connections

Proto	Local Address	Foreign Address	State
TCP	default:1026	204.153.163.2:80	ESTABLISHED
TCP	default:1027	204.153.163.2:80	ESTABLISHED
TCP	default:1028	204.153.163.2:80	ESTABLISHED
TCP	default:1029	204.153.163.2:80	ESTABLISHED
UDP	default:nbname	*:*	
UDP	default:nbdatagram	*:*	

The last two entries in Figure 5.2 show a protocol type of UDP and the source port of nbname and nbdatagram. These port addresses are commonly seen on networks that broadcast the NetBIOS name of a workstation on the TCP/IP network. You can tell that this is a broadcast because the destination address is listed as *:*, meaning "any address, any port."

The State column has no entry because UDP is not a connection-oriented protocol and, therefore, has no connection state.

The most common use for the –a switch is to check the status of a TCP/IP connection that appears to be hung. You determine if the connection is simply busy or is actually hung and no longer responding.

The –e Switch

This switch displays a summary of all the packets that have been sent over the NIC (Network Interface Card) as of that instant. The two columns in Figure 5.3 show packets coming in as well as being sent.

FIGURE 5.3   Sample output of the netstat –e command

```
C:\NETSTAT -e

Interface Statistics

                         Received        Sent

Bytes                    3126759       648563
Unicast packets             4688         4233
Non-unicast packets          226          193
Discards                       0            0
Errors                         0            0
Unknown protocols            487
```

You can use the –e switch to display the following categories of statistics:

Bytes   The number of bytes transmitted or received since the computer was turned on. This statistic is useful in helping to determine if data is actually being transmitted and received or if the network interface isn't doing anything.

Unicast packets   The number of packets sent from or received at this computer. To register in one of these columns, the packet must be addressed directly from one computer to another, and the computer's address must be in either the source or destination address section of the packet.

Non-unicast packets   The number of packets not sent directly from one workstation to another. For example, a broadcast packet is a non-unicast packet. The number of non-unicast packets should be smaller than the number of unicast packets. If the number of non-unicast packets is as high or higher than that of unicast packets, too many broadcast packets are being sent on your network. You should find the source of these packets and make any necessary adjustments.

Discards The number of packets that were discarded by the NIC during either transmission or reception because they weren't assembled correctly.

Errors The number of errors that occur during transmission or reception. These numbers may indicate problems with the network card.

Unknown protocols The number of received packets that the Windows networking stack couldn't interpret. This statistic only shows up in the Received column, because if the computer sent them, they wouldn't be unknown, would they?

Unfortunately, statistics don't mean much unless they can be colored with time information. For example, if the Errors column shows 100 errors, is that a problem? It might be if the computer has only been on for a few minutes. But 100 errors could be par for the course if the computer has been operating for several days. Unfortunately, the netstat utility doesn't have a way of indicating how much time has elapsed for these statistics.

Outsmarting netstat

If you place a number after the netstat –e command, like so:

```
netstat –e 15
```

The command executes, waits the number of seconds specified by the number (in this case, 15), and then repeats until you press Ctrl+C.

You can use this feature with any combination of switches.

The –r Switch

You use the –r switch to display the current route table for a workstation so that you can see how TCP/IP information is being routed. Figure 5.4 shows sample output using this switch. You can tell from this output which interface is being used to route to a particular network (useful if computers have multiple NICs).

FIGURE 5.4 Sample output of the netstat –r command

```
C:\NETSTAT -r
Route Table

Active Routes:
```

Network Address	Netmask	Gateway Address	Interface	Metric
127.0.0.0	255.0.0.0	127.0.0.1	127.0.0.1	1
204.153.163.0	255.255.255.0	204.153.163.4	204.153.163.4	1
204.153.163.4	255.255.255.255	127.0.0.1	127.0.0.1	1
204.153.163.255	255.255.255.255	204.153.163.4	204.153.163.4	1
224.0.0.0	224.0.0.0	204.153.163.4	204.153.163.4	1
255.255.255.255	255.255.255.255	204.153.163.4	0.0.0.0	1

```
Active Connections
```

Proto	Local Address	Foreign Address	State
TCP	default:1026	204.153.163.2:80	ESTABLISHED
TCP	default:1027	204.153.163.2:80	ESTABLISHED
TCP	default:1028	204.153.163.2:80	ESTABLISHED
TCP	default:1029	204.153.163.2:80	ESTABLISHED

The –s Switch

Using the –s switch displays a variety of TCP, UDP, IP, and ICMP (Internet Control Message Protocol) protocol statistics. Below is some sample output using this switch.

```
C:\NETSTAT -s

IP Statistics

    Packets Received              = 17455
    Received Header Errors        = 0
    Received Address Errors       = 108
    Datagrams Forwarded           = 0
    Unknown Protocols Received    = 0
    Received Packets Discarded    = 0
    Received Packets Delivered    = 17346
    Output Requests               = 16374
    Routing Discards              = 255
    Discarded Output Packets      = 0
    Output Packet No Route        = 0
```

```
       Reassembly Required                  = 2
       Reassembly Successful                = 1
       Reassembly Failures                  = 0
       Datagrams Successfully Fragmented    = 0
       Datagrams Failing Fragmentation      = 0
       Fragments Created                    = 0
```

ICMP Statistics

```
                              Received      Sent
       Messages               12            19
       Errors                 0             0
       Destination Unreachable 0            7
       Time Exceeded          0             0
       Parameter Problems     0             0
       Source Quenchs         0             0
       Redirects              0             0
       Echos                  4             8
       Echo Replies           8             4
       Timestamps             0             0
       Timestamp Replies      0             0
       Address Masks          0             0
       Address Mask Replies   0             0
```

TCP Statistics

```
       Active Opens                  = 715
       Passive Opens                 = 0
       Failed Connection Attempts    = 35
       Reset Connections             = 638
       Current Connections           = 1
       Segments Received             = 15815
       Segments Sent                 = 15806
       Segments Retransmitted        = 61
```

```
UDP Statistics

   Datagrams Received    = 573
   No Ports              = 946
   Receive Errors        = 0
   Datagrams Sent        = 492
```

Since the Network+ exam doesn't cover them, we won't go into detail on what all these statistics mean. You can probably figure out some of them, such as Packets Received. For details, go to Microsoft's support Web site at www.microsoft.com/support/.

The –n Switch

This switch is a modifier for the other switches. When used with other switches, it reverses the natural tendency of netstat to use names instead of network addresses. In other words, when you use the –n switch, the output always displays network addresses instead of their associated network names.

The –p Switch

Like the –n switch, the –p switch is a modifier. Typically used with the –s switch (discussed earlier), it specifies which protocol statistics to list in the output (IP, TCP, UDP, or ICMP). For example, if you want to view only ICMP statistics, you use the –p switch, like so:

```
netstat –s –p ICMP
```

The netstat utility then displays the ICMP statistics instead of the entire gamut of TCP/IP statistics that the –s switch normally produces.

The nbtstat Utility

If you'll remember from the last chapter, NetBIOS associates names with workstations. But NetBIOS is only an upper-layer interface and requires a transport protocol. In many cases, TCP/IP is used. You use the *nbtstat* utility to do the following:

- Track NetBIOS over TCP/IP statistics
- Show the details of incoming and outgoing NetBIOS over TCP/IP connections
- Resolve NetBIOS names

Because NetBIOS name resolution is primarily a Windows 95/98 or Windows NT network issue, the nbtstat command is available only on Windows 95/98 and NT networked computers. To display a basic description of nbtstat and its associated options, type **nbtstat** at the command line. You use these options to configure the display of information about NetBIOS over TCP/IP hosts. Here are some of the switches you can use:

```
-a
-A
-c
-n
-r
-R
-S
-s
```

All nbtstat switches are case-sensitive. Generally speaking, lowercase switches deal with NetBIOS names of hosts, and uppercase switches deal with the TCP/IP address of hosts.

The –a Switch

The –a switch displays a remote machine's NetBIOS name table, which is a list of all the NetBIOS names that that particular machine "knows about." The following command produced the output for the server S1 shown in Figure 5.5:

```
C:\nbtstat –a S1
```

FIGURE 5.5   Sample output of the nbtstat –a command

C:\>nbtstat -a s1

NetBIOS Remote Machine Name Table

Name	Type		Status
S1	<20>	UNIQUE	Registered
S1	<00>	UNIQUE	Registered
ACME	<00>	GROUP	Registered
ACME	<1C>	GROUP	Registered
ACME	<1B>	UNIQUE	Registered
S1	<03>	UNIQUE	Registered
ACME	<1E>	GROUP	Registered
ACME	<1D>	UNIQUE	Registered
..__MSBROWSE__.	<01>	GROUP	Registered
INet~Services	<1C>	GROUP	Registered
IS~S1...................	<00>	UNIQUE	Registered

MAC Address = 00-A0-C9-D4-BC-DC

As you can see, using this switch produces an output with four columns. The Name column gives the NetBIOS name entry of the host in the NetBIOS name table of the remote machine. The next column displays a two-digit, unique hexadecimal identifier for the NetBIOS name. This identifier represents the last byte of the NetBIOS name shown in the Name column. This identifier is necessary because the same name might be used several times on the same station. It uniquely identifies which service on the host the name is referencing. Tables 5.1 and 5.2 list the hexadecimal identifiers for Unique and Group host names (discussed next).

TABLE 5.1   Last Byte Identifiers for Unique Names

Hex ID	Description
00	The general name for the computer.
03	Messenger service ID used to send messages between a WINS server and a workstation. This is the ID registered with a WINS server.
06	Remote Access Server (RAS) server service ID.

TABLE 5.1   Last Byte Identifiers for Unique Names *(continued)*

Hex ID	Description
20	File-serving service ID.
21	RAS client.
1B	Domain master browser ID. A NetBIOS name with this ID indicates the domain master browser.
1F	NetDDE service ID.
BE	Network monitor agent ID.
BF	Network monitor utility ID.

TABLE 5.2   Last Byte Identifiers for Group Names

Hex ID	Description
01	Indicates the master browser for a domain to other master browsers.
20	The Internet group name ID. This ID is registered with the WINS server to indicate which computers are used for administrative purposes.
1C	The Domain group name ID.
1D	The Master browser name.
1E	The Normal group name.

The Type column refers to the type of NetBIOS name being referenced:

- Unique NetBIOS names refer to individual hosts.
- Group names refer to the names of logical groupings of workstations, either Domains or Workgroups.

The Status column refers to the status of the NetBIOS name for the specified host, regardless of whether the name has been registered with the rest of the network.

The –A Switch

The –A switch works in the exact same way as the -a switch and produces the same output; only the syntax of the command is different. First, you use a capital A instead of a lowercase a. Second, you use the IP address of the host whose NetBIOS name table you want to view instead of the NetBIOS name. The syntax includes the nbtstat command, followed by the –A switch, and finally the IP address of the host whose NetBIOS table you want to view, like so:

```
nbtstat -A 199.153.163.2
```

The –c Switch

The function of the –c switch is to display the local NetBIOS name cache on the workstation on which its run. Figure 5.6 shows sample output of the nbtstat –c command.

FIGURE 5.6   Sample output of the nbtstat –c command

```
Node IpAddress: [204.153.163.4] Scope Id: []

             NetBIOS Remote Cache Name Table

        Name             Type      Host Address    Life [sec]
    ---------------------------------------------------------
    S1              <00>  UNIQUE     204.153.163.2      420
```

Each entry in this display shows the NetBIOS name, the hex ID for the service that was accessed, the type of NetBIOS name (Unique or Group), the IP address that the name resolves to, and Life (in seconds). Life (in seconds) dictates how long (in seconds) each entry will live in the cache. When this time expires, the entry is deleted from the cache.

If you run nbtstat to display the cache and you get the result "No names in the cache," all entries in the cache have expired. This will happen often if you don't regularly access machines or services with NetBIOS names.

The –n Switch

You use the –n switch to display the local NetBIOS name table on a Windows 95/98 or Windows NT station. The output (shown in Figure 5.7) is similar to the output of the –a switch, except instead of displaying the NetBIOS name table of another host, you are displaying it for the machine on which you are running the command.

FIGURE 5.7 Sample output of the nbtstat –n command

```
C:\NBTSTAT -n

Node IpAddress: [204.153.163.4] Scope Id: []

          NetBIOS Local Name Table

    Name              Type      Status
---------------------------------------------
DEFAULT        <00>  UNIQUE    Registered
WORKGROUP      <00>  GROUP     Registered
DEFAULT        <03>  UNIQUE    Registered
DEFAULT        <20>  UNIQUE    Registered
WORKGROUP      <1E>  GROUP     Registered
WORKGROUP      <1D>  UNIQUE    Registered
.._MSBROWSE_.<01>   GROUP     Registered
ADMINISTRATOR  <03>  UNIQUE    Registered
```

The –r Switch

This switch is probably the most commonly used switch when checking NBT (NetBIOS over TCP/IP) statistics. The –r switch displays the statistics of how many NetBIOS names have been resolved to TCP/IP addresses. Figure 5.8 shows sample output of the nbtstat –r command.

FIGURE 5.8   Sample output of the nbtstat –r command

```
C:\>nbtstat -r


NetBIOS Names Resolution and Registration Statistics
------------------------------------------------------
Resolved By Broadcast    = 2
Resolved By Name Server  = 0

Registered By Broadcast   = 12
Registered By Name Server = 0

    NetBIOS Names Resolved By Broadcast
------------------------------------------------
        ACME            <1B>
        ACME            <00>
```

As you can see, the statistics are divided into categories. The first category is NetBIOS name resolution and registration statistics, which shows how many names have been resolved or registered by either broadcasts on the local segment or by lookup from a WINS name server. The second category gives the NetBIOS unique and group names and their associated hex IDs that were resolved or registered. In Figure 5.8, no WINS server is operating, so all NetBIOS names were resolved by broadcast only. This is evident from the lack of statistics of names resolved by a name server.

The –r switch is useful in determining how a workstation is resolving NetBIOS names and whether WINS is configured correctly. If WINS is not configured correctly, the numbers under Resolved by Name Server or Registered by Name Server will always be zero.

The –R Switch

Let's say that you have a bad name in the NetBIOS name cache, but the right name is in the LMHOSTS file. If you'll remember from Chapter 4, the LMHOSTS file contains NetBIOS names of stations and their associated IP addresses. Also remember that the cache is consulted first and then the LMHOSTS file. The problem exists because the bad address will be in the cache (until it expires). To purge the NetBIOS name table cache and reload the LMHOSTS file into memory, simply use the nbtstat command with the –R switch, like so:

```
nbtstat -R
```

The –S Switch

You use this switch to display the NetBIOS sessions table, which lists all the NetBIOS sessions, incoming and outgoing, from the host where you issue the command. The –S switch displays both workstation and server sessions, but lists remote addresses by IP address only.

Figure 5.9 shows sample output of the nbtstat –S command. The NetBIOS name is displayed along with its hex ID. The state of each session is also shown. An entry in the In/Out column determines whether the connection is initiated from the computer you are running nbtstat on (outbound) or whether another computer initiated the connection to this computer (inbound). The numbers in the Input and Output columns indicate (in bytes) the amount of data transferred between this station and the station listed in that entry.

FIGURE 5.9 Sample output of the nbtstat –S command

```
C:\NBTSTAT -S

               NetBIOS Connection Table
Local Name          State     In/Out  Remote Host          Input   Output
-------------------------------------------------------------------------
S1         <00>     Connected   Out    204.153.163.4        256B    432B
S1         <03>     Listening
```

The –s Switch

As with the –A and –a switches, the lowercase –s switch is similar to its uppercase brother. The nbtstat -s command produces the same output as nbtstat –S, except that it tries to resolve remote host IP addresses into hostnames, if possible. Figure 5.10 shows sample output from the nbtstat –s switch. Note the similarities between Figure 5.10 and Figure 5.9.

FIGURE 5.10 Sample output of the nbtstat –s command

```
C:\NBTSTAT -s

               NetBIOS Connection Table
Local Name          State     In/Out  Remote Host          Input   Output
-------------------------------------------------------------------------
S1         <00>     Connected   Out    DEFAULT      <20>    256B    432B
S1         <03>     Listening
```

As you can with the netstat command, you can place a number at the end of any nbtstat command so that the command executes once every so many seconds (specified by the number) until you press Ctrl+C.

The File Transfer Protocol (FTP) Utility

In the last chapter, we discussed the *File Transfer Protocol (FTP)* as a subset of TCP/IP. Additionally, we discussed how FTP is used during transfer of files between Unix boxes. In recent years, FTP has become a truly cross platform protocol for file transfer. Because Internet (and, thus, TCP/IP) use has skyrocketed, almost every client (and server) platform has implemented FTP. Windows 95/98 and NT are no exception. Both of their TCP/IP stacks come with a command line FTP utility (as a matter of fact, they're basically the same utility).

To start the FTP utility, type FTP at a command prompt. The result is an FTP command prompt:

FTP>

From this command prompt, you can upload and download files, as well as change the way FTP operates. To display a list of all the commands you can use at the FTP command prompt, type **HELP** and press Enter. To get help on a specific command, type **HELP,** a space, and then the name of the command.

The Network+ exam doesn't ask specific details about how to upload and download files using FTP. You primarily need to know what the protocol is and does. We're going to give you a brief introduction to uploading and downloading files in this section, because every network technician and administrator needs to know how to do this. As they come up, we'll discuss the specific commands necessary to perform those two operations, as well as commands that relate to those processes. But first, let's look at how to start the process.

Starting FTP and Logging In to an FTP Server

Of the two FTP file operations (download and upload), the ability to download files is an important skill for a network technician or administrator to master, because network and client operating system drivers and patches are located on FTP servers throughout the Internet.

The first step in starting an FTP download session is to determine the address of the FTP site and start the FTP utility. The FTP site typically has the same name as the Web site, except the first three characters are FTP instead of WWW. For example, Novell, Inc.'s Web site is www.novell.com. Its FTP site, on the other hand, is ftp.novell.com. We'll use this FTP site as an example for the rest of this section.

First, start the FTP utility as discussed earlier, and then follow these steps:

1. At the FTP command prompt, type **OPEN**, a space, and the name of the FTP server. For example:

```
FTP> open ftp.novell.com
```

You can also start an FTP session by typing FTP, a space, and the address of the FTP server (for example, FTP ftp.novell.com). This allows you to start the FTP utility and open a connection in one step.

If the FTP server is available and running, you will receive a response welcoming you to the server and asking you for a username, like so:

```
ftp> open ftp.novell.com
Connected to ftp.novell.com.
220 nemesis FTP server (Version wu-2.4.2-academ[BETA-
14](4) Tue Oct 14 17:57:04
MDT 1997) ready.
User (ftp.novell.com:(none)):
```

2. Enter a valid username, and press Enter.

Most Internet Web servers that allow just about anyone to download files allow the username anonymous. Remember to type the username exactly and to double-check as you enter it because usernames are case-sensitive. In addition to anonymous, you can use the username *ftp* to gain access to a public FTP server. They are both anonymous usernames. Remember that FTP (and Unix) usernames are case-sensitive.

3. Enter your password, and press Enter.

If you are accessing a private FTP server, the administrator gave you your username and password. If you are accessing a public FTP server with a username such as anonymous, you can use your e-mail address as the password.

You don't have to enter your entire e-mail address to log in with anonymous. Most FTP server software doesn't verify the e-mail address, just that it is, in fact, an e-mail address. To do this, it checks for an @ sign and two words separated by a period. Just enter a very short e-mail address to bypass the password (like u@me.com). This is especially helpful if you have a long e-mail address. It's also more secure if you don't want lots of junk e-mail.

If you enter the wrong username and/or password, the server will tell you so by displaying the following and leaving you at the FTP command prompt:

```
530 Login Incorrect
Login failed.
```

You must now start over with the login process. If you are successful, the FTP server will welcome you and drop you back at the FTP command prompt. You're now ready to start uploading or downloading files.

Downloading Files

After you log in to the FTP server, you navigate to the directory that contains the files you want. Thankfully, the FTP command-line interface is similar to the DOS command-line interface. This is no surprise since DOS is based on Unix, and FTP is a Unix utility. Table 5.3 lists and describes the common navigation commands for FTP. Remember, these are also case-sensitive.

TABLE 5.3   Common FTP Navigation Commands

Command	Description
ls	Short for list, this command displays a directory listing. Very similar to the DIR command in MS-DOS.
cd	Short for change directory, this command works almost identically to the MS-DOS CD command. Use it to change to a different directory and navigate the server's directory structure.
pwd	Short for print working directory, this command displays the current directory on the server. Useful if you forget where you are when changing to several locations on the server.
lcd	Short for local change directory, this command displays and changes the current directory on the local machine. Useful when you are downloading a file and aren't in the directory where you want to put the file.

After you navigate to the directory and find the file you want to download, you must set the parameters for the type of file. Files come in two types:

- ASCII, which contains text
- Binary, which is all other files

If you set FTP to the wrong type, the file you download will contain gibberish. When in doubt, set FTP to download files as binary files.

To set the file type to ASCII, type **ASCII** at the FTP command prompt. FTP will respond by telling you that the file type has been set to A (ASCII), like so:

```
FTP> ASCII
Type set to A
```

To set the file type to binary, type binary at the FTP command prompt. FTP will respond by telling you that the file type has been set to I (binary), like so:

```
FTP> binary
Type set to I
```

To download the file, you use the get command, like so:

```
FTP> get scrsav.exe
200 PORT command successful.
150 Opening BINARY mode data connection for 'scrsav.exe'
(567018 bytes).
```

The file will start downloading to your hard drive. Unfortunately, the FTP utility doesn't give you any indication of the progress of the transfer. When the file is done downloading, the FTP utility will display the following message and return you to the FTP command prompt:

```
226 Transfer complete.
567018 bytes received in 116.27 seconds (4.88 Kbytes/sec)
```

You can download multiple files using the mget command. Simply type **mget**, a space, and then a wildcard that specifies the files you want to get. For example, to download all the text files in a directory, **type mget *.txt**.

Uploading Files

To upload a file to an FTP server, you must have rights on that server. These rights are assigned on a directory-by-directory basis. To upload a file, log in and then follow these steps:

1. At the FTP command prompt, **type lcd** to navigate to the directory on the local machine where the file resides.

2. Type cd to navigate to the destination directory.

3. Set the file type to ASCII or binary.

4. Use the put command to upload the file.

The syntax of the put command is:

```
FTP> put <local file> <destination file>
```

For example, if you want to upload a file that is called 1.txt on the local server, but you want it to be called my.txt on the destination server, use the following command:

```
FTP> put 1.txt my.txt
```

You'll see the following response:

```
200 PORT command successful.
150 Opening BINARY mode data connection for collwin.zip
226 Transfer complete.
743622 bytes sent in 0.55 seconds (1352.04 Kbytes/sec)
```

You can upload multiple files using the mput command. Simply type **mput**, a space, and then a wildcard that specifies the files. For example, to upload all the text files in a directory, type **mput *.txt**.

When you're finished with the FTP utility, simply type **quit** to return to the command prompt.

The Ping Utility

*P*ing is the most basic TCP/IP utility and is included with most TCP/IP stacks for most platforms. Windows 95/98 and NT are no exception. In most cases, Ping is a command line-utility (although there have been some GUI implementations). You use the Ping utility for two primary purposes:

- To find out if you can reach a host

- To find out if a host is responding

The syntax is:

```
ping <hostname or IP address>
```

If you ping any station that has an IP address, the ICMP (Internet Control Message Protocol) protocol that is part of that host's TCP/IP stack will respond to the request. This ICMP test and response might look something like this:

```
ping 204.153.163.2
```

```
Pinging 204.153.163.2 with 32 bytes of data:

Reply from 204.153.163.2: bytes=32 time<10ms TTL=128
Reply from 204.153.163.2: bytes=32 time=1ms TTL=128
Reply from 204.153.163.2: bytes=32 time<10ms TTL=128
Reply from 204.153.163.2: bytes=32 time<10ms TTL=128
```

Because we receive a reply from the destination station (204.153.163.2 in this case), we know that we can reach the host and that it is responding to basic IP requests.

Most versions of Ping work in the same fashion, although there are some switches you can use to specify—for example, the number of packets to send, how big a packet to send, and so on. If you are running the Windows 95/98 or NT command-line versions of Ping, use the -? switch to display a list of the available switches, like so:

```
ping -?
```

Table 5.4 lists and describes some of the most common switches for the Windows 95/98 and NT Ping utility.

TABLE 5.4   Windows Ping Utility Switches

Switch	Description
-?	Displays a list of switches that can be used with Ping.
-a	Resolves the pinged address to a hostname simultaneously.
-n #	Pings the specified host multiple times (the number of times is specified by the number, #).
-t	Pings the host continuously until you press Ctrl+C.
-r #	Records the route taken during the Ping hops. Requires a number (#) to indicate the number of hops to record. Similar to the tracert command (discussed later).

You can ping your local TCP/IP interface by typing **ping 127.0.0.1** or **ping local-host**. Both addresses represent the local interface.

The winipcfg and ipconfig Utilities

Of all the TCP/IP utilities that come with Windows 95/98 or NT, the IP configuration utilities are probably the most overlooked. These utilities display the current configuration of TCP/IP on that workstation, including the current IP address, DNS configuration, WINS configuration, and default gateway.

Using the winipcfg Utility

The IP configuration utility for Windows 95/98 is *winipcfg*. You use it to display the current TCP/IP configuration on a Windows 95/98 workstation. Follow these two steps:

1. Choose Start ➢ Run, type **winipcfg**, and click OK to display the IP Configuration dialog box:

2. Click the down arrow to choose the network interface for which you want to view statistics. The screen in the graphic shows this information for the Intel Ether Express.

To display more detailed configuration information, click the More Info button to open the following IP Configuration dialog box:

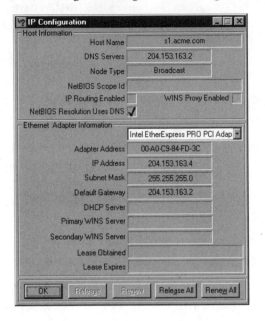

If you are using DHCP to get IP address information, click the Release All button to remove all information obtained from a DHCP server (including an IP address). Click the Renew All button to release all DHCP information and request new TCP/IP configuration information.

The top of this screen shows the DNS name of the machine and the IP address of the DNS server that this workstation is using. Below that are several lines of NetBIOS over TCP/IP information. The bottom section contains the same information shown in the first screen but also includes additional information, such as the addresses of the DHCP and WINS servers (if present) and the lease information (how long the DHCP information is current) for the addresses obtained from a DHCP server.

The winipcfg utility comes in handy when you're resolving TCP/IP address conflicts and configuring a workstation. For example, if this workstation is experiencing Duplicate IP Address errors, you can run winipcfg to determine the IP address of this station. Also, if the address was obtained from a DHCP server, you can release it and obtain a new IP address by clicking the Renew All button.

The ipconfig Utility

Because Windows NT was designed to be Unix compatible, Windows NT and Unix have several functions and utilities in common. You can use many Unix command-line utilities at the Windows NT command prompt, including:

- FTP

- Ping

- tracert

- ipconfig

The Windows NT utility *ipconfig* does the same job as its Windows 95/98 counterpart, winipcfg. With Windows NT ipconfig, however, the display is command-line based.

You can also use the ipconfig utility in Windows 98.

To use ipconfig, follow these steps:

1. Choose Start ➢ Programs ➢ Command Prompt to display the command prompt.

2. Type **ipconfig**, which produces output similar to the following:

```
C:\>ipconfig

Windows NT IP Configuration

Ethernet adapter E100B1:

        IP Address. . . . . . . . . : 204.153.163.2
        Subnet Mask . . . . . . . . : 255.255.255.0
        Default Gateway . . . . . . :
```

As you can see, this output is similar to the information in the Windows 95/98 IP Configuration dialog box, except that the MAC address is not listed.

Only four switches can be used with the ipconfig command. Figure 5.11 shows the output produced by using the /All switch. Table 5.5 lists and describes all four switches.

TABLE 5.5   ipconfig Switches

Switch	Description
/?	Displays the available switches and a description of each.
/All	Displays all TCP/IP configuration information; similar to clicking the More Info button in the Windows 95/98 IP Configuration dialog box.
/Release	Releases all TCP/IP configuration information obtained from DHCP; similar to clicking the Release All button in the Windows 95/98 IP Configuration dialog box.
/Renew	Releases and then renews all TCP/IP configuration information obtained from a DHCP server.

FIGURE 5.11   Sample output produced by using the /all switch

```
C:\>ipconfig /all

Windows NT IP Configuration

        Host Name . . . . . . . . . : s1.devarim.com
        DNS Servers . . . . . . . . :
        Node Type . . . . . . . . . : Broadcast
        NetBIOS Scope ID. . . . . . :
        IP Routing Enabled. . . . . : No
        WINS Proxy Enabled. . . . . : No
        NetBIOS Resolution Uses DNS : No

Ethernet adapter E100B1:

        Description . . . . . . . . : Intel EtherExpress PRO PCI Adapter

        Physical Address. . . . . . : 00-A0-C9-D4-BC-DC
        DHCP Enabled. . . . . . . . : No
        IP Address. . . . . . . . . : 204.153.163.2
        Subnet Mask . . . . . . . . : 255.255.255.0
        Default Gateway . . . . . . :
```

Because NT servers can (and often do) have more than one TCP/IP interface, you can specify which interface you want to view statistics for by placing its address on the command line with the switches. If you don't specify, ipconfig displays information for all interfaces.

The tracert Utility

Have you ever wondered where the packets go when you send them over the Internet? The TCP/IP *Trace Route (tracert)* command-line utility will show you every router interface a TCP/IP packet passes through on its way to a destination.

To use tracert, at a Windows 95/98 or NT command prompt, type **tracert**, a space, and the DNS name or IP address of the host for which you want to find the route. The tracert utility responds with a list of all the DNS names and IP addresses of the routers the packet is passing through on its way. Additionally, tracert indicates the time it takes for each attempt. Figure 5.12 shows sample tracert output from a workstation connected to an ISP (Corporate Communications, in Fargo, ND, in this case) to the search engine Yahoo.

FIGURE 5.12   Sample tracert output

```
C:\>tracert www.yahoo.com
Tracing route to www10.yahoo.com [204.71.200.75]
over a maximum of 30 hops:

  1   110 ms    96 ms   107 ms   fgo1.corpcomm.net [209.74.93.10]
  2    96 ms   126 ms    95 ms   someone.corpcomm.net [209.74.93.1]
  3   113 ms   119 ms   112 ms   Serial5-1-1.GW2.MSP1.alter.net [157.130.100.185]
  4   133 ms   123 ms   126 ms   152.ATM3-0.XR2.CHI6.ALTER.NET [146.188.209.126]
  5   176 ms   133 ms   129 ms   290.ATM2-0.TR2.CHI4.ALTER.NET [146.188.209.10]
  6   196 ms   184 ms   218 ms   106.ATM7-0.TR2.SCL1.ALTER.NET [146.188.136.162]
  7   182 ms   187 ms   187 ms   298.ATM7-0.XR2.SJC1.ALTER.NET [146.188.146.61]
  8   204 ms   176 ms   186 ms   192.ATM3-0-0.SAN-JOSE9-GW.ALTER.NET [146.188.144.133]
  9   202 ms   198 ms   212 ms   atm3-0-622M.cr1.sjc.globalcenter.net [206.57.16.17]
 10   209 ms   202 ms   195 ms   pos3-1-155M.br4.SJC.globalcenter.net [206.132.150.98]
 11   190 ms      *      191 ms   pos0-0-0-155M.hr3.SNV.globalcenter.net [206.251.5.93]
 12   195 ms   188 ms   188 ms   pos4-1-0-155M.hr2.SNV.globalcenter.net [206.132.150.206]
 13   198 ms   202 ms   197 ms   www10.yahoo.com [204.71.200.75]

Trace complete.
```

As you can see, the packet bounces through several routers before arriving at its destination. This utility is useful if you are having problems reaching a Web server on the Internet and you want to know if a WAN link is down or if the server just isn't responding. In Figure 5.12, every router is up and is, in fact, responding. The asterisk indicates that the attempt for that router took longer than the default timeout value. This usually means that either the router is extremely busy or that particular link is slow.

You can use tracert to ascertain how many hops a particular host is from your workstation. This is useful in determining how fast a link should be. Usually if a host is only a couple of hops away, access should be relatively quick.

The Telnet Utility

Telnet is an acronym formed from Terminal EmuLation for NETworks and was originally developed to open terminal sessions from remote Unix workstations to Unix server. Although still used for that purpose, it has evolved into a troubleshooting tool. Figure 5.13 shows the basic Telnet interface as it is being used to start a terminal session on a remote Unix host.

FIGURE 5.13   The Windows 95/98 and NT Telnet utility

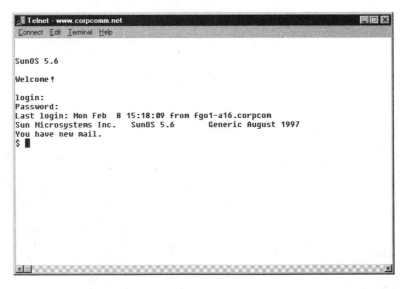

In today's Windows 95/98 and NT environments, Telnet is a basic GUI tool for testing TCP connections. You can telnet to any TCP port to see if it is responding, which is especially useful when checking SMTP and HTTP (Web) ports. If you'll remember from Chapter 4, each upper layer service in a TCP stack has a number for its address. Each network service that uses a particular address will respond to a TCP request on this port (if the defaults are used). Table 5.6 lists the most commonly referenced port numbers and their associated services.

TABLE 5.6 TCP Port Addresses and Services

Port	TCP/IP Service
21	FTP
23	Terminal Emulation (Telnet)
25	Simple Mail Transfer Protocol (SMTP)
80	Hypertext Transfer Protocol (HTTP) Session Start
110	POP3 Mail transfer protocol

This list is by no means comprehensive. For a complete list, go to www.microsoft.com/support/ or support.novell.com.

To find out if a TCP service is responding, follow these steps:

1. Choose Start ➢ Run.

2. Enter **telnet**, and click OK to open the Telnet utility.

3. Choose Connect ➢ Remote System to open the Connect dialog box:

Connect	✕
Host Name:	204.153.163.2 ▾
Port:	80 ▾
TermType:	vt100 ▾
Connect	Cancel

4. In the Host Name box, type the IP address or DNS host name of the host running the TCP service to which you want to connect.

For example, to find out if a Web server is responding to TCP port 80 (its default port), enter the IP address or DNS host name of the Web server (204.153.163.2 in this case).

5. In the Port box, enter the number from Table 5.6 that corresponds to the service you want to check.

6. Click Connect.

If you successfully connect to the Web server, you won't be notified that is the case. If the Web server doesn't respond, you'll receive a Connect Failed message.

If you're attempting to connect to an SMTP server, telnet to port 25, and you'll see a screen similar to that in Figure 5.14. Theoretically, you could send an e-mail message using Telnet to see if your SMTP system is functioning.

FIGURE 5.14 Using Telnet to find out if your SMTP mail system is responding

Key Terms

Before you take the exam, be certain you are familiar with the following terms:

ARP table

Dynamic ARP table entries

File Transfer Protocol (FTP)

ipconfig

nbtstat

netstat

Ping

Static ARP table entries

Telnet

Trace Route (tracert)

winipcfg

Review Questions

1. Which TCP/IP utility is most often used to test whether an IP host is up and functional?

   A. FTP

   B. Telnet

   C. Ping

   D. netstat

2. Which TCP/IP utility will produce this result?

   ```
   Interface: 199.102.30.152
     Internet Address    Physical Address    Type
     199.102.30.152      A0-ee-00-5b-0e-ac   dynamic
   ```

   A. ARP

   B. netstat

   C. tracert

   D. nbtstat

3. Which Windows 95/98 or NT utility can you use to display NetBIOS over TCP/IP statistics?

   A. nbtstat

   B. netstat

   C. ARP

   D. ipconfig

4. Which TCP/IP utility might produce this output?

```
Pinging 204.153.163.2 with 32 bytes of data:
Reply from 204.153.163.2: bytes=32 time=1ms TTL=128
Reply from 204.153.163.2: bytes=32 time=1ms TTL=128
Reply from 204.153.163.2: bytes=32 time=1ms TTL=128
Reply from 204.153.163.2: bytes=32 time<10ms TTL=128
```

A. tracert

B. Ping

C. WINS

D. winipcfg

5. Which utility can you use to find the MAC and TCP/IP address of your Windows 95 workstation?

A. Ping

B. winipcfg

C. ipconfig

D. tracert

E. Telnet

6. Which Ping commands will verify that your local TCP/IP interface is working?

A. ping 204.153.163.2

B. ping 127.0.0.1

C. ping localif

D. ping localhost

E. ping iphost

7. Which switch for the Windows 95/98 nbtstat utility will display all NetBIOS name resolution statistics and each name's associated IP address?

    A. −r

    B. /r

    C. −R

    D. /R

8. Which program can you use to download files from a Unix server?

    A. nbtstat

    B. netstat

    C. ARP

    D. FTP

9. Which nbtstat utility switch will purge and reload the remote NetBIOS name table cache?

    A. −r

    B. −R

    C. /r

    D. /R

10. Which Windows NT utility will display the current TCP/IP configuration of that host?

    A. ARP

    B. ipconfig

    C. winipcfg

    D. winipconfig

11. Which utility produces an output similar to this:

```
1   110 ms   96 ms   107 ms  fgo1.corpcomm.net
[209.74.93.10]
2   96 ms   126 ms   95 ms someone.corpcomm.net
[209.74.93.1]
3   113 ms   119 ms   112 ms  Serial5-1-
1.GW2.MSP1.alter.net
    [157.130.100.185]
4  133 ms  123 ms  126 ms 152.ATM3-0.XR2.CHI6.ALTER.NET
    [146.188.209.126]
5  176 ms   133 ms   129 ms 290.ATM2-0.TR2.CHI4.ALTER.NET
    [146.188.209.10]
6  196 ms   184 ms   218 ms 106.ATM7-0.TR2.SCL1.ALTER.NET
    [146.188.136.162]
7  182 ms   187 ms   187 ms 298.ATM7-0.XR2.SJC1.ALTER.NET
    [146.188.146.61]
8  204 ms   176 ms   186 ms 192.ATM3-0-0.SAN-JOSE9-
    GW.ALTER.NET [146.188.144.133]
9  202 ms   198 ms   212 ms atm3-0-
    622M.cr1.sjc.globalcenter.net [206.57.16.17]
10 209 ms   202 ms   195 ms pos3-1-
    155M.br4.SJC.globalcenter.net [206.132.150.98]
11 190 ms    *     191 ms pos0-0-0-
    155M.hr3.SNV.globalcenter.net [206.251.5.93]
12 195 ms   188 ms   188 ms pos4-1-0-
    155M.hr2.SNV.globalcenter.net [206.132.150.206]
13 198 ms   202 ms   197 ms www10.yahoo.com
[204.71.200.75]
```

A. ARP

B. tracert

C. nbtstat

D. netstat

12. You are the network administrator. A user calls you complaining that the performance of the intranet web server is sluggish. When you try to ping the server, it takes several seconds for the server to respond. You suspect the problem is related to a router that is seriously overloaded. Which workstation utility could you use to find out which router is causing this problem?

    A. netstat

    B. nbtstat

    C. tracert

    D. Ping

    E. ARP

13. Which ipconfig switch will display the most complete listing of IP configuration information for that station?

    A. /All

    B. /Renew

    C. /Release

    D. /?

14. Which utility will display a list of all the routers a packet passes through on the way to an IP destination?

    A. netstat

    B. nbtstat

    C. tracert

    D. Ping

    E. ARP

15. Which Windows 95/98 TCP/IP utility could you use to find out if a server is responding on TCP port 21?

   A. TCP

   B. PORT

   C. Ping

   D. netstat

   E. Telnet

16. Which ARP command can you use to display the currently cached ARP entries?

   A. ARP

   B. ARP –A

   C. ARP –a

   D. ARP /A

   E. ARP /a

17. Which FTP command line command will initiate the download of a file?

   A. ARP

   B. GET

   C. PUT

   D. LCD

18. Which utility on a Windows 95 computer can be used to view IP address configuration information?

   A. winipcfg

   B. ipconfig

   C. netstat

   D. nbtstat

19. Which netstat switch will enable you to view the number of ICMP packets your workstation has sent and received?

    A. -a

    B. -r

    C. -s

    D. -I

20. Which nbtstat switch displays a list of all the NetBIOS sessions currently active on the local workstation?

    A. -a

    B. -r

    C. -s

    D. -I

Answers to Review Questions

1. C. Although all utilities can be used to test the functionality of an IP host in one way or another, the Ping utility is used specifically to test whether an IP host is up and responding.

2. A. The ARP utility is used to display the contents of the ARP cache, which tracks the resolution of IP addresses to Physical (MAC) addresses and will produce the displayed output.

3. A. The "nbt" in "nbtstat" stands for "NetBIOS over TCP/IP." The purpose of nbtstat is to display the NetBIOS over TCP/IP statistics for a computer running both protocols.

4. B. The purpose of the Ping utility is to test the communications channel between two IP hosts, as well as how long it takes the packets to get from one host to another.

5. B. The winipcfg utility is for Windows 95/98. It displays information like the MAC and TCP/IP address of your workstation as well as other TCP/IP configuration information for your workstation.

6. B, D. The address 127.0.0.1 is the special IP address designated for the local TCP/IP interface. The hostname "localhost" is the hostname given to the local interface. So pinging either the IP address or hostname for the local interface will tell you whether or not the local interface is working.

7. A. The -r switch for nbtstat (nbtstat -r) displays all the name resolutions performed by the local client as well as their associated IP addresses.

8. D. The only utility listed that can be used to download files from a Unix server is the FTP utility.

9. B. To purge and reload the remote NetBIOS name cache, you must use the -R switch with the nbtstat utility (nbtstat -R). Additionally, the "R" must be capitalized and it will not work correctly without the dash in front.

10. B. The NT utility ipconfig is similar to the Windows 95/98 utility winipcfg in that it displays the current TCP/IP configuration of that station. However, ipconfig is a Windows NT-only utility.

11. B. The tracert utility traces the route from the source IP host to the destination host.

12. C. The tracert utility will tell you which router is having the performance problem, how long it would take to get between each host, and can be used to located problem areas in a network.

13. A. The ipconfig /all switch will display the most complete listing of TCP/IP configuration information for a Windows NT computer.

14. C. The tracert utility returns all router names and addresses through which a packet passes on its way to a destination host.

15. E. The Telnet utility can be used to test to see if a particular IP host is responding on a particular TCP port.

16. C. The ARP -a command will display the current contents of the ARP cache on the local workstation.

17. B. The GET command, followed by the name of the file you want to download, will initiate the download of that particular file.

18. A. The winipcfg utility can be used to view the configuration of a Windows 95/98 workstation.

19. C. The -s switch will enable you to view the statistics about how many of a particular TCP/IP protocol's packets have been sent and received.

20. C. Nbtstat -s will list all NetBIOS sessions, incoming and outgoing, from that PC.

Chapter

6

Network Installation and Upgrades

NETWORK+ EXAM OBJECTIVES COVERED IN THIS CHAPTER:

✓ Demonstrate awareness that administrative and test accounts, passwords, IP addresses, IP configurations, relevant SOPs, and so on must be obtained prior to network implementation.

✓ Explain the impact of environmental factors on computer networks. Given a network installation scenario, identify unexpected or atypical conditions that could either cause problems for the network or signify that a problem already exists, including:

- Room conditions (for example, humidity, heat, and so on)
- The placement of building contents and personal effects (for example, space heaters, TVs, and radios)
- Computer equipment
- Error messages

✓ Recognize visually or by description common peripheral ports, external SCSI (especially DB-25 connectors), and common network componentry, including:

- Print servers
- Peripherals
- Hubs
- Routers
- Brouters
- Bridges
- Patch panels
- UPSs

- NICs
- Token ring media filters

✓ **Given an installation scenario, demonstrate awareness of the following compatibility and cabling issues:**

- The consequences of trying to install an analog modem in a digital jack
- That the uses of RJ-45 connectors may differ greatly depending on the cabling
- That patch cables contribute to the overall length of the cabling segment

✓ **Given an installation, configuration, or troubleshooting scenario, select an appropriate course of action if a client workstation does not connect to the network after installing or replacing a network interface card. Explain why a given action is warranted. The following issues may be covered:**

- Knowledge of how the network card is usually configured, including EEPROM, jumpers, and Plug-and-Play software
- Use of network card diagnostics, including the loopback test and vendor-supplied diagnostics
- The ability to resolve hardware resource conflicts, including IRQ, DMA, and I/O base address

✓ **Identify the kinds of test documentation that are usually available regarding a vendor's patches, fixes, upgrades, and so on.**

This chapter brings you to the most important test of all: your ability to install new network hardware and software as well as upgrade older network hardware and software. As your network grows and changes, you will be called upon frequently to update obsolete hardware and software. The Network+ exam tests your knowledge of the basic network hardware components that you might install as well as how to successfully upgrade outdated hardware or software. In this chapter, we're going to examine what you should consider before you upgrade, some common network components you might install, and how you connect them.

Before You Install New Hardware or Software

Before you add a new hardware component to a network, upgrade the operating system, install a new application, or make any other such change, you need a clear picture of the current condition of the network. Additionally, you need to have an understanding of how a network behaves when it is functioning normally, so you will be able to tell when the network is malfunctioning. This includes an understanding of standard operating procedures and how they are being implemented and an awareness of any environmental issues that affect the way the network is set up. You also need to take a close look at error messages and log files, which will give you a lot of information about the health of the network, and be sure you are familiar with the current configuration and baselines. In addition, don't forget to review the manufacturers' documentation that you should have at hand. A 15-minute perusal of the documentation beforehand could save you hours of work later.

Standard Operating Procedures

Standard operating procedures (SOPs) are part of company policy and typically cover everything from sick day accrual to how the computer systems are used. In particular, network administrators need to be aware of company policies regarding the following:

- Internet access
- Printing
- Storage allocation
- E-mail usage
- User administration

Policies about these issues will be reflected in the network's naming conventions, protocol standards, and workstation configuration, and will affect the location of network devices.

Naming Conventions

Naming conventions specify how network entities are named, within the guidelines of the network operating system being used. Each entity name must be unique on the network, including the names you give to the following:

- Servers
- Printers
- User accounts
- Group accounts
- Test and service accounts

Naming Servers

In general, you name servers according to their location or function; sometimes it makes sense to use a combination. For example, a server located in Seattle might be named SEATTLE, or a server in the sales department might be named SALES. Or you might name a server that stores data DATA1, a server that stores applications APPS1, a server that stores a database DB1, and so on.

Another common practice is to name file servers FS followed by a number, such as FS1, FS2, FS3, and so on. Unfortunately, this naming convention doesn't provide the user with any information about what the server stores.

The X.500 Standard

Novell Directory Service (NDS) and Active Directory (included with Windows 2000 Server) are modeled after a standard known as X.500. X.500 is a type of a global phone book. The delimiter for NDS, Active Directory, and X.500 entries is the period. Suppose a user's name is Bob. Bob works in the accounts department of the finance division, at a company known as YourCo. His full address would be `Bob.Accounts.Finance.YourCo`.

In NDS and Active Directory, each name is known as an *object*. A graphical tree displays each object. Thus, it is efficient to begin at a higher level and administer policies to an entire network, for example, at YourCo. Furthermore, it is possible to drill down and work on a smaller unit level. Additional policy information can be applied to the Finance level.

Using periods as the delimiter, NDS and Active Directory look similar to DNS, or the Domain Name Service.

Domain Name Service is an Internet standard. This standard is like NDS in that it is based on X.500 and the period is used as a delimiter. It's time to put one misconception to rest here and now. Not all Internet addresses need www. Try `http://research.Microsoft.com` to prove this to yourself.

Another point needs to be made about DNS entries. All URLs don't end with .com, .org, or .edu. *Country codes* are common final entries in a *URL*. Here are some of them:

- TW (Taiwan)

- TZ (Tanzania)

- UA (Ukraine)

- UG (Uganda)

- UK (United Kingdom)

- UM (U.S. Minor Outlying Islands)

- US (United States of America)

- UY (Uruguay)

- UZ (Uzbekistan)

- VA (Vatican City State)

The most common naming convention in use today is a combination of location and function. Using this approach, you might specify that the first four characters of the name identify the server's location, the next two, the server's function, and the last two, the server's rank for that type of server. For example, the FRGOFS02 server is located in Fargo, it's a file server, and it is the second server of that type in Fargo.

Naming Printers

As with server names, printer names are often derived from their function, location, or both. Naming a printer after its function or location makes the printer easier to locate for the users. If, for example, your dot-matrix printer is used to print multiple-part forms, you might name it Forms. If you have more than one forms printer, you might need to use two-word names, such as Forms-Ship or Forms-Finance. You might name high-quality printers Laser or Laser-Legal, indicating that this printer is always loaded with legal-size paper.

This is not intended to reflect a right or a wrong way to address naming conventions. There is only one right way for any organization—the method it follows.

Naming User Accounts

Generally speaking, the simplest user name is the user's first name. This works well in a company with only a few users and fits the often-found informality of a small office. This method is fairly insecure, however, because hackers can easily guess a user name. It also won't work in a larger organization that could easily include two people with the same first name.

The user naming convention you use should allow for unique IDs and ensure that there are no duplicates. Larger firms typically use a first initial followed by part or all of the last name. For example, Tim Catura-Houser would be TCaturaHouser. This is still a long username and might even cause a problem with maximum character lengths allowed in some operating systems. In this example, Tcat might be used as a short, yet unique, login name.

Naming Groups

Groups are network entities that logically associate users by function. They are designed to make network administration easier: you can assign rights to a group of users all at once, rather than to each individual. Because the group of users is organized by function, it would stand to reason that groups should be named by function. Additionally, the names should be short, fewer than 15 characters if possible. For example, if you have a group of users from the sales department that all use the same printer, you might name the group SALES_PRN. On the other hand, if you just want a general group for security and rights assignment purposes, you might name that group of users SALES.

We'll discuss groups in detail in Chapter 8.

Naming Test and Service Accounts

When you install new services on the network, such as printers, applications, and so on, it is always a good idea to test the functionality of these services first. It is not good practice to do this testing logged in using an administrative account because administrative accounts usually have all-encompassing rights to the network, and thus problems related to accessing the service are less likely to occur. It is better to use an account that is equivalent to a user's account who will be using the service. For this reason, it makes sense to create *test accounts* that you can use to test access to and functionality of new services.

Service accounts, on the other hand, give outside network maintenance personnel the ability to perform administrator-level functions on your network. This is necessary whenever you must call in outside personnel.

The naming conventions document should also specify naming conventions for these accounts and define their security rights.

Protocol Standards

You have already learned that protocols have different properties. If your firm has nothing but NetWare servers that are either version 3.*x* or 4.*x*, using IPX (Internet Packet eXchange) as the standard protocol would make sense. Alternatively, suppose there is a small group called New Product Development. Because of the sensitive nature of this group's work and because data should not leave the department, a routable protocol might be forbidden. In this case, NetBEUI (NetBIOS Extended User Interface) would be a wise choice, since it cannot be routed and serves a small group without much maintenance. Today, because of its prevalence and to reduce training and operational expenses, a great number of companies are standardizing on TCP/IP (Transmission Control Protocol/Internet Protocol).

Regardless of the protocol you choose, you must obtain all network addresses before installing or upgrading a network device. This brings its own set of considerations. As you saw in Chapter 4, using TCP/IP as an example, each IP address must be unique, and just guessing at one is bound to create havoc. Clearly, you need a well-documented IP address and associated parameters, such as where the IP address comes from. Your SOPs should specify how network addresses are to be formatted and distributed.

Workstation Configuration

A standardized workstation configuration serves a company well for a couple of reasons:

- You can narrow the scope of problems at a client station.

- You can more easily troubleshoot if everyone uses the same operating system, network client, and productivity software.

This is not to say that everyone in the office has to have the exact same software. The engineering group would most likely need a CAD (computer-aided design) program, along with the appropriate horsepower and RAM. Giving everyone in the company a CAD program would not only waste resources, it would be difficult for the accounting department to use a CAD program to create a paycheck for each employee. Therefore, a standard for workstation configuration is usually mandated by a group's function. However, once an application is chosen, only that application (preferably the same version) should be used by anyone who requires access to that type of program. Which applications and which versions of each application can be used on the network should be documented in your SOPs.

Some network management applications simplify the process of distributing unique applications to those users who need them, while maintaining the same basic workstation software configuration. Examples of these include Microsoft's Systems Management Server (SMS) and Novell's Z.E.N.works.

It is also important to define minimum workstation hardware standards. Typically, the minimum requirement is one or two generations behind what is considered the hottest, fastest new system. A standards document might specify the following:

- Type, brand, and speed of CPU

- Minimum RAM

- Minimum hard disk size

- Type and brand of NIC

- Minimum monitor size (14", 15", or 17")

Network Device Placement

The network SOP may also specify where network devices are to be placed. Many of these specifications relate to safety, for example, where cables are to be run and where to place network devices so that they are immune to sources of extreme heat or cold. Critical network components (such as servers and routers) should be placed in a room away from "busy fingers."

You should also consider the needs of users when you are deciding where to place network devices. For example, although placing a printer in the middle of the office might seem logical, it probably makes more sense to place it near the employees who use it the most.

Environmental Issues

Environmental conditions, as they relate to installing or upgrading a network and its components, are important. Just like human beings, computers require a proper environment in order to function correctly. If the environment is harsh, the device will not function at peak efficiency. Surprisingly, environmental conditions and their consequences may be the most over-looked topic in the entire industry of networking. Often problems that seem to appear out of nowhere and appear to make no sense are caused by environmental conditions. Let's examine the frequently elusive challenges that we all face at one time or another, including:

- Power problems
- ESD problems
- EMI problems
- RFI problems
- Climate problems

Power Problems

Alternating current (AC), which is "food" to PCs and other network devices, is normally 110 volts and changes polarity 60 times a second (or 60 Hertz). These values are referred to as *line voltage*. Any deviation from these values can create problems for a PC or other network device. Power problems fall into three categories:

- Overage
- Underage
- Quality

Power Overage Problems

During a power overage, too much power is coming into the computer. Power overage can take two forms:

- A *power spike* occurs when the power level rises above normal levels and then drops back to normal in less than one second.
- A *power surge* occurs when the power level rises above normal levels and stays there for more than one or two seconds.

Typically, power surges last longer than a second or two, and they may last for several minutes. For this reason, surges are usually more damaging than spikes (although a very large spike can damage a computer's power supply just as much as a surge). Figure 6.1 shows the difference between a spike and a surge.

FIGURE 6.1   Comparing a power spike and a power surge

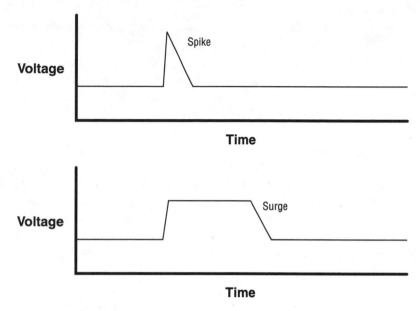

Two types of devices are used to protect computers and other network devices from power overage problems:

- Surge protectors

- Line conditioners

A *surge protector* contains a special electronic circuit that monitors the incoming voltage level and trips a circuit breaker when the overvoltage reaches a certain level (called the *overvoltage threshold*). The problem with surge protectors is that the threshold is set too high to be safe. By the time the circuit breaker trips, some overvoltage has gotten to the power supply of the computer, possibly damaging it. Nor does a surge protector protect against power surges and spikes that are lower than the threshold. For the most part, a surge protector is better than nothing, but not by much. It is really only a multiple outlet strip and should not be considered anything more.

Surge protectors with a very low overvoltage threshold cost upward of $50. They sacrifice themselves in the event of any significant overvoltage but are smart enough not to trip for just a small amount over the standard power levels. Additionally, most of these protectors contain electronic circuits that can "shave off" any overvoltage and ensure that the powered devices receive only the voltage they need.

Line conditioners are a much better choice for protecting against surges and spikes. Line conditioners use several electronic methods to "clean" all power coming into the line conditioner. The best models can be prohibitively expensive, but there is a way to get a kind of "natural" line conditioner. An *uninterruptible power supply (UPS)* uses a battery and power inverter to run the computer equipment that plugs into it. A battery charger continuously charges the battery. The battery charger is the only thing that runs off line voltage. The computer itself runs off steady voltage supplied by the UPS. When power problems occur, the battery charger stops operating, and the equipment continues to run off the battery. The power coming from the UPS is always a continuous 110 volts, 60 Hertz. Because the AC power from the wall never crosses over the battery charger to run the computer components, it's considered a "natural" line conditioner. As you will see, the UPS is the solution for a number of power problems.

Power Underage Problems

Power underages occur when power levels drop below the standard, and they are almost as common as power overages. There are three types of power underages:

- A *sag* is an inverted spike. Sags occur when power levels drop below normal and rise back to normal within a brief period of time (usually less than one second). It is doubtful that you would be aware of sags (you might see a light flicker off and then on), although your computer might reboot.

- A *brownout*, on the other hand, occurs when power drops below normal levels for several seconds or longer. In other words, a brownout is an inverted surge. The lights in the room will dim for a short period of time and then come back to full brightness.

- *A blackout* is a total loss of power for several seconds, several minutes, or several hours.

Any one of these problems will cause your computers and other network devices to malfunction. Figure 6.2 contrasts these power problems.

FIGURE 6.2 Comparing power underage problems

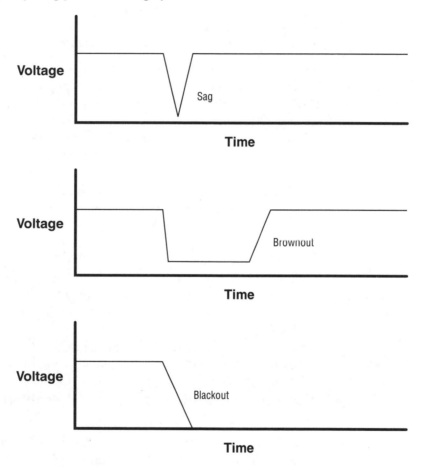

To ward off power underage problems, you need only one device, a UPS, which allows network devices to continue to function even in the complete absence of power. Some are intelligent and can shut down your computer in the case of a blackout.

Power Quality Problems

Power quality problems generally indicate that stray frequencies have entered the power supply through the power cord. Stray frequencies can cause strange problems (such as intermittent reboots or hangs) and can damage a device's power supply. You can detect problems in power quality only with an oscilloscope. If you're having power quality problems, you need either a UPS or a line conditioner.

Electrostatic Discharge (ESD) Problems

ESD occurs when two items with dissimilar static electrical charges are brought together. Nature doesn't like things to be unequal, so static electrical charges will "jump" from the item with more electrons. This "jump" is seen as an electrical spark and thus is called an *electrostatic discharge*. ESD can damage electronic components because the several thousand electrons moving through delicate circuit junctions of silicon chips render the chips useless.

Static can be damaging to equipment and uncomfortable for users at the same time. One worker had the habit of walking around the office without shoes. Walking across a nylon carpet in cotton socks created an immense static charge. When he got within 15 centimeters (not a typo) of the keyboard, the static charge jumped from his fingers to the keyboard. This not only caused him considerable pain, but it also burned out one of the horizontal scan rows on the keyboard, destroying it forever. Fortunately, the computer was properly grounded; otherwise, much more damage could have been done.

Properly grounding equipment can prevent static, as can maintaining room humidity in the 40 percent to 60 percent range.

Electromagnetic Interference (EMI) Problems

EMI occurs when magnetic fields intersect network or computer cables, causing interference in that cable. Motors and transformers, which are ubiquitous in an office (in air conditioners, heaters, and so on), are a typical source of EMI. A common mistake is to run network cable through an elevator shaft or through a ceiling that hides a bank of transformers in fluorescent lights.

Finding the source of EMI can be a challenge. The best approach is to follow a cable with an inexpensive compass, noting strong, odd needle movement. When you find the source of the EMI, you can protect the cable against it by either replacing the cable with a shielded cable (or fiber-optic cable, which is immune to both EMI and RFI) or by moving the cable far away from the source of the EMI.

Radio Frequency Interference (RFI) Problems

RFI occurs when radio signals interfere with the normal operation of electronic circuits (computers in particular). Everyday sources of RFI include television and radio transmitters, which by nature create a specific radio frequency as part of the transmission process. Other sources are two-way radios and cellular phones.

The only way to protect against both EMI and RFI is to use shielded network cables. Shielded cable, as is used in shielded twisted-pair (STP) and coaxial cable, can reduce the effects of RFI. You could also use fiber-optic cable, which is immune to EMI and RFI, throughout your entire network, although this option can get a little pricey.

"Let's Be Careful Out There!"

In one of the strangest cases of RFI we have ever seen, a server was resetting almost every night, right about 3 a.m., while doing a tape backup. Changing the tape drive, the power supply, and other components were of no avail. The log files showed that the tape drive was operating normally and that the server would simply go down and restart, returning to normal operation.

Frustrated with dead-ends, an engineer was on-site at 3 a.m. to observe the failure. He noticed that a police patrol car was parked nearby, radioing in status reports. Separated only by a wall, the server didn't have a chance with 25 watts of VHF radio signal being transmitted from only a few meters away. The radio signal was resetting the server, and once the policeman was done filing reports, the RFI was gone and the server restarted.

Climate Problems

Network devices (including computers and servers) are very sensitive to temperature extremes and can fail prematurely if subjected to them. The environment for network devices should be roughly the same as that for human beings. Keep the temperature consistently at 70° F, and keep the relative humidity between 40 and 60 percent. Maintaining consistent temperature and humidity can be a challenge, because every computer constantly generates heat. Larger companies usually place network equipment in a special room that is climate controlled.

Even if your company can't provide a climate-controlled server room, you can do at least one thing to avoid climate problems: *never* put servers in a network closet without ventilation. It is better to put servers out in the open, locked to a desk, than to lock them up in an unventilated closet. Also never put an electronic device of any kind directly in front of a heat source, such as a space heater. This can cause the components to fail prematurely because excessive heat can damage electronic components.

Error Messages and Log Files

A careful perusal of error messages and log files can give you a good sense of the health of a network. This is important because you may not want to add a new network device to a network that is experiencing problems. *Log files* record every action that occurs on a computer. For example, a log file can contain a record of who logged in to the network when, from which machine, and at what time. Figure 6.3 shows a sample log file.

Each network operating system includes special tools for creating and maintaining log files. In Windows NT, for example, you use Event Viewer (as shown in Figure 6.3) to display System Logs, Security Logs, and Application Logs. NetWare tracks events in the ABEND.LOG, SYS$LOG.ERR, and CONSOLE.LOG files. In Chapter 10, we'll look at log files and error messages in detail.

FIGURE 6.3 A sample log file from the Windows NT Event Viewer

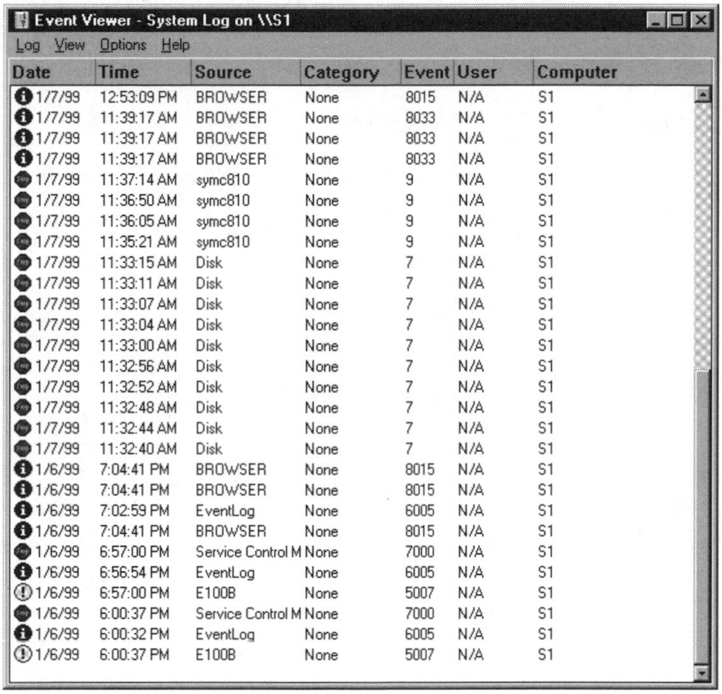

Date	Time	Source	Category	Event	User	Computer
1/7/99	12:53:09 PM	BROWSER	None	8015	N/A	S1
1/7/99	11:39:17 AM	BROWSER	None	8033	N/A	S1
1/7/99	11:39:17 AM	BROWSER	None	8033	N/A	S1
1/7/99	11:39:17 AM	BROWSER	None	8033	N/A	S1
1/7/99	11:37:14 AM	symc810	None	9	N/A	S1
1/7/99	11:36:50 AM	symc810	None	9	N/A	S1
1/7/99	11:36:05 AM	symc810	None	9	N/A	S1
1/7/99	11:35:21 AM	symc810	None	9	N/A	S1
1/7/99	11:33:15 AM	Disk	None	7	N/A	S1
1/7/99	11:33:11 AM	Disk	None	7	N/A	S1
1/7/99	11:33:07 AM	Disk	None	7	N/A	S1
1/7/99	11:33:04 AM	Disk	None	7	N/A	S1
1/7/99	11:33:00 AM	Disk	None	7	N/A	S1
1/7/99	11:32:56 AM	Disk	None	7	N/A	S1
1/7/99	11:32:52 AM	Disk	None	7	N/A	S1
1/7/99	11:32:48 AM	Disk	None	7	N/A	S1
1/7/99	11:32:44 AM	Disk	None	7	N/A	S1
1/7/99	11:32:40 AM	Disk	None	7	N/A	S1
1/6/99	7:04:41 PM	BROWSER	None	8015	N/A	S1
1/6/99	7:04:41 PM	BROWSER	None	8015	N/A	S1
1/6/99	7:02:59 PM	EventLog	None	6005	N/A	S1
1/6/99	7:04:41 PM	BROWSER	None	8015	N/A	S1
1/6/99	6:57:00 PM	Service Control M	None	7000	N/A	S1
1/6/99	6:56:54 PM	EventLog	None	6005	N/A	S1
1/6/99	6:57:00 PM	E100B	None	5007	N/A	S1
1/6/99	6:00:37 PM	Service Control M	None	7000	N/A	S1
1/6/99	6:00:32 PM	EventLog	None	6005	N/A	S1
1/6/99	6:00:37 PM	E100B	None	5007	N/A	S1

Current Configuration and Baselines

Of particular value when you are upgrading a network or installing new hardware or software are the *server and client configuration* documents. If these have been properly maintained, they include information about the current hardware configuration (including I/O address, IRQ, DMA, and memory address), the installed software, any patches, and any special settings.

Configuration documentation should also include *cable maps* that indicate each network cable's source (workstation/server) and destination (typically, a port in a hub), as well as where each network cable runs. (We'll discuss cabling in detail in Chapter 10.)

Baseline documentation indicates how the network normally runs. It includes network traffic statistics, server utilization trends, and processor performance statistics. Baselines indicate how things currently are, not how they should be. Creating and maintaining these types of documents provides a valuable reference point should a client or server fail or malfunction after an upgrade.

Other Documentation

You have at your disposal three more resources that can be of value before, during, and after upgrading or installing new hardware or software:

- README files
- The manufacturer's technical support CD-ROM
- The manufacturer's technical support Web site

We discuss all these in detail in Chapter 10.

All three of these resources can come in handy when you are unable to get through to technical support phone numbers. But some people feel that talking with a human is worth the effort it sometimes takes. Be aware that this is not necessarily free. See Chapter 10 for more information.

Network Components

Now that we have discussed what you need to do before you install or upgrade, let's examine some of the components you may actually be installing. In this section, we'll look at a typical UTP (unshielded twisted-pair) installation to illustrate the components that connect a LAN. Figure 6.4 shows some of these components. Notice that the only hard-wired cables (those you can't simply unplug) run from the wall jack to the patch panel. The workstation connects to the cable run through the wall jack via a patch cable, which is usually less than 3 meters (about 10 feet). Also, the hub connects to the patch panel with multiple patch cables (although in Figure 6.4, only one cable is shown to illustrate a single connection from end to end). In addition to the components shown in Figure 6.4, we will also discuss some of the network connectivity devices you will need when installing the network.

FIGURE 6.4   A typical UTP installation

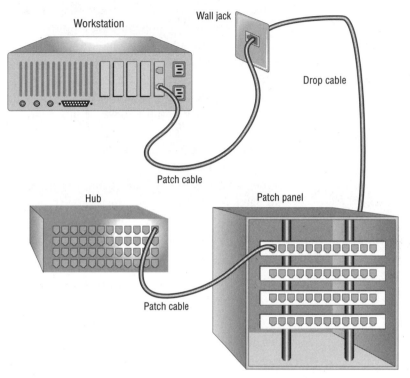

Patch Panel

A *patch panel* is a central wiring point for multiple devices on a UTP network and itself contains no electronic circuits. The following advantages are associated with using a patch panel:

- Upgrading is easier.

- Troubleshooting is easier.

- You can avoid physical damage to the cable since it isn't necessary to move it when you upgrade the network.

When you use a patch panel on a UTP network, you connect components with patch cables. A *patch cable* is any cable that connects one network device to the main cable. For example, patch cables can connect worksta-tions to the main cable and connect the main cable through the patch panel to the hub. Instead of plugging the long run of cable directly into the hub, you connect it to a patch panel and then connect the patch panel port that represents that cable into the hub using a patch cable.

Be careful, though, because the total segment length of the network includes the patch cables at both ends. For example, let's say you are using Ethernet over UTP in the 10BaseT configuration. The maximum segment length is 100 meters (a little more than 300 feet). Thus, the maximum dis-tance from hub to NIC can be 100 meters. Some people mistake this and put in a 100-meter cable run from patch panel to wall plate. They then install a 10-meter workstation to wall-plate patch cable and a 3-meter patch panel to hub patch cable. This brings the total distance to 113 meters, and the work-station using that cable run may not be able to communicate correctly with the rest of the network.

WARNING Be sure to match or exceed the rating for existing cabling. Using a Category 3 Patch Panel with Category 5 cabling makes the network a Category 3 network.

The Repeater

As we discussed in Chapter 2, a *repeater* amplifies (or repeats) network sig-nals to extend the maximum reach of a network. Repeaters receive network signals on one port, amplify them, and repeat them out the other port. Since they operate only at the Physical layer of the OSI model, repeaters can inter-connect different media types but cannot convert protocols.

The main purpose of a repeater is to extend the maximum distance of a single network segment. Let's say you have a workstation that is 150 meters (about 450 feet) from a hub. If your network is 10BaseT Ethernet, you won't be able to connect the workstation directly to the hub because the distance between the hub and the workstation is longer than the maximum segment length of 10BaseT Ethernet (100 meters). For this reason, you place a repeater about 50 to 100 meters between the two.

If it's practical, you could also move the hub. But since hubs are usually close to where all wires come together, this is often neither the best nor the most practical solution.

A repeater is the least expensive of all network devices, but since a repeater can do nothing to segment network traffic, it does little to decrease network traffic. A repeater can actually do more harm than good because it propagates everything, including noise and error packets.

The Hub

A *hub*, which we also discussed in Chapter 2, is the central device in a star topology. Hubs are most commonly used in 10BaseT or 100BaseT Ethernet networks. Most hubs are simple multiport repeaters. That is, they receive a signal on one port and repeat it to all other ports. As with repeaters, though, they also repeat any noise or corrupt signals to all ports.

There are three types of hubs:

- A *passive hub* simply makes physical, electrical connections between all incoming cables and stations so that stations can communicate. Because they don't do any repeating, passive hubs don't require power. ARCNet is an example of a topology that uses passive hubs.

- An *active hub* is powered and contains circuitry to amplify the network signals it receives. Active hubs are used most often in UTP installations of Ethernet (the most common method of cabling for Ethernet). The majority of hubs are active hubs.

- An *intelligent hub* is really a subtype of active hub. All intelligent hubs are active, but not all active hubs are intelligent. An intelligent hub is any hub that contains special features for management and configuration. Many hubs today can manage individual ports, collect traffic statistics, and power up/power down from a remote station on the network. These features make an intelligent hub more complex and, thus, more expensive.

When you install a hub, you simply plug patch cables from the patch panel into the ports on the hub. These hub–to–patch-panel patch cables are typically very short (less than 1 meter, or about 3 feet). If you have an intelligent hub, you may be able to configure ports to be active or inactive using special hub-configuration software.

Remember that hub and workstation patch cables are included in the total length of a network segment.

The Bridge

A *bridge* is a network device that logically separates a single network into two segments. The primary use for a bridge is to keep traffic meant for stations on one segment on that side of the bridge and not let that traffic pass to the other side. It does this by creating a table of MAC (media access control) addresses of all stations, indicating which stations are on which segment. When the bridge receives an incoming packet, it examines the MAC address, determines which segment that station is on, and sends the packet only to that segment.

If power to a bridge is lost, the MAC address table is lost, requiring a rebuild when power is restored. Working at the Data Link layer of the OSI model (IEEE MAC sublayer), a bridge knows nothing about protocols and simply passes packets to the correct segment. Bridges can improve network performance because traffic is not propagated unnecessarily on all network segments. It is possible to create a bridge by placing two NICs in one computer. This is commonly called an *internal bridge*.

The Router

Routers connect logical networks and provide a way for data to move between those networks. A router is more like a special-purpose computer than a simple electronic device. The classic definition of a router is a device that reads the source and destination address of a packet and forwards it based on the information it gathers about the network. Routers can make intelligent decisions about the best way to forward packets, based on Network layer information. These decisions are based primarily on *hop count* (also referred to as *cost*). A hop occurs each time a packet traverses a router to get from one network to another. Hop count is established through communication with other routers. The router chooses the route with the lowest hop count to the packet's destination. If a link in the network is down, the router may choose a route that does not have the lowest hop count.

Do not power off a router whose configuration has not yet been saved.

You usually configure a router via a serial port connection to a computer that contains configuration software. Others may use a command-line interface and require either a terminal or PC-emulated terminal for configuration. Some routers are expandable with plug-in modules. These expansion modules allow you to make a router that uses any of the different types of port configuration, including Ethernet, Token Ring, FDDI (Fiber Distributed Data Interface), ATM (Asynchronous Transfer Mode), and any other network topology.

The Network+ exam—and most networking tests—requires you to know the classic definition of a router. Some of today's routers can actually perform the functions of both a router and a gateway. Configuring routers can be a career in itself. Do not configure a router without clear instructions and permission to do so.

The Brouter

A *brouter* is a network device that combines the features of a router and a bridge. It routes all protocols that can be routed. If the brouter detects a protocol that is not routable (such as NetBEUI), it tries to bridge it to the destination network. Most true routers can perform this function. A brouter is seldom used in today's networks.

The Network Interface Card (NIC)

As we discussed in Chapter 2, you install a NIC in a computer so that the computer can connect to the network. Each type of NIC is specific to a topology and a connection type. To determine a NIC's type, review the documentation and examine the NIC. Even though two NICs look alike, one may be a Token Ring NIC and the other an Ethernet NIC.

You can't connect an Ethernet NIC to a Token Ring network (even though they may use similar cable types) because the technologies are different. But you can use a device called a *media converter* (sometimes called a *transceiver* or *media filter*) to connect a NIC to a different cable type within the same type of network. For example, you can connect a Token Ring NIC (which normally uses Type 1 STP cable and IBM data connectors) to a Token Ring network using UTP as long as you use the correct media converter. This device is, in fact, often found on Token Ring networks to change between cable types.

In the desktop arena, be sure you have a NIC that matches the bus slot available in your computer, and be sure that a slot is open. Although this sounds obvious, it is amazing how often this is overlooked, often due to inadequate documentation.

We'll look at how to install a NIC into a computer later in this chapter.

The Print Server

In a typical production network, it is common to find servers with specialized duties, such as database, proxy, and remote access servers. Today, the most common type of specialized server is the print server.

A *print server* is a centralized device that controls and manages all network printers. The print server can be hardware, software, or a combination. Some print servers are actually built into the network interface (as is the case with the Hewlett-Packard JetDirect network interface cards).

Print servers do not require as many resources as application servers. Thus, instead of using a new computer for a print server, you might want to consider migrating a current file server to a new machine and then using the older computer as a print server.

Placing a printer appropriately may require running a new connection to the patch panel. Keep this in mind when staking out an old server's new home.

The Disk Subsystem

A disk subsystem is the entire set of hard disks, controllers, and software that make up the storage component of a workstation or a server. Even a client-based computer that has only one drive inside the case has a disk subsystem. Some disk subsystems can be directly connected to a network, providing network disk access to servers and workstations.

Disk subsystems can be internal or external and can consist of one or more disk drives. Many disk subsystems now support "hot swapping," meaning that you can remove a drive from a computer (usually a server) without having to stop the operation of the computer.

Redundant, fault-tolerant disk configurations (such as mirroring and other RAID configurations) are covered in detail in Chapter 9.

External disk subsystems typically connect to the server in one of two ways:

- Via Fibre Channel
- Via Small Computer System Interface (SCSI)

Fibre Channel is a relatively new technology. It uses fiber optics to connect the server and storage system. Currently, the most common way to connect external disk subsystems to computers is via the SCSI interface.

SCSI is a high-speed parallel interface that can connect many types of peripherals, including disks, scanners, and CD-ROMs. It requires the addition of a special SCSI adapter (usually an add-on card) and comes in many speeds, from 10MBps to 80 MBps (for Ultra-2). In addition, SCSI connectors come in three styles:

- DB-25 female
- Centronics-50
- SCSI-2 (a special, high-density, 68-pin connector)

The DB-25 female is commonly found on the back of older Macintosh computers and is used to connect to an external disk drive. These connectors have not been widely used in the PC world. Figure 6.5 shows a sample DB-25 female connector.

FIGURE 6.5 A sample DB-25 female SCSI connector

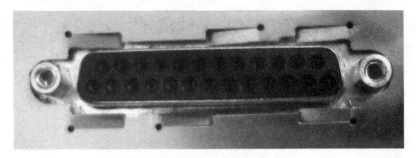

More commonplace is the Centronics-50 interface, which is considered the standard SCSI connector. Centronics-50 connectors have both male and female connectors and typically are used in SCSI-1 implementations. Figure 6.6 shows sample male and female Centronics-50 connectors.

FIGURE 6.6 Male Centronics-50 SCSI connector

The SCSI-2 connector was so dubbed because it was introduced on systems at the same time as the introduction of the SCSI-2 interface. Typically, a cable connects to the 68-pin connector on one end and connects to either another 68-pin connector or a standard Centronics-50 connector on the other. Figure 6.7 shows a sample high-density, 68-pin connector.

FIGURE 6.7 A high-density, 68-pin SCSI connector

Peripherals

When you connect computers to a network, you may have to deal with the peripherals attached to those computers. A *peripheral* is any device that is not an actual part of a computer, but is directly attached to it. Some examples of peripherals are printers, modems, speakers, and backup devices. In a network, peripherals can be attached to servers or workstations (and sometimes also directly to the network cable), and "hosted" for other computers on the network. This means you can buy one peripheral and then share it with other computers on the network. It's important to note that not every peripheral can be hosted, but many, such as printers and modems, can.

A peripheral is connected to the applicable peripheral port on a computer, such as serial, parallel and USB ports. Once peripherals are connected, you can install software so that they can be hosted on the network.

Network Connectors

In addition to testing you on the various components you might find on a network, the Network+ exam will ask you to identify the types of connectors found on a network. When installing a network, you need to know which type of connector to use for which component. The type of connector you use depends on the type of network and the type of cable (copper or fiber-optic). In this section, we'll discuss the connectors commonly used with copper cable:

- D-type
- BNC
- RJ-series
- IBM data

D-type Connectors

The first type of networking connector was the *D-type connector*. Coincidentally, it's also used to connect many peripherals to a PC. A D-type connector is characterized by its shape. Turned on its side, a D-type connector looks like the letter *D* and contains rows of pins (male) or sockets (female). Figure 6.8 shows a male and female D-type connector.

FIGURE 6.8 A sample male and female D-type connector

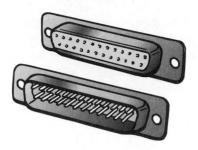

D-type connectors are also called D-sub or DB connectors.

The Attachment Unit Interface (AUI) connector used with the original DIX Ethernet implementation is a D-type connector and is included with many types of Ethernet NICs for compatibility. You can use an AUI connector with an external transceiver to change to a different media type (such as UTP to coax). To prevent the connector from disconnecting, two screws secure the male and female halves.

BNC Connectors

Most commonly used with coaxial cable, *BNC connectors* are tube-shaped, as Figure 6.9 shows. A twist-lock mechanism prevents the cable from disconnecting. You must push the cable's connector onto the connector on the NIC and then twist the connector on the cable to lock it in place.

BNC connectors are most commonly found in 10Base2 Ethernet networks, as well as in ARCNet, but they can be used on any network that is connected by coaxial cable.

FIGURE 6.9 A sample BNC connector

The abbreviation for the BNC connector has been the topic of debate for years. Some people think that it is named after its developers (Bayonet, Neil, and Concelman). Others think the abbreviation comes from the description of the connector (Bayonet Nut Connector) or from its first use (British Naval Connector).

RJ Connectors

You are probably familiar with the *RJ (Registered Jack)* family of connectors. The little clip connector at the end of the telephone cable that connects most home phones to the wall jack is an RJ-11 connector. RJ-45 connectors are most commonly found on both 10BaseT and Token Ring networks, but they can be found on any network that uses four-pair, UTP cable. Figure 6.10 shows an RJ-series connector. An RJ-11 connector is smaller than an RJ-45 connector, and RJ-11 uses four (or six) wires; the RJ-45 has eight wires housed in its case. Figure 6.10 shows an RJ-45 connector that might be used in 10BaseT Ethernet.

FIGURE 6.10   A typical RJ-45 connector

The RJ-45 is very popular, even outside networking. Frequently, this connector is used for digital phone systems in offices and motels.

RJ-45 connectors use a small tab to lock the connector in place. Unfortunately, this tab, after many uses, can break. Fortunately, network connectors aren't commonly connected and disconnected, so the instances of breakage are minimal. Plus, you can easily replace a connector by cutting off the old one and crimping on a new one.

The IBM Data Connector

The *IBM data connector* is unique in many ways. First, it isn't as universal as the other types of network connectors. Second, there aren't male and female versions, as with the others. The IBM data connector is both male and female. Any two data connectors can connect. This connector (shown in Figure 6.11) is most commonly used with IBM's Token Ring technology and Type 1 or 2 STP cable.

Analog vs. Digital Connections

The typical traveling office worker has a laptop and an analog modem. You just saw that an RJ-45 connector is similar to an RJ-11 connector, only wider. Yes, this means that an RJ-11 plug will make a perfect physical connection inside an RJ-45 jack. You also saw that this jack is used in many commercial phone systems. Connecting an analog modem (RJ-11 connector) to a digital system (RJ-45 jack) carrying a higher voltage is never a pretty picture. One of two outcomes is possible:

- The connection will not function.

- The analog modem will never function again.

Clearly, when an analog device receives a digital signal, there is no basis for a successful connection. The second possibility arises when a higher voltage from the digital connection burns out the modem. Yes, we told you it could get ugly.

Additionally, some digital phone systems might also be using RJ-11 connectors and jacks. In this case, it is imperative that the jack be clearly labeled. If you're on the road, pay careful attention to the type of wall jack you encounter.

FIGURE 6.11   An IBM data connector

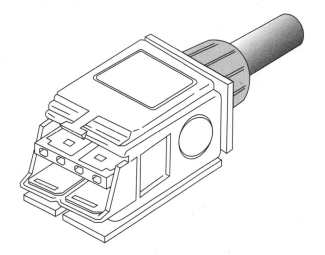

The IBM data connector also uses a tab to hold the connectors together, but this tab is a little more rigid than the tab on the RJ-series connectors and doesn't move as much. Therefore, breakage is not much of an issue.

Installing a Network Interface Card (NIC)

Installing a NIC is typically a nonevent, except when the NIC doesn't work. In most cases, success or failure in troubleshooting the NIC rests entirely on your decisions and also on your ability to master much of what we've talked about thus far in this chapter. Let's take a look at the proper procedures for installing a NIC.

Before you get started, there is one item of note. In many cases, when a NIC doesn't work, it REALLY doesn't work and the indications are obvious. Troubleshooting the NIC then simply becomes a matter of replacing the NIC. When you have a temperamental NIC card, don't waste too much time on troubleshooting the NIC. Just replace it.

Getting Started

Lacking current and complete documentation for the NIC-less computer, your first step is a physical examination of the following:

- The type of network (Ethernet/Token Ring/ARCNet)
- The type of available bus in the computer (ISA/EISA/VLB/PCI, and so on)
- The available IRQ and memory address
- The type of cable connection

Although this may seem obvious, more than one network engineer has traveled some distance to install a NIC, only to find that the cabling wasn't what she expected or that no slots were available for the type of NIC that she brought along.

Physical Inspection

Be sure to check with the user about saving work before shutting down the system. Once the computer is turned off, take precautions to eliminate static electricity before removing the case.

Have your toolkit ready! A popular computer requires a Torx screwdriver. Another one will need a flat tip. Yet a third type will require a cross or Phillips screwdriver. First, visually inspect the area where you want to put the NIC. You need to know the following:

- The type of bus slot that is available
- Whether the card will interfere with cables, fans, or other obstructions

- The type of connector the NIC will need (UTP or coax)
- The location of the drivers for this NIC

The second part of a physical inspection of the computer involves computer logic:

- Which IRQ choices are available?
- Which I/O addresses are available?
- Which memory address choices are possible?

Not all NICs have every possible memory address available. Eight-bit NICs cannot have an IRQ address that is beyond IRQ 7. Most of the interrupts in the 8-bit range are usually already consumed by basic PC functions, such as the floppy drive or keyboard. Typically, an 8-bit NIC can be installed on IRQ 5. That is the common home of either a second parallel port or a sound card. So be prepared to resolve conflicts.

You will have more IRQ choices with a 16-bit NIC. In most computers today, both IRQ 14 and 15 are used by IDE controllers. Add a SCSI device, and another IRQ becomes unavailable. Sound cards typically use IRQ 5 or IRQ 10. IRQ 8 is used by the Real Time Clock (RTC). The wise installer avoids IRQ 9 since that is cascaded to IRQ 2. That leaves only two choices if a SCSI card is installed. A PS/2 mouse might absorb one of those, with IRQ 12. Will the NIC you are planning to install offer you IRQ 13, the only one left? No? This requires reconfiguring the SCSI card or removing something. The latter choice at a minimum will make you unpopular with users. Clearly some homework is required on your part to complete the job and not upset users.

The same issues exist with I/O addresses. You must configure a NIC with the appropriate I/O address before you can even use most configuration utilities. Most commonly, NICs are set to I/O address 300; however, if another device in the computer is already using that address, the address must be changed.

This leads us to the tools you can use to find out which IRQ and I/O address you can use. Let's take a look.

Identifying Free IRQ and Memory Addresses

If the computer is running Microsoft operating systems, you can use some simple tools. MSD.EXE has been available since MS-DOS 5. Although not perfect, it can tell you which IRQs and I/O addresses appear to be in use. In

Windows 95/98, you can use Device Manager (choose Start ≻ Settings ≻ Control Panel ≻ System ≻ Device Manager).

After you identify the available settings, enter this information in the logbook for that computer. If no logbook exists, this is the perfect time to start one.

If you are not installing the NIC at this time, put your tools away, power up the computer, and spend a little time with the user to make sure the computer is as it was when you powered it down. You don't want a phone call complaining that you broke the computer when you looked at it. It is not unheard of for a cable to come loose when you're inspecting a PC.

At this point, let's assume you have all the data you need, the proper NIC, and the correct drivers for a successful install. Now it is time to actually physically install the NIC.

Removing the Slot Cover

It is always important to keep a computer as sealed as possible to reduce the effects of EMI or RFI and to properly cool the system. However, since you are planning to install a new device, you will have to open the computer's cover and remove one of the slot covers. Properly ground yourself to avoid static electricity. The opening created by removing the slot cover will be closed again when the NIC is installed. Store this slot cover so that it can be replaced if the card needs to be removed in the future.

Antistatic Enclosures

Removing an electronic device from an antistatic protective bag or hard enclosure requires a static-free area. Some old hands would leave the PC plugged in and turned off during this process. Touching the metal case would create a ground strap. Technically, this works with AT cases; however, company policy may require a more official approach. This does not work with ATX cases. ATX cases use a power supply that always has a small amount of power going to the system board. This is so that the system board can continue to power a few of its devices and thus "wake" the rest of the computer when it receives data from the network (this feature is known as Wake on LAN). If you accidentally plug a device into a motherboard while there is power to the power supply, you may damage the device, the system board, or both and possibly the entire system. *Always* unplug the computer's power cable when working with ATX cases to avoid system damage.

Inserting the NIC

After you determine the appropriate slot for the NIC, you need to remove that slot's associated blank. A *blank* is a piece of metal that covers the back of the computer where an expansion card's ports would normally go. You must remove the blank and the screw that holds it in before you can install any expansion card (including a NIC). You can remove the blank by removing the screw that holds it in and lifting the blank out of the computer. Save the blank for future use in case you ever need to remove a device.

Some blanks are die-stamped into the metal framing of the case. To remove them, push them inward, bending them up so that the metal tab that's securing them will break. This type of blank is becoming scarce and is now seen only in the "cheaper" cases.

After you remove the blank, you can insert the NIC in the slot you selected. The metal "fingers" on the bottom side of the NIC should engage with the metal tabs inside the slot. When you insert the NIC, use gentle, even pressure straight down on the card. The card should seat firmly in its slot.

If the NIC doesn't go into the expansion slot easily, don't force it. You may break the tab on the NIC, the expansion slot connector, or both.

Once you have inserted the card, you MUST secure it to the case using the screw you removed with the blank earlier. Many people don't do this step and the card will eventually work its way loose, causing the NIC to stop working, or worse, cause shorts inside the computer, thus damaging other components.

Now that the NIC is installed in the system, it is time to configure it.

Configuring the NIC

Until you give the NIC some command logic, the computer and the network will be unable to communicate. How you do this varies with the design of the NIC. The most common methods are:

- Jumpers
- DIP switches

- EEPROM
- Plug and Play

Setting Jumpers

Jumpers are small connectors that are used to complete a circuit by connecting two pins, indicating a setting to the device, either On or Off. One disadvantage of jumpers is that you can easily drop the cap that makes the connection inside the computer when changing a jumper setting. Be sure you always have tweezers in your toolkit to retrieve "lost" jumpers. Figure 6.12 shows a jumper and how it is used.

FIGURE 6.12 A jumper and how it is used

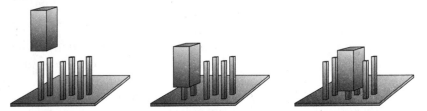

A jumper (above left) can be used to make a connection between various pairs of pins in an array of pins. On some devices you may need to jumper multiple pairs, using several jumpers. This arrangement of six pins offers eight different jumper settings.

You'll often see devices with just three pins. These are common for devices that require only two settings, like on and off, or enabled and disabled.

Some jumpered cards are clearly labeled on the circuit board with a nomenclature such as IRQ 3 4 5 7 9 10 11 12 13 14 15. Simply put a jumper on the numbered jumper to establish the needed IRQ. Other cards may have labels such as JP8 A B C D E F G H I J K. You will have to refer to the NIC's documentation to determine the appropriate setting. The NIC's documentation will usually include a table of configuration settings and which pins to jumper to get them. Table 6.1 shows an example of an IRQ jumper configuration table.

WARNING   Not all jumper tables look alike!

TABLE 6.1   A Sample NIC Jumper Configuration Table

IRQ	Jumper This Set of Pins
3	A1
4	A2
5	A3
6	A4
7	A5
8	A6
10	A7
11	A8
12	A9

Dual Inline Package (DIP) Switches

To create an On or Off state, you slide or rock a DIP switch (as shown in Figure 6.13), depending on whether it is a slider or rocker type. Unlike a jumper, it is impossible to lose a DIP switch. Nevertheless, DIP switches are more expensive, and so some manufacturers prefer jumpers.

FIGURE 6.13   The DIP switch

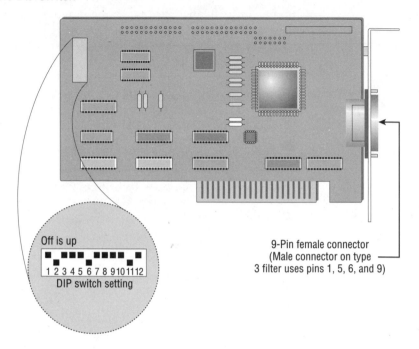

Off is up

1 2 3 4 5 6 7 8 9 10 11 12
DIP switch setting

9-Pin female connector
(Male connector on type
3 filter uses pins 1, 5, 6, and 9)

At first glance, network nirvana may seem to be at hand with DIP switches. In fact, nothing could be further from the truth. Depending on the make and model of a NIC, it may be just as easy or ugly to configure, depending on the card and how well it is labeled and documented.

DIP switches are very small and as such, it is next to impossible to use your fingers to move the switch. You should use a small probe or paper clip to move them. NEVER use a pencil because the lead tip could break off inside the switch.

The EEPROM Chip

EEPROM is an acronym formed from *electrically erasable programmable read-only memory* and is a chip whose settings can be configured with software. NICs use these chips to hold their configuration settings, including IRQ, I/O, and DMA addresses. Rather than configure the hardware settings

> ### NIC Documentation
>
> Attempting to configure a device such as a NIC without documentation is an exercise in futility. The permutations, while not technically endless, are numerous enough that it could take several hours to find even a pattern to the settings. This is no fun whatsoever and is completely avoidable if you save the documentation for all devices in each client or server in your domain.
>
> The settings for a particular NIC are in the documentation can that comes with it. So, while it may appear that all those loose papers are so much junk, this junk can later be worth its weight in gold.

of a NIC using jumpers or DIP switches, with EEPROMs on a NIC, you can configure the hardware settings with special configuration software. The configuration software is specific to each NIC and usually comes with the NIC on a disk.

An EEPROM together with software-based NIC configuration software is a real treat to use after installing a NIC configuring JP 8, 10, and 14, all the while attempting to decipher what the tiny little table of jumper settings is trying to tell you. Typically these software configuration utilities can even test the system to determine which IRQ and memory addresses are available in a system before you begin setup of the EEPROM.

The Plug-and-Play Standard

Plug and Play is a standard that defines automatic techniques for configuring ISA expansion boards. This standard was originally developed by a consortium of companies, including Microsoft, Intel, Compaq, and Phoenix. With this technology, a Plug-and-Play expansion card is configured automatically by the computer's BIOS with the correct, available hardware settings (that is, IRQ, DMA, and I/O address) for that computer. After the settings are configured, all you have to do is install the software driver for the expansion card.

Unfortunately this process works correctly only if all devices in the computer are Plug-and-Play compliant. Plug and Play has become known as Plug and Pray because of the difficulties in properly configuring a non–Plug-and-Play ISA card in a Plug-and-Play system. If you manually assign an IRQ address, for example, to a non–Plug-and-Play ISA card, install that card in the system, and then come back and install a Plug-and-Play card, the Plug-and-Play card may take the IRQ address manually assigned to the other card. It does this because the BIOS doesn't know that the non–Plug-and-Play card exists. Some BIOSes allow you to enter the IRQ, I/O, and DMA addresses that are being used by non–Plug-and-Play cards. In this way, when a new Plug-and-Play card is inserted, the BIOS will be able to choose a setting that doesn't conflict with any existing hardware.

Resource Conflicts

A resource conflict occurs when two devices are set to the same IRQ, I/O, or DMA address. It can (and does) happen with Plug-and-Play cards in a mixed (non–Plug-and-Play system) environment, as already mentioned. Additionally, most expansion cards (including NICs) are set by default to settings that other hardware device manufacturers aren't using for their devices. For example, most sound cards are set, by default, to IRQ 5, I/O address 220h. Network cards are often set to IRQ 10, I/O address 300h.

NIC Drivers

A *NIC driver* provides a software interface between the NIC hardware and the host operating system. Normally, you'll find a driver for the NIC you're installing on a diskette that came with the NIC. Sometimes, however, the driver for the NIC is included with the operating system.

Check the README file on the disk before installing the driver. If you suspect that the driver may be on the old side, check the manufacturer's Web site for an updated driver. In addition, you may want to update the driver as a result of any of the following:

- Security holes

- Updates from other subsystems

- Performance enhancements

- Changes within the operating system itself

Standardize the NICs you use throughout your network. You can reduce capital expenditures by purchasing in bulk, reducing the learning curve, and becoming adept at installation.

Testing the NIC

Today, most NICs come with some sort of software utility that you can use to verify that the NIC is functioning correctly and to test every aspect of its operation. This software is known as *NIC diagnostics*. Even if the NIC vendor did not include any diagnostics, you can check proper NIC operation by installing client software and logging in. If you can log in to the network, generally speaking, the NIC is functioning.

The tests that these diagnostics can perform fall into two categories:

- Hardware

- Software

Hardware diagnostics examine the individual parts of the NIC and verify the functions of each component. If there's a problem, the diagnostics will report it. This functionality is typically part of the software configuration program for the NIC.

Unfortunately, most diagnostics for UTP-based NICs can't determine whether the NIC is transmitting or receiving data successfully without a device known as a *hardware loopback*. A hardware loopback connects the transmission pins directly to the receiving pins, allowing the diagnostics to test this aspect of the NIC. You can't get a full suite of diagnostic information without one. Loopbacks are discussed in detail in Chapter 10.

Software diagnostics test the higher-level functions of the NIC, such as network communication with other stations. These programs typically consist of a sender and receiver portion. Each portion is run on one of a pair of computers connected to the network. The sender sends a test packet out to the receiver. When the receiver receives the packet, it immediately sends a response. This function is similar to the TCP/IP Ping command, but is protocol-independent.

Network Upgrade Considerations

In addition to testing you on how to plan for a new network installation, the Network+ exam requires you to know how to upgrade network hardware and software. An *upgrade* is a procedure that brings older or out-of-date hardware or software to a more current level. Upgrades solve problems (for example, through bug fixes) or provide better performance (for example, by upgrading your 486 server to a newer, faster processor).

The Network+ exam will test your knowledge of what to do before, during, and after an upgrade and will require that you know how to test an upgrade.

Before You Begin an Upgrade

Upgrades always introduce an element of the unknown: you don't know how the new hardware or software will interact with the rest of the network. For this reason, you must prepare yourself and your network before upgrading your hardware or software. Here are some tips:

- Install a test network representative of your network and then upgrade it.

- Ask the manufacturer of the hardware or software you are upgrading if they are aware of any potential trouble spots.

- Be sure that you have a complete, reliable backup system. This means that you have done a restore that works.

During an Upgrade

Each upgrade is different. Some (such as updating software) may take only a few minutes (if the process is simple enough). Others, such as replacing server hardware, may take several hours. Regardless of the type of upgrade, be sure to allow enough time, and be sure to notify the users and give them an estimate of how long the system will be down.

When upgrading software, be sure to note any error messages that you see during the installation. If the upgrade fails, you can then search technical support documentation to find out exactly what went wrong and how to fix it.

Preparing for Location Changes

Moving a computer or a network to a new location is not an upgrade, but also requires proper preparation. To ensure that a move goes smoothly:

- Be sure that proper power is available at the new location.

- Be sure that the network connections are active at the new location.

Even though these two items seem simple enough, it's amazing how many network location changes fail because the network administrator didn't check these out.

Testing an Upgrade

When the upgrade is complete, test the system to ensure that nothing was damaged or is now inoperable. For example, log in, transfer files, and browse the Internet. If you were able to perform an operation before an upgrade but not afterward, you'll need to determine the source of the problem.

Two DLLs are overwritten during a software upgrade: VBRUN*x*00 .DLL (*x* is the version number) and ODBC.DLL. The former is the Visual Basic Runtime Library, which stores many of the basic subroutines for programs based on Visual Basic. The latter is the Open Database Connectivity DLL, which is used to connect workstations to many types of databases, including Access, SQL, and DB/2 databases. If either DLL is overwritten, you will have problems running programs that use them for functionality.

After an Upgrade

After you finish testing your equipment, it's time for some post-upgrade cleanup:

- Remove outdated drivers. You'll usually find hardware drivers in the packaging materials for any hardware you upgrade. Sometimes these aren't the most current. Check the manufacturer's Web site for more up-to-date drivers.

- Remove any unneeded hardware so that it doesn't become a possible source for network failure.

- Gradually give clients access. The best way to get users back on the network is to give access to one group at a time. "Ramping up" enables you to see how the new component functions under varying conditions and prevents all users from being affected if there are difficulties.

Key Terms

Before you take the exam, be certain you are familiar with the following terms:

active hub

baseline

blackout

blank

bridge

brouter

brownout

cable map

cost

country code

electrically erasable programmable read-only memory (EEPROM)

hardware loopback

hop count

hub

intelligent hub

internal bridge

line conditioner

line voltage

media converter

NIC diagnostics

object

overvoltage threshold

passive hub

patch cable

peripheral

power spike

power surge

print server

router

sag

server and client configuration

service accounts

surge protector

test account

uninterruptible power supply (UPS)

upgrade

URL

Review Questions

1. Which piece of software allows the computer's operating system to access the NIC hardware?

    A. NIC driver

    B. Operating system driver

    C. System driver

    D. Protocol driver

2. Which component of a NIC can store the settings like IRQ, I/O address, and DMA address?

    A. DIP switch

    B. Software driver

    C. ISA Interface

    D. EEPROM

3. The three forms of electrical interference are _____.

    A. ERI

    B. EMI

    C. ESD

    D. RFI

4. You are running UTP cable in an Ethernet network from a workstation to a hub. Which item(s) are included in the total length measurement of the cable segment (as needed in determining the longest segment length)?

    A. Workstation patch cable

    B. Main cable run

    C. Hub internal network

    D. Hub patch cable

5. Besides the documentation that is supplied by a vendor, updated information for a product may be found on/at _____.

   A. Any update sheets supplied with the product

   B. The vendor's Web site

   C. A README file on the diskette or CD

   D. All of the above

6. SCSI connections can use which of the following connectors? Choose all that apply.

   A. BNC

   B. DB-25

   C. Centronics-50

   D. RJ-11

   E. IBM Data Connector

7. Depending on the Windows client operating system version, which commands can you use to find out what is installed on a system? Choose all that apply.

   A. netstat

   B. MSD

   C. Ping

   D. All of the above

8. Which network connectivity device is specifically designed to extend the maximum reach of a network segment?

   A. Bridge

   B. Router

   C. Repeater

   D. Brouter

9. A bridge can increase network efficiency by _____.

   A. Copying packets of data sent to storage and resending them as requested without rereading the needed data

   B. Learning and storing the MAC address for each NIC on each side of the bridge and then, based on this information, forwarding packets only to the appropriate segment

   C. Defining traffic order by using Quality of Service (QoS)

   D. All of the above

10. Updating old NIC drivers on systems _____.

   A. Can correct bugs

   B. Can be a good way to look like you are doing useful work

   C. Can act as a protocol converter

   D. All of the above

11. EEPROM is short for _____.

   A. Electronically Erasable Programmable Read Only Memory

   B. Electrically Erasable Programmable Read Only Memory

   C. Electronically Erasable Periodical Only Memory

   D. Electrically Erasable Powered Read Only Memory

12. Plug-and-Play expansion cards sometimes have problems working correctly with _____ expansion cards.

   A. PCI

   B. Token Ring

   C. Legacy ISA

   D. EISA

13. A brouter combines which functions? Choose all that apply.

    A. Router

    B. Bridge

    C. Gateway

    D. Repeater

14. The 10Base2 implementation of Ethernet, for the most part, uses which type of connector?

    A. RJ-11

    B. BNC

    C. RJ-45

    D. All of the above

15. You are a consultant. You have been asked to upgrade the network operating system version for one of your clients on a TCP/IP network. What kinds of information do you need to obtain before starting the upgrade?

    A. The president's password

    B. The administrative password

    C. The network documentation

    D. The IP address scheme

    E. The hub manufacturer

    F. The network cable diameter

16. Which locations would be a poor choice for a network server?

    A. Nonventilated wiring closet

    B. Ventilated wiring closet

    C. Factory production floor

    D. Shelf in front of a southern-facing window

17. Which network component "shares out" a printer so that printing services can be provided to the entire network?

   A. Print server

   B. Print facilitator

   C. PCONSOLE.EXE

   D. Print manager

18. Which power condition occurs when the voltage level increases quickly and falls just as quickly?

   A. Surge

   B. Spike

   C. Brownout

   D. Blackout

19. Which power condition occurs when the voltage level increases quickly and remains at the high level for an extended period of time (several seconds)?

   A. Surge

   B. Spike

   C. Brownout

   D. Blackout

20. Which power condition occurs when the voltage level drops below 120 volts and stays below for an extended period of time?

   A. Surge

   B. Spike

   C. Brownout

   D. Blackout

Answers to Review Questions

1. A. The NIC driver is a software component that an operating system uses to interface with the NIC hardware.

2. D. The EEPROM is the part of some (not all) NICs that can store card resource settings that are made or changed with configuration software.

3. B, C, D. Electromagnetic Interference (EMI), Electrostatic Discharge (ESD), and Radio Frequency Interference are the three major forms of electrical interference.

4. A, B, D. The total length of the segment is measured from the hub port to the workstation NIC interface. So, the workstation patch cable, the main cable run (from wall port to cabling closet), and the hub patch cable (from hub to main cable run) are all considered part of this distance measurement. For a 10BaseT Ethernet network, this total distance cannot be longer than 100 meters.

5. D. Vendors are constantly coming out with updated information about their software. All the listed methods are ways the software vendor can release updated information after the main documentation has been printed/released.

6. B, C. Although there are other connectors used for SCSI, of those listed, the only connectors that are currently used for SCSI connections are the DB-25 and Centronics-50.

7. B. The only command listed that will tell you what hardware or software is installed on a system is the MSD utility (normally supplied with DOS versions after 6).

8. C. Although many of these devices CAN extend the maximum reach of a network, the only one listed that was specifically designed to extend the maximum segment length of a network is a repeater.

9. B. A bridge learns the MAC addresses of stations on both sides of the bridge and keeps track of which side individual stations are on. Then, when the bridge intercepts a packet, the bridge examines the destination field of the packet and compares the destination address to its list of MAC addresses. The bridge then forwards or rejects the packet based on whether or not the destination station is on the local segment.

10. A. Updating older drivers on a system can correct various bugs. When a hardware manufacturer detects a bug in a driver, they develop and release a new version to correct the problem.

11. B. The correct expansion for EEPROM is Electrically Erasable Programmable Read Only Memory.

12. C. Because Plug-and-Play expansion cards automatically assign a computer's resources, they can be set to a resource that conflicts with a Legacy ISA card (which doesn't always register itself with the Plug-and-Play software).

13. A, B. As its name suggests, a brouter combines certain functionalities of both a bridge and a router.

14. B. 10Base2 Ethernet normally uses BNC connectors for making its connections.

15. B, C, D. When upgrading a network operating system, the first piece of information you'll need is the network documentation, which will tell you how the network is put together. Additionally, you will need the administrative password (or equivalent) to be able to have the rights and permissions to make changes to the network. Finally, since this network is a TCP/IP network, you will need the addressing scheme, as the NOS may ask you what IP addresses that computer should have.

16. A, C, D. All the locations listed will give poor air quality, poor ventilation, or bad environmental conditions. The ventilated wiring closet is actually a good location for a server, assuming the climate can be controlled sufficiently.

17. A. The only network component listed that actually provides network printing service to network clients is the Print server.

18. B. Spikes are an overvoltage condition in which the power level quickly increases, then decreases just as quickly.

19. A. Surges are an overvoltage condition in which the power level increases quickly and stays at a higher level for several seconds.

20. C. Brownouts are an undervoltage condition in which the voltage level drops and stays low for several seconds. During a brownout, the lights usually dim and then become bright again.

Chapter

7

Network Remote Access

NETWORK+ EXAM OBJECTIVES COVERED IN THIS CHAPTER:

✓ **Explain the following remote connectivity concepts:**

- The distinction between PPP and SLIP
- The purpose and function of PPTP and the conditions under which it is useful
- The attributes, advantages, and disadvantages of ISDN and PSTN (POTS)

✓ **Specify the following elements of dial-up networking:**

- The modem configuration parameters that must be set, including serial port IRQ, I/O address, and maximum port speed
- The requirements for a remote connection

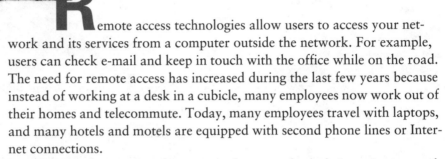

Remote access technologies allow users to access your network and its services from a computer outside the network. For example, users can check e-mail and keep in touch with the office while on the road. The need for remote access has increased during the last few years because instead of working at a desk in a cubicle, many employees now work out of their homes and telecommute. Today, many employees travel with laptops, and many hotels and motels are equipped with second phone lines or Internet connections.

Before employees can telecommute, however, both their equipment and the corporate network must be set up for remote access. This involves acquiring the appropriate hardware, installing the appropriate software, configuring this hardware and software, and ensuring that the proper protocols are in place. In this chapter, we'll look at all this from the standpoint of what you as a network administrator will need to know in the workplace and for the Network+ exam.

Remote Access Connection Configuration Requirements

Remote access requires two basic components: a remote computer (typically, a laptop) and a remote access system on the network (typically, a computer or device running special software called the Remote Access Server). The remote computer connects to the remote access server and then operates just as it would if it were a workstation on the network.

The most common remote access connection (and, therefore, the one that the Network+ exam tests you on) is a dial-up connection over a regular analog phone line. This section covers only one type of remote access configuration. Each NOS (network operating system) has many options for remote access to your network. Check your NOS documentation for these options.

Hardware Requirements

The device most commonly used to connect computers over a public analog phone line is a *modem* (a contraction of MOdulator/DEModulator). A sending modem converts digital signals from the computer into analog signals that can be transmitted over telephone lines and other analog media. On the receiving end, the modem changes the analog signals back to digital signals. Because telephone lines can be found almost everywhere, this method of remote communication is readily available to everyone with access to a phone line.

Modems change the digital ones and zeros into analog signals that can be transmitted over telephone lines. The pattern of these analog signals encodes the data for transmission to the receiving computer. The receiving modem then takes the analog signals and turns them back into ones and zeros. This method is slower than a completely digital transmission, but data can travel over longer distances with fewer errors.

A modem can be either internal or external. The key difference between the two is the amount of configuration required. You must configure internal modems with an IRQ and an I/O address as well as a virtual COM port address, to ensure that they function properly. External modems simply hook to a serial port and don't require nearly as much configuration.

Configuring an Internal Modem

Internal modems are on expansion cards that fit into a computer's expansion bus. To that end, the modem you install must be designed to work in the type of expansion bus slot in that computer. Configuring an internal modem is much like configuring any other hardware device. You must set the IRQ, I/O address, and virtual COM port so that they don't conflict with other devices.

The only one of these configuration parameters that you haven't seen before is the virtual COM port. A *virtual COM* port is a logical designation given by the operating system for a serial port. A computer can have only two physical serial ports, but it can have as many as four logical ports. Each physical port must be associated with a logical port so that the operating system can use it. The same is true for modems (since they are, in fact, serial devices). You must set a modem to use a COM port that is not being used by any other device.

You usually configure the IRQ, I/O addresses, and virtual COM port using jumpers, DIP switches, or software programs, just like any other expansion card. See Chapter 6 for information on configuring expansion cards.

Each COM port shares an IRQ address with another port. COM 1 and COM 3 share IRQ 4, and COM 2 and COM 4 share IRQ 3. If two devices are set to different COM ports (COM1 and COM3, for example) but have the same IRQ, the modem may not function properly. It is usually best to set an internal modem to COM4, because COM1 is most likely to be in use, while COM2 (which shares the IRQ with COM4) is less likely to be used. Table 7.1 lists the virtual COM ports, their associated IRQs, and default I/O addresses. Note which COM ports share IRQ addresses.

TABLE 7.1 COM Port IRQ and Default I/O Addresses

Port	IRQ	I/O
COM1	4	3F8
COM2	3	2F8
COM3	4	3E8
COM4	3	2E8

Configuring an External Modem

Many people prefer external modems to internal ones because they can see the modem's status lights. Most internal modems use software status lights, which don't work if the hardware or software is failing. When using external modems, you have two considerations: available serial ports and the UART type.

Available Serial Ports

With the large number of external serial expansion devices available—including modems, cameras, and printers—a spare serial port is often not available, and so you have to purchase an internal modem. A technology called the Universal Serial Bus (USB) is now available on most new computers. The USB allows multiple devices (including modems) to be chained off a single serial port. This technology will eventually eliminate the current need for multiple serial ports on a computer.

UART Type

UART stands for Universal Asynchronous Receiver-Transmitter and is the chip that manages serial communications. Each set of serial ports shares a UART. The type of UART chip determines the maximum port speed that a particular serial port can handle. There are two main types: the 8250 and 16550 series. The primary difference between them is the capacity of the port buffers. Internal modems have built-in, high-speed UART chips, so this isn't an issue with internal modems.

The 8250 chips have 8-bit buffers that are limited to a maximum speed of 9600bps and are typically found in PCs manufactured before 1986 (before the IBM AT).

Starting with the IBM AT, computers have the faster 16450 and 16550 UARTs. These chips use 16-bit buffers and transmit data at a maximum speed of 115,200bps. Any modem faster than 9600bps that will be connected to a PC for remote access requires the use of 16550 UARTs in the PC to get the maximum possible speed. Otherwise, connection speed will be limited to the fastest output speed of the 8250 UART, 9600bps.

Software Requirements

When configuring a workstation for remote access, in addition to configuring the hardware, you must configure the software to recognize the modem. In Windows 95/98, you do so using Device Manager (choose Start ➤ Settings ➤ Control Panel ➤ System to open the System Properties dialog box, and click the Device Manager tab). Additionally, you must configure the software to initiate and maintain the connection. This means configuring the dialer software (the client software that uses a local modem to dial the remote access server) and the network protocols that the communications will use, including TCP/IP (Transmission Control Protocol/Internet Protocol), IPX (Internet Packet eXchange), PPP (Point-to-Point Protocol), and PPTP (Point-to-Point Tunneling Protocol). Even if the hardware is configured properly, the software may not initiate a connection.

You can configure remote access from Windows 95/98/NT workstations using the built-in Dial-Up Networking software.

Remote Access Connection Methods

Because a computer using remote access is not connected to your network, it will not use LAN technologies to connect to the network. The remote computer will instead use connection methods to connect to the LAN, including:

- Public Switched Telephone Network (PSTN, also called Plain Old Telephone Services, or POTS)

- Integrated Services Digital Network (ISDN)

- Other digital connection methods (including one of the Digital Subscriber Lines [DSLs] and T-series connections)

The Public Switched Telephone Network

Almost everyone outside the phone companies refer to PSTN as POTS. This is the wiring system that runs from your house to the rest of the world. It is the most popular method for connecting a remote user to a local network because of its low cost, ease of installation, and simplicity.

Even the employees of most phone companies refer to PSTN as POTS when discussing work inside the phone company. The only time the acronym PSTN is used is when making a technical presentation or when the phone company marketing department is making a public statement.

Attributes of the Public Switched Telephone Network

Two key concepts when discussing PSTN are *public* and *switched*. Public, of course, is the opposite of private and means that for a fee, anyone can lease the use of the network, without the need to run cabling. The term switched explains how the phone system works. Although one or more wires are connected to your home and/or office, they are not always in use. In effect, your wiring and equipment is *offline*, or not part of the network. Yet, in this offline state, you have a standing reservation so that you can join at almost any time. Your identification for this reservation is your phone number, which is what makes the phone companies a viable communications network. You initiate a connection by dialing a phone number. Can you see how it would be technically impractical if every phone number were connected all the time? The cabling issues would be almost impossible.

Let's take an example from the U.S. telephone system. The actual numbering sequence varies in other countries, though the concept is identical. The phone company runs a UTP (unshielded twisted-pair) cable (called the *local loop)* from your location (called the *demarcation point* or *demarc,* for short) to a phone company building called the *Central Office.* All the pairs from all the local loop cables that are distributed throughout a small regional area come together at a central point, similar to a patch panel in a UTP-based LAN.

This centralized point has a piece of equipment called a switch attached. This switch functions almost exactly like the switches we mentioned in Chapter 2, in that a communications session, once initiated by dialing the phone number of the receiver, exists until the conversation is closed. The switch can then close the connection. On one side of the switch is the neighborhood wiring. On the other side are lines that may connect to another switch or to a local set of wiring. The number of lines on the other side of the switch depends on the usage of that particular exchange. Figure 7.1 shows a PSTN system that utilizes these components.

When you want to make a call, you pick up the phone. This completes a circuit, which in most cases gives you a dial tone. The tone is the switch's way of saying, "I'm ready to accept your commands." Failure to get a dial tone indicates either a break in the equipment chain or that the switch is too busy at the moment processing other commands. In many areas of the world, you may hear a fast on and off tone after giving a command string (phone number) to the local switch. This means that other switches with which the local switch is attempting to communicate are too busy right now. Recently, this has been replaced with a localized voice, which typically says, "We're sorry. All circuits are busy. Hang up and try your call later." This happens frequently on holidays or during natural disasters. The phone company in a local area uses only a few wires (called *trunk lines*) for normal capacity and some auxiliary lines for unexpected usage. This is because wiring and switches are very expensive. It is a tradeoff between 100 percent uptime and keeping the costs of leasing the connection from the phone company affordable.

FIGURE 7.1 A local PSTN (POTS) network

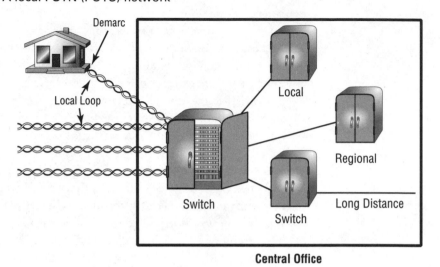

 Use caution when working with bare phone wires as they may carry a current. In POTS, the phone company uses a battery to supply power to the line, which is sometimes referred to as *self-powered*. It isn't truly self-powered, as the power comes from the phone system.

POTS has many advantages, including:

- It is inexpensive to set up. Almost every home in the United States has or can have a telephone connection.

- There are no LAN cabling costs.

- Connections are available in many countries throughout the world.

POTS is the most popular remote access connection method because only one primary disadva ntage is associated with it: limited bandwidth and thus a limited maximum data transfer rate. At most, 64Kbps data transmissions are possible, though rarely achieved by the traveling user connecting remotely to the corporate network.

Integrated Services Digital Network (ISDN)

ISDN is a digital, point-to-point network capable of maximum transmission speeds of about 2Mbps, although speeds of 128Kbps are more common. Because it is capable of much higher data rates, at a fairly low cost, ISDN is becoming a viable remote user connection method, especially for those who work out of their homes. ISDN uses the same UTP wiring as POTS, but can transmit data at much higher speeds. But that's where the similarity ends. What makes ISDN different from a regular POTS line is how it uses the copper wiring. Instead of carrying an analog (voice) signal, it carries digital signals. This is the source of several differences.

A computer connects to an ISDN line via an ISDN terminal adapter (often incorrectly referred to as an ISDN modem). An ISDN terminal adapter is not a modem because it does not convert a digital signal to an analog signal; ISDN signals are digital.

An ISDN line has two types of channels. The data is carried on special *Bearer*, or *B*, channels, each of which can carry 64Kbps of data. A typical ISDN line has two B channels. One channel can be used for a voice call while the other is being used for data transmissions, and this occurs on one pair of copper wires. The second type of channel is used for call setup and link management and is known as the *signal*, or *D*, channel (also referred to as the *Delta* channel). This channel has only 16Kbps of bandwidth.

In many cases, to maximize throughput, the two Bearer channels are combined into one data connection for a total bandwidth of 128Kbps. This is known as *bonding* or *inverse multiplexing*. This still leaves the Delta channel free for signaling purposes. In rare cases, you may see user data, such as e-mail, on the D line. This was introduced as an additional feature of ISDN, but it hasn't caught on.

The main advantages of ISDN are:

- Fast connection.

- Higher bandwidth than POTS. Bonding yields 128Kb bandwidth.

- No conversion from digital to analog.

However, ISDN does have a few disadvantages:

- It's more expensive than POTS.

- Specialized equipment is required at the phone company and at the remote computer.

- Not all ISDN equipment can connect to every other type of equipment.

- ISDN is a type of dial-up connection and therefore the connection must be initiated.

Other Digital Options

Digital connections provide one main benefit to remote access users: increased bandwidth over older technologies. The digital nature of ISDN and other digital connection types makes them excellent choices for remote access connections. Some of the more important types are:

- xDSL
- Frame relay
- T-series

 These options are here for clarification only. They are not tested on the exam. You will see them in the field as a network professional, however.

xDSL Technology

xDSL is a general category of copper access technologies that is becoming popular because it uses regular, POTS phone wires to transmit digital signals, and is extremely inexpensive compared with the other digital communications methods. xDSL implementations cost hundreds instead of the thousands of dollars that you would pay for a dedicated, digital point-to-point link (such as a T1). They include Digital Subscriber Line (DSL), High Data-Rate Digital Subscriber Line (HDSL), Single Line Digital Subscriber Line (SDSL), Very High Data-Rate Digital Subscriber Line (VDSL), and Asymmetric Digital Subscriber Line (ADSL), which is currently the most popular. It is beyond the scope of this book to cover all the DSL types.

ADSL is winning the race because it focuses on providing reasonably fast upstream transmission speeds (up to 640Kbps) and very fast downstream transmission speeds (up to 9Mbps). This makes downloading graphics, audio, video, or data files from any remote computer very fast. The majority of Web traffic, for example, is downstream. The best part is that ADSL works on a single phone line without losing voice call capability. This is accomplished with what is called a *splitter*, which enables the use of multiple frequencies on the POTS line.

As with ISDN, communicating via xDSL requires an interface to the PC. All xDSL configurations require a modem, called an *endpoint*, and a NIC. Often the modem and NIC are on a single expansion card.

Frame Relay Technology

Frame relay is a WAN technology in which variable-length packets are transmitted by switching. Packet switching involves breaking messages into chunks at the sending router. Each packet can be sent over any number of routes on its way to its destination. The packets are then reassembled in the correct order at the receiver. Since the exact path is unknown, a cloud is used when creating a diagram to illustrate how data travels throughout the service. Figure 7.2 shows a frame relay WAN connecting smaller LANs.

FIGURE 7.2 A typical frame relay configuration

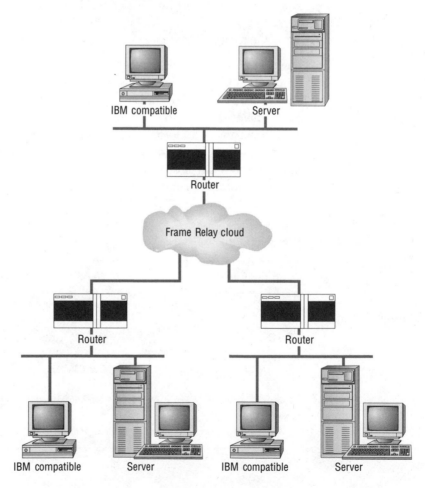

Frame relay uses permanent virtual circuits (PVCs). PVCs allow virtual data communications circuits between sender and receiver over a packet-switched network. This ensures that all data that enters a frame relay cloud at one side comes out at the other over a similar connection.

The beauty of using a shared network is that sometimes you can get much better throughput than you are paying for. When signing up for one of these connections, you specify and pay for a Committed Information Rate (CIR) or, in other words, a minimum bandwidth. If the total traffic on the shared network is light, you may get much faster throughput, without paying for it. Frame relay begins at this CIR speed and can reach as much as 1.544Mbps, the equivalent of a T1 line, which we'll discuss next.

T-Series Connections

The T-series connections are digital connections that you can lease from the telephone company. They can use regular copper pairs like regular phone lines, or they can be brought in as part of a backbone (also called a trunk line). At this point, T-series connections use time-division multiplexing (TDM) to divide the bandwidth into 24 channels plus a control line.

The T-series connection types are rated by the letter T plus a number. Each connection type differs primarily in its speed. Table 7.2 lists some of the T-series connections and their maximum data rates. The most commonly used T-series lines are T-1 and T-3.

TABLE 7.2 T-series Connections

Connection	Maximum Speed
T-1	1.544Mbps
T-1C	3.152Mbps
T-2	6.312Mbps
T-3	44.736Mbps
T-4	274.176Mbps

The T-1 Connection

A T-1 is a 1.544Mbps digital connection that is typically carried over two pair of UTP wires. This 1.544Mbps connection is divided into 24 discrete, 64Kbps channels (called DS0 channels). Each channel can carry either voice or data. In the POTS world, T-1 lines are used to bundle analog phone conversations over great distances, using much less wiring that would be needed if each pair carried only one call. This splitting into channels allows a company to combine voice and data over one T-1 connection. You can also order a fractional T-1 channel that uses fewer than the 24 channels of a full T-1.

The T-3 Connection

A T-3 line works similarly to a T-1 connection, but carries a whopping 44.736Mbps. This is equivalent to 28 T-1 channels (or a total of 672 DS0 channels). Currently this service requires fiber-optic cable or microwave technology. Many local ISPs have T-3 connections to the major ISPs, including SprintNet, AT&T, and MCI. Also, very large, multinational companies use T-3 connections to send voice and data between their major regional offices.

Remote Access Protocols

A *remote access protocol* manages the connection between a remote computer and a remote access server. Three primary remote access protocols are in use today:

- Serial Line Internet Protocol (SLIP)
- Point-to-Point Protocol (PPP)
- Point-to-Point Tunneling Protocol (PPTP)

Serial Line Internet Protocol (SLIP)

In 1984, students at the University of California at Berkeley developed SLIP for Unix as a way to transmit TCP/IP over serial connections (such as modem connections over POTS). SLIP operates at both the Physical and Data Link layers of the OSI model. Today, SLIP is found in many network operating systems in addition to Unix. It is being used less frequently with each passing year, though, because it lacks features when compared with other protocols. Although a low overhead is associated with using SLIP and you can use it to transport TCP/IP over serial connections, it does no error checking or packet addressing and can only be used on serial connections. SLIP is used today primarily to connect a workstation to the Internet or to another network running TCP/IP.

SLIP does not support encrypted passwords and therefore transmits passwords in clear text, which is not secure at all.

Setting up SLIP for a remote connection requires a SLIP account on the host machine and usually a batch file or a script on the workstation. When using SLIP to log in to a remote machine, a terminal mode must be configured after login to the remote site so that the script can enter each parameter. If you don't use a script, you will have to establish the connection and then open a terminal window to log in to the remote access server manually.

It is difficult to create a batch file that correctly configures SLIP. Our advice is to avoid SLIP when possible.

Point-to-Point Protocol (PPP)

PPP is used to implement TCP/IP over point-to-point connections (for example, serial and parallel connections). It is most commonly used for remote connections to ISPs and LANs.

PPP uses the Link Control Protocol (LCP) to communicate between PPP client and host. LCP tests the link between client and PPP host and specifies PPP client configuration. PPP can support several network protocols, and because it features error checking and can run over many types of physical media, PPP has almost completely replaced SLIP. In addition, PPP can automatically configure TCP/IP and other protocol parameters. On the down side, high overhead is associated with using PPP, and it is not compatible with some older configurations.

From the technician's standpoint, PPP is easy to configure. Once you connect to a router using PPP, the router assigns all other TCP/IP parameters. This is typically done with the DHCP (Dynamic Host Configuration Protocol) protocol. DHCP is the protocol within the TCP/IP protocol stack that is used to assign TCP/IP addressing information, including host IP address, subnet mask, and DNS (Domain Naming System) configuration. This information can be assigned over a LAN connection or a dial-up connection. When you connect to an ISP, you are most likely getting your IP address from a DHCP server.

To configure a client with Windows 95/98 to dial up a remote access server and connect using PPP, follow these steps:

1. Choose Start ➢ Programs ➢ Accessories ➢ Communications ➢ Dial-up Networking to open the Dial-up Networking dialog box.

2. Double-click Make New Connection.

3. Type the name of the system you will be dialing in to in the *Type a name for the computer you are dialing* field. This field defaults to My Connection. Select the modem installed in your computer that you want to use for this connection from the Select a Device drop-down list.

4. Click Next. Enter the area code and phone numbers, and click Next.

5. The last screen informs you that you have successfully created the connection. Click Finish to return to the Dial-up Networking dialog box.

6. Right-click the connection you just made, and choose Properties from the shortcut menu.

7. Click the Server Types tab, and from the Type of Dial-Up Server drop-down list, choose PPP: Windows 95, Windows NT 3.5, Internet.

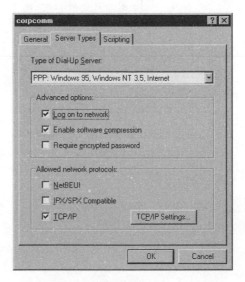

8. Clear the options you won't be using to connect to the server. For PPP connections, you can usually clear Logon to Network, IPX/SPX Compatible, and NetBEUI.

9. Click OK to save the settings.

You can now double-click the connection you made, enter your username and password, and click Connect to establish the connection.

Point-to-Point Tunneling Protocol (PPTP)

PPTP is the Microsoft-created sibling to PPP. It is used to create virtual connections across the Internet using TCP/IP and PPP so that two networks can use the Internet as their WAN link, yet retain private network security. PPTP is both simple and secure.

To use PPTP, you set up a PPP session between the client and server, typically over the Internet. Once the session is established, you create a second dial-up session that dials through the existing PPP session, using PPTP. The PPTP session tunnels through the existing PPP connection, creating a secure session. In this way, you can use the Internet to create a secure session between the client and the server. Also called a Virtual Private Network, this type of connection is very inexpensive when compared with a direct connection.

PPTP is a good idea for network administrators who want to connect several LANs, but don't want to pay for dedicated leased lines. But, as with any network technology, there can be disadvantages, including:

- PPTP is not available on all types of servers.

- PPTP is not a fully accepted standard.

- PPTP is more difficult to set up than PPP.

- Tunneling can reduce throughput.

You can implement PPTP in two ways. First, you can set up a server to act as the gateway to the Internet and the one that does all the tunneling. The workstations will run normally without any additional configuration. You would normally use this method to connect entire networks. Figure 7.3 shows two networks connected using PPTP. Notice how the TCP/IP packets are tunneled through an intermediate TCP/IP network (in this case, the Internet).

FIGURE 7.3 A PPTP implementation connecting two LANs over the Internet

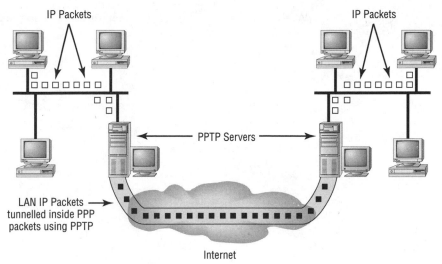

The second way to use PPTP is to configure a single, remote workstation to connect to a corporate network over the Internet. The workstation is configured to connect to the Internet via an ISP, and the VPN client is configured with the address of the VPN remote access server as shown in Figure 7.4. PPTP is often used to connect remote workstations to corporate LANs when a workstation must communicate with a corporate network over a dial-up PPP link through an ISP and the link must be secure.

FIGURE 7.4 A workstation is connected to a corporate LAN over the Internet using PPTP

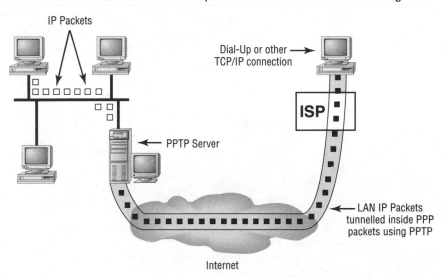

Windows 98 and Windows NT 4 include PPTP. You must add it to Windows 95.

Key Terms

Before you take the exam, be certain you are familiar with the following terms:

B (bearer) channel

bonding

Central Office

D (Delta) channel

demarc

demarcation point

endpoint

internal modems

inverse multiplexing

local loop

modem

offline

public

remote access protocol

self-powered

signal

splitter

switched

trunk lines

virtual COM

Review Questions

1. As part of your daily duties, you are configuring a workstation to connect to your ISP. Already installed are a Web browser, client-side FTP, and a dial-up networking connection by using SLIP. A remote DHCP server will assign an IP address automatically. When you dial and connect, you are unable to browse the Internet. Upon further investigation, you find you also cannot retrieve files from an FTP site. The results that you want require that you are able to browse the Internet and access FTP files. You, therefore, configure the TCP/IP client so that IP addresses are assigned by a DHCP server. This solution achieves which of the following?

   A. Both required results

   B. Only one of the required results

   C. None of the required results

2. As part of your daily duties, you are configuring a workstation to connect to your ISP. Already installed are a Web browser, client-side FTP, and a dial-up networking connection by using SLIP. A remote DHCP server will assign an IP address automatically. When you dial and connect, you are unable to browse the Internet. Upon further investigation, you find you also cannot retrieve files from an FTP site. The results that you want require that you can browse the Internet and access FTP files. Therefore, you change the dial-up connection protocol to PPP. This solution achieves which of the following?

   A. Both required results

   B. Only one of the required results

   C. None of the required results

3. Your CEO read in a popular magazine that it is possible to reduce remote access connection costs by using the Internet as a WAN. You already have a connection from the head office to the Internet. He is requiring that you provide a connection from the remote office to headquarters over the Internet. Optionally, he requires both a dial-up connection to the Internet and a secure connection over the Internet for Road Warriors. The proposed solution is to install PPTP over a dial-up connection from the remote office to the local ISP. This solution achieves which of the following?

   A. The required result only

   B. The required and one of the optional results

   C. The required and both of the optional results

   D. Does not meet the required result

4. Which transport protocol does PPTP use?

   A. IPX/SPX

   B. SNA

   C. AppleTalk

   D. TCP/IP

5. Which of the following is an advantage of PSTN (POTS)?

   A. Readily available

   B. Greater than 64Kbps data rates

   C. Fault tolerant

   D. Not available in all markets

6. Which of the following is an advantage of ISDN?

   A. Readily available

   B. Easy to configure

   C. Least expensive implementation

   D. Greater than 64Kbps possible

7. Which WAN technology uses digital signaling from sender to receiver?

   A. X.25

   B. POTS

   C. X2

   D. Kflex

   E. T-series

8. The UART in your PC is an 8250. You have installed an external ISDN terminal adapter on your computer. You are not getting the full speed of an ISDN line. You must replace the UART with which chip set?

   A. 8550

   B. 11500

   C. 12550

   D. 16550

9. You require which of the following components for a remote, asynchronous connection?

   A. Keyboard

   B. Modem

   C. Mouse

   D. Monitor

10. What must be set on an Internal modem to use it in a PC?

    A. COM port

    B. I/O address

    C. DMA Channel

    D. IRQ

11. You bought a Windows 98 computer by mail order. You can see that the modem is installed because you have plugged a phone line into the RJ-11 modem jack. Everything else has worked from the first time you plugged in the modem, but the modem fails to respond. What should you check next?

    A. Device Manager

    B. Explorer

    C. The vendor's Web site

    D. The Start menu

12. You have a server with two external modems. The modems work one at a time but not together. COM1 is set to IRQ 4, I/O 3F8h. COM 2 is configured for IRQ 3, I/O 3F8h. What should you do to ensure that both modems work simultaneously?

    A. Change the IRQ of modem 1

    B. Change the I/O address of COM 2

    C. Change the IRQ of modem 2

    D. Change the COM port of modem 2

13. Which of the following protocols works at both the Physical and Data Link layers of the OSI?

    A. SLIP

    B. PPP

    C. TCP/IP

14. You are setting up a remote workstation for remote access to the office. The office has a modem pool configured, and it is working correctly. The required results are that the remote workstation and modem bank must establish a connection and that the server at the office must authenticate the workstation. Optionally, the workstation and office must be able to communicate by using a single protocol, and the workstation must be able to access all network devices at the office. The proposed solution is to install a POTS telephone line, modem cable, and modem at the workstation.

NetBEUI is installed and configured on the workstation. TCP/IP and IPX are installed and configured on the office server. You configure the software settings on the modem. You dial into your headquarters. The appropriate modem lights turn on, and you hear a connection tone from the speaker of the workstation modem. The office network is set up to allow the entire network to be accessed via a dial-in connection. The proposed solution meets which of the following?

A. The required results.

B. The required results and one of the optional results.

C. The required results and both of the optional results.

D. Neither the required nor the optional results.

15. You are setting up a workstation for remote access to the office. The office has a modem pool configured, and it is working correctly. The required results are that the workstation and modem bank must establish a connection and that the server at the office must authenticate the workstation. Optionally, the workstation and office must be able to communicate by using a single protocol, and the workstation must be able to access all network devices at the office. The proposed solution is to install a POTS telephone line, modem cable, and modem connected to the workstation. TCP/IP is installed and configured on the workstation. TCP/IP with DHCP, as well as IPX, are installed and configured on the office server. You configure the software settings on the modem. You dial into your headquarters. The appropriate modem lights turn on, and you hear a connection tone from the speaker of the workstation modem. The office network is set up to allow the entire network to be viewed via dial-in. The proposed solution achieves which of the following?

A. The required results.

B. The required results and one of the optional results.

C. The required results and both of the optional results.

D. Does not meet the required results.

16. You are setting up a workstation for remote access to the office. The office has a modem pool configured, and it is working correctly. The required results are that the workstation and modem bank must establish a connection and that the server at the office must authenticate the workstation. Optionally, the workstation and office must be able to communicate by using a single protocol, and the workstation must be able to access all network devices at the office. The proposed solution is to install a POTS telephone line, modem cable, and modem connected to the workstation. TCP/IP is installed and configured to have a DHCP server automatically assign an IP address. TCP/IP and IP routing are installed and configured on the office server. You configure the software settings on the modem. You dial into your headquarters. The appropriate modem lights turn on, and you hear a connection tone from the speaker of the workstation modem. The office network is set up to allow the entire network to be viewed via dial-in. The proposed solution achieves which of the following?

    A. The required results

    B. The required results and one of the optional results

    C. The required results and both of the optional results

    D. Does not meet the required results

17. You want to order analog ISDN. You call around and can't seem to find the equipment you want. What could be the possible reason for this?

    A. Everyone is out of stock because of unexpected customer demand.

    B. ISDN equipment is only available in PC card format.

    C. You must order this with external termination.

    D. You can't order analog ISDN.

18. Which remote access protocol can run over both serial and parallel connections?

    A. PPP

    B. SLIP

19. _____ is the Microsoft TCP/IP protocol that can be used over the Internet to create a secure, virtual network.

A. SLIP

B. PPTP

C. TCP

D. HTTP

20. What is the standard I/O port of COM3?

A. 2E8

B. 2F8

C. 3E8

D. 3F8

Answers to Review Questions

1. C. Because SLIP does not support DHCP, you won't be able to receive an IP address over the dial-up connection. In order to resolve this situation, you must configure PPP as your dial up protocol and configure that station to use DHCP to get its IP address.

2. A. As discussed in the last question, because PPP supports DHCP and SLIP does not, by configuring the workstation to use PPP instead of SLIP, you can achieve both required results.

3. A. By using PPTP only to the ISP, you are just providing a secure connection between your company and the ISP. Because the required result is to establish an Internet connection from the remote office to HQ, you've done that by connecting your remote network to the Internet. To provide a secure connection between HQ and the remote office (the optional result), you would have to install PPTP on the connection between HQ and HQ's ISP.

4. D. The point-to-point tunneling protocol uses TCP/IP as a transport.

5. A. The major advantage to the Public Switched Telephone Network (Plain Old Telephone System) is that it is readily available in almost every part of the world.

6. D. Of the advantages listed, the one most often associated with ISDN is the higher bandwidth available.

7. E. The T-series of WAN connection (such as T1, T3, and so on) uses digital signaling completely from sending hardware to receiving hardware.

8. D. For the serial buffers to keep up with the high bandwidth of ISDN connections, you must have a 16-bit UART on the serial port that the Terminal Adapter is connected to. The only fully 16-bit UART listed is the 16550.

9. B. Although with a computer, some of these items (keyboard, mouse, monitor) are required for browsing the Web, the only one absolutely required for a remote, asynchronous connection is a modem.

10. A, B, D. When you install an internal modem into a PC, the COM port, I/O address, and IRQ must be set. This is done either manually in the case of most ISA cards, or automatic in the case of PCI.

11. A. The device manager is the built-in utility for Windows 98 that shows whether or not a particular device is installed correctly.

12. B. The I/O addresses of both modems are conflicting as they are both set to the same I/O address. If you change the I/O address of COM2, both modems will work at the same time.

13. A. The SLIP protocol specifies both a Data Link portion and a Physical portion. The Physical portion specifies that the protocol will only work over a serial link (the first two letters in SLIP).

14. D. The workstation is only running NetBEUI, the servers running TCP/IP and IPX. Because the workstation and server are running separate protocols, they can't communicate. Thus, neither the required nor the optional results can be achieved since both fundamentally have to do with the workstation and server communicating.

15. C. This question is similar to question #14; however, in this case, the protocols match. Because the server and workstation are both running the same protocol (TCP/IP), and there is a connection between them, they can both communicate.

16. C. In exactly the same situation as question #15, both workstation and server are running the same protocol and the server has IP routing installed. Thus, the workstation can communicate with the server over the POTS line. And because routing is installed, the workstation can communicate with the entire network.

17. D. ISDN is a digital services network. There is no such thing as analog ISDN.

18. A. Because PPP doesn't contain a physical layer specification as part of the protocol, it can run over any kind of medium.

19. B. The point-to-point tunneling protocol (PPTP) allows you to create a secure, virtual connection between two points by tunneling one protocol inside another. Usually, a PPP connection is opened over a TCP/IP link.

20. C. Every COM port is assigned a default I/O port. The default I/O port of COM3 is 3E8.

Chapter

8

Network Access and Security

✓ **Identify good practices to ensure network security, including:**

- Selection of a security model (user and share level)
- Standard password practices and procedures
- The need to employ data encryption to protect network data
- The use of a firewall

here are two prerequisites that you should keep in mind when you access a resource on the network: network access and the proper security clearance. These items work together to allow you access to a particular resource.

The first topic of these two is *network access*. Network access involves installing *client software* on your computer. This software gives your computer the instructions that it needs to be able to access the network.

Network security involves ensuring that only authorized users have access to the network and that they access it only in authorized ways. You want to ensure that hardware, software, and data are available to authorized users when they are needed, but you also want to ensure that hardware, software, and data are not compromised or threatened. In addition to providing network access, client software works with the network operating system to provide network security.

As a network administrator, you can create an effective security plan in a number of ways and by using a variety of tools and procedures. Some of these are practical, common sense safeguards, and others involve implementing protective systems and technologies. Although numerous recent examples indicate that almost no network is completely immune to security breaches, taking advantage of the measures we'll look at in this chapter gives you a head start.

We'll start by discussing the different types of clients and how they are installed. You'll then learn some of the simplest of security measures, usernames, and passwords, and give you some good and bad examples. We'll move on to the more complex ways to secure your network—firewalls and proxies. Finally, we'll discuss some threats that may exist for your network. The Network+ exam covers all these topics.

One aspect we don't discuss in this chapter is physical security, which the Network+ exam doesn't include. But remember: If someone can walk in and take your server or backup tapes, you don't have much security at all. In the real world, you'll want to ensure that all appropriate and necessary physical mechanisms are in place to protect your network.

Accessing Network Resources

Generally speaking, computers don't know how to access the various resources on your network. Each workstation OS (such as DOS and Window 95/98, for example) knows how to access only its own local resources (such as local printers and local disk storage). For this reason, network operating systems use various methods to enable workstations to access network resources.

Windows 95/98 computers can use both the various built-in software clients and third-party client software to achieve network connectivity. As a network administrator, you need to tailor the connection software to your network. This is known as *proper client selection*. Once the client and the server are communicating, the PC can connect to network directories. Drive mappings allow reproducible connections from the local workstation to a network drive. Additionally, local print jobs on the PC are redirected instead of being sent out a physical LPT port. The job is then sent to a network printer. This is achieved through printer port captures. Let's look at each of these in detail.

Client Selection

A workstation communicates with the server over a certain protocol using client software. The protocol might be IPX/SPX (Internet Packet eXchange/Sequenced Packet eXchange), TCP/IP (Transmission Control Protocol/Internet Protocol), or NetBEUI. Protocols are separate from the client software, but in some instances, the installation of protocols is integrated into the installation of client software. In Windows 95/98, installed protocols and clients are listed together. To display a listing of the protocol(s) and client(s) currently installed, follow these steps:

1. Choose Start ≻ Settings ≻ Control Panel to open the Control Panel.

2. Double-click Network to open the Network dialog box.

Installed clients are listed in the Configuration tab, at the top of the list above installed protocols and network adapters.

Installing the Windows 95/98 and NT Client

Not surprisingly, Windows 95/98 comes with a client to connect to Microsoft servers and PCs. The Client for Microsoft Networks is the preferred client to access Microsoft networks. You also need this client to run the server tools for Windows NT on a Windows 95/98 computer to be able to perform domain administrative tasks.

Additionally, the network administrator will also have to authenticate (provide username and password at a login screen) again when using the server tools versions of administrative utilities on a Windows 95/98 machine. Therefore, the best combination for a network administrator's desktop machine is Windows NT Workstation or Server with the Client for Microsoft Networks.

Follow these steps to install the Microsoft Client for Networks on a Windows 95/98 computer:

1. Be sure that your network interface card is installed properly and configured. The operating system must already recognize the card. Locate your Windows 95/98 CD and have it ready.

2. Connect your network cable, and ensure that the link light on the NIC (network interface card) is on.

3. Make sure you are at the Windows 95/98 desktop.

4. Choose Start ≻ Settings ≻ Control Panel to open Control Panel.

5. Double-click Network to open the Network dialog box.

6. Click Add to open the Select Network Component Type dialog box.

7. Click the Client icon in the list, and then click Add to open the Select Network Client dialog box.

   8. In the Manufacturers box, click Microsoft.

   9. In the Network Clients box, click Client for Microsoft Networks, and then click OK.

   10. Click OK in the Network dialog box.

   11. Place the Windows 95/98 CD in the drive if prompted to do so. Locate the install CAB files, and click OK if prompted. The Copying Windows Files screen opens and then closes.

   12. In the System Settings Change dialog box, click Yes. The system will now reboot.

Installing the NetWare Client

You have two options for setting up user workstations to connect to a NetWare network:

- Novell NetWare Client
- Microsoft Client for NetWare Networks

The one you select depends on your network and users. If you have a predominantly Windows NT network, the Microsoft client might better fit your needs. If you have a NetWare network or a hybrid network with a substantial Novell base, you need to use the Novell client; the latest version is available from Novell. Stay away from the clients distributed with Microsoft Windows 95/98 and NT.

You can find the Novell Client for NetWare on the following:

- Novell's Web site at `www.novell.com`
- NetWare Client CD as part of the NetWare installation CD set or floppies (only with older versions)
- The Z.E.N.works CD
- The SYS volume of a NetWare server

What happens when you lose connectivity with your NetWare server and you need to install client software? If you are using IPX/SPX without a Web proxy server, downloading the software from the Novell Web site is out. Many companies place software media under lock and key, and require support staff to install from the network. If that is the case with your company, that cuts out installing from CDs and floppies. The SYS volume is useless if you can't access the server. To avoid these problems, place a copy of the client installation software on your local PC the first time you connect to a NetWare server.

Regardless of the vendor you choose, a good practice is to download the installation files for your operating system (CABs for Windows 95/98, i386 directory for NT), client software, video drivers, and NIC drivers as soon as you connect to a server.

Don't forget about yourself. The best combination for the network administrator's computer is a Windows 95/98 or NT operating system with the Novell NetWare Client. Novell's NDS takes care of authentication, thus addressing network security. Use Windows NT if you want additional security on your local machine. As an administrator, you have no choice about the client. Without Novell's client you will not get the full functionality of the NetWare Administrator utility, and besides, Novell's client is free.

To install the Novell Client for NetWare on a Windows 95/98 computer, follow these steps:

1. Download the latest Novell Client for NetWare from the Novell Web site, and run the self-extracting file. Or insert your NetWare Client CD.

2. Double-click the setup.exe file. (This is true for the non-Z.E.N.works version of the client software.) The Novell client license agreement window opens.

3. Read the license agreement, and then click Yes to accept the agreement and to open the Welcome dialog box.

4. In the Select an Installation Option section, click Typical.

5. Click Install to open the Building Driver Information Database and Copying Files windows.

6. You'll be asked if you want to set the preferred server proper for NetWare 3.x servers or the preferred tree, context, and server properties for NetWare 4.x and later servers. If you click Yes, you will have an opportunity to set these properties in the Novell NetWare Client Properties dialog box. Click OK when you finish entering the information, and the installation continues. If you click No, the installation continues.

On Windows 95/98 computers, some files need to be copied from the Windows 95/98 CABs. If these are not in the `Windows\Options\Cabs` directory, you will be prompted to insert the Windows 95/98 installation CD.

7. When the installation is finished and you are prompted to restart the computer, click Reboot.

Be sure that your IPX/SPX or TCP/IP protocol stacks are properly configured. See Chapter 4 for details.

Installing the Unix Client

Windows 95/98 needs the client portion of the Network File System (NFS) to connect to the Unix Network File Systems. If a computer has this client installed, NFS Client or a similar wording will appear in the listing in the Network dialog box.

Windows 95/98 computers without an NFS client can connect directly to a Unix system that is running Samba. Samba is a free server-based solution that uses Server Message Blocks (SMBs) to allow Microsoft clients to see the Unix file system. Samba is available from `ftp://samba.anu.edu.au/pub/samba/`. Samba is designed for Unix servers and will not install on a Windows 95/98 PC.

The client portion of NFS is currently available only from third-party vendors. No NFS client is distributed with Windows 95/98 or NT. (Microsoft may incorporate one into Windows 2000.) Two popular NFS client vendors are Sun and NetManage. Sun Microsystems offers server and client products for Unix server to PC connectivity. Its client-based product is Solstice NFS Client. NetManage offers several products, including Chameleon Unix Link. Select the vendor and product based on your individual needs and budget and after evaluating the demo software. Since third-party options tend to be more popular than their primary vendor counterparts, we're going to demonstrate the installation of NetManage's Chameleon.

You can get a demo of Chameleon from the NetManage Web site at www .netmanage.com/. This is a demo; after 30 days, the software ceases to function.

To install the NetManage Chameleon Unix Link on a Windows 95/98 PC, follow these steps:

1. Double-click setup.exe in the Cham_95\NFS directory. This directory is on your CD or in your download directory after extraction. The NetManage Setup and License Notice windows open.

2. Read the License Notice, and click Accept to open the Setup Option dialog box.

3. Click Typical, and then click Next to open the Serial Number dialog box.

4. Enter your serial number and key in their fields, and then click Next to open the Select Directory dialog box.

The serial number and key are typically included on a document that comes with the software. You can also obtain them from a Web site.

5. Verify the installation directory. By default it is C:\NETMANAG.95. If you want to install to a different directory, enter the path or browse to the directory. When you are finished, click Next. Files are installed when the Copy Files dialog box opens.

6. The Building Driver Information Database and Copying Files windows open. You may be prompted for your Windows 95/98 CD if the CAB files are not on your local hard drive.

7. The Information screen opens, telling you that it will now install support programs. Click OK to open the Choose Program Destination Location dialog box.

8. Click Next. The NetManage Setup window tells you that components are being installed.

9. In the Finish window, click Finish. The NetManage setup window opens, telling you that you must restart Windows for the changes to take effect.

10. Click Yes to restart Windows.

Selecting a Primary Client

Now you have connections to your NT, NetWare, and Unix servers. You now must determine which client will be the primary client on your Windows 95/98 machines. The first question you must ask yourself is: Which servers do your users most often access? For your CAD/CAM engineers, it may be Unix; for Web design, it could be either NT or NetWare. Each user will want their favorite servers to appear in the Network Neighborhood first. As an administrator, you will want to gain quick access to the network you spend the most time managing. The network administrator can set a primary type of client to speed access and searches.

To set a primary client on a Windows 95/98 PC, follow these steps:

1. Choose Start ➢ Settings ➢ Control Panel to open Control Panel.

2. Double-click Network to open the Network dialog box with the Configuration tab selected. Notice the Client for Microsoft Networks, the NetManage Unix Link NFS Client, and the Novell NetWare Client at the top of the dialog box.

3. Click the drop-down button to the right of the Primary Network Logon text field to display the drop-down list.

4. Scroll down through the options, and select the primary client of your choice. Your selection now appears in the Primary Network Logon text field.

5. Click OK to save the change. The System Settings Change dialog box opens, asking you to restart your computer.

6. Click Yes to restart your computer.

Managing User Account and Password Security

Usernames and passwords are key to network security, and you use them to control initial access to your system. Although the network administrator assigns usernames and passwords, users can generally change their passwords. Thus, you need to ensure that users have information about what constitutes a good password. In this section, we'll look at the security issues related to user accounts and passwords, including resource-sharing models and user account and password management.

Network Resource-Sharing Security Models

You can secure files that are shared over the network in two ways:

- At the share level
- At the user level

Although user-level security provides more control over files and is the preferred model, implementing share-level security is easier for the network administrator. Let's examine these two security models and their features.

Share-Level Security

In a network that uses share-level security, you assign passwords to individual files or other network resources (such as printers) instead of assigning rights to users. You then give these passwords to all users that need access to these resources. All resources are visible from anywhere in the network, and any user who knows the password for a particular network resource can make changes to it. With this type of security, the network support staff will have no way of knowing who is manipulating each resource. Share-level security is best used in smaller networks, where resources are more easily tracked.

Windows 95/98 and Windows NT support share-level security.

User-Level Security

In a network that uses user-level security, rights to network resources (such as files, directories, and printers) are assigned to specific users who gain access to the network through individually assigned usernames and passwords. Thus, only users who have a valid username and password and have been assigned the appropriate rights to network resources can see and access those resources. User-level security provides greater control over who is accessing which resources because users do not share their usernames and passwords with other users (or at least they shouldn't). Thus, user-level security is the preferred method for securing files.

Windows NT, NetWare, and Unix support user-level security.

Managing Accounts

First and foremost, you manage access to network resources through a user account and the rights given to that account. The network administrator is charged with the daily maintenance of these accounts. Common security duties include renaming accounts and setting the number of concurrent connections. You can also specify where users can log in, how often they can log in, at what times they can log in, how often their passwords expire, and when their accounts expire.

Disabling Accounts

When a user leaves the organization, you have three options:

- Leave the account in place.

- Delete the account.

- Disable the account.

If you leave the account in place, anyone (including the user to whom it belonged) can log in as that user if they know that user's password. Therefore, leaving the account in place is a security breach. Deleting the account presents its own set of problems. If you delete an account and then create a new one, the numeric ID associated with that user (UID in Unix, SID in Windows Server) is lost. It is through this number that passwords and rights to network resources are associated with the user account. If you create a new user account with the same name as the user account you deleted, the identification number of the new account will be different from that of the old account, and thus none of the settings of the old account will be in place for the new account.

This same concept holds true for NetWare, although NetWare does not use a number to uniquely identify each entity. Each NDS object (including users) is a unique object ID.

Your best practice is to disable an account until a decision has been made as to what should happen to the account. Perhaps you'll want to simply rename the account when a new person is hired. When you disable an account, it still exists, but no one can use it to log in. You might also disable an account (rather than deleting it) if someone leaves for an extended period (for example, on maternity/paternity leave or medical leave). In most network operating systems, disabling an account involves changing a setting that says something like Account Disabled.

Disabling Temporary Accounts

Because of the proliferation of contract and temporary employees in the information technology industry, you need to know how to manage temporary accounts. A temporary account is used for only a short period (less than a month or so) and then disabled.

Managing the accounts of temporary employees is easy. You can simply set the account to expire on the employee's anticipated last day of work. The NOS then disables, but does not delete, these accounts on the expiration date.

Setting Up Anonymous Accounts

Anonymous accounts provide extremely limited access for a large number of users who all log in with the same username, which is often Anonymous or Guest. An anonymous login is frequently used to access FTP files. You log in with the username Anonymous and enter your e-mail address as the password.

Users don't necessarily enter their correct e-mail address. If you really want to know where on the Internet the user is located, use third-party software to verify IP addresses and Internet domain names.

Avoid using anonymous accounts for regular network access. If someone is using an anonymous account, you cannot track who manipulated a file. Windows NT comes with the anonymous account Guest disabled. NetWare does not automatically create a guest account. Don't change these default setups.

Some Web servers create an Internet user account to allow anonymous access to the Web site. The Internet user account is automatically created and allowed to access the Web server over the network. The password is always blank. You never see a request to log in to the server. This is done automatically. Without this account, no one would be able to access your Web pages.

Do not rename the Internet user account or set a password. If you do so, the general public will not be able to view your Web site. If you want to secure documents, use another Web server, secure HTTP, Windows NT domain and file security, or NetWare Directory Services security.

Limiting Connections

You may want to limit the number of times a user can connect to the network. Users should normally be logged in to the network for only one instance, because they can only be in one place at a time. If the system indicates they are logged in from more than one place, someone else might be using their account. When you limit concurrent connections to one, only a single user at a single workstation can gain access to the network using a particular user account. Some users, however, might need to log in multiple times in order to use certain applications or perform certain functions. In that case, you can allow the user to have multiple concurrent connections.

Limiting the location from which a user logs in can be important also, because typical users shouldn't log in to the network from any place but their own workstation. Although in theory this is true, it is not often implemented in most corporations. Users move stations, often not taking their computers with them. Or they have to log in at someone else's station to perform some function. Unless you require really tight security, this restriction requires too much administrative effort. Both NetWare and Windows NT can limit which station(s) a user is allowed to log in from; however, by default, user accounts are not restricted in this respect. This is probably acceptable in most cases. If you really want to tighten security, restrict users to logging in from their assigned workstations. By default, Windows NT servers do not allow a regular user to log in at the console because most users should not be working directly on a server. They can do too much damage accidentally. In NetWare, the console interface is entirely different and is not used to access network resources, so this is not an issue.

Renaming the Maintenance Account

Network operating systems automatically give the network maintenance (or administration) account a default name. In Windows NT, this account is named Administrator; in Unix, it is root, and in NetWare, it is Admin. If you don't change this account name, hackers already have half the information they need to break in to your network. The only thing they're missing is the password.

Rename the account to something innocuous. For example, *jmorris* is a much better choice than *super*. Rename the account using the same naming convention that is used for regular users. Here is a list of common names that you should not use:

- Admin
- Administrator
- Analyst
- Audit
- Comptroller
- Controller
- Manager
- Root
- Super
- Superuser
- Supervisor

- Wizard

- Any variation on the above

Managing Passwords

Like any other aspect of network security, passwords must be managed. Managing passwords involves ensuring that all passwords for user accounts follow security guidelines so that they cannot be easily guessed or cracked, as well as implementing features of your network operating system to prevent unauthorized access.

What Makes a Strong Password?

Generally speaking, a strong password is a combination of alphanumeric and special characters that is easy for you to remember and difficult for someone else to guess. Unfortunately, many users try to make things easy on themselves and choose passwords that are easy to guess. Let's look at some characteristics of strong passwords.

Minimum Length

Strong passwords should be at least 8 characters, if not more. They shouldn't be any longer than 15 characters so that they are easy to remember. You need to specify a minimum length for passwords because a short password is easily cracked. For example, there are only so many combinations of three characters. The upper limit depends on the capabilities of your operating system and the ability of your users to remember complex passwords. Users will forget passwords that are too long, so you must balance ease of remembrance with the level of security you need to implement.

The Weak List

Here are some passwords that you should never use:

- The word *password*

- Proper names

- Your pet's name

- Your spouse's name

- Your children's names

- Any word in the dictionary
- A license plate number
- Birth dates
- Anniversary dates
- Your username
- The word server
- Any text or label on the PC or monitor
- Your company's name
- Your occupation
- Your favorite color
- Any of the above with a leading number
- Any of the above with a trailing number
- Any of the above backward

There are others, but these are the most commonly used weak passwords.

Strong Password Character Use

Difficult-to-crack passwords do not have to be difficult to remember and include a combination of numbers, letters, and special characters (not just letters, not just numbers, not just special characters, but a combination of all three). Special characters are those that cannot be considered letters or numbers (for example, $ % ^ # @). An example of a strong password is tqbf4#jotld. Such a password may look hard to remember, but it is not. The following sentence uses every letter in the English alphabet: The quick brown fox jumped over the lazy dog. Take the first letter of each word, put the number 4 and a pound (#) symbol in the middle, and you have a strong password.

To consistently get strong passwords, you can use auditing tools such as a crack program that tries to guess passwords. If you use strong passwords, the crack program should have great difficulty guessing a password.

Use special characters and numbers in the middle of the password, for example, under43gate@w#ay. Do not just use a regular word preceded or ended by a special character. Good crack programs strip off the leading and trailing characters in their decryption attempts.

Here are a few examples of strong passwords:

- run4!cover

- iron$steel4

- four$score

We'd include a few more, but we don't want to give away all our secrets!

Never write your password on a note and stick it under your keyboard or on your monitor. This is the most common network security breach.

NOS Password Management Features

All network operating systems (including NetWare, Unix, and Windows NT) include functions for managing passwords so that the system remains secure and that passwords cannot be easily hacked with crack programs.

Automatic Account Lockouts

Hackers (as well as users who forgot their password) attempt to log in by guessing the user's password. To ensure that a password can't be guessed by repeatedly inputting different passwords, most network operating systems have a feature that allows the account to be disabled, or locked out, after several unsuccessful login attempts. Once this feature is enabled, the user cannot log in with that account even if the correct password is entered. This feature prevents a potential hacker from running an automated script to continuously attempt logins using different character combinations for the password.

After a lock-out is activated, to log in successfully the user must ask the network support staff to unlock the account if the network operating system doesn't unlock it after a preset period. In high-security networks, it is usually advisable for an administrator to manually unlock every locked account (rather than letting the NOS do it automatically). In this way, the administrator is notified of a possible security breach.

Be careful not to lock yourself out. With many network operating systems, only administrators can reset passwords. If you are the administrator and you lock yourself out, only another administrator can unlock your account. If you are the only administrator, you have a problem. Many NOS vendors do have solutions to this problem, but the solution will cost you.

Password Expiration

Passwords, even the best ones, do not age well over time. Eventually someone will guess or crack a password if it never changes. The impact of someone guessing your password is reduced—even if a password is guessed—if passwords are set to expire after a certain amount of time. After this time (which varies and can be set by the administrator), the old password is considered invalid, and a new one must be specified. This new password is valid until it expires and another password must be specified.

Most organizations expire passwords every 30 days. After that, users must reset their password immediately or during the allotted grace period. Some systems give the user a few grace logins after the password has expired. Limit this grace period to a number of times or days.

Each network operating system specifies a password expiration period. If your organization's policy states that users must change their password every 30 days, check to see if your operating system is enforcing that. For example, in NetWare the default expiration date is every 40 days and might need to be changed.

Unique Passwords and Password Histories

In older versions of many network operating systems, users could reset their password to its original form after using an intermediary password for a while. More recent network operating systems prevent this practice by using password histories.

A *password history* is a record of the past several passwords used by the user. When the user attempts to use any password stored in the password history, the password fails. The operating system then requests a password change again. When implementing a password history policy, be sure to make the password history large enough to contain at least a year's worth of password changes. For a standard 30-day life span password, a history of 12 or 13 passwords will suffice.

Advanced users know about the history feature. Creating a good password takes some time. Once a user finds a password, the human tendency is to want to keep it and use it for everything, which is counter to good security policy. If a user really likes a particular password or does not want to remember a new one, he or she will try to find a way around password histories.

One user admitted changing her password as many times as it took to defeat the history log. She then changed the password one last time back to her original password. This can take less than five minutes of a user's time.

Administrators can force users to change their password so that it is unique. The latest operating systems (including NetWare 4.*x* and later, as well as Windows NT 4) require unique passwords. All passwords are stored, and depending on the NOS, more than 20 passwords can be stored. Reverting to any of the previous passwords is not allowed.

Using Firewalls

It is popular these days to connect a corporate network to the Internet. By connecting your *private network* (only authorized users have access to the data) to a *public network* (everyone connected has access to the data), you introduce the possibility for security break-ins. For this reason, firewalls are implemented. A *firewall* protects a private network from unauthorized users on a public network.

Firewalls are usually a combination of hardware and software. The hardware is typically a computer or a dedicated piece of hardware (often called a black box) that contains two network cards. One connects to the public side; the other, to the private side. The software controls how the firewall operates and protects your network. It examines each incoming and outgoing packet and rejects any suspicious packets. In general, firewalls work by allowing only packets that pass security restrictions to be forwarded through the firewall.

The Network+ certified system administrator usually does not have the resources to design, install, and manage a firewall. This section is to help you work in an environment where a firewall is already installed. You might also work as part of a team to install or upgrade your company's firewall solution. This section will give you the tools you need to understand the basic operation of a firewall.

Firewalls can be placed on top of an existing operating system or be self-contained. Black box systems are proprietary systems that have external controls and are not controlled by the operating system. If you want to use a general-purpose operating system, you have two options, Unix and Windows NT. Both can support third-party firewall products. Novell makes its own firewall product, BorderManager, which is excellent and runs on NetWare. But at the time of this writing, there are few third-party firewall products for NetWare.

All Windows NT firewalls should be installed on Windows NT Server computers rather than Windows NT Workstation computers.

Firewall Technologies

There are many firewall technologies, and they differ in the method they use to restrict information flow. Some, such as Access Control Lists and dynamic packet filtering, are themselves used as firewalls. Others, such as proxies and demilitarized zones, are implemented with other firewall technologies to make a more robust, complete implementation.

Access Control Lists (ACL)

The first form of defense for every network connected to the Internet is Access Control Lists (ACL). These lists reside on your routers and determine which machines (that is, which IP addresses) can use the router and in what direction. ACLs have been around for decades and have other uses, apart from a firewall. In Figure 8.1, these lists prevent people on Network B from accessing Network A.

FIGURE 8.1   Two networks with an ACL-enabled router

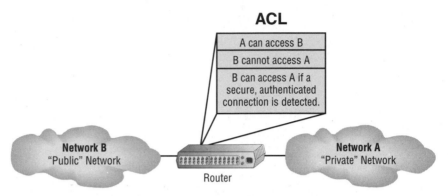

Note that data from users in Network A can pass through the router into Network B. IP spoofing attacks (in which someone, presumably a hacker, pretends to have a network address on the inside of a firewall to gain access to a network) can still occur if a user in Network B pretends to be located in Network A. (We'll discuss IP spoofing in a later section in this chapter.)

The Demilitarized Zone (DMZ)

Most firewalls in use today implement a feature called a DMZ, which is a network segment that is neither public nor local, but halfway between. People outside your network primarily access your Web servers, FTP servers, and mail-relay servers. Because hackers tend to go after these servers first, place them in the DMZ. A standard DMZ setup has three network cards in the firewall computer. The first goes to the Internet. The second goes to the network segment where the aforementioned servers are located, the DMZ. The third connects to your intranet.

When hackers break into the DMZ, they can see only public information. If they break into a server, they are breaking into a server that holds only public information. Thus, the entire corporate network is not compromised. Last, no e-mail messages are vulnerable; only the relay server can be accessed. All actual messages are stored and viewed on e-mail servers inside the network. As you can see in Figure 8.2, the e-mail router, the FTP server, and the Web server are all in the DMZ, and all critical servers are inside the firewall.

FIGURE 8.2   A firewall with a DMZ

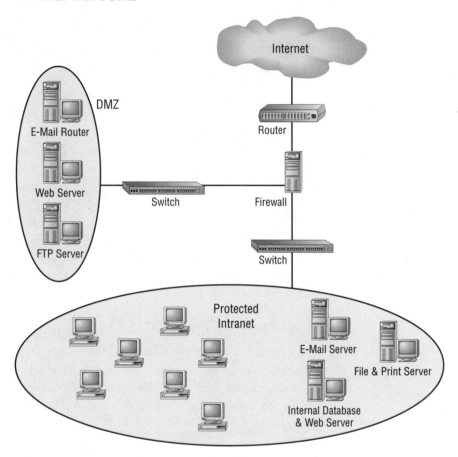

Protocol Switching

Protocol switching protects data on the inside of a firewall. Because TCP/IP (Transmission Control Protocol/Internet Protocol) is the protocol used on the Internet, many external types of attacks, including the Ping of Death and SYN floods (discussed later), are based on this protocol stack.

You can choose between two common approaches:

- Use a different protocol on the internal network (not TCP/IP) inside the firewall. For example, IP-based attacks aimed at your development server will never have any effect if you are using IPX (Internet Packet eXchange) on the internal network side of a router. This approach makes a router a natural firewall.

- Use TCP/IP on both the internal network and the Internet, and use a different protocol in a dead zone between them. For example, switch from IP to IPX in a dead zone, and then switch back to IP again once inside your network.

You can see both approaches in Figure 8.3. Notice the position of the dead zone between two of the routers, and also notice that the only protocol on the inside of either router is IPX. Any TCP/IP packet from the Internet is unable to pass into the local network because of the difference in protocols.

FIGURE 8.3   Protocol switching with and without a dead zone

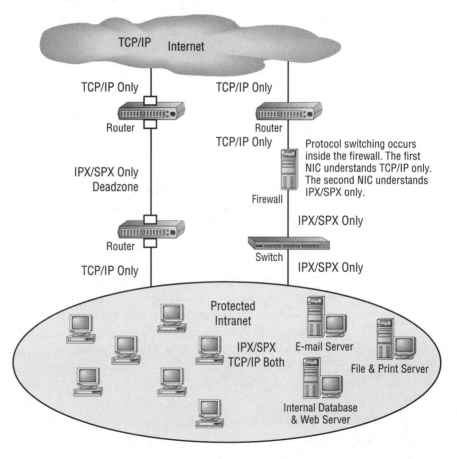

In both approaches, only the internal network is protected. You still need a firewall to handle any attacks on your network's access point and protocol-switching device.

Dynamic Packet Filtering

Packet filtering is the ability of a router or a firewall to discard packets that don't meet certain criteria. Firewalls use *dynamic packet filtering* to ensure that the packets it forwards match sessions initiated on the private side of a firewall. A *dynamic state list* (also known as a *state table*), held on a firewall, keeps track of all communications sessions between stations inside the firewall and stations outside the firewall. This list changes as communication sessions are added and deleted. Dynamic state lists allow a firewall to filter packets dynamically.

In dynamic packet filtering, only packets for current (and valid) communications sessions are allowed to pass. Someone trying to play back a communications session (such as a login) to gain access will be unsuccessful if the firewall is using dynamic packet filtering with a dynamic state list, because the data sent would not be recognized as part of a currently valid session. The firewall will filter out (or "drop") all packets that don't correspond to a current session using information found in the dynamic state list. For example, a computer in Network A requests a Telnet session with a server in Network B. The firewall in between the two keeps a log of the communication packets that are sent each way. Only packets that are part of this current communication session are allowed back into Network A through the firewall.

Figure 8.4 shows a failed attempt to infiltrate a network that is protected with a dynamic state list. Notice that the hacker attempts to insert a packet into the communication stream but fails because he did not have the correct packet number. The firewall was waiting for a specific order of packets, and the hacker's packet was out of sequence.

FIGURE 8.4   A hacker is denied by a dynamic state list.

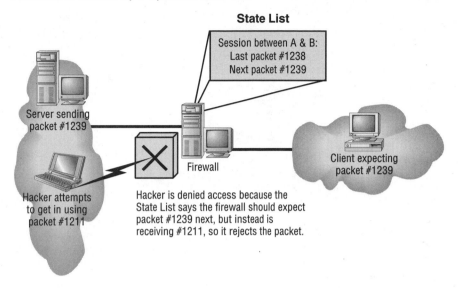

State List

Session between A & B:
Last packet #1238
Next packet #1239

Server sending
packet #1239

Firewall

Client expecting
packet #1239

Hacker attempts
to get in using
packet #1211

Hacker is denied access because the
State List says the firewall should expect
packet #1239 next, but instead is
receiving #1211, so it rejects the packet.

Proxy Servers

Proxy servers (also called proxies, for short) act on behalf of a network entity (either client or server) to completely separate packets from internal hosts and from external hosts. Let's say an internal client sends a request to an external host on the Internet. The request is first sent to a proxy server, where it is examined, broken down, and handled by an application. That application then creates a new packet requesting information from the external server. Figure 8.5 shows the process. Note that this exchange is between applications at the Application layer of the OSI model.

FIGURE 8.5 A packet going to a proxy

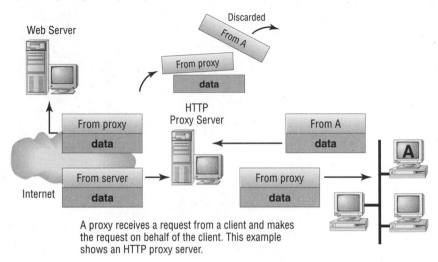

A proxy receives a request from a client and makes the request on behalf of the client. This example shows an HTTP proxy server.

Proxies are good firewalls because the entire packet is dissected, and each section can be examined for invalid data at each layer of the OSI model. For example, a proxy can examine a packet for information contained in everything from the packet header to the contents of the message. Attachments can also be checked for viruses. Messages can be searched for keywords that might indicate the source of a packet.

You can use this type of searching to prevent sensitive information from exiting your organization with the outbound data stream. If your sensitive documents contain a header or footer that includes the words *MyCompanyName Confidential*, you can set up your proxy server software to search for those keywords. This level of detailed searching degrades performance, however, because it is more time-intensive than checking state lists.

There are many types of proxy servers, including IP, Web, FTP (File Transport Protocol), and SMTP (Simple Mail Transfer Protocol). Each type is used for a different purpose and uses different methods.

IP Proxy

An *IP Proxy* hides the IP addresses of all stations on the internal network by exchanging its IP address for the address of any requesting station. You do not want a hacker to know IP addresses specific to your internal network. Web servers on the Internet will also be unable to determine the specific IP address from which a request is being sent. All communications look as if they originate from the proxy server. This type of proxy is also known as *network address translation (NAT)*.

Web (HTTP) Proxy

Web proxies (also called HTTP [Hypertext Transfer Protocol] proxies) handle HTTP requests. The HTTP proxy makes HTTP requests on behalf of the sending workstation. When implemented correctly, a client's Web browser asks a Web server on the Internet for a Web page using an HTTP request. Because the browser is configured to make HTTP requests using an HTTP proxy, the browser sends the request to the proxy server. The proxy server changes the From address of the HTTP request to its own network address and sends it to the Internet Web server. The response to the HTTP request goes directly to the proxy (because it replaced the sender's address with its own). The proxy server then replaces its address with the address of the original sender, and the response is delivered to the original sender.

The most popular implementation of a Web proxy is a *proxy cache server*. This server receives an HTTP request from a Web browser and then makes the request on behalf of the sending workstation. When the requested page is returned, the proxy server caches a copy of the page locally. The next time someone requests the same Web page or Internet information, the page can be delivered from the local cache instead of the proxy server having to formulate a new request to the Web server on the Internet. This speeds up Web surfing for commonly accessed pages. Web proxies can also increase network security by filtering out content that is considered insecure, such as executables, scripts, or viruses.

FTP Proxy

FTP proxies handle uploading and downloading of files from a server on behalf of a workstation. An FTP proxy operates in a fashion similar to that of a Web proxy. Just like Web proxies, FTP proxies can filter undesirable content (viruses and the like).

SMTP Proxy

SMTP proxies handle Internet e-mail. Here, the actual contents of the packet and mail can be automatically searched. Any packets or messages that contain material that is considered not secure can be blocked. Many SMTP proxies allow network virus protection software to scan inbound mail.

Not every firewall falls into a category. Traditional firewall vendors are adding features to their firewalls to make them difficult to classify. Vendors who traditionally offered packet-filtering solutions are now also offering proxy solutions, and vendors who traditionally offered proxy solutions are now also offering packet-filtering solutions. The network administrator can now get a packet-filtering firewall and a proxy firewall combined into one product. Dual-style firewalls are considered hybrids.

Comparing Firewall Operating System Platforms

Most firewalls are implemented as a combination of hardware and software. The hardware is typically a server-class machine. The software is usually specially written and sits on top of an NOS. Firewalls are typically dedicated computers (that is, they don't do file/print serving or perform any other network function).

Let's briefly look at each of the four major network operating systems and how each implements a firewall.

Remember that in addition to firewall software, you need at least two NICs (some firewall products use three) to have a functional firewall.

The Unix Operating System

Unix is the NOS on which the Internet is based and, as such, is also the NOS on which firewalls are based. In Unix, you can unload and lock down individual services. This means that you can configure a Unix server so that only the firewall service is up and running. Proponents of Unix argue that it is more secure because nonessential services can be removed, though knowledgeable Microsoft or Novell administrators can do the same with Windows and NetWare.

To support multiple segments, the firewall needs a number of network interface cards. An advantage of using Unix-based firewalls it that they allow the most network cards (more than 32). NetWare has a practical limit of 16, and Windows is currently limited to four.

As we discussed in Chapter 3, Unix is a command-line based operating system and, thus, doesn't lend itself to the most friendly firewall platform in the world. However, since the introduction of the X Window interface (and firewall software's adoption of it), Unix-based firewalls have become easier to use.

Finally, because firewalls must examine hundreds, even thousands, of packets per second, speed is a major factor in all firewall platforms. Many companies make security products for both Unix and Windows NT. Unix implementations tend to be significantly faster than Windows NT implementations. If you're communicating over a T1 line, however, platform speed won't create a bottleneck. This only becomes a problem when your corporation gets into higher connection speeds that T3, OC3, and other connections provide (and, therefore, your firewall must be examining more packets per second). In these cases, you should consider Unix-based firewall implementations.

NetWare

NetWare, through the leverage of NDS, provides for easy network administration through NetWare Administrator, the graphical utility that runs on Windows 95/98 and Windows NT. The primary firewall is Novell's own product, BorderManager. BorderManager installs onto NetWare servers and has a NetWare Administrator snap-in. With this feature, you can continue to use familiar NetWare tools to manage the many aspects of your network, including the firewall.

NetWare as a firewall platform offers two major benefits: speed (which is discussed below) and client compatibility. NetWare is compatible with just about every client platform, including Mac OS, Windows 95/98, Windows NT, DOS, and OS/2. NetWare (with BorderManager) can offer firewall protection for all these client platforms.

BorderManager integrates into NDS and thus can be managed with NetWare's single administration utility, NetWare Administrator. This makes BorderManger an easy-to-use firewall product, especially for experienced NetWare network administrators.

NetWare's core operating system has been optimized for the Intel platform, which is cheap and widely available. Apart from Unix running on a RISC processor, NetWare is considered by the IT industry the fastest, and most efficient, network operating system. BorderManager running on NetWare is one of the fastest firewall software packages available.

Windows NT

As Windows NT becomes more and more popular, firewall developers are porting their software from Unix to NT. However, because of security problems associated with Windows NT (see the WinNuke discussion later in this chapter), it doesn't rival Unix or NetWare for firewall installations. As these problems are solved (through patches, other fixes, and likely the Windows 2000 product), Windows NT will gain ground in the firewall market.

Most third-party, Windows-based firewalls can integrate with Windows NT Domain security. This allows proxies to use Windows NT Domain usernames and passwords.

The primary advantage of an NT firewall is that it can be managed through a graphical user interface, as can Windows NT itself. Windows NT servers (and thus firewalls based on them) are more intuitive to the general user than a Unix operating system, with almost the same level of features. If your network support staff is well versed in Windows, the learning curve for a new firewall will not be as steep as that for another operating system.

Windows NT, however, isn't the fastest NOS platform, mainly because of the overhead required to maintain the graphical interface; thus, firewalls running on it aren't the fastest. To address this issue, some firewall vendors are adding hardware accelerator cards to increase firewall throughput. Microsoft is advancing the line of Windows Servers to utilize more than a dozen CPUs and gigabytes of memory in one box so that performance can be increased to much higher levels. These new features will make Windows NT much faster and thus more effective as a firewall platform. With the advent of Windows 2000 servers, high-end throughput speeds will be possible.

The Black Box

A black box firewall implementation is your fourth choice. You do not know what operating system is inside the box, but it is definitely not Windows. It might be a special implementation of Unix or a completely proprietary system. These implementations tend to have the fastest throughput because they are designed specifically as firewalls, rather than as file and print network operating systems that run firewall software. Cisco's PIX Firewall is an example of a proprietary black box system.

The major feature of a black box firewall is simplicity. You don't have to worry about extraneous features you don't need, such as file or print services. The box is only a firewall, not a server and a firewall.

Ease of use is not, however, a feature of a black box, which often lacks a screen or an input device. The administrator must rely on connecting to the black box using an external keyboard or terminal to change firewall configuration data. This is not typically a problem with firewalls that don't require significant configuration (as in simpler network implementations). In this case, once the firewall is configured, you can pretty much leave it alone.

Given the dedicated nature of black box firewalls (they aren't used to provide other network services) and that they are designed from the ground up as firewalls, they are often very efficient and fast. They use RISC processors and operating systems designed specifically for a firewall. Unfortunately, black boxes cannot be upgraded easily and often must be replaced as new technology is released.

Attack and Defense

You can view the interaction between a hacker and a network administrator in different ways. You can see a harmless game of cat and mouse or a terrorist attack on national security. In either case, a person attempts to break into or crash your system. You, as the network administrator, work at preventing and tracking the attacks.

Hacker Tools—Common Network Attacks

Network attacks that are directed by a hacker are called directed attacks. For example, a hacker sending a WinNuke packet (generated by the WinNuke utility, discussed later in this chapter) to a specific machine is considered a directed attack. Viruses are traditionally not directed attacks. The virus is unknowingly copied from user to user. (Traditional viruses are covered in Chapter 10.) Viruses are some of the most prevalent attacks used on the Internet. In this section, we'll discuss some of the techniques that hackers commonly use to attack a network. Then, in the next section, we'll discuss some tools and procedures you can use to defend against them.

IP Spoofing

IP spoofing is the process of sending packets with a fake source address, pretending that the packet is coming from within the network the hacker is trying to attack. The address can be considered stolen from the hacker's target network. A router (even a packet-filtering router) is going to treat this packet as coming from within the network and will let it pass; however, a firewall can prevent this type of packet from passing into the secured network. In Figure 8.6, a hacker is attempting an IP spoof. Notice that the hacker with the spoofed IP address is denied access to the network by the firewall.

FIGURE 8.6   IP spoofing

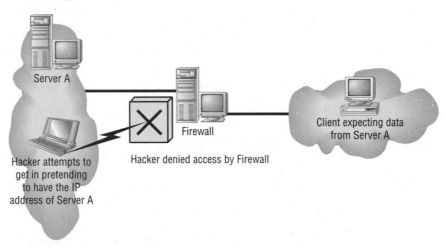

The Ping of Death

The *Ping of Death* is a type of *Denial of Service (DoS) attack*. A DoS attack prevents any users, even legitimate ones, from using the system. Ping is primarily used to see if a computer is responding to IP requests. Normally, when you ping a remote host, four normal-sized ICMP (Internet Control Message Protocol) packets are sent to the remote host to see if it is available. In a Ping of Death attack, a very large ICMP packet is sent to the remote host, whose buffer is flooded by this packet. Typically, this causes a system to reboot or hang. Patches to prevent a Ping of Death attack from working are available for most operating systems.

WinNuke

WinNuke is a Windows program that sends special TCP/IP packets with an invalid TCP header. Windows 95/98 and Windows NT computers will crash when they receive one of these packets because of the way the Windows 95/98 or Windows NT TCP/IP stack handles bad data in the TCP header. Instead of returning an error code or rejecting the bad data (Microsoft calls it out-of-band data), it sends the computer to the Blue Screen of Death (BSoD). Figuratively speaking, the hacker causes the computer to blow up or to be nuked. This type of attack does not affect Unix boxes and NetWare servers.

There is a patch to solve this particular problem, making machines invulnerable to WinNuke attacks. You can obtain it by going to Microsoft's support Web site at http://support.microsoft.com/servicedesks/technet/ and searching for WinNuke.

SYN Flood

A *SYN flood* is also a Denial of Service attack because it can barrage the receiving machine with dozens of meaningless packets. In normal communications, a workstation that wants to open a TCP/IP communication with a server sends a TCP/IP packet with the SYN flag set to 1. The server automatically responds to the request, indicating it is ready to start communicating. Only new communications use SYN flags. If you are in the middle of a file download, SYNs are not used. A new SYN packet is only used if you lose your connection and must reestablish communications.

To initiate a SYN flood, a hacker sends a barrage of SYN packets. The receiving station normally can't help itself and tries to respond to each SYN request for a connection. The receiving device soon expends its resources trying to reply, and all incoming connections are rejected until all current connections can be answered. The victim machine cannot respond to any other requests because its buffers are overfilled, and it therefore rejects all packets, including valid requests for connections. Patches that can help with this problem are available for the various network operating systems.

Intruder Detection—Defense Techniques

There are three main types of intruder detection and defense:

- Active detection involves constantly scanning the network for possible break-ins.

- Passive detection involves logging all network events to a file.

- Proactive defense involves using tools to shore up your network walls against attack.

Active Detection

Active detection is analogous to a security guard walking down the hallway rattling doors. The guard is checking for a break-in. Special network software can search for hackers trying known attack methods, including suspicious activity as they travel over the network. Some sophisticated active systems actually take action, such as shutting down the communication sessions that the hacker is using, as well as e-mailing or paging you. Some packages actually go as far as trying to cripple the computer from which the hacker is attacking. Cisco's NetRanger, Memco's SessionWall, and SATAN are all forms of active intrusion-detection software.

Because SATAN is free, both sides have access to it. Consequently, hackers can (and often do) use SATAN to look for security holes. Many other intrusion-detection programs will also look for SATAN-type intrusions.

Passive Detection

Video cameras are an example of passive intrusion-detection systems. Their counterparts in networking are files that log events that occur on the network. Tripwire for Unix systems is one of the earliest programs of this type. With passive detection systems, files and data are looked at, and checksums are calculated for each file and piece of data. These checksums are then stored in a log file. If the network administrator notices a security breach on the network, he or she can access the log files to find clues regarding the security breach.

Proactive Defense

The main feature of the proactive defense is to make sure your network is invulnerable to attack. You can do this through research and maintenance. You must stay current on all known security holes on your network. You can use tools such as SATAN to find the holes in your security walls and plug them with software patches. Unfortunately, before you can patch a hole, it must be discovered. And the war against attackers is ongoing. As soon as you patch a hole, the hacker will find and exploit two other weaknesses. It usually takes some time for a patch to be developed, and in that time, companies lose resources to a hacker.

DOD Security Standards

The U.S. Department of Defense (DOD) gave responsibility for computer security to the National Security Agency (NSA) in 1981 via directive 5215.1, and the National Computing Security Center (NCSC) was formed. The NCSC Web site states the center's mission as "technical standards and criteria for the security evaluation of trusted computer systems that can be incorporated into the Department of Defense component life-cycle management process."

In this section, we will briefly examine some NCSC standards and their impact on network security. The Network+ exam asks you do identify each level.

You can find the evaluation criteria for the DOD computer standards (called the *Rainbow Series* because of the color of the books) at `http://www.radium.ncsc.mil/tpep/library/rainbow`.

Trusted Computer System

The NCSC first released *A Trusted Computer System Evaluation Criteria* (TCSEC) in 1983 for stand-alone, non-networked computers. The current DOD Standard release is 5200.28-STD and is commonly referred to as the Orange Book. The Orange Book defines the standard parameters of a trusted computer in several classes, indicated by letter and number: the higher the letter, the higher the certification. For example, class A is the highest class, and class D is the lowest class. The most publicized class is C2, Controlled Access Protection, which indicates that, within the trusted computer guidelines, the computer must have accountability for the data. In other words, each person that uses the computer must have a unique username and password, and the use of a file can be traced to that user. This is the highest NCSC class for local operating systems. Higher-level classes require that operating systems be specifically written to incorporate security-level information as the data is input.

Generally speaking, a stand-alone computer system can qualify for Trusted Computer certification if it meets the objectives in the DOD document 5200.28-STD and passes the DOD's evaluation process. Several vendors put their operating systems through this process. Although Microsoft makes the operating systems for the majority of desktop computers, only its Windows NT product has been submitted and approved for the Trusted Computer certification.

For the exam, you must know that Windows NT Server is C2-level certified for Trusted Computer (Orange Book). If the computer on which Windows NT Server is installed is connected to a network, however, it loses the C2 Trusted Computer certification.

Trusted Network Interpretation

In 1987, the NCSC released enhanced testing criteria based on the Orange Book standard. The new standard, NCSC-TG-005, is called the Red Book and is the *Trusted Network Interpretation Environmental Guideline (TNIEG)*. Trusted computers are addressed in the Orange Book. The Red Book defines the certification criteria for trusted networks. They both use the D through A levels. As with the C2 class in the Trusted Computer implementation, the C2 class is the highest class for generic network operating systems. Higher-level classes require that operating systems be specifically written to incorporate security-level information as the data is input.

With a C2 Trusted Network certification, network operating systems must provide a unique user account for each person on the network and provide accountability for the information the user uses. Additionally, the network communications must be secure.

Currently, several network operating systems are under evaluation for C2 Trusted Network certification. However, the only currently available network operating system that achieved C2 Trusted Network certification is NetWare 4.1.

Certified Operating Systems and Networks

Not all versions of an operating system are certified. This is the case even within the same vendor's product line. The NCSC requires that products adhere to a specific implementation in order to maintain their security certification. Be sure to check these out if you want to take advantage of the security rating.

The Cray Research and Harris Computer Systems versions of Unix are B-level certified. Unix and Windows NT 3.5 are Trusted Computer (Orange Book) certified (C-level). NetWare is certified C2 Red Book, allowing it to operate as a trusted network. Tables 8.1 and 8.2 list C2 and above certified Microsoft Windows, Novell NetWare, and Unix products as of this writing.

TABLE 8.1 National Security Agency Trusted Products—B Certified

Certification	Operating System	Vendor	Product Version(s)
B3 Orange Book	Unix	Wang Government Services, Inc.	XTS-200 STOP 3.1E and 3.2E, XTS-300 STOP 4.1, 4.1a, and 4.4.2
B2 Orange Book	Unix	Trusted Information Systems, Inc.	Trusted XENIX 3 and 4
B1 Orange Book	Unix	Amdahl Corporation	UTS/MLS, Version 2.15+
B1 Orange Book	Unix	Digital Equipment Corporation	ULTRIX MLS+ Version 2.1 on VAX Station 3100
B1 Orange Book	Unix	Harris Computer Systems Corporation	CX/SX 6.1.1 and 6.2.1

TABLE 8.1 National Security Agency Trusted Products—B Certified *(continued)*

Certification	Operating System	Vendor	Product Version(s)
B1 Orange Book	Unix	Hewlett-Packard Corporation	HP-UX BLS release 8.04 and 9.0.9+
B1 Orange Book	Unix	Silicon Graphics, Inc.	Trusted IRIX/B release 4.0.5EPL
B1 Red Book	Unix	Cray Research, Inc.	Trusted UNICOS 8 release 8.0.2
B1 Red Book	Unix	Harris Computer Systems Corporation	CX/SX with LAN/SX 6.1.1 and 6.2.1

TABLE 8.2 National Security Agency Trusted Products—C Certified

Cert.	OS	Vendor	Product Version(s)
C2 Orange Book	Unix	IBM	RS/6000 Distributed System
C2 Orange Book	Windows NT	Microsoft Corporation	Windows NT Server and Workstation, Version 3.5 with Service Pack 3
C2 Red Book	NetWare	Novell, Inc.	NetWare 4 Network System Architecture and Design, and NetWare 4.11
C2 Red Book	Proprietary	SISTex, Inc.	Assure EC 4.11 for Novell

There are no A level certified Microsoft Windows, Novell NetWare, or Unix operating systems yet. C1 has been discontinued as a certification.

To verify security certification or check out officially released documents or books, go to the NCSC Web site at www.radium.ncsc.mil/tpep/epl/index .html. Products may be added or removed by the National Security Agency at any time. The tables here are for informational purposes only.

Assure EC 4.11 for Novell is included in Table 8.2 because it has ties to Windows 3.*x*, Windows 95/98, and NetWare. The NSA has certified SISTex's product as being the trusted workstation component of a NetWare 4/4.11 network. The Assure workstation can run DOS and Windows 3.*x* programs. Windows 95/98 is allowed although it was not specifically tested. Assure is not a Microsoft or Novell product; however, this operating system/hardware combination works with both companies' products.

Understanding Encryption

Occasionally company data has to be sent over public networks, such as the Internet, and just about anyone with the desire to do so (including a company's competitors) can view the data in transit. Companies that want to ensure that their data is secure during transit encrypt their data before transmission. Encryption is the process that encodes and decodes data. The encrypted data is sent over the public network and is decrypted by the intended recipient. Generally speaking, encryption works by running the data (represented as numbers) through a special encryption formula (called a *key*). Both the sender and the receiver know the key. The key, generally speaking, is used to encrypt and decrypt the data.

The NSA has classified encryption tools and formulas as munitions since 1979 and therefore regulates them. The agency is concerned that unfriendly nations, terrorists, and criminals will use encrypted communications to plan crimes and go undetected. You can export weak encryption methods, but they cannot compete commercially with the tools designed overseas.

RSA Data Security, a U.S. company, has side-stepped this issue by opening another company in Australia. We will have to wait and see what becomes of RSA's move.

One way to measure an encryption algorithm is by its bit strength. Until 1998, only 40-bit and lesser strength software could be exported. That limit has been increased to 56-bit by special consideration of the U.S. Department of Commerce.

To ensure the security of monetary transfers, the NSA allows U.S. banks to use more secure encryption methods. Banks need to communicate with their overseas branches, customers, and affiliates.

Uses for Encryption

In internal networks, some encryption is necessary, such as encrypting passwords that are being sent from workstation to server at login. This is done automatically by the network operating system. Encryption is also used by e-mail systems, giving the user the option to encrypt individual or all e-mail messages. Encryption is also used for data transmission over VPNs (Virtual Private Networks), using the Internet to connect remote users securely to internal networks. Finally, encryption has become important with the advent of e-commerce, online banking, and online investing. Buying products and handling finances online would not be possible if the data sent between all involved parties over the Internet were not encrypted.

How Encryption Works

The encryption process involves taking each character of data and comparing it against a key. For example, we could encrypt the following string of data in any number of ways:

The quick brown fox

For example purposes, let's use a simple letter-number method. In this method, each letter in the alphabet corresponds to a particular number. You may have used this method as a kid when you got a decoder wheel in your Cracker Jack or breakfast cereal box. If we use a straight alphabetic-to-number encryption (for example, A=1, B=2, C=3, and so on), the data translate into the following:

> 20 8 5 17 21 9 3 11 2 18 15 23 14 6 15 24

We can then transmit this series of numbers over a network, and the receiver can decrypt the string using the same key in reverse. From left to right, the number 20 translates to the letter T, 8 to H, 5 to E, and so on. Eventually, the receiver gets the entire message:

> The quick brown fox

Most encryption methods use much more complex formulas and methods. Our key was about 8 bits long; some keys are extremely complex and can be a maximum of 128 bits. The larger the key (in bits), the more complex the encryption and the more difficult it is to crack.

Encryption Keys

To encode a message and decode an encrypted message, you need the proper encryption key or keys. The *encryption key* is the table or formula that defines which character in the data translates to which encoded character. Encryption keys fall into two categories—public and private. Let's look at how these two types of encryption keys are used.

Private Key Encryption

Private keys are known as *symmetrical keys*. In private key encryption technology, both the sender and receiver have the same key and use it to encrypt and decrypt all messages. This makes it difficult to initiate communication the first time. How do you securely transmit the single key to each user? You use public keys, which we'll discuss shortly.

The Data Encryption Standard (DES)

International Business Machines (IBM) developed one of the most commonly used private key systems, DES. In 1977, the United States made DES a government standard, defined in the Federal Information Processing Standards Publication 46-2 (FIPS 46-2). It has been reaffirmed about every five years, most recently in 1993. DES uses lookup table functions and is incredibly fast when compared with public key systems. A 56-bit private key is used. RSA Data Systems issued a challenge to break the DES standard. Several Internet users worked in concert, each tackling a portion of the 72 quadrillion possible combinations. The key used in RSA's challenge was broken in June 1997, after searching only 18 quadrillion keys out of the possible 72 quadrillion. The plain text message read: "Strong cryptography makes the world a safer place."

Skipjack and Clipper

The replacement for DES might be the NSA's recent algorithm called *skipjack*. Skipjack is officially called the Escrowed Encryption Standard (EES), defined in FIPS 185, and uses an 80-bit key rather than the DES standard 56-bit key. The functions and complexity of each algorithm are different as well. Classified as secret (or classified) by the NSA, the skipjack formulas remain unknown. Skipjack was supposed to be integrated into the clipper chip.

A *clipper chip* is a hardware implementation of skipjack. Clipper chips were proposed for use in U.S. telephone lines. Many civil liberties and privacy activists became upset because the government would be able to decrypt secure telephone conversations.

Public Key Encryption

Public key encryption, or a Diffie-Hellman algorithm, uses two keys to encrypt and decrypt data: a public key and a private key. The receiver's public key is used to encrypt a message to the receiver. The message is sent to the receiver who can then decrypt the message using the private key. This is a one-way communication. If the receiver wants to send a return message, the same principle is used. The message is encrypted with the original sender's public key (that person is going to be the receiver of this new message) and can only be decrypted with his or her private key. If the original sender does not have a public key, a message can still be sent with a digital certificate (also sometimes referred to as a digital ID). The digital ID verifies the sender of the message.

Figure 8.7 shows public-key encrypted communication between two people, User X and User Y.

FIGURE 8.7 Public key encryption

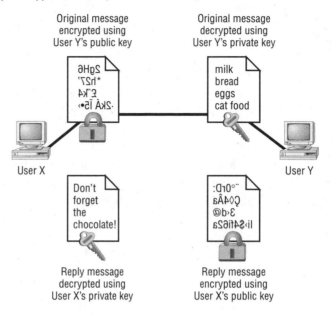

The term *Diffie-Hellman* refers to all public key algorithms. Whitfield Diffie and Martin Hellman from the Stanford Research Institute invented public key encryption. They introduced the dual key concept in their 1976 paper, "New Directions in Cryptography."

RSA Data Security

Rivest, Shamir, and Adleman (RSA) encryption is a public key encryption algorithm named after the three scientists from the Massachusetts Institute of Technology (MIT) who developed it. They created a commercial company in 1977 to develop asymmetric keys and received several U.S. patents. Their encryption software is used in several products today, including Netscape Navigator and Novell's latest NetWare Client.

For more information on RSA Data Security, go to www.rsa.com.

Pretty Good Privacy (PGP)

PGP is an encryption utility based on public key encryption. In the early 1990s, Phil Zimmerman, also from MIT, wrote the majority of the code for this freely available version of public key encryption. The software was designed to encrypt data for e-mail transmission. Zimmerman compared e-mail to postcards. As the e-mail message is passed from server to server on the Internet, anyone can read it, just as anyone can read a postcard as it travels through the postal service. He compared an encrypted message to a letter mailed inside an envelope.

Zimmerman distributed the software for personal use only and restricted commercial use. The name *PGP* denotes that nothing is 100 percent secure. Both RSA Data Security and the U.S. federal government had problems with Zimmerman's product. RSA complained about patent infringement (a license fee is now paid to RSA). The government decided to prosecute Zimmerman for exporting munitions grade software; however, the charges were eventually dropped. Many years later, PGP and other public key–related products are readily available.

Security Policies

A *security policy* defines how security will be implemented in an organization, including physical security, document security, and network security.

Security policies must be implemented completely because random implementation is similar to blocks of Swiss cheese. Some areas are covered, and others are full of holes. Before a network can be truly secure, the network support staff must implement a total network security policy that includes posting company information on bulletin boards, clean desks, audits, recording, and the consequences of not complying with the security policy.

Security Audit

A security audit is a review of your network to identify components that aren't secure. Although you can do a security audit yourself, you can also contract an audit with a third party. This is a good idea if you want the level of security to be certified. A consultant's audit is a good follow-up to an internal audit.

Government agencies may also require that your network be certified before granting you contract work, especially if the work is considered confidential, secret, or top secret.

Clean Desk Policy

A clean desk policy does not mean that employees must wipe the bread crumbs from their last lunch. (Being clean with food is still a good idea. Mice and ants are difficult to get rid of once an infestation occurs.) A clean desk policy means that all important documents, such as books, schematics, confidential letters, and the like are removed from a desk (and locked away) when employees leave their workstation. This goes for offices, laboratories, workbenches, and desks and is especially important for employees who share space. It is easy to grab something off someone's desk without that person's knowledge, and most security problems involve people on the inside. Implementing a clean desk policy is the number-one way to reduce such breaches.

The International Computer Security Association (www.icsa.net) reports that as much as 80 percent of all network break-ins occur from within the company by employees. Thus, protecting your data with a firewall is just the beginning of establishing network security.

For a clean desk policy to be effective, users must clean up their desks every time they walk away from it, without exception. The day this is not done will be the day when prospective building tenants are being shown the layout of the building, and an important document ends up missing. Additionally, workstations should be locked to desks, and you should spot-check to help enforce the clean desk policy. Spot-check randomly, for example, before the company picnic or before a child-at-work day.

The ICSA is a vendor-neutral organization that certifies the functionality of security products as well as makes recommendations on security.

Recording Equipment

Recording equipment, such as tape recorders and video cameras, can contain sensitive, confidential information. A security policy should prohibit their unauthorized presence and use.

When you walk into almost any large technology company, you are confronted with signs. A common sign is a camera with a circle surrounding it and a slash through the center of the circle. The text below the sign usually indicates that you cannot bring any recording devices onto the premises. This applies to, but is not limited to, still cameras, video cameras, and tape recorders of any kind.

The NSA recently updated its policy to disallow the Furby doll on government premises. Why would a government not allow dolls on its premises? Well, the Furby doll has a sophisticated computer inside with a digital recording device. The doll repeats what it hears at an interval of time later. This is quite harmless in the playroom at a children's daycare center. A recording of conversations at the NSA, however, cannot be allowed.

Other Common Security Policies

Security policies can cover hundreds of items. Here are some of the more common:

Notification   What good is a security policy if no one knows about it? Give users a copy of the security policy when you give them their username and password. Computers should also display a shortened version of the policy when a user attempts to connect. For example, "Unauthorized access is prohibited and will be prosecuted to the fullest extent of the law." One hacker argued that since a computer did not tell him otherwise, anyone was free to connect to and use the system.

Equipment Access   Disable all unused network ports so that non-employees who happen to be in the building cannot connect a laptop to an unused port and gain access to the network. Also, place all network equipment under lock and key.

Wiring   Network wires should not run along the floor where they can be easily accessed. Routers, switches, and concentrators should also not be hooked up in open office space. They should be in locked closets or rooms, with access to those rooms controlled by badge-swiping systems.

Door Locks/Swipe Mechanisms   Be sure that only a few, key people know the combination to the cipher lock on data center doors or that only the appropriate people have badges that will allow access to the data center. Change lock combinations often, and never leave server room doors open or unlocked.

Badges   Require everyone to wear an ID badge, including contractors and visitors, and assign appropriate access levels to contractors, visitors, and employees.

Tracking   Require badge access to all entrances to buildings and internal computer rooms. Track and record all entry and exit to these rooms.

Passwords   Reset passwords at least every month. Train everyone on how to create strong passwords. Set BIOS passwords on every client and server computer to prevent BIOS changes.

Monitor Viewing   Block computer monitors so that visitors or people looking through windows can't see them. Be sure that unauthorized users/persons cannot see security guard stations and server monitors.

Accounts   Each user should have their own, unique user account, and employees should not share user accounts. Even temporary employees should have their own account. Otherwise, you will not be able to isolate a security breach.

Testing   Review and audit your network security at least once a year.

Background Checks   Do background checks on all network support staff. This may include calling their previous employers, verifying their college degrees, requiring a drug test, and checking for any criminal background.

Firewalls   Use a firewall to protect all Internet connections, and use the appropriate proxies and dynamic packet-filtering equipment to control access to the network. Your firewall should provide as much security as your company requires and your budget allows.

Intrusion Detection   Use intrusion detection and logging software to determine a breach of security. Be sure that you are logging the events you want to monitor.

Cameras   Cameras should cover all entrances to the building and the entire parking lot. Be sure that cameras are in weather-proof and tamper-proof housings, and review the output at a security monitoring office. Record everything on extended-length tape recorders.

Mail Servers   Provide each person with their own e-mail mailbox, and attach an individual network account to each mailbox. If several people need to access a mailbox, do not give them all the password to a single network account. Assign privileges to each person's network account. You can then track activity to a single person, even with a generic address such as info@mycompany.com.

DMZ   Use a demilitarized zone for all publicly viewable servers, including Web servers, FTP servers, and e-mail relay servers. Do not put them outside the firewall. Servers outside the firewall defeat the purpose of the firewall.

Mail Relay   Use a mail-relay server for e-mail. E-mail traffic should not go straight to your production servers. That would enable a hacker to directly access your server as well. Use a relay server in a DMZ.

Patches   Make sure the latest security updates are installed after being properly tested on a nonproduction computer.

Backups   Store backup tape cartridges securely, not on a shelf or table within reach of someone working at the server. Lock tapes in a water-proof, fireproof safe, and keep at least some of your backups offsite.

Modems   Do not allow desktop modems for any reason. They allow users to get to the Internet without your knowledge. Restrict modem access to approved server-based modem pools.

Guards   In some cases, security guards are necessary. Guards should not patrol the same station all the time. As people become familiar with an environment and situation, they tend to become less observant about that environment. Thus, it makes sense to rotate guards to keep their concentration at the highest possible levels. Guards should receive sufficient breaks to ensure alertness. All patrol areas should be covered during shift changes, rotations, and breaks. Guards should also receive periodic training. Test to ensure that guards can recognize a threat and take appropriate action.

Covering all these bases does not ensure that your network or facility is secure. This is just a starting point to head you in the right direction.

Breaking Policy

A security policy is not effective unless it is enforced, and enforced consistently. You cannot exempt certain individuals from policies or the consequences of breaking them. Your network users need to have a clearly written document that identifies and explains what users are and are not allowed to do. Additionally, it is important to state that breaking the policy will result in punishment, as well as which types of policy breaks result in which kind of punishment. Punishment may vary depending on the severity of the incident. If a policy is broken, the appropriate punishment should be administered immediately.

Major Infractions

As far back as the mid-1980s, employees were being immediately terminated for technology policy infractions. One employee was immediately terminated from a large computer company when pornography was found on his computer's hard drive. A manager and a security guard visited the employee. The manager informed the employee that he was being summarily terminated. The guard was there to ensure that the employee touched only personal items. The manager logged out the computer session. The former employee could now touch no computer equipment, including storage media such as floppy disks. The manager then informed the guard that the employee had one hour to vacate the premises.

Minor Infractions

A lesser infraction might be accidentally corrupting your desktop computer by installing software from the Internet. Beta products, new releases of software, and patches need to be tested by the IS department before implementation. One episode of downloading and installing a beta release of a Web browser invoked action at a national telephone company. After installing the beta version and rebooting, the production Windows NT Server became inoperable. The employee's Internet FTP privileges were revoked for three months.

The Exit Interview

The exit interview is the process in which employers ask employees who are leaving the company about their employment experience. The exit interview is used to minimize risks whether the employee is leaving under favorable circumstances or is being terminated. During the exit interview, a manager, a human resources representative, a network administrator, and a security guard may be involved to different extents.

Returning and Logging Property

When an employee leaves the company, all company property needs to be turned in and logged. This includes, but is not limited to, cellular phones, pagers, tool kits, keys, badges, security tokens, models, and all documents. Obviously, coffee mugs and photos of the spouse do not count. The manager, security guard, or both handle this, depending on whether the employee is being terminated or leaving voluntarily.

Disabling Accounts

The information systems division or department needs to disable all accounts immediately, including those for network and voice mail. This should coincide with the announcement that the employee is leaving (either voluntarily or forcefully). This is especially important when the employee has access to sensitive documents. Even if the person is leaving under favorable conditions, she may still be able to log in and copy data to floppy disks to take with her for her own use. Common practice has extended this from just system administrators to everyone.

Salespeople can easily hurt a company by taking client information with them. One salesperson accessed his former company's voice mail system and stole sales leads. For total security, you need to look beyond the obvious disgruntled ex-network administrator who demolishes your Web site after leaving.

Key Terms

Before you take the exam, be certain you are familiar with the following terms:

clipper chip

Denial of Service (DoS) attack

dynamic packet filtering

dynamic state list

encryption key

firewall

IP Proxy

IP spoofing

key

network address translation (NAT)

packet filtering

password history

Ping of Death

private network

proxy servers

proxy cache server

public network

security policy

skipjack

state table

symmetrical keys

SYN flood

Web proxies

Review Questions

1. Which of the following is an appropriate name for the network administration account?

   A. super

   B. superuser

   C. tswilliam

   D. administrator

   E. Leave the original name

2. Which type of firewall checks for a current communication and the next packet needed?

   A. Access Control Lists

   B. Member Control Lists

   C. Static State Lists

   D. Dynamic packet filtering

   E. Proxy

3. Which version(s) of Windows is/are certified by the DOD?

   A. Windows NT 3.5

   B. Windows NT 3.51

   C. Windows NT 4

   D. Windows 2000

4. Which version(s) of NetWare is/are certified by the DOD?

   A. 2

   B. 3.12

   C. 4

   D. 4.1

   E. 4.11

5. For security reasons, where should you store backup tapes?

    A. Next to the server

    B. Next to the monitor

    C. In a drawer

    D. Locked in a cabinet

    E. Sealed in an envelope

    F. Offsite

6. Which operating system(s) has/have achieved a National Security Agency certification allowing it/them to be used in a networked B or C certified environment?

    A. Unix

    B. NetWare

    C. Windows

    D. Linux

7. Which group of books does the DOD publish that deal with network security?

    A. The Rainbow Series

    B. The Colored Book Series

    C. The Orange Book Series

    D. The Red Book Series

    E. The Brown Book Series

8. Which government agency did the U.S. Department of Defense (DOD) task to handle computer security certification?

    A. EPA

    B. DOE

    C. DIS

    D. DSS

    E. NSA

9. The Diffie-Hellman algorithm is used to _____.

   A. Encrypt data using public key cryptography

   B. Encrypt data using private key cryptography

   C. Encrypt data using symmetric cryptography

   D. Run a key manager that distributes tokens

   E. Revoke distributed security tokens

10. What is the strongest bit-strength encryption that the U.S. government normally allows to be exported?

   A. 32-bit

   B. 40-bit

   C. 64-bit

   D. 128-bit

   E. 250-bit

   F. 256-bit

11. Which type of security uses a file that identifies predefined IP addresses that are allowed to send data through a router?

   A. Access Control Lists

   B. Dynamic State List

   C. Proxy

   D. Interpreter

   E. Translator

12. Which of the following passwords are considered weak?

  A. tempest4@wiND

  B. gwashington

  C. MargeS

  D. MSmith

  E. os2Cys&BtDel?

  F. wwater7D$walkEr

13. How often should regular users be forced to reset their passwords?

  A. Never

  B. Every day

  C. Once a week

  D. Once a month

  E. Once a semester

  F. Once a fiscal quarter

14. Which of the following are good criteria for a strong password?

  A. Three characters or longer

  B. Eight characters or longer

  C. Use both alphanumeric and special characters

  D. The license plate number of your truck

  E. Not found in a dictionary

15. What is the proper action to take before you leave your workstation? You are going to get a glass of water and will return in five minutes.

  A. Power down your workstation.

  B. Log out.

  C. Unplug the monitor.

  D. Unplug the computer.

16. Whose accounts should immediately be disabled when their employment is terminated?

A. Secretaries

B. Lab assistants

C. Engineers

D. Managers

E. Security guards

F. Network administrators

17. What should be collected in an exit interview of a terminated employee?

A. Schematics

B. Blood sample

C. Coffee mug

D. Office keys

E. Badge

F. Pager

G. Spouse's photo

18. What types of recording devices are typically allowed inside technology companies?

A. The Furby doll

B. Hand-held still cameras

C. Mounted company security video cameras

D. Dictation tape recorders

E. Newspaper reporter tape recorders

19. Active intrusion detection systems have which of the following characteristics?

    A. Capability to scan communications in near real time

    B. Record actions of attackers without raising an alarm

    C. Act to terminate the communications of the attacker

    D. Shut themselves down to hide from the attacker

    E. Shut down the entire network to protect against attacks

20. Which of the following attacks affects only Windows operating systems?

    A. PingNuke

    B. Ping of Death

    C. WinNuke

    D. Win of Death

    E. SYNNuke

    F. SYN of Death

Answers to Review Questions

1. C. It's considered a "best practice" to not use the names super, superuser, or administrator because those are default accounts. The best choice is to pick a user and give them administrative privileges. Then, delete or disable the built-in administration accounts.

2. D. A proxy provides firewall services by keeping track of all communications sessions and "pre-fetching" the next packets.

3. A. The only version of Windows that is currently certified as a secure workstation platform is Windows NT version 3.5.

4. C, E. Versions 4 and 4.11 were certified by the DOD as secure.

5. D, F. The best two locations for backup tapes are locked in some kind of cabinet or offsite. That way, it would be difficult for someone to steal the backups.

6. A, B. Of the OSes listed, only Unix and NetWare have been certified for use in a networked environment. Windows NT 3.5 was certified, but only as a workstation environment.

7. A. The Rainbow Series is the series of books that the DOD publishes for standards of secure networking.

8. E. The National Security Agency (NSA) is responsible for handling computer security certification.

9. A. Diffie-Hellman is a public key cryptography algorithm.

10. B. At the time of the writing of this exam, a 40-bit encryption algorithm was the strongest you could export. That restriction is currently being revised.

11. A. Access Control List security uses a file (the ACL) that identifies which addresses can send data through a particular firewall or router.

12. B, C, D. The best passwords are those that don't use any part of a person's name or a dictionary word. Thus, since, B, C, and D all are essentially usernames, they would be considered weak passwords.

13. D. It has been found that, for ease of remembrance and maximum possible security, a user should be forced to change their password at least once a month (or every 30 days). Any sooner and the user will forget their new password frequently; any later and they may complain that they would just like to keep their same password all the time.

14. B, C, E. The best passwords are eight characters are longer, use both numbers and letters, and are words not necessarily found in a dictionary. Any word that can be found in a dictionary, proper name, or other names of sentimental value is considered a bad/weak password.

15. B. It would be inefficient to shut down your workstation or unplug the computer because it takes so long to restart it. Unplugging the monitor would still leave the computer accessible (an intruder could simply plug it back in). The only convenient way to secure the computer for that short a time is to simply log out.

16. A, B, C, D, E, F. For security reasons, all accounts should be disabled when the employee quits or is terminated. You don't necessarily have to delete the account, but it should be disabled so that the employee can't use it.

17. A, D, E, F. Any item that could be used to gain access to a company's resources should be collected during the exit interview of an employee. Keys, badges, important papers (like schematics) should be obtained along with any company property (intellectual or otherwise).

18. C. For an absolutely secure installation, the only recording devices that should be on the premises are the company-owned and-operated devices like security cameras.

19. A, C. Active intrusion systems detect intrusions or possible intrusions the moment they occur and take actions to prevent the intrusion. These systems, if working correctly, should only affect the intruder.

20. C. Although many of these attacks can affect Windows systems, only one: WinNuke, was designed specifically to attack Windows systems. It works because of a bug in the Windows TCP/IP stack.

Chapter 9

Fault Tolerance and Disaster Recovery

NETWORK+ EXAM OBJECTIVES COVERED IN THIS CHAPTER:

✓ **Define the following terms and explain how each relates to fault tolerance or high availability:**

- Mirroring
- Duplexing
- Striping (with and without parity)
- Volumes
- Tape backup

✓ **Identify the kinds of test documentation that are usually available regarding a vendor's patches, fixes, upgrades, and so on.**

✓ **Given a network maintenance scenario, demonstrate the awareness of the following issues:**

- Standard backup procedures and backup media storage practices
- The need for periodic applications of software patches and other fixes to the network
- The need to install antivirus software on the server and workstations
- The need to frequently update virus signatures

Computers are not perfect. They can (and do) have problems that affect their users' productivity. These problems range from small errors to total system failure. Errors and failures can be the result of environmental problems, hardware and software failure, hacking (malicious, unauthorized use of a computer or a network), as well as natural disasters.

In all cases, you can take measures to minimize the impact of computer and network problems. These measures fall into two major categories: fault tolerance and disaster recovery. *Fault tolerance* is the capability of a computer or a network system to respond to a condition automatically, usually resolving it and thus reducing the impact on the system. If fault tolerant measures have been implemented, it is unlikely that a user would know that a problem existed. *Disaster recovery*, as its name suggests, is the ability to get a system functional after a total system failure (a disaster for a company and the network administrator) in the least amount of time. Strictly speaking, if enough fault tolerance methods are in place, you shouldn't need disaster recovery.

Both methods are important and are implemented on most, if not all, networks. Because of this, the Network+ exam will test you on your knowledge of the most popular implementations of fault tolerance and disaster recovery. In this chapter, we will look at the following:

- How to assess fault tolerance and disaster recovery needs

- Power management

- Disk system fault tolerance methods

- Backup considerations

- Virus protection

Assessing Fault Tolerance and Disaster Recovery Needs

Before implementing fault tolerance or disaster recovery, you should determine how critical your systems are to daily business operations. Additionally, you should determine how long each system could afford to be non-functional (down). Making these determinations will dictate which fault tolerance and disaster recovery methods you implement and to what extent. The more vital the system, the greater lengths (and, thus, greater expense) you should go to to protect it from downtime. Less critical systems may call for simpler measures. For example, banks, insurance companies, the U.S. government, and airlines all run highly critical computer and network systems. Thus, they all have complex and expensive fault tolerance and disaster recovery systems in place.

In terms of how fault tolerance and disaster recovery are implemented, sites can be described as hot, warm, or cold. As the temperature decreases, so does the level of fault tolerance and disaster recovery that are implemented at a site.

Hot Sites

In a hot site, every computer system and piece of information has a redundant copy (possibly multiple redundancies). This level of fault tolerance is used when systems must be up 100 percent of the time. Hot sites are strictly fault-tolerant implementations, not disaster recovery implementations (as no downtime is allowed). Budgets for this type of fault-tolerant implementation are typically large.

In a system that has 100 percent redundancy, the redundant system(s) will take over for the failed system without any downtime. The technology used to implement hot sites is *clustering*, which is grouping multiple computers to provide increased performance and fault tolerance.

Clustering Technologies

Although servers are commonly clustered, workstations are normally not clustered because they are simple and cheap to replace. Each computer in the cluster is connected to the other computers in the cluster by high-speed, redundant links (usually multiple fiber-optic cable). Each computer runs special clustering software that makes the cluster of computers appear as a single entity to clients.

There are two levels of cluster service: failover and true.

Failover Clustering

A failover cluster includes two entities (usually servers). The first is the active device (the device that responds to network requests), and the second is the failover device. The *failover device* is an exact duplicate of the active device, but it is inactive and connected to the active device by a high-speed link. The failover device monitors the active device and its condition by using what is known as a *heartbeat*. A heartbeat is a signal that comes from the active device at a specified interval. If the failover device doesn't receive a heartbeat from the active device in the specified interval, the failover device considers the active device inactive, and the failover device comes online (becomes active) and is now the active device.

When the previously active device comes back online, it starts sending out the heartbeat. The failover device, which currently is responding to requests as the active device, hears the heartbeat and detects that the active device is now back online. The failover device then goes back into standby mode and starts listening to the heartbeat of the active device again.

In a failover cluster, both servers must be running failover clustering software, for example, Novell's SFTIII (System Fault Tolerance, Level III), Standby Server and High Availability Server (with Novell's High Availability software, either of the servers can fail and the other takes over), and Microsoft's Cluster Server (MSCS) for Windows NT servers. Each software package provides failover functionality.

Here are some advantages to this approach to fault tolerance:

- Resources are almost always available. This approach ensures that the network service(s) that the device provides will be available as much as 99 percent of the time. Each network service and all data are exactly duplicated on each device, and when one experiences problems, the other takes over for virtually uninterrupted service.

- It is relatively inexpensive when compared with true clustering (discussed in the next section).

But, as with any technology, there are disadvantages, and failover clustering has its fair share:

- There is only one level of fault tolerance. This technology works great if the active device fails, but if the failover device fails as well, the network will totally lose that device's functionality.

- There is no load balancing. Servers in a failover clustering configuration are either in active or standby mode. There is no balancing of network service load across both servers in the cluster. The active server responds to network requests, and the failover server simply monitors the active server, wasting its processor resources.

- During cutover time, the server can't respond to requests. Failover clusters take anywhere from a few seconds to a few minutes to detect and recover from a failed server. This is called cutover time. During cutover time, the server can't respond to network client requests, so the server is effectively down. This time is indeed short, but, nevertheless, clients can't get access to their services during it.

- Hardware and software must be exactly duplicated. In most failover configurations, the hardware for both active and failover devices must be *identical*. If it's not, the transition of the failover device to active device may be hindered. These differences may even cause the failover to fail. This is a disadvantage because it involves checking all aspects of the hardware (for servers this means disk types and sizes, NICs, processor speed and type, and RAM).

Even though we described Microsoft Cluster Server (MSCS) as a failover clustering technology, it does have some capability for load balancing (according to Microsoft). It currently supports only a two-device configuration, so it primarily fits into this category of clustering.

True Clustering

True clustering differs from failover clustering in two major ways:

- It supports multiple devices.
- It provides load balancing.

In true clustering (also called *multiple server clustering*), multiple servers (or any network devices) act together as kind of super server. True clusters must provide load balancing. For example, 20 servers can act as one big server. All network services are duplicated across all servers, and network requests are distributed across all servers. Each server is connected to the other servers through a high-speed, dedicated link. If one server in the cluster malfunctions, the other servers automatically take over the burden of the failed server. When the failed server comes back online, it resumes responding to requests as part of the cluster.

This technology can provide greater than 99 percent availability for network services hosted by the cluster. Unfortunately, most NOS vendors (including Novell and Microsoft) don't currently ship true clustering software solutions. One notable exception is VMS, by Digital Equipment Corporation. However, both Novell and Microsoft have announced plans to release true clustering server solutions by the end of the year 2000.

Several advantages are associated with true clustering, including:

More than 99 percent availability for network services   With multiple servers, the impact of a single or even more than one server in the cluster going down is minimized because other servers take over the functionality.

Increased performance   Because each server is taking part of the load of the cluster, much higher total performance is possible.

No cutover time   Because multiple servers are always responding to network requests, true clusters don't suffer from the cutover time even when a server goes down. The remaining servers do receive an increased load, and clients may see a Server Busy or Not Found error message if they should by some chance try to communicate with the server that is going down. But if the user tries the operation again, one of the remaining servers will respond to the request.

Replication   If the clustering software supports it, a few servers can be located off site in case the main site is destroyed by fire, flood, or other disaster. Because there is replica (copy) of all data in a different location, this technology is known as *replication*.

But these advantages don't come without their price. Here are a couple of disadvantages to true clustering:

The more servers, the more complex the cluster   As you add servers to the cluster to increase performance, you also increase the complexity. For this reason, most clustering software is limited to a maximum of 64 servers. As technology develops, this limit will increase. The minimum number of servers in a true cluster is 2.

Much more expensive   Because of the hardware involved and the complexity of the clustering software, true clustering requires a serious financial commitment. To justify the expense, ask the keepers of the purse strings how much money would be lost if the system were down for a day.

Warm Site

In a warm site (also called a *nearline site*), the network service and data are available most of the time (more than 85 percent of the time). The data and services are less critical than those in a hot site. With hot site technologies, all fault-tolerance procedures are automatic and are controlled by the NOS. Warm site technologies require a little more administrator intervention, but they aren't as expensive.

The most commonly used warm site technology is a duplicate server. A *duplicate server*, as its name suggests, is currently not being used and is available to replace any server that fails. When a server fails, the administrator installs the new server and restores the data; the network services are available to users with a minimum of downtime. The administrator sends the failed server out to be repaired. Once the repaired server comes back, it is now the spare server and is available when another server fails.

Using a duplicate server is a disaster recovery method because the entire server is replaced, but in a shorter time than if all the components had to be ordered and configured at the time of the system failure. The major advantage of using duplicate servers rather than clustering is that it's less expensive. A single duplicate server costs much less than a comparable cluster solution.

Corporate networks don't often use duplicate servers, and that's because there are some major disadvantages associated with duplicate servers:

- You must keep current backups. Because the duplicate server relies on a current backup, you must back up every day and verify every backup, which is time-consuming. To stay as current as possible, some companies run continuous backups.

- You can lose data. If a server fails in mid-afternoon and the backup was run the evening before, you will lose any data that was placed on the server since the last backup. This may not be a big problem on servers that aren't updated frequently.

Cold Site

A cold site cannot guarantee server uptime. Generally speaking, cold sites have little or no fault tolerance and rely completely on efficient disaster recovery methods to ensure data integrity. If a server fails, the IT personnel do their best to recover and fix the problem. If a major component needs to be replaced, the server stays down until the component is replaced. Errors and failures are handled as they occur. Apart from regular system backups, no fault tolerance or disaster recovery methods are implemented.

This type of site has one major advantage: it is the cheapest way to deal with errors and system failures. No extra hardware is required (except hardware required for backing up).

Power Management

A key element of any fault tolerance plan is a power management strategy. Electricity powers the network, switches, hubs, PCs, and computer servers. Variations in power can cause problems ranging from a reboot after a short loss of service to damaged equipment and data. Fortunately, a number of products are available to help protect sensitive systems from the dangers of lightning strikes, dirty (uneven) power, and accidental power cable disconnection, including surge protectors, Standby Power Supplies, uninterruptible power supplies, and line conditioners. What you use depends on how critical your system is (decide whether it is a hot, warm, or cold site). At a minimum, connect individual workstations to surge protectors; network hardware and servers should use uninterruptible power supplies or line conditioners. Critical operations, such as ambulance corps and hospitals, typically go one step further and also have a gas-powered backup generator to provide long-term supplemental power to all systems.

Surge Protectors

Surge protectors (also commonly referred to as *surge suppressors*) are typically power blocks or power strips with electronics that limit the amount of voltage, current (amps), and noise that can get through to your equipment. They are designed to protect your equipment from long-lasting increases in voltage (surges) and high, short bursts of voltage (spikes). The unit does not provide any power, however. Rather, it blocks harmful electricity from reaching your equipment. The surge protector detects a surge or a spike and clamps down on the incoming voltage, reducing it to safe levels. If the surge is large enough, it can trip the built-in safety mechanism. You may then lose power and have to reset the equipment you are protecting. Common causes of surges and spikes are fluctuations in power from the electricity company, additions of equipment to the power grid by customers, and natural storms.

Level of Protection

Unfortunately, surge protectors provide only a limited amount of protection. Surge protectors are simple devices that can only protect against large spikes and surges. Small increases in voltage are allowed to pass. Small increases may not cause immediate damage, but over time, they can damage sensitive computer equipment. It is definitely better to have a surge protector than not have one, but the surge protector must be of high quality (these usually cost more than $30.00).

The $5.99 power strips you find at Wal-Mart and similar stores are not true surge protectors. They are simply multiple-outlet strips with a single circuit breaker and provide only the most basic protection. Don't use them with computer equipment.

Common Components/Features

Tripp Lite's Isobar and American Power Conversion's (APC) SurgeArrest are two leading surge protector products. When selecting a surge protector, look for these components and features:

Active Protection Light When this light is illuminated, the unit is properly functioning. It should be on at all times.

Site Wiring Fault Light When this light is illuminated, there is a wiring fault in the circuit to which the surge protector is connected. This light should be off at all times.

Ground Make sure that the unit has three prongs on the plug, the third, middle plug, being for ground. If the ground is missing, the user can receive a lethal shock. This may seem obvious, but it is important to remember.

IEEE 587 A Let-Through Rating Check the value of the IEEE 587 A Let-Through rating. This value indicates how much voltage is let through when the surge protector clamps down on the incoming spike or surge. The lower this rating, the lower the voltage let through, and the better you are protected. A 330V rating is excellent protection.

UL Listing United Laboratories is an independent testing laboratory that certifies electrical equipment specifications. A UL listing indicates that the surge protector meets national electrical code and safety standards.

Circuit Breaker   This button pops out after a large spike or surge. When the circuit breaker trips, you will lose all power to your equipment. Press the button back in to reset the surge protector.

Additional Ports   New protectors protect much more than power cables. Today's surge protectors have RJ-45 and coaxial connectors for protecting network cards from extremely high surges. Also, RJ-11 and ISDN ports protect modems from telephone pole lightning strikes (these strikes can follow the phone line right into the modem, damaging it).

 IEEE stands for International Electrical and Electronics Engineers, an organization that is involved in creating standards. For more information, visit www.ieee.com.

Battery Backup Systems

Battery backup systems protect computer systems from power failures. These systems use a battery to power the computer and its assorted peripherals. Generally speaking, when these devices are activated due to a power failure, they permit the user to save data and initiate a graceful shutdown of the system. They normally aren't used to run the system for an extended period (unless the units use a *very large* capacity battery).

There are two main types of battery backup systems:

- Standby Power Supply (SPS)

- Uninterruptible Power Supply (UPS)

 Never plug a laser printer or copier into a battery backup device. These devices draw tremendous amounts of current when they are turned on (much more than any computer or network device would ever draw). If you do this, you may permanently damage or disable your battery backup device.

Power output from battery-powered inverters isn't exactly perfect. Normal power output alternates polarity 60 times a second (60 Hertz). When graphed, this output looks like a sine wave. Output from inverters is stepped to approximate this sine wave output, but it really never duplicates it. Today's inverter technology can come extremely close, but the differences between inverter and true AC power can cause damage to computer power supplies over the long run.

Standby Power Supply (SPS)

A Standby Power Supply (SPS) contains a battery, a switchover circuit, and an inverter (a device to convert the DC voltage from the battery into AC voltage that the computer and peripherals need). The outlets on the SPS are connected to the switching circuit, which is in turn connected to the incoming AC power (called line voltage). The switching circuit monitors the line voltage. When it drops below a factory preset threshold, the switching circuit switches from line voltage to the battery and inverter. The battery and inverter power the outlets (and, thus, the computers or devices plugged into them) until the switching circuit detects that line voltage is present again at the correct levels. The switching circuit then switches the outlets back to line voltage.

Level of Protection

Standby Power Supplies can provide some protection against power outages (more so than surge protectors, at any rate). Unfortunately, because the switching circuit must switch between power sources, there is a short period of time when the outlets have no power. Computers and network devices can usually handle this infinitesimally short period of time without power, but they don't always handle it gracefully. Some devices will lock up or experience errors. Others can even reboot (thus negating the reason for having a battery backup system).

For this reason, Standby Power Supplies have never been really popular with computer and electronic equipment users. They are inexpensive, and they can provide a basic level of protection, but this is usually not sufficient for sites that require 100 percent uptime.

Common Components/Features

Most Standby Power Supplies will have one or more of these features or components:

Multiple Outlets   Each SPS will have at least one outlet for connecting computers or network devices to the SPS. Most have multiple outlets. The number of outlets depends on the capacity of the battery, the inverter, and the switching circuit in the SPS.

Line Voltage Indicator   This light or indicator, when illuminated, indicates that the SPS is receiving sufficient AC line voltage to power the equipment plugged into the SPS.

Battery Power Indicator   This light or indicator, when illuminated, indicates that the equipment plugged into the SPS is running off the battery and inverter in the SPS. When this indicator is initially illuminated, a beep will sound, warning that power to the SPS has failed.

System Management Port   This is usually a standard serial port (although USB ports are becoming more popular). It allows the SPS to connect to the host computer (or server) it is protecting. The host computer runs SPS management software that gathers statistics about the power the SPS is using and providing. Also, when a power failure occurs, this port is used to send a signal from the SPS informing the management software on the host computer that the power to the SPS has failed. The management software can then initiate a graceful shutdown of the workstation computer or server.

Uninterruptible Power Supply (UPS)

A UPS is another type of battery backup often found on computers and network devices today. It is similar to an SPS in that it has outlets, a battery, and an inverter. The similarities end there, though. A UPS uses an entirely different method to provide continuous AC voltage to the equipment it supports.

In a UPS, the equipment is always running off the inverter and battery. A UPS contains a charging/monitoring circuit that charges the battery constantly. It also monitors the AC line voltage. When a power failure occurs, the charger just stops charging the battery. The equipment never senses any change in power. The monitoring part of the circuit senses the change and emits a beep to tell the user the power has failed.

Level of Protection

A UPS provides a significant amount of protection against many types of power problems because the computer is always running off the battery and inverter. Problems with the input line voltage don't really affect the output voltage. They only affect the efficiency of the charging circuit. A UPS is the most popular form of power protection because it provides significant protection at a fairly low cost.

Common Components/Features

When buying a UPS, you must look for the features that will solve your particular power problems or that meet your needs in general. Some of the features of a UPS include:

Multiple Outlets Each UPS will have at least one outlet for connecting computers or network devices to the UPS. Most have multiple outlets. The number of outlets depends on the capacity of the battery, inverter, and switching circuit in the UPS.

Line Voltage Indicator This light or indicator, when illuminated, indicates that the UPS is receiving sufficient AC line voltage to power the charging circuit of the UPS.

Battery Power Indicator This light or indicator, when illuminated, indicates that the equipment plugged into the UPS is running off the battery and inverter in the UPS and that the charging circuit is not active. When this indicator is initially illuminated, a beep will sound, warning that power to the UPS has failed.

System Management Port This is usually a standard serial port (although USB ports are becoming more popular). It allows the UPS to connect to the host computer (or server) it is protecting. The host computer runs UPS management software that gathers statistics about the power the UPS is using and providing. Also, when a power failure occurs, this port is used to send a signal to the management software on the host computer that the power to the UPS has failed. The management software can then initiate a graceful shutdown of the workstation computer or server.

Line Conditioners

The AC voltage that powers our everyday devices comes from power sources usually located far from where we use it. The power is conducted through wires and stepping stations over many miles on its trip from where it's generated to where it's used. At any point along this trip, erroneous electrical patterns or signals can be introduced into the power that computers may not be able to handle properly. These erroneous signals are known as *line noise* and can cause many types of problems, including random lockups, random reboots, and system crashes.

All power signals have varying degrees of line noise. In areas that have particularly bad line noise, a device known as a *line conditioner* is used. This device filters out the erroneous signals in the power, leaving the devices it supplies with clean, 110 Volt, 60Hz power.

Line conditioners are complex (and, thus, expensive) devices that incorporate a number of power correction technologies to provide electronic devices with clean power. Some of these technologies include UPS, surge suppression, and power filtering.

Level of Protection

Line conditioners provide the highest level of power protection for electronic devices. Hot sites will have a large line conditioner (or multiple line conditioners) that service every computer in an organization. These conditioners are often wired directly into the electrical system of a company. Special outlets (with markings that indicate they are protected outlets) are wired in each room. Wires from these outlets lead directly back to the line conditioner. These devices are usually cost-prohibitive for smaller companies or for a single computer, although, some small companies will invest in a small line conditioner for their main server, if it is a critical server.

Common Components/Features

Line conditioners usually have control panel interfaces. Some manufacturers replace the control panel interface with a computer and power management software. These interfaces can report both incoming and outgoing voltages, as well as any problems these interfaces might be experiencing. These devices are so complex and large that they typically require large cooling fans and an adequate supply of cool air.

Disk System Fault Tolerance

A hard disk is a temporary storage device, and every hard disk will eventually fail. The most common problem is a complete hard disk failure (also known as a hard disk crash). When this happens, all stored data is irretrievable. Therefore, if you want your data to be accessible 90 to 100 percent of the time (as with warm and hot sites), you need to use some method of disk fault tolerance. Typically, disk fault tolerance is achieved through disk management technologies such as mirroring, striping, and duplexing drives and provides some level of data protection. As with other methods of fault tolerance, disk fault tolerance means that a disk system is able to recover from an error condition of some kind.

The methods that provide fault tolerance for hard disk systems include:

- Mirroring

- Duplexing

- Data striping

- Redundant array of independent (or inexpensive) disks (RAID)

Understanding Disk Volumes

Before we can discuss the various methods of providing fault tolerance for disk systems, we must discuss one important concept: volumes. When you install a new hard disk into a computer and prepare it for use, the NOS sets up the disk so that you can store data on it in a process known as formatting. Once this has been achieved, the NOS can access the disk. Before it can store data on the disk, it must set up what is known as a volume. A *volume*, for all practical purposes, is a named chunk of disk space. This chunk can exist on part of a disk, can exist on all of a disk, or can span multiple disks. Volumes provide a way of organizing disk storage, as you can see in this illustration:

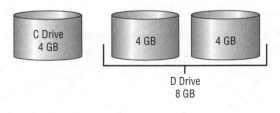

Disk Mirroring

Mirroring a drive means designating a hard disk drive in the computer as a mirror or duplicate to another, specified drive. The two drives are attached to a single disk controller. This disk fault tolerance feature is provided by most network operating systems. When the NOS writes data to the specified drive, the same data is also written to the drive designated as the mirror. If the first drive fails, the mirror drive is already online, and since it has a duplicate of the information contained on the specified drive, the users won't know that a disk drive in the server has failed. The NOS notifies the administrator that the failure has occurred. The down side is that if the disk controller fails, neither drive is available. Figure 9.1 shows how disk mirroring works.

FIGURE 9.1 Disk mirroring

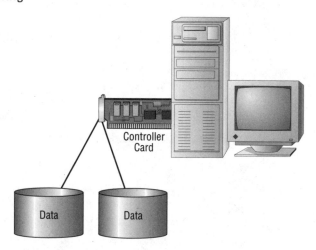

The drives do not need to be identical; but this helps. Both drives must have the same amount of free space to allow a mirror to be formed. For example, you have two 4GB drives; one has 3GB free, and the other has 2GB free. You can create one 2GB mirrored system.

Mirroring is an implementation of RAID Level 1, which is discussed in more detail later in this chapter.

Disk Duplexing

As with mirroring, duplexing also saves data to a mirror drive. In fact, the only major difference between duplexing and mirroring is that duplexing uses two separate disk controllers (one for each disk). Thus, duplexing provides not only a redundant disk, but a redundant controller as well. Duplexing provides fault tolerance even if one of the controllers fails. Figure 9.2 shows a duplexed disk system. Compare this with Figure 9.1. Notice that there is now an extra disk controller in the system.

FIGURE 9.2   Disk duplexing

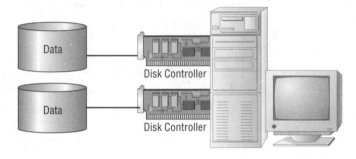

 Duplexing is also an implementation of RAID level 1.

Disk Striping

From a performance point of view, writing data to a single drive is slow. When three drives are configured as a single volume, information must fill the first drive before it can go to the second, as well as fill the second before filling the third. If you configure that volume to use disk striping, you will see a definite performance gain. Disk striping breaks up the data to be saved to disk into small portions and sequentially writes the portions to all disks simultaneously in small areas called stripes. These stripes maximize performance because all the read/write heads are working constantly. Figure 9.3 shows an example of striping data across multiple disks. Notice that the data is broken into sections and that each section is sequentially written to a separate disk.

FIGURE 9.3 How disk striping works

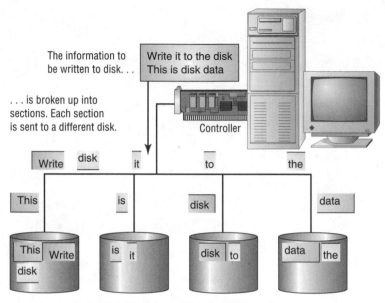

The information to be written to disk. . .

Write it to the disk
This is disk data

. . . is broken up into sections. Each section is sent to a different disk.

Controller

Each disk holds a piece of the original information.

Striping data across multiple disks improves only performance; it does not improve fault tolerance. To add fault tolerance to disk striping, it is necessary to use parity.

Parity Information

Parity, as it relates to disk fault tolerance, is a general term for the fault tolerance information computed for each chunk of data written to a disk. This parity information can be used to reconstruct missing data should a disk fail. Striping can use parity or not, but if the striping technology doesn't use parity, you won't gain any fault tolerance. When using striping with parity, the parity information is computed for each block and written to the drive.

The advantage to using parity with striping is gaining fault tolerance. If any part of the data gets lost or destroyed, the information can be rebuilt from the parity information. The down side to using parity is that computing and writing parity information reduces the total performance of a disk system that uses striping. The parity information also reduces the total amount of free disk space.

Redundant Array of Inexpensive (or Independent) Disks (RAID)

RAID is a technology that uses an array of less-expensive hard disks instead of one enormous hard disk and that provides several methods for writing to those disks to ensure redundancy. Those methods are described as *levels,* and each level is designed for a specific purpose:

RAID 0 (Commonly used)   This method is the fastest because all read/write heads are constantly being used without the burden of parity or duplicate data being written. A system using this method has multiple disks, and the information to be stored is striped across the disks in blocks without parity. This RAID level only improves performance; it does not provide fault tolerance.

RAID 1 (Commonly used)   This level uses two hard disks, one mirrored to the other (commonly known as mirroring; duplexing is also an implementation of RAID 1). This is the most basic level of disk fault tolerance. If the first hard disk fails, the second automatically takes over. No parity or error-checking information is stored. Rather, each drive has duplicate information of the other. If both drives fail, a new drive must be installed and configured, and the data must be restored from a backup.

RAID 2   Individual bits are striped across multiple disks. One drive (designated as the parity drive) in this configuration is dedicated to storing parity data. If any data drive (a drive in this configuration that is not the parity drive) fails, the data on that drive can be rebuilt from parity data stored on the parity drive. At least three disk drives are required in this configuration. This is not a commonly used implementation.

RAID 3 (Commonly used)   Data is striped across multiple hard drives using a parity drive (similar to RAID 2). The main difference is that the data is striped in bytes, not bits, as in RAID 2. This configuration is popular because more data is written and read in one operation, increasing overall disk performance.

RAID 4   This is similar to RAID 2 and 3 (striping with parity drive), except data is striped in blocks, which facilitates fast reads from one drive. Raid 4 is the same as RAID 0, with the addition of a parity drive. This is not a popular implementation.

RAID 5 (Commonly used)   The data and parity are striped across several drives. This allows for fast writes and reads. The parity information for data on one disk is stored with the data on another disk, so if any one disk fails, the drive can be replaced, and its data can be rebuilt from the parity data stored on the other drives. A minimum of three disks is required. Five or more disks are most often used.

There are other levels of RAID, including RAID 53, 6, 7, and 10, but because they aren't covered on the exam, we won't discuss them here.

Backup Considerations

Although you can never be completely prepared for every natural disaster or human foible that can bring down your network, you can make sure that you have a solid backup plan in place to minimize the impact of lost data. Even if the worst happens, you don't have to lose days or weeks of work, provided that you have a solid plan in place. A *backup plan* is the set of guidelines and schedules that determine which data should be backed up and how often. A backup plan includes information such as:

- What to back up

- Where to back it up

- When to back up

- How often to back up

- Who should be responsible for backups

- Where media should be stored

- How often to test backups

- The procedure to follow in case of data loss

This section covers some of the items that are contained in a common backup plan, including:

- Backup media options

- Backup utilities

- Backup types
- Tape rotation schedule

Backup Media Options

When you back up your network's data, you must have something on which to store that data, which is called the backup medium. You have several options, including:

- Small-capacity removable disks
- Large-capacity removable disks
- Removable optical disks
- Magnetic tape

Let's examine the advantages and disadvantages of each type, starting with small-capacity removable disks.

Small-Capacity Removable Disks

Small-capacity disks are magnetic media disks, with a capacity of less than 500MB, which can be removed from their drives and replaced as they get filled. They are popular because of their low cost and ease of use. Additionally, because they are inexpensive, many computers come with one or more of these drives. Table 9.1 lists some examples of this type of backup medium and their popular capacities.

TABLE 9.1 Popular Small-Capacity Removable Disks

Medium	Capacity
Floppy disk	1.44MB, 2.88MB
SyQuest cartridges	44MB, 88MB, 105MB, 200MB, 230MB
Iomega ZIP disk	100MB, 250MB
Imation SuperDisk	120MB
Removable hard disk drive	Varies

Large-Capacity Removable Disks

Large-capacity removable disks are virtually the same as small-capacity removable disks except they can store more data (more than 500MB per disk). The drives and media cost more, but the increase in capacity easily offsets the increased cost. Large-capacity removable disks are good for backing up a workstation that has only one or two disks. You can also use them to back up a server, but because they don't have the capacity to back up a server with a single removable disk (multiple disks would be required for each backup), their use is limited. Table 9.2 lists a few of the common large-capacity removable disks and their capacities.

TABLE 9.2   Popular Large-Capacity Removable Disks

Medium	Capacity
Iomega Jaz	1GB, 2GB
Sharq	1.5GB
Syquest cartridges	1GB, 1.5GB
Removable hard disk drive	Varies

Removable Optical Disks

Removable optical disks use a laser (or some kind of light beam) to read and write information stored on a removable disk. They typically have large capacities and are fairly slow (more than 100 milliseconds as opposed to less than 50 milliseconds for magnetic) access times. The advantage to optical disks is that the capacities start at about 128MB and go up from there (although 650MB is a common size). There are even special optical jukeboxes, containing hundreds of disks and a robotic arm to select disks and put them in the drive(s), that have capacities in the hundreds of terabytes (1 tera-byte is 1000 gigabytes). Table 9.3 lists some of the popular optical formats and their capacities.

TABLE 9.3   Popular Removable Optical Disk Capacities

Medium	Common Capacities
CD-ROM, CD-R, CD-RW	650MB
Magneto Optical disk	650MB, 1.3GB, 4.6GB
DVD	4.7GB up to 17GB

CD-R and CD-RW are writable CD-ROM implementations.

Magnetic Tape

Magnetic tape is the oldest and most popular backup medium for offline (not readily accessible) data storage. It stores data in the form of magnetically oriented metal particles (either copper oxide or chromium dioxide) on a polyester tape. It is popular because it is simple, inexpensive, and has a high capacity. Most networks use a magnetic tape backup of some kind. Table 9.4 lists a few of the most common magnetic tape backup technologies and their common capacities.

TABLE 9.4   Common Magnetic Tape Capacities

Technology	Common Capacities
QIC	100MB to gigabytes and up
DDS Cartridges for DAT drives	Gigabytes
DLT	35GB and up
AIT	25GB, 50GB

Copying Workstation Data to the Network

Servers must be backed up because they contain all the data for the entire network. In most networks, workstations are not backed up because they usually don't contain any data of major importance. This is only the case if the users are trained properly and store all their data on the network. Users can mistakenly save their data to their local workstation. Also, user application configuration data are normally stored on the workstation. If a workstation's hard disk goes down, the configuration is lost.

For backups to be successful, users need to ensure that all necessary data is located on the network. You can do this in two ways: user training and folder replication. Training is time-consuming and costly, but productive in the long run. Users should understand the general network layout and know how to save their data in the proper place. This keeps all user data centralized and makes it easy for the administrator to back up the data.

When you replicate folders, client platforms that support replication will share out their hard disks (or portions of it) to the rest of the network. The network backup software then backs up those portions of the workstation that the administrator specifies.

Backup Utilities

A backup utility is a software program that can archive the data on a hard disk to a removable medium. Backup utilities can compress data before they store it, making it more efficient to use a backup program to archive data than to simply copy it to the backup medium.

Most operating systems include backup utilities, but these are usually simple programs that lack the advanced features of full-fledged, third-party programs (such as Seagate Backup Exec and Computer Associate's ARCSERVE):

- Windows 98 comes with Microsoft Backup.

- Windows NT has a backup program with a similar interface.

- Novell's NetWare comes with SBackup.

- Unix comes with a command-based tape archive utility called tar.

All these backup utilities are good for an initial backup of your system. For a complete set of features including scheduling and managing tape sets, purchase a third-party product that fits your platforms and specific backup requirements.

Backup Types

After you choose your backup medium and backup utility, you must decide what type of backup to run. The types vary by how much data they back up each time and by how many tapes it takes to restore data after a complete system crash. The three backup types are:

- Full
- Differential
- Incremental

Full Backup

In a full backup, all network data is backed up (without skipping any files). This type of backup is straightforward because you simply tell the software which servers (and, if applicable, workstations) to back up, where to back the data up, and start the backup. If you have to do a restore after a crash, you have only one set of tapes to restore from (as many tapes as it took to back up everything). Simply insert the most recent full backup into the drive and start the restore.

If you have a tape system with a maximum capacity of half the size of all the data on your server, the backup utility will stop the backup halfway through and ask you to insert the next tape. Normally, full backups take several hours, and most companies can't afford to have a user sit in front of the tape drive and change tapes. So you need a backup drive and medium with enough capacity, or a backup system that can automatically change its own tapes (such as a DAT autoloader).

Figure 9.4 shows the amount of data backed up each day in a full backup scheme. Note that if you are working with 20GB of data, approximately 20GB is stored on a new tape each night, along with any additional data from that day. However, you are basically backing up the same data each day.

FIGURE 9.4 The amount of data backed up with a full backup

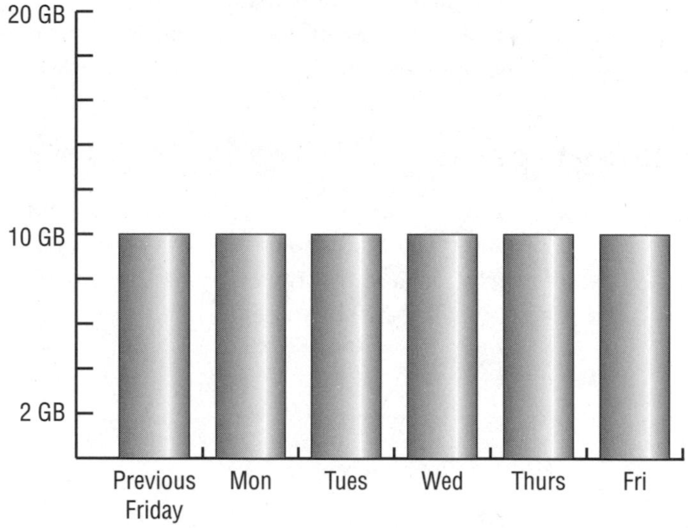

Differential Backup

In a differential backup strategy, a single, full backup is done typically once a week. Every night for the next six nights, the backup utility backs up all files that have changed since the last full backup (the actual differential backup). After a week's worth of differential backups, another full backup is done, starting the cycle all over again. With differential backups, you use a maximum of two backup sessions to restore a file or group of files.

Here's how it works: The backup utility keeps track of which files have been backed up through the use of the archive bit, which is simply an attribute that indicates a file's status with respect to the current backup type. The archive bit is cleared for each file backed up during the full backup. After that, any time a program opens and changes a file, the NOS sets the archive bit, indicating that the file has changed and needs to be backed up. Then each night, in a differential backup, the backup program copies every item that has its archive bit set, indicating the file has changed since the last full backup. The archive bit is not touched during each differential backup.

When restoring a server after a complete server failure, you must restore two sets of tapes: the last full backup and the most current differential backup. A full restoration may take longer, but each differential backup takes much less time than a full backup. This type of backup is used when the amount of time each day available to perform a system backup (called the *backup window*) is smaller during the week and larger on the weekend.

Figure 9.5 shows the amount of data being backed up each day in a differential backup. Notice that the amount of data becomes gradually larger every day as the number of files that need to get backed up increases. Remember that the archive bit isn't cleared each day; so by the end of the week, the files that changed at the beginning of the week may have been backed up several times, even though they haven't changed since the first part of the week.

FIGURE 9.5 The amount of data backed up in a differential backup

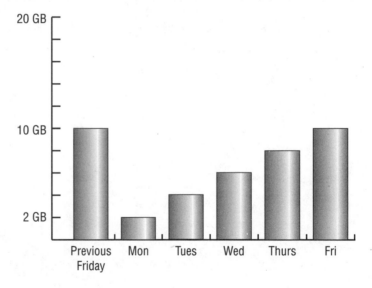

Incremental Backup

In an incremental backup, a full backup is used in conjunction with daily partial backups to back up the entire server, thus reducing the amount of time it takes for a daily backup. With an incremental backup, the weekly full backup takes place as it does during a differential backup, and the archive bit is cleared during the full backup. The incremental, daily backups back up only the data that has changed since the *last* backup (*not* the last full backup). The archive bit is cleared each time a backup occurs. With this method, only files that change since the previous day's backup are backed up. Each day's backup is a different size because a different number of files are modified each day.

This method provides the fastest daily backups for networks whose daily backup window is extremely small. However, the network administrator does pay a price for shortened backup sessions. The restores after a server failure take the longest of the three methods. The full backup set is restored plus every tape from the day of the failure back to the preceding full backup.

Figure 9.6 shows the incremental backup scenario. Note that the amount of data backed up each day is different from day to day, but it is also much smaller than doing a differential or full backup.

FIGURE 9.6 The amount of data backed up with an incremental backup

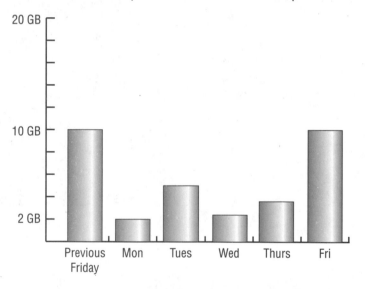

Each backup type is used for a different purpose. Full backups are used when restore time is at a premium. Incremental backups are used when

backup time is at a premium. Differential backups are a compromise between the two methods. Table 9.5 summarizes the backup types.

TABLE 9.5 Backup Types

Type	What Is Backed Up	Archive Bit Cleared?	Number of Sets to Restore after Server Crash
Full	All data on the server (network)	Y	Full only
Differential	Data since the last full backup	N	Full plus last differential
Incremental	Data since the last backup	Y	Full plus every daily incremental since last full backup

Tape Rotation Schedule

Rotating backup tapes is the most practical way to manage a tape backup scheme, since the costs of using a new tape every day are prohibitive. Tapes are the cheapest form of storage compared with other media. That does not mean that tapes are cheap, though. A single DLT cartridge can cost $40.00. If you use a tape for every day of the month, plus one for every month, you will be spending more than $1600, not counting taxes, for just one server. To go back to any day in the year on a single tape would require a tape per day. When you use a tape for every day of the year, the cost is more than $14,000. Most companies also have more then one server. Advanced backup programs can remotely back up users' workstations as well.

The solution is tape rotation. Do not use a different tape each day. Instead, reuse tapes from previous months and weeks. We will look at some simple rotations, such as weekly, along with some rather complicated schemes.

Weekly Rotation

In a weekly rotation, you use a different backup tape or tapes for each day of the week. Weekly rotations are the simplest to understand and set up. You first assign a tape to each weekday and label the tape with the name of the day. You have five tapes, and you overwrite each tape as the day of the week comes again. The furthest you can go back to do a restore is one business week. On Friday, before the backup, you can go back to any day for one week, but no further.

Monthly Rotation

Rotating tapes on a monthly basis allows you to restore data for an entire month. Managing this type of backup scheme is more complicated because you must keep track of many more tapes. A straightforward solution is to assign 31 tapes and do a full backup each day. This becomes unwieldy if a full backup takes many tapes. For example, a thousand-user corporation's e-mail, file, and print servers can take multiple high-capacity DLT tapes per session.

Most of your restore requests will be reported shortly after the file is accidentally deleted or corrupted. Take your typical user who accidentally deletes his home directory. Using a GUI interface, this is as easy as right-clicking a folder and then left-clicking delete. The user will immediately call network support and plead for quick rescue. In this case, you only have to go back to the previous day's tape. To plan for this scenario, have daily backups that go back a week. Supplement this with a weekly backup for an entire month.

In this configuration, you would use no more than nine tapes. You will use one tape for each day of the week, Monday through Thursday (= 4 tapes) and one tape for each Friday of the month (= 4 or 5 tapes, depending on how many Fridays there are in a month). A maximum of nine tapes will give you daily backups for a week and weekly backups for a month. Label the tapes Monday through Thursday, and Friday Week 1 through Friday Week 5.

Yearly Rotation

You can build a yearly backup on top of the monthly system. You'll need 12 tapes, one for each month labeled with the names of the months. Rename the last weekly, full backup of each month to the corresponding month. You go from nine tapes to 21 tapes and gain the capability of going back a year to restore data. Only one day out of each month is available after you go back further than your current month.

Grandfather-Father-Son Rotation

A standard rotation scheme for tapes is the Grandfather-Father-Son (GFS) method. Daily backups are differential, incremental, or full. Full backups are done once a week. The daily backups are known as the Son. The last full backup of the week is known as the Father. Because the daily tapes are reused after a week, they age only five days. The weekly tapes stay around for a month and are reused during the next month. The last full backup of the month is known as the monthly backup, or the Grandfather. The Grandfather tapes become the oldest, and you retain them for a year before reusing them. Figure 9.7 is an example of a GFS tape scheme.

FIGURE 9.7 Grandfather-Father-Son rotation

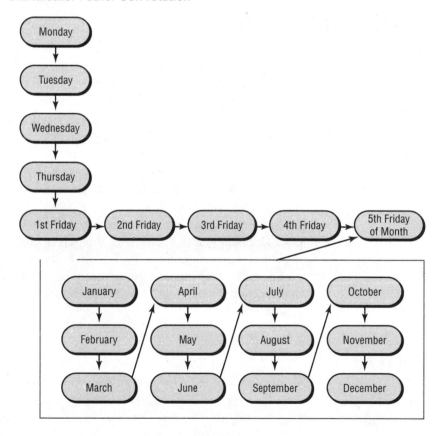

Long-Term Configurations

In addition to daily, weekly, and yearly backups, some companies, for archival purposes, do an end-of-year backup, which is then kept offsite in long-term storage. They do this to keep a record of the year's financial and transactional data so that they can refer to it in case of tax problems (the IRS may require businesses to keep transactional data for seven years).

Some companies do two end-of-year backups—one before closing out the fiscal year, and another after closing out. They do this in case they mess up the closing and need to start over. When the closing out is finished, they back up the closed-out system and place the tape in long-term storage.

Virus Protection

A *virus* is a program that causes malicious change in your computer and makes copies of itself. Sophisticated viruses encrypt and hide themselves to thwart detection. There are tens of thousands of viruses that your computer can catch. Known viruses are referred to as being "in the wild." Research laboratories and universities study viruses for commercial and academic purposes. These viruses are known as being "in the zoo," or not out in the wild. Every month, the number of viruses in the wild increase.

Viruses can be little more than hindrances, or they can shut down an entire corporation. The types vary, but the approach to handling them does not. You need to install virus protection software on all computer equipment. This is similar to vaccinating your entire family, not just the children who are going to summer camp. Workstations, personal computer, servers, and firewalls all must have virus protection, even if they never connect to your network. They can still get viruses from floppy disks or Internet downloads (via modem).

Types of Viruses

Several types of viruses exist, but the two most popular are macro and boot sector. Each type differs slightly in the way it works and how it infects your system. Many viruses attack popular applications such as Microsoft Word, Excel, and PowerPoint, which are easy to use and for which it is easy to create a virus. Because writing a unique virus is considered a challenge to a bored programmer, viruses are becoming more and more complex and harder to eradicate.

Macro Viruses

A macro is a script of commonly enacted commands that are used to automatically perform operations without a user's intervention. Macro viruses use the Visual Basic macro scripting language to perform malicious or mischievous functions in Microsoft Office products. Macro viruses are among the most harmless (but also the most annoying). Since macros are easy to write, macro viruses are among the most common viruses and are frequently found in Microsoft Word and PowerPoint. They affect the file you are working on. For example, you might be unable to save the file even though the Save function is working, or you might be unable to open a new document— you can only open a template. These viruses will not crash your system, but they are annoying. Cap and Cap A are examples of macro viruses.

Boot Sector Viruses

Boot sector viruses get into the master boot record. This is track one, sector one on your hard disk. No applications are supposed to reside there. The computer at boot up checks this section to find a pointer for the operating system. If you have a multioperating system boot between Windows 95/98, Windows NT, and Unix, this is where the pointers are stored. A boot sector virus will overwrite the boot sector, thereby making it look as if there is no pointer to your operating system. When you power up the computer, you will see a Missing Operating System or Hard Disk Not Found error message. Monkey B, Stealth, and Stealth Boot are examples of boot sector viruses.

These are only a few of the types of viruses out there. For a more complete list, see your antivirus software manufacturer's Web site, or go to Symantec's Web site at www.symantec.com/.

Updating Antivirus Components

A typical antivirus program consists of two components:

- The definition files
- The engine

The definition files list the various viruses, their type, and footprints and specify how to remove the specific virus. More than 100 new viruses are found in the wild each month. An antivirus program would be useless if it did not keep up with all the new viruses. The engine accesses the definition files, or database, runs the virus scans, cleans the files, and notifies the appropriate people and accounts. Eventually viruses become so sophisticated that a new engine and new technology are needed to combat them effectively.

Heuristic scanning is a technology that allows an antivirus program to search for a virus even if there is no definition for that specific virus. The engine looks for suspicious activity that might indicate a virus. Be careful if you have this feature turned on. A heuristic scan might detect more than viruses.

For an antivirus program to be effect, you must upgrade, update, and scan in a specific order:

1. Upgrade the antivirus engine.
2. Update the definition files.
3. Create an antivirus emergency boot disk.
4. Configure and run a full on-demand scan.
5. Schedule monthly full on-demand scans.
6. Configure and activate on-access scans.
7. Update the definition files monthly.
8. Make a new antivirus emergency boot disk monthly.
9. Get the latest update when fighting a virus outbreak.
10. Repeat all steps when you get a new engine.

If you think this is a lot of work, you are right. However, not doing it can be a lot more work and a lot more trouble.

Upgrading an Antivirus Engine

An antivirus engine is the core program that runs the scanning process; virus definitions are keyed to an engine version number. For example, a 3.*x* engine will not work with 4.*x* definition files. When the manufacturer releases a new engine, consider both the cost to upgrade and the added benefits.

Before installing new or upgraded software, back up your entire computer system, including all data.

Updating Definition Files

Every month you need to update your list of known viruses—called the virus definition files. You can do this manually or automatically through the manufacturer's Web site. You can use a staging server within your company to download and then distribute the updates, or you can set up each computer to download updates.

Scanning for Viruses

An antivirus scan is the process in which an antivirus program examines the computer suspected of having a virus and eradicates any viruses it finds. There are two types of antivirus scans:

- On-demand
- On-access

An on-demand scan searches a file, a directory, a drive, or an entire computer. An on-access scan checks only the files you are currently accessing. To maximize protection, you should use a combination of both types.

On-Demand Scans

An on-demand scan is a virus scan initiated by either a network administrator or a user. You can manually or automatically initiate an on-demand scan. Typically, you schedule a monthly on-demand scan, but you also want to do an on-demand scan in the following situations:

- After you first install the antivirus software
- When you upgrade the antivirus software engine
- When you suspect a virus outbreak

Before you initiate an on-demand scan, be sure that you have the latest virus definitions.

When you encounter a virus, scan all potentially affected hard disks and any floppy disks that could be suspicious. Establish a cleaning station, and quarantine the infected area. The support staff will have a difficult time if a user continues to use the computer while it is infected. Ask all users in the infected area to stop using their computers. Suggest a short break. If it is lunchtime, all the better. Have one person remove all floppies from all disk drives. Perform a scan and clean at the cleaning station. For computers that are operational, update their virus definitions. For computers that are not operational or are operational but infected, boot to an antivirus emergency boot disk. Run a full scan and clean the entire system on all computers in the office space. With luck, you will be done before your users return from lunch.

On-Access Scans

An on-access scan runs in the background when you open a file or use a program. For example, an on-access scan can run when you do any of the following:

- Insert a floppy disk
- Download a file with ftp
- Receive e-mail messages and attachments
- View a Web page

The scan slows the processing speed of other programs, but is worth the inconvenience.

A relatively new form of malicious attack makes its way to your computer through ActiveX and Java programs (applets). These are miniature programs that run on a Web server or that you download to your local machine. Most ActiveX and Java applets are safe, but some contain viruses or snoop programs. The snoop programs allow a hacker to look at everything on your hard drive from a remote location without your knowing. Be sure that you properly configure your on-access component of antivirus software to check and clean for all these types of attacks.

Many programs will not install unless you disable the on-access portion of your antivirus software. This is dangerous if the program has a virus. Your safest bet is to do an on-demand scan of the software before installation. Disable on-access scanning during installation, and then reactivate it when the installation is complete.

Emergency Scans

In an emergency scan, only the operating system and the antivirus program are running. An emergency scan is called for after a virus has invaded your system and taken control of a machine. In this situation, insert your antivirus emergency boot disk and boot the infected computer from it. Then scan and clean the entire computer.

If you don't have your boot disk, go to another computer and create one.

Software Patches

Patches, fixes, service packs, and updates are all the same thing—free software revisions. These are intermediary solutions until a new version of the product is released. A patch may solve a particular problem, as does a security patch, or change the way your system works, as does an update. You can apply a so-called hot patch without rebooting your computer; in other cases, applying a patch requires that the server go down.

Is It Necessary?

Because patches are designed to fix problems, it would seem that you would want to download the most current patches and apply them immediately. That is not always the best thing to do. Patches can sometimes cause problems with existing, older software. Different philosophies exist regarding the application of the newest patches. The first philosophy is to keep your systems only as up-to-date as necessary to keep them running. This is the "If it ain't broke, don't fix it" approach. After all, the point of a patch is to fix your software. Why fix it if it isn't broken? The other philosophy is to keep the software as up-to-date as possible because of the additional features that a patch will sometimes provide.

You must choose the approach that is best for your situation. If you have little time to devote to chasing down and fixing problems, go with the first philosophy. If you always need the latest and greatest features, even at the expense of stability, go with the second.

Where to Get Patches

Patches are available from several locations:

- The manufacturer's Web site

- The manufacturer's CD or DVD

- The manufacturer's support subscriptions on CD or DVD

- The manufacturer's bulletin (less frequently an option)

You'll notice that in every case the source of the patch, regardless of the medium being used to distribute it, is the manufacturer. You cannot be sure that patches available through online magazines, other companies, and shareware Web sites are safe. Patches for the operating system are also sometimes included when you purchase a new computer.

How to Apply Patches

Just as you always need to plan for an upgrade, you need to plan for a patch. Never blindly install patches (or any other new software) without examining the potential impact on the network. Although patches are designed to fix known problems, they may create new ones. It is best to try patches on a test network or system before installing them on all systems on the network.

Follow these steps to apply a patch:

1. Research the enhancements and changes that the patch provides. Go to the manufacturer's Web site, or take a look at the official documentation.

2. Download the patch and related documentation to an isolated test network (or computer if you don't have an entire test network).

3. Decompress any documentation files and read them. (Yes, the manual is something you read before installation, not after things crash.)

4. Note the changes, and define a way to test the new features.

5. Install the patch on a test workstation/server.

6. Select the installation method that allows you to save previous configurations so that you uninstall if necessary.

7. Record any options and your selections, such as retaining or replacing drivers.

8. Reboot the computer.

9. If the operating system does not load or work properly, start over with a clean test machine. Select to keep your original drivers. (NIC drivers are commonly updated and may not work.)

10. Try out the new features. Test all patches to see if they work as advertised.

11. Run the test workstation/server for two weeks. Reboot it and try different tasks during this time.

12. If all goes well, do a limited roll out of the update to your support staff's personal computers and applicable servers, and have them test the patch.

13. After the IS support staff determines the product is safe, do a limited roll out to some users' workstations and applicable servers.

14. Roll out the patch to all production servers and all workstations via an automated procedure.

15. Ensure proper revision control. Make sure that all equipment has the same approved patch.

Remember that these are general steps. Refer to the documentation that comes with the patch (most likely a README.TXT file) for specific instructions on installing a specific patch.

You can see that this process can take a long time, even with multiple test machines and people helping you. The process can be speeded up a little, but do not skip any steps. If at any point you cannot get a system to work, even with changing the install options, stop the installation and refer to the support documentation for the patch to see if you are doing something wrong. Do not roll out a patch until it has been proven stable in all test environments.

If you use your operating system or application CDs to make changes to the operating system or an application after applying the patch, you may overwrite the updates made by the patch. You will need to reapply the patch after accessing these files.

Key Terms

Before you take the exam, be certain you are familiar with the following terms:

backup plan

backup window

clustering

Disaster recovery

duplicate server

failover device

Fault tolerance

heartbeat

levels

line conditioner

line noise

multiple server clustering

nearline site

replication

surge suppressors

virus

volume

Review Questions

1. What type of communication does a failover server typically have with the primary server?

   A. Total. They are two virtual servers in the same box.

   B. The two machines are in different sites connected by a modem.

   C. The two machines are in different sites connected by sleeping NICs.

   D. A dedicated network cable links the two servers.

   E. None. The failover server is on a separate network for protection.

2. What does the failover server listen for to determine if it needs to take over services?

   A. Ping

   B. Heartbeat

   C. Shutdown sequence

   D. Startup sequence

   E. Telnet session

3. What technology does VMS use to allow multiple servers to access the same resources to provide load balancing and fault tolerance?

   A. Clusters

   B. Proxies

   C. Slave servers

   D. Master servers

   E. Failover servers

4. What benefit does a backup system give you?

    A. A master/slave server combination

    B. A clustered network up 100 percent of the time

    C. Copies of data on tape or removable media

    D. A power conditioner

    E. A UPS with a built-in surge protector

5. What RAID level provides the fastest access times with no fault tolerance?

    A. 0

    B. 1

    C. 3

    D. 5

    E. 10

6. RAID level 1 is more commonly known as _____.

    A. Striping

    B. Striping with parity

    C. Duplicating

    D. Mirroring

    E. Master/slave

7. What is the minimum number of hard disks required for RAID 5?

   A. one

   B. two

   C. three

   D. four

   E. five

8. What are the differences between disk duplexing and disk mirroring?

   A. Disk duplexing uses one controller card, whereas mirroring uses two.

   B. Disk duplexing uses two controller cards, whereas mirroring uses one.

   C. Disk duplexing is slower because it uses only two disks, whereas mirroring uses three.

   D. Disk duplexing is faster because it uses three disks, whereas mirroring uses two.

   E. Disk duplexing can have a controller fail and not lose access to data.

   F. Mirroring can have a controller fail and not lose access to data.

9. You are newly hired as a network administrator for a group. The workgroup server has two 6GB disks. The first has 3GB used and the second has 2GB used.

   Required Results: Without reformatting the hard disks, implement a fault-tolerant partition.

   Optional Results: Provide for the highest level of fault tolerance without buying another hard disk. Use the maximum amount of space that will work with your RAID solution.

Proposed Solution: Purchase two RAID 1 duplexing controllers. Implement hardware-based duplexing. Use all the available free space on both hard disks to create a 7GB duplexed partition.

A. The proposed solution meets the required results.

B. The proposed solution meets the required results and one of the optional results.

C. The proposed solution meet the required results and both the optional results.

D. The proposed solution does not meet the required results.

10. What power management device should be connected to every server?

    A. SPS

    B. UPS

    C. APS

    D. USPS

    E. SPSS

11. What power management device is best suited for noncritical workstations and home stereo equipment?

    A. Standby Power Supply

    B. Uninterruptible power supply

    C. Power conditioner

    D. Gas generator

    E. Surge protector

12. A brownout is _____.

    A. A long increase in power

    B. A change from AC to DC power

    C. A reduction in power

    D. A short decrease in power

13. What is an electrical spike?

    A. A long increase in power

    B. A change from AC to DC power

    C. A reduction in power

    D. A short increase in power

14. A full backup does what to the archive bit once a backup has completed?

    A. Clears it

    B. Activates it

    C. Does nothing

    D. Sets it to 100

    E. Resets it to 1000

15. In which type of backup do you use a maximum of two backup sessions to restore a file or a group of files?

    A. Full

    B. Partial

    C. Incremental

    D. Additional

    E. Differential

16. An incremental backup copies _____ to tape.

    A. Data files only

    B. Operating system files only

    C. Files with the archive clear

    D. Files that have changed since the last full backup only

    E. Files changed since the last full or incremental backup

17. Compared with other backup schemes required to fully restore a server, the restore time from a full backup is _____.

    A. The shortest because multiple sessions are accessed

    B. The shortest because a single session is accessed

    C. The longest because multiple sessions are accessed

    D. The longest because a single session is accessed

    E. The same length of time as all other backup schemes

18. Which type of backup tape has the greatest capacity?

    A. QIC

    B. AIT

    C. DAT

    D. DLT

    E. Travan

19. How often should you update your virus definition files?

    A. Daily

    B. Weekly

    C. Monthly

    D. Quarterly

    E. Yearly

20. You should get your updates from which source(s)?

A. Manufacturer

B. Online magazine

C. Postal magazine

D. Original Equipment Manufacturer

E. Shareware Web site

Answers to Review Questions

1. D. A failover server must have a connection available to the other server in case the other server goes down. Thus, there is a dedicated network between the two to ensure that the other server will be available when the failover must occur.

2. B. Failover servers send a signal to the backup failover server every few seconds. When the backup server detects that the primary server has not sent the signal after a specified time, the failover takes over until the primary comes back online. This signal is known as a "heartbeat."

3. A. VMS clustering makes many servers appear as one. If one server malfunctions, the others stay functioning, thus allowing no breaks in network services.

4. C. Backup systems are designed to provide a backup copy of existing data in case of system failure. These copies are typically stored on magnetic tape or some other kind of removable media.

5. A. RAID 0 is where you use multiple disks as a single volume and the data is striped across all drives. This RAID level gives you increased performance, but doesn't provide any increased reliability.

6. D. RAID level 1 is more commonly known as mirroring or duplexing. Mirroring is where you have two disks of the same size and data is written to both disks at once. If one fails, the other is available to service disk requests.

7. C. Although five or more disks are commonly used, the minimum number of hard disk drives needed for a RAID level 5 configuration is three.

8. B, E. By definition, the major differences between disk duplexing and mirroring are that in a duplex configuration, the disks are mirrored, but each disk has its own disk controller adapter card installed in the computer. The reason for this is that in a mirrored configuration, if a disk controller fails, both mirrored disks are lost. Duplexing provides an extra level of protection.

9. D. RAID 1 doesn't provide any fault tolerance. It simply stripes the data across two separate disks to increase performance.

10. B. An uninterruptable power supply (UPS) provides the most power protection and management features of those listed. It should be connected to every server to protect the server from power problems.

11. E. A surge protector only provides a basic level protection against specific power overage problems. It won't protect a server against power underage (sags, brownouts, blackouts) problems.

12. D. A brownout occurs when the power dips below standard levels for several seconds and then returns to normal level.

13. D. A spike is an extremely short increase in power that immediately returns to normal voltage levels. It gets its name because a graph of this condition looks like a spike.

14. A. A full backup will clear the archive bit on every file it backs up.

15. E. A differential backup uses a full backup and a daily backup that backs up everything that has changed since the last full backup. When a restore needs to happen, only two tapes will be used.

16. E. An incremental backup backs up the files that have changed since the last full or incremental backup. Each time an incremental backs up files, it clears the archive bit.

17. B. Because you are only restoring a single backup session, it doesn't take as long as it would if you had to restore from either a differential or incremental where you have, at the very least, two sessions or more.

18. D. At the time of the writing of this book, Digital Linear Tape (DLT) has the highest capacity (hundreds of gigabytes) of those backup tape technologies listed.

19. C. Because new viruses are introduced often (approximately once or twice a month), the generally accepted guidelines are to update the virus definition files for your antivirus software approximately once a month.

20. A, D. The best places to get updates (such as patches, fixes, upgrades) for a particular software or hardware item is from either the manufacturer of that item or the OEM distributor. They can provide patches and more on a Web site or via a CD mailing.

Chapter 10

Network Troubleshooting

NETWORK+ EXAM OBJECTIVES COVERED IN THIS CHAPTER:

✓ **Identify the following steps as a systematic approach to identifying the extent of a network problem, and given a problem scenario, select the appropriate next step based on this approach:**

- Determine whether the problem exists across the network
- Determine whether the problem is workstation, workgroup, LAN, or WAN
- Determine whether the problem is consistent and replicable
- Use standard troubleshooting methods

✓ **Identify the following steps as a systematic approach for troubleshooting network problems, and, given a problem scenario, select the appropriate next step based on this approach:**

- Identify the exact issue
- Re-create the problem
- Isolate the cause
- Formulate a correction
- Implement the correction
- Test
- Document the problem and the solution
- Give feedback

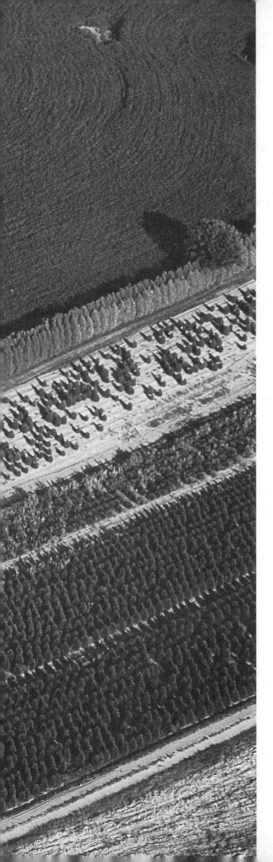

✓ **Identify the following steps as a systematic approach to determining whether a problem is attributable to the operator or the system, and, given a problem scenario, select the appropriate next step based on this approach:**

- Have a second operator perform the same task on an equivalent workstation
- Have a second operator perform the same task on the original operator's workstation
- See whether operators are following standard operating procedure

✓ **Given a network troubleshooting scenario, demonstrate awareness of the need to check for physical and logical indicators of trouble, including:**

- Link lights
- Power lights
- Error displays
- Error logs and displays
- Performance monitors

✓ **Given a network problem scenario, including symptoms, determine the most likely cause or causes of the problem based on the available information. Select the most appropriate course of action based on this inference. Issues that may be covered include:**

- Recognizing abnormal physical conditions
- Isolating and correcting problems in cases where there is a fault in the physical media (patch cable)
- Checking the status of servers
- Checking for configuration problems with DNS, WINS, and HOST file
- Checking for viruses
- Checking the validity of the account name and password
- Rechecking operator logon procedures
- Selecting and running appropriate diagnostics

✓ **Specify the tools that are commonly used to resolve network equipment problems. Identify the purpose and function of common network tools, including:**

- Crossover cable
- Hardware loopback
- Tone generator
- Tone locator (fox and hound)

here is no doubt about it. The only way to get good at troubleshooting computers and networks is the same way to get good at any other art: practice, practice, practice. As with any art, you must learn some basic skills before you can start practicing.

This chapter introduces you to some items to keep in mind when troubleshooting networks as well as to the troubleshooting topics covered on the Network+ exam. In this chapter, we'll examine some basic troubleshooting techniques. First, we'll look at how to check quickly for simple problems. Then, we'll discuss a common troubleshooting model that you can use to identify many network problems. Finally, we'll look at some common troubleshooting resources and tips and tricks that you can use to make troubleshooting easier. Let's start with how you go about narrowing down the problem.

Narrowing Down the Problem

roubleshooting a network problem can be daunting. That's why it's best to start by trying to narrow down the source of the problem. You do this by checking a few key areas, and you begin with the simple stuff.

Checking for the Simple Stuff

The first thing to check, as most people will tell you, is the simple stuff. There's a saying that "all things being equal, the simplest explanation is probably the correct one." For computers, it's rather hard to categorize simple stuff because what's simple to one person might be complex to another. We like to define simple stuff (as it relates to troubleshooting) as those items that you don't think to check, but when it turns out that one of those items is the problem, you say, "Oh, DUH!" Almost everyone can agree on a few items that fall into this category:

- Correct login procedure and rights
- Link lights
- Power switch
- Operator error

Can the Problem Be Reproduced?

The first question to ask anyone who reports a network or computer problem is, Can you show me what "not working" looks like? If you can reproduce the problem, you can identify the conditions under which it occurs. And if you can identify the conditions, you can start to determine the source.

Unfortunately, not every problem can be reproduced. The hardest problems to solve are those that can't be reproduced, but instead appear randomly and with no pattern.

The Correct Login Procedure and Rights

To gain access to the network, users must follow the correct login procedure exactly. If they don't, they will be denied access. Considering everything that must be done correctly and in the correct order, it's a miracle that anyone logs in to a network correctly, because there are so many opportunities for making a mistake.

First, a user must enter the username and password correctly. As easy as this sounds, users frequently enter this information incorrectly, don't realize it, and report to the network administrator that the network is broken or that they can't log in. The most common problem is accidentally typing the wrong username or password incorrectly. In some operating systems, this can happen when you accidentally leave the Caps Lock key pressed. In network operating systems such as Unix, in which passwords are case-sensitive, the user will not be able to log in (unless her password is in all capital letters).

Additionally, in NetWare and Windows NT the network administrator can restrict the times and conditions under which users can log in. If a user doesn't log in at the right time or from the right workstation, the network operating system will reject the login request, even though it might be a valid request in terms of the username and password being spelled correctly. Additionally, a network administrator might restrict how many times a user can log in to the network simultaneously. If that user tries to establish more connections than are allowed, access will be denied. Any time a user is denied access to the network, they are likely to interpret that as a problem, even though the network operating system might be doing what it should.

To test for these types of problems, first check to see if the username and password are being typed correctly, including whether the Caps Lock key is pressed. Try the login yourself from another workstation (assuming that doesn't violate the security policy). If it works, you might try asking the user to check to see if the Caps Lock light on the keyboard is on (indicating that the Caps Lock key has been pressed). If that doesn't solve the problem, check the network documentation to see if the aforementioned kinds of restrictions are in place.

If intruder detection is enabled on the network, the user's account will be locked after a specified number of incorrect login attempts. In this case, the user cannot log in until the administrator has unlocked the account, or until a certain amount of time specified by the administrator has elapsed, after which the account is unlocked.

The Link Lights

The *link light* is a small light-emitting diode (LED) found on both the NIC (network interface card) and the hub. It is typically green and is labeled *link* (or some abbreviation). A link light indicates that the NIC and hub (in the case of 10BaseT) are making a logical (Data Link layer) connection. You usually assume that the workstation and hub are communicating if the link lights are lit on both the workstation's NIC and the hub port to which the workstation is connected.

The link lights on some NICs aren't activated until the operating system driver is loaded for that NIC. So, if the link light isn't on when the system is first turned on, you may have to wait until the operating system loads the NIC driver.

The Power Switch

To function properly, all computer and network components must be turned on and powered up! As obvious as this is, network administrators often hear a user complain, "My computer is on, but my monitor is dark." In this case, our response is to ask, "Is the monitor turned on?" After a pause, the voice on the other end usually says sheepishly, "Oh. Thanks."

Most systems include a power indicator such as a Power or PWR light, and the power switch typically has a 1 or an On indicator. However, the unit could be powerless even if the power switch is in the On position. Thus, you need to check that all power cables are plugged in, including the power strip.

Remember, every cable has two ends, and both must be plugged in to something.

When troubleshooting power problems, start with the most obvious device and work your way back to the power service panel. There could be any number of power problems between the device and the service panel, including a bad power cable, bad outlet, bad electrical wire, tripped circuit breaker, or blown fuse. Any of these items can cause power problems at the device.

Operator Error

The problem may be that the user simply doesn't know how to perform the operation correctly; in other words, *OE (operator error)*. Those in the computer and networking industry have devised several colorful expressions to describe operator error:

- EEOC (Equipment Exceeds Operator Capability)
- PEBCAK (Problem Exists Between Chair And Keyboard)
- ID Ten T Error (written as ID10T)

Assuming that all problems are related to operator error, however, is a mistake. Before you attribute any problem to operator error, ask the user to reproduce the problem in your presence, and pay close attention. You may find out that the user is having a problem because he is using an incorrect procedure; for example, flipping the power switch without following proper shutdown procedures. You may also find out that the user was trained incorrectly, in which case you might want to see if others are having the same difficulty. If the problem and solution are not obvious, try the procedure yourself, or ask someone else at another workstation to do so.

This is only a partial list of simple stuff. You'll come up with our own expanded list over time, as you troubleshoot more and more systems.

Is Hardware or Software Causing the Problem?

A hardware problem typically manifests itself as a device in your computer that fails to operate correctly. You can usually tell that a hardware failure has occurred because you will try to use that piece of hardware, and the computer will issue an error indicating that this has happened. Some failures, such as hard disk failures, may give warning signs; for example, a Disk I/O error or something similar. Other components may just suddenly fail. The device will be operating fine and then simply fail.

The solution to hardware problems usually involves either changing hardware settings or replacing hardware. As we have discussed in previous chapters, I/O address, IRQ (interrupt requests), and DMA (direct memory access) conflicts can cause computers (including workstations and servers) to malfunction. Change the hardware settings to solve these types of problems.

If the hardware has actually failed, however, you must get out your tools and start replacing components. If this is not one of your skills, you can send the device out for repair. In either case, because the system can be down for anywhere from an hour to several days, it's always prudent to have backup hardware on hand.

Software problems are little more evasive. Some problems might result in General Protection Fault messages, which indicate a Windows or Windows program error of some type. Also, a program might suddenly stop responding (hang), or the entire machine might lock up randomly. The solution to these problems generally involves a trip to the manufacturer's support Web site to get software updates and patches or to search for the answer in a knowledgebase.

Sometimes software will give you a precise message regarding the source of the problem, such as the software is missing a file or that a file has become corrupt. In this case, you can either provide the file or, if necessary, reinstall the software. Either solution doesn't take long, and the user will be up and running in a short time.

Sometimes fragmented memory, which occurs after you open and close too many programs, is the source of the problem. The solution may be to reboot the computer, thus clearing memory. Be sure to add this to your network-troubleshooting bag of tricks.

Is a Particular Workstation Causing the Problem, or Is It the Server?

Troubleshooting this problem involves first determining whether one person or a group of people are affected. If only one person is affected, think workstation. If several people are affected, the server or, more generally speaking, a portion of the network is probably experiencing problems.

If a single user is affected, your first line of defense is to try to log in from another workstation within the same group of users. If you can do so, the problem is related to the user's workstation. Look for a cabling fault, a bad NIC, or some other problem.

On the other hand, if several people in a group (such as a whole department) can't access a server, the problem may be related to that server. Go to the server in question, and check for user connections. If everyone is logged in, the problem could be related to something else, such as individual rights or permissions. If no one can log in to that server, including the administrator, the server may have a communication problem with the rest of the network. If it has crashed, you might see messages to that effect on the server's monitor; or the screen might be blank, indicating that the server is no longer running. These symptoms vary among network operating systems.

Which Segment(s) of the Network Are Affected?

Making this determination can be tough. If multiple segments are affected, the problem could be a network address conflict. As you may remember from Chapter 4, network addresses must be unique across an entire network. If two segments have the same IPX network address, for example, all the routers and NetWare servers will complain bitterly and send out error messages, hoping that it's just a simple problem that a router can correct. This is rarely the case, however, and, thus, the administrator must find and resolve the issue. Also keep in mind that the continuous broadcasting of error messages will negatively impact network performance.

If all users of the network are experiencing the problem, it could be related to a different device, such as a server that everyone accesses. Or, a main router or hub could be down, making network transmissions impossible.

Additionally, if the network has WAN connections, you can determine if a network problem is related to the WAN connection by checking to see if stations on both sides can communicate. If they can, the problem isn't related to the WAN. If they can't communicate, you must check everything between the sending station and the receiving one, including the WAN hardware. Usually, the WAN devices have built-in diagnostics that can indicate whether the WAN link is functioning correctly to help you determine if the fault is related to the WAN link or to the hardware involved.

Cabling Issues

After you determine whether the problem is related to the whole network, to a single segment, or to a single workstation, you must determine whether the problem is related to network cabling. First, check to see if the cables are properly connected to the correct port. More than once, we've seen a wall phone cable plugged into a modem in the In jack.

Additionally, patch cables from workstation to wall jack can and do go bad, especially if they get moved or tripped over often. This problem is often characterized by connection problems. If you test the NIC and there is no link light (discussed later), the problem could be related to a bad patch cable.

Next, check the MDI/MDX port setting on small, workgroup hubs, a potential source of trouble that is often overlooked. This port is used to uplink, for example, to a hub on the network's backbone. The port setting has to be set to either MDI or MDX, depending on the type of cable used for the hub-to-hub connection. A crossover cable (discussed later) requires that the port be set to MDI; a standard network patch cable requires that the port be set to MDX (sometimes this is also labeled MDI-X). You can usually adjust the setting via a regular switch or a DIP (dual in-line package) switch. Check the hub's documentation.

Some hubs just have a port labeled MDX, since the MDI setting is really just another standard port, for all intents and purposes. If you connect hubs using a standard patch cable, you must connect the MDX port to a standard port on the backbone hub.

Troubleshooting Steps

In the Network+ troubleshooting model, there are eight steps:

1. Identify the exact issue.
2. Re-create the problem.
3. Isolate the cause.
4. Formulate a correction.
5. Implement the correction.
6. Test the solution.
7. Document the problem and the solution.
8. Give feedback.

To facilitate our discussion of the troubleshooting steps, let's assume that a user has called you, the network administrator, to complain about not being able to connect to the Internet.

Step 1: Identify the Exact Issue

Obviously, if you can't identify a problem, you can't begin to solve it. Typically, you need to ask some questions to begin to clarify exactly what is happening. In our example, we asked the following:

- Which part of the Internet can't you access?
- A particular Web site? A particular address? Any Web site?
- Can you use your Web browser?

We found out that the user couldn't access the corporate intranet or get to any sites on the Internet. He could, however, use his Web browser to access the corporate FTP site, which he had bookmarked (by IP address 10.0.0.2). We can, therefore, rule out the Web browser as the source of the problem.

Step 2: Re-create the Problem

Computers and networks are fickle; they can work fine for months, suddenly malfunction horribly, and then continue to work fine for several more months, never again exhibiting that particular problem. And that's why it's important to be able to reproduce the problem.

One of your goals is to make problems easier to troubleshoot and, thus, get users working again as soon as possible. Therefore, the best advice you can give when training users is that when something isn't working, try it again and then write down exactly what is and is not happening. Most users' knee-jerk reaction is to call you immediately when they experience a problem. This isn't necessarily the best thing to do, because your response is most likely, What were you doing? And most users don't know precisely what they were doing at the computer because they were primarily trying to get their job done. Therefore, if you train users to reproduce the problem first, they'll be able to give you the information you need to start troubleshooting it.

In our example, we found out that when the user tries to access the corporate intranet, he gets the following error message:

We're in luck—we can re-create this problem.

It is a definite advantage to be able to watch the user try to reproduce the problem. That way, you can determine whether the user is performing the operation correctly.

Step 3: Isolate the Cause

If you can reproduce the problem, your next step is to attempt to determine the cause. Drawing on your knowledge of networking, you might ask yourself and your user questions such as the following:

Were you ever able to do this?   If not, then maybe this is not an operation the hardware or software is designed to do. You can inform the user that the system won't do the operation (or that she may need additional hardware or software to do it).

If so, when did you become unable to do it?   If the computer was able to do the operation and then suddenly could not, the conditions that surround this change become extremely important. You may be able to discover the cause of the problem if you know what happened immediately before the change. It is likely that the cause of the problem is related to the conditions surrounding the change.

Has anything changed since you were last able to do this?   This question can give you insight into a possible source for the problem. Most often, the thing that changed before the problem started is the source of the problem. When you ask this question of a user, the answer is typically that nothing has changed, so you might need to rephrase it. For example, Did anyone add anything to your computer? Or, Are you doing anything differently from the way you normally proceed?

Were any error messages displayed?   This is one of the best indicators of the cause of a problem. Error messages are designed by programmers to help them determine what aspect of a computer system is not functioning correctly. These error messages are sometimes clear, such as Disk Full (indicating that the disk cannot store any more files on it because it is full), or cryptic, such as "A random bit has been flipped in the I/O subsystem of memory junction 44FA380h" (this is a fictitious error, but you may encounter those just as complex). If you get a cryptic error message, you can go to the software or hardware vendor's support Web site and usually get a translation of the "programmerese" of the error message into English.

Are other people experiencing this problem? This is one question you must ask yourself. That way you might be able to narrow the problem down to a specific item that may be causing the problem. Try to duplicate the problem yourself from your own workstation. If you can't duplicate the problem on another workstation, it may be related to only one user or group of users (or possibly their workstations). If more than one user is experiencing this problem, you may know this already because several people will be calling in with the same problem.

Is the problem always the same? Generally speaking, when problems crop up, they are almost always the same problem each time they occur. But their symptoms may change ever so slightly as conditions surrounding them change. A related question is, If you do x, does the problem get better or worse? For example, you might ask a user, If you use a different file, does the problem get better or worse? If the symptoms become less severe, it might indicate that the problem is related to the original file being used.

These are just a few of the questions you can use to isolate the cause of the problem.

In our example, we found out that the problem was unique to one user, indicating that the problem was specific to his workstation. We watched him as he attempted to reproduce the problem and noticed that he was typing the address correctly. The error message leads us to believe that the problem has something to with DNS (Domain Name Service) lookups on his workstation.

Step 4: Formulate a Correction

After you observe the problem and isolate the cause, your next step is to formulate a solution. Trust us, this gets easier with time and experience.

You must come up with at least one possible solution, even though it may not be correct. And you don't always have to come up with the solution yourself. Someone else in the group may have the answer. Also, don't forget to check online sources and vendor documentation.

In our example, we determined earlier that the cause was improperly configured DNS lookup on the workstation. The correction, then, is to reconfigure DNS on the workstation.

Step 5: Implement the Correction

In this step, you implement your formulated correction. In our example, we need to reconfigure DNS on the workstation. Here are the steps we took:

1. Choose Start ➢ Settings ➢Control Panel ➢Network to open the Network dialog box.

2. Click the TCP/IP binding for your network card (indicated by TCP/IP ➢*name of network card*.

3. Click Properties to open the TCP/IP Properties dialog box for that binding.

4. Click the DNS Configuration tab.

As you can see in Figure 10.1, DNS has been disabled on this workstation. At this point, it doesn't matter how it was disabled. We could probably assume that the user did something by accident to cause this to happen or that it was the result of a software installation, but anything is possible. To re-enable DNS, click the Enable DNS button. You may have to reboot the workstation to get the changes to take effect.

FIGURE   10.1   The TCP/IP DNS properties for the misconfigured workstation

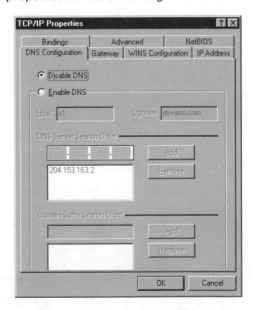

Step 6: Test the Solution

Now that you have made the changes, you must test your solution to see if it solves the problem. In our example, we'd ask the user to try to access the intranet (since that was the problem reported). In general terms, ask the user to repeat the operation that previously did not work. If it works, great! The problem is solved. If it doesn't, try the operation yourself.

If the problem isn't solved, you may have to go back to step 4, formulate a new correction, and redo steps 5 and 6. But it is important to make note of what worked and what didn't so that you don't make the same mistakes twice.

Step 7: Document the Problem and the Solution

As we mentioned in Chapter 6, network documentation is very important. You definitely want to document problems and solutions so that you have the information at hand when a similar problem arises in the future. With documented solutions to documented problems, you can assemble your own database of information that you can use to troubleshoot other problems. Be sure to include information such as the following:

- A description of the conditions surrounding the problem
- The NOS version, the software version, the type of computer, and the type of NIC
- Whether you were able to reproduce the problem
- The solutions you tried
- The ultimate solution

Step 8: Give Feedback

Of all the steps in the troubleshooting model, this is probably the most important. You want to give feedback to the persons who need to know, including the person experiencing the problem and possibly the person reporting the problem. The person reporting the problem and the person experiencing the problem are often one and the same. However, in larger companies, there may be help desk personnel that report the problems users are having to outside service agencies or in-house service personnel. You should report the solutions to both people so that the user knows the problem is fixed and the help desk person knows the problem is fixed.

Most network administrators have a system for tracking work orders, so they know when the problem is fixed. In addition to letting the user know that the problem has been fixed, explain the problem and the solution. It may be to your benefit to show the user exactly what happened. Fifteen minutes of training may go a long way toward preventing a recurrence of the problem. Additionally, you may find out how the problem happened in the first case.

During this feedback session, first apologize to the person for the time he was without the use of the computer. Then tell him what happened, why, and what you did to solve the problem. You should also tell him that you tested the solution. Above all, however, you must be able to gauge your user's knowledge level and level of interest. Be sure that you use words and terms he understands. In our sample case, you might say the following to a user:

> I'm sorry for the downtime you experienced. However, we've located the source of the problem and have fixed it, and we are now able to do what you couldn't do before. Your workstation was misconfigured with the wrong Internet settings. If you'd like to try it yourself, you can double-check that everything is functioning the way it normally should be.

On the other hand, you might say something like the following to the network administrator (if appropriate) or help desk person that reported the problem:

> I'm sorry for the downtime you experienced. However, we've located the source of the problem and have fixed it, and we are now able to do what the user couldn't do before. His workstation's DNS requester had been disabled. It is possible that the user was exploring his computer and accidentally shut it off. I re-enabled DNS and had the user test his ability to connect to Web sites. He was able to connect to both the intranet and the Internet with no problems. Do you have any questions for me? <Answer questions> OK. Thanks for calling.

Note the difference in technical language. We mentioned *Internet settings* to the user because when discussing the computer with him, we determined his level of knowledge to be introductory. He knows what the Internet is, but more than likely, he doesn't know what DNS is. The administrator or help desk person, on the other hand, knows what DNS is and will want to know *exactly* what the problem was and *exactly* how it was solved.

The Troubleshooter's Resources

In the process of troubleshooting a workstation, a server, or other network component, you have many resources at your disposal. In this section, we'll take a brief look at some of them. Those you use depend on the situation and your personal preferences. Most of us eventually have our favorites.

Log Files

As we mentioned in Chapter 6, *log files* can indicate the general health of a server. Each log file format is different, but generally speaking, the log files contain a running list of all errors and notices, the time and date they occurred, and any other pertinent information. Let's look at a couple of the log files from the most commonly used network operating systems, NetWare 5 and Windows NT 4.

NetWare Log Files

NetWare uses three log files that can help you diagnose problems on a NetWare server:

- The Console Log file (CONSOLE.LOG)

- The Abend Log file (ABEND.LOG)

- The Server Log file (SYS$LOG.ERR)

Each file has different uses in the troubleshooting processes.

The CONSOLE.LOG File

The Console Log file (CONSOLE.LOG) keeps a history of all errors and information that have been displayed on the server's console. It is located in the SYS:\ETC directory on the server and is created and maintained by the utility CONLOG.NLM that comes with NetWare versions 3.12 and later. You must load this utility manually (or place the load command in the AUTOEXEC.NCF file so that it starts automatically upon server startup) by typing the following at the console prompt:

```
LOAD CONLOG
```

Once this utility is loaded, it erases whatever CONSOLE.LOG file currently exists and starts logging to the new file.

This command works with any version of NetWare, including 3.12 or later. However, if you are using NetWare 5 or later, the LOAD command is optional. It is required in versions 3.12 to 4.1*x*.

Figure 10.2 shows a sample CONSOLE.LOG file. From this log file, we can tell that someone edited the AUTO-EXEC.NCF file and then restarted the server. This indicates a major change on the server. If we were trying to troubleshoot a server that was starting to exhibit strange problems after a recent reboot, this might be a source to check.

FIGURE 10.2   A sample CONSOLE.LOG file

```
CONLOG-1.04-10: System console logging started Fri Feb 12 13:52:40 1999.
CONLOG-1.04-9: Logging system console to sys:etc\console.log.
S1:edit autoexec.ncf
Loading module EDIT.NLM
  NetWare Text Editor
  Version 4.15     March 23, 1998
  Copyright 1989-1998 Novell, Inc.  All rights reserved.
File OWL501F.DLL in use by user ADMIN on station 23
File NWCORE32.DLL in use by user ADMIN on station 23
File WANMAN.DLL in use by user ADMIN on station 23
File SLP-SP.ZIP in use by user ADMIN on station 23
*** WARNING *** There are active files open.
Down server? y
IPXRTR: IPX link state router down.
Java: Cleaning up resources, Please Wait.

Module JAVA.NLM unloaded
Notifying stations that file server is down
Dismounting volume DATA

 2-12-1999   1:57:26 pm:    DS-7.9-23
     Bindery close requested by the SERVER


 2-12-1999   1:57:26 pm:    DS-7.9-20
     Directory Services:  Local database has been closed

Dismounting volume SYS
```

The information in the CONSOLE.LOG file is lost every time the CONLOG .NLM is unloaded and reloaded. It doesn't keep a history of every command ever issued, only those since CONLOG.NLM was loaded. However, you can configure the ARCHIVE=YES parameter to configure CONLOG to keep a history of all the conlog files. The first file is saved with a .000 extension, the next with a .001 extension, and so forth. The complete command to run at the console (or add to Autoexec.ncf) is Conlog archive=yes.

The ABEND.LOG File

This log file registers all Abends on a NetWare server. An Abend (ABnormal END) is an error condition that can halt the proper operation of the Net-Ware server. Abends can be serious enough to lock the server, or they can simply force an NLM to shut down. You know an Abend has occurred when you see an error message that contains the word *Abend* on the console. Additionally, the server command prompt will include a number in angle brackets (for example, <1>) that indicates the number of times the server has Abended since it was brought online.

Because the server may reboot after an Abend, these error messages and what they mean can be lost. NetWare versions 4.11 and later include a routine to capture the output of the Abend both to the console and to the ABEND.LOG file. ABEND.LOG is located in the SYS:SYSTEM directory on the server.

The ABEND.LOG file contains all the information that is output to the console screen during an Abend, plus much more:

- The exact flags and registers of the processor at the time of the Abend

- The NLMs that were in memory, including their versions, descriptions, memory settings, and exact time and date

Here is a portion of our ABEND.LOG file.

```
*************************************************************


Server S1 halted Friday, February 12, 1999   2:37:03 pm
Abend 1 on P00: Server-5.00a: Page Fault Processor
Exception (Error code 00000002)


Registers:
    CS = 0008 DS = 0010 ES = 0010 FS = 0010 GS = 0010
      SS = 0010
    EAX = 00000000 EBX = D0AC2238 ECX = 0697DEF0
      EDX = 00000009
    ESI = D0C5C040 EDI = 00000000 EBP = 0697DED0
      ESP = 0697DEC0
    EIP = D0AC2232 FLAGS = 00014246
    D0AC2232 C600CC         MOV      [EAX]=?,CC
    EIP in ABENDEMO.NLM at code start +00000232h
```

```
Running process: Abendemo Process
Created by: NetWare Application
Thread Owned by NLM: ABENDEMO.NLM
Stack pointer: 697DCE0
OS Stack limit: 697A000
Scheduling priority: 67371008
Wait state: 5050170  (Blocked on keyboard)
Stack: D0AC22C1  (ABENDEMO.NLM|MenuAction+89)
       D1FEA602  (NWSNUT.NLM|NWSShowPortalLine+3602)
       --00000008  ?
       --00000000  ?
       --0697DF20  ?
       --D0134080  ?
       --00000001  ?
       D1FEA949  (NWSNUT.NLM|NWSShowPortalLine+3949)
       --00000010  ?
       --0697DEF0  ?
       --0697DEF4  ?
       --0697DFAC  ?
       --D0C2E100
(CONNMGR.NLM|WaitForBroadcastsToClear+C90C)
       --00000003  ?
       --00000008  ?
       --00000012  ?
       --00000000  ?
       --00000019  ?
       --00000050  ?
       --000000FF  ?
       --00000001  ?
       --00000010  ?
       --00000001  ?
       --00000000  ?
       --00000011  ?
       --0697DFDC  ?
       --0000000B  ?
       --00000000  ?
```

```
        D1FEABD9  (NWSNUT.NLM|NWSShowPortalLine+3BD9)
        --0000000B  ?
        --00000000  ?
        --00000000  ?


Additional Information:
    The CPU encountered a problem executing code in
ABENDEMO.NLM.  The problem may be in that module or in
data passed to that module by a process owned by
ABENDEMO.NLM.


Loaded Modules:
SERVER.NLM        NetWare Server Operating System
  Version 5.00    August 27, 1998
    Code Address: FC000000h  Length: 000A5000h
    Data Address: FC5A5000h  Length: 000C9000h
LOADER.EXE        NetWare OS Loader
    Code Address: 000133D0h  Length: 0001D000h
    Data Address: 000303D0h  Length: 00020C30h
CDBE.NLM          NetWare Configuration DB Engine
  Version 5.00    August 12, 1998
    Code Address: D087E000h  Length: 00007211h
    Data Address: D0887000h  Length: 0000684Ch
```

This information can be useful when determining the source of an Abend. For example, any time you see the words *Page Fault* or *Stack* in the output, the Abend occurred because of something to do with memory. Usually, a program or process tried to take memory that didn't belong to it (for example, from another program). When NetWare detects this, it shuts down the offending process and issues an Abend.

The SYS$LOG.ERR File

The general Server Log file, found in the SYS:SYSTEM directory, lists any errors that occur on the server, including Abends and NDS errors and the time and date of their occurrence. An error in the SYS$LOG.ERR file might look something like this:

```
1-07-1999  11:51:10 am:    DS-7.9-17
    Severity = 1  Locus = 17  Class = 19
    Directory Services:  Could not open local database,
    error: -723
```

The Severity, Locus, and Class designations in the second line substitute for lengthy text descriptions of the error and can provide more information:

- Severity indicates the seriousness of the problem.

- Locus indicates which system component is affected by the error (for example, memory, disk, LAN cards).

- Class indicates the type of error.

Tables 10.1, 10.2, and 10.3 explain the codes used for Severity, Locus, and Class. Based on the information in these tables, we can determine that the Severity of 1 indicates a warning condition (so the problem isn't really serious), a Locus of 17 indicates that the error relates to the operating system (which would make sense because this is a Directory Services error), and the Class of 19 indicates the problem is with a domain, meaning that the problem is defined by the operating system, but not an operating system problem. These designations tell us the reported error is related to NDS and that it's not really serious. In fact, this particular error might occur when you bring up the server and the database hasn't yet been opened by the operating system.

TABLE 10.1   SYS$LOG.ERR Severity Code Descriptions

Number	Description
0	**Informational**. Indicates that the information is non-threatening, usually just to record some kind of entry in the SYS$LOG.ERR file.
1	**Warning**. Indicates a potential problem that does not cause damage.
2	**Recoverable**. Indicates an error condition has occurred that can be recovered by the operating system.
3	**Critical**. Indicates a condition that should be taken care of soon and that might cause a server failure in the near future. For example, mirrored partitions are out of sync or the Abend recovery routine is invoked.
4	**Fatal**. Indicates that something has occurred that will cause the imminent shutdown of the server or that a shutdown has occurred. This type of error might occur when a disk driver unloads because of a software failure.

TABLE 10.1 SYS$LOG.ERR Severity Code Descriptions *(continued)*

Number	Description
5	**Operation Aborted**. Indicates that an attempted operation could not be completed because of an error. For example, a disk save could not be completed because the disk was full.
6	**No NOS Unrecoverable**. Indicates that the operation could not be completed, but that it will not affect the operating system. For example, a compressed file is corrupt and unrecoverable.

TABLE 10.2 SYS$LOG.ERR Locus Code Descriptions

Number	Description
0	Unknown
1	Memory
2	File System
3	Disks
4	LAN Boards
5	COM Stacks (Communication Protocols)
6	No definition
7	TTS (Transaction Tracking System)
8	Bindery
9	Station
10	Router
11	Locks
12	Kernel

TABLE 10.2 SYS$LOG.ERR Locus Code Descriptions *(continued)*

Number	Description
13	UPS
14	SFT_III
15	Resource Tracking
16	NLM
17	OS Information
18	Cache
19	Domain

TABLE 10.3 SYS$LOG.ERR Class Code Descriptions

Number	Description
0	Class Unknown
1	Out of Resources
2	Temporary Situation
3	Authorization Failure
4	Internal Error
5	Hardware Failure
6	System Failure
7	Request Error
8	Not Found
9	Bad Format

TABLE 10.3 SYS$LOG.ERR Class Code Descriptions *(continued)*

Number	Description
10	Locked
11	Media Failure
12	Item Exists
13	Station Failure
14	Limit Exceeded
15	Configuration Error
16	Limit Almost Exceeded
17	Security Audit Information
18	Disk Information
19	General Information
20	File Compressions
21	Protection Violation

Windows NT 4 Log Files

Windows NT, like other network operating systems, employs comprehensive error and informational logging routines. Every program and process theoretically could have its own logging utility, but Microsoft has come up with a rather slick utility, Event Viewer, which, through log files, tracks all events on a particular Windows NT computer. Normally, though, you must be an administrator or a member of the Administrators group to have access to Event Viewer.

To use Event Viewer, follow these steps:

1. Choose Start ≻ Programs ≻ Administrative Tools (Common) to open the Select Computer dialog box:

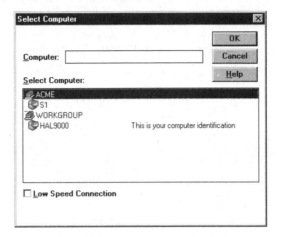

2. In the Computer field, enter the UNC (Universal Naming Convention) name of the computer whose events you want to view.

You can also simply double-click the computer's name in the list in the Select Computer section.

3. If you are connected to a Windows NT network over a slower link, such as a slow WAN link or a dial-up connection, click the Low Speed Connection check box to optimize Event Viewer for running over the lower-speed connection.

4. Click OK.

5. To view a log file, select it from the list.

6. To view a different log file, choose Log ≻ Select Computer.

The first time you open Event Viewer, you will automatically be brought to the System log. Subsequently, when you open Event Viewer, the first log you see is the one you were last viewing.

Even though this list displays Windows 95/98 computers, you cannot view log files on those computers because their logging system isn't designed to interface with Event Viewer.

Using Event Viewer, you can take a look at three types of files:

- The System Log
- The Security Log
- The Application Log

To view the log files of any Windows NT machine from your Windows 95/98 client, copy the Server Tools from the Windows NT Server CD to your hard disk and create a shortcut for them. The server tools directory is located in the \CLIENTS\SRVTOOLS\ directory on the Windows NT Server Installation CD.

The System Log

This log file tracks just about every event that occurs on that computer. It is similar to NetWare's SYS$LOG.ERR file. However, whereas the SYS$LOG .ERR file tracks many categories of errors, the System Log tracks only three main types of events:

- Information (an event occurred, especially when a service fails)
- Warning (an event occurred that could cause problems)
- Error (a component has failed and needs immediate attention)

In a log file, the icon that precedes the date indicates the event's type. Figure 10.3 shows the three types of events found in the System Log.

FIGURE 10.3 System Log event types and their associated icons

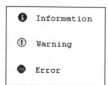

Two other types of events (Audit Success and Audit Failure) normally appear only in the Security Log (discussed later).

Figure 10.4 shows a sample system log. This list contains several categories of information, including the date and time the event occurred, the source of the event (which process the event came from), which user (if applicable) initiated the process, the name of the computer the event happened on, and the Event ID number (in the Event column). The Event ID number is the unique error type of a particular event. For an explanation of each Event ID number, check the Help file, or go to www.microsoft.com/technet/ and search for Event ID.

FIGURE 10.4   A sample System Log. Note the different error types and event IDs.

	Date	Time	Source	Category	Event	User	Computer
ℹ	1/7/99	12:53:09 PM	BROWSER	None	8015	N/A	S1
ℹ	1/7/99	11:39:17 AM	BROWSER	None	8033	N/A	S1
ℹ	1/7/99	11:39:17 AM	BROWSER	None	8033	N/A	S1
ℹ	1/7/99	11:39:17 AM	BROWSER	None	8033	N/A	S1
⊗	1/7/99	11:37:14 AM	symc810	None	9	N/A	S1
⊗	1/7/99	11:36:50 AM	symc810	None	9	N/A	S1
⊗	1/7/99	11:36:05 AM	symc810	None	9	N/A	S1
⊗	1/7/99	11:35:21 AM	symc810	None	9	N/A	S1
⊗	1/7/99	11:33:15 AM	Disk	None	7	N/A	S1
⊗	1/7/99	11:33:11 AM	Disk	None	7	N/A	S1
⊗	1/7/99	11:33:07 AM	Disk	None	7	N/A	S1
⊗	1/7/99	11:33:04 AM	Disk	None	7	N/A	S1
⊗	1/7/99	11:33:00 AM	Disk	None	7	N/A	S1
⊗	1/7/99	11:32:56 AM	Disk	None	7	N/A	S1
⊗	1/7/99	11:32:52 AM	Disk	None	7	N/A	S1
⊗	1/7/99	11:32:48 AM	Disk	None	7	N/A	S1
⊗	1/7/99	11:32:44 AM	Disk	None	7	N/A	S1
⊗	1/7/99	11:32:40 AM	Disk	None	7	N/A	S1
ℹ	1/6/99	7:04:41 PM	BROWSER	None	8015	N/A	S1
ℹ	1/6/99	7:04:41 PM	BROWSER	None	8015	N/A	S1
ℹ	1/6/99	7:02:59 PM	EventLog	None	6005	N/A	S1
ℹ	1/6/99	7:04:41 PM	BROWSER	None	8015	N/A	S1
⊗	1/6/99	6:57:00 PM	Service Control M	None	7000	N/A	S1
ℹ	1/6/99	6:56:54 PM	EventLog	None	6005	N/A	S1
⚠	1/6/99	6:57:00 PM	E100B	None	5007	N/A	S1
⊗	1/6/99	6:00:37 PM	Service Control M	None	7000	N/A	S1
ℹ	1/6/99	6:00:32 PM	EventLog	None	6005	N/A	S1
⚠	1/6/99	6:00:37 PM	E100B	None	5007	N/A	S1

Event Viewer - System Log on \\S1
Log View Options Help

If you want more detail on a specific event, double-click it. Figure 10.5 shows the event detail for the following event in Figure 10.4:

`1/7/9911:33:15 AMDiskNone7N/AS1`

FIGURE 10.5 The Event Detail dialog box for an event listed in Figure 10.4

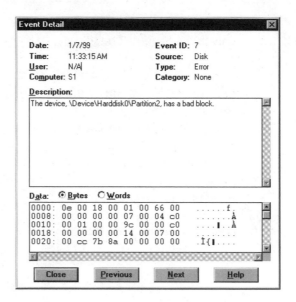

The note in the Description box indicates that Windows NT found a bad disk block. Even though this is an error event, it is not serious. One bad block is not a problem, unless several disk blocks start going bad at once. The Data box lists the exact data the Event Viewer received about the error condition. This may be useful in determining the source of the problem. More than likely, if you have a serious problem that you can't fix, this is the information that you will send to the vendor (or to Microsoft) to help troubleshoot the problem.

The Security Log

This log tracks security events specified by the domain's Audit policy. The Audit policy is set in User Manager for Domains and specifies which security items will be tracked in Event Viewer. To set the Audit policy, follow these steps:

1. Choose Start ➢ Programs ➢ User Manager for Domains to open User Manager for Domains.

2. Choose Policy ➤ Audit to open the Audit Policy dialog box:

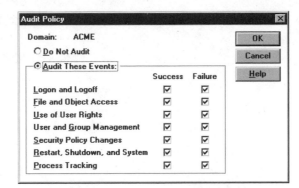

3. Indicate the events that you want logged and check the Success or Failure check boxes to track the success and failure of those events. Since these are security settings, most often you'll want to log failures.

4. Click OK, and these events will be logged for all users and systems in the domain.

After you set the Audit Policy for a domain, you can view the Security Log for any computer in that domain. Follow these steps:

1. Choose Start ➤ Programs ➤ Administrative Tools (Common) to open the Select Computer dialog box.

2. In the Computer field, enter the UNC (Universal Naming Convention) name of the computer whose events you want to view.

3. If you are connected to a Windows NT network over a slower link, such as a slow WAN link or a dial-up connection, click the Low Speed Connection check box to optimize Event Viewer for running over the lower-speed connection.

4. Click OK.

5. Choose Log ➤ Security to open the Security Log (see Figure 10.6) for that computer.

FIGURE 10.6 The Security Log in Event Viewer

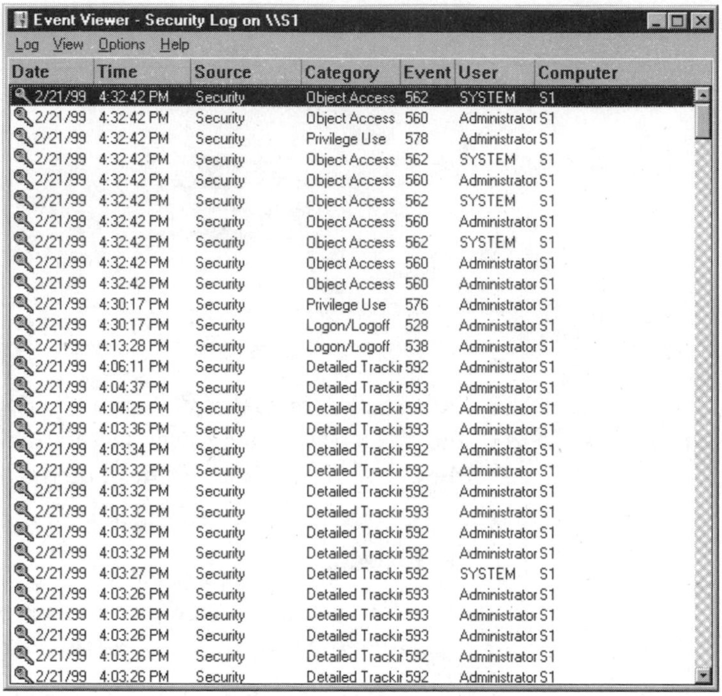

As you can see, this log looks similar to the System Log in most respects. The main differences are the icons and the types of events recorded here. To view the detail for an event, double-click it.

The Security Log displays two types of events:

- Success Audit (the event passed the security audit)

- Failure Audit (the event failed the security audit)

Figure 10.7 shows the icons associated with each of these types of events. When an item fails a security audit, something security-related failed. For example, a common entry (assuming the Logon Failure check box is checked in the Audit Policy dialog box) is a Failure Audit with a value of Logon/ Logoff in the category. This means that the user failed to log on. If you look at the log shown previously in Figure 10.6, you can see that a user successfully logged on as administrator and that no failures have occurred.

FIGURE 10.7 The Security Log event types and their associated icons

This log is especially useful in troubleshooting when someone can't access a resource. If your domain security policy has been set to log Failures of Use of User Rights, you can see every instance of a user not having enough rights to access a resource. The username appears in the User column of the Failure Audit event for the resource the user is trying to access.

The Application Log

This log is similar to the other two logs, except that it tracks events for network services and applications (for example, SQL Server and other Back-Office products). It uses the same event types (and their associated icons) as the System Log. Figure 10.8 shows an example of an Application log.

FIGURE 10.8 A sample Application event log

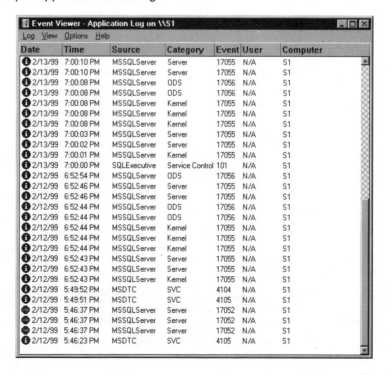

To access the Application Log, in Event Viewer, choose Log ➤ Application. The Sources column indicates which service logged which event. For example, in Figure 10.8, you can see three Error events that came from Microsoft SQL Server (the MSSQL entry).

All together, the log files present a picture of the general health of a Windows NT server. Generally speaking, if you see an error message, open Event Viewer and check the System Log. If you don't see the event here, check the other two logs.

Manufacturers' Troubleshooting Resources

In addition to viewing log files, you can use several types of troubleshooting tools that manufacturers make available for their network operating systems. You can use these resources to augment your own knowledge, as well as to solve those pesky problems that have no pattern or few recognizable symptoms. Each type of resource provides different information or different levels of support (some of which have been discussed in previous chapters, but their importance to troubleshooting necessitates discussing them again here). Let's examine the most popular, including:

- README files

- Telephone support

- Technical support CD-ROM

- Technical support Web site

README Files

As we discussed in Chapter 6, *README files* contain information that did not make it into the manual. Also, they may contain tips, default settings, and installation information (so you don't have to read the entire first chapter to install the software).

When troubleshooting application or networking software, check out the README file before you try any of the other manufacturers' resources. It is usually found on the first installation disk or CD.

Telephone Support

Many people prefer telephone support over other forms of support. You actually get to talk to a human being from the software manufacturer about the problem. Most, if not all, software manufacturers have toll-free support numbers. The people on their end of the line can provide anything from basic how-to answers to complex, technical answers.

Unfortunately, because of their popularity, technical support phone lines are often busy. When the line is finally free, you might, however, find yourself in "voicemail hell." We've all been through it: Press 1 for support for products A, B, and C. Press 2 for Products D, E, and F, and so on and so on. Most people don't want this and hang up. They prefer to speak with a human being as soon as the call is answered. Today, phone support is often not free (the 800 number to reach support might be, but the support itself is not), but must be purchased via either a time-limited contract or on an incident-by-incident basis. This is particularly true for network operating system software support. To solve this problem, companies have devised other methods, such as the Technical Support CD-ROM and Web site, which we will discuss next.

The Technical Support CD-ROM

With the development of CD-ROM technology, it became possible to put volumes of textual information on a readily accessible medium. The CD-ROM was, thus, a logical distribution vehicle for technical support information. In addition, the CD was portable and searchable. Introduced in the early 1990s, Novell's Network Support Encyclopedia (NSE) CD-ROM was one of the first products of this kind. Microsoft's TechNet came soon after. Both companies charge a nominal fee for a yearly subscription to these CDs (anywhere from $100-$500).

To be sure, the first editions of these products (as with the first editions of most software products) left much to be desired. Search engines were often clumsy and slow, and the CDs were released only about twice a year. As these products evolved, however, their search engines became more advanced, they included more documents, and they were released more often. And, probably most important, manufacturers began to include software updates, drivers, and patches on the CD.

The Technical Support Web Site

The technical support CDs were great, but people started to complain (as people are wont to do) that because this information was vital to the health of their network, they should get it for free. Well, that is, in fact, what happened. The Internet proved to be the perfect medium for allowing network support personnel access to the same information that was on the technical support CD-ROMs. Additionally, Web sites can be instantly updated and accessed, so they provide the most up-to-date network support information. Since Web sites are hosted on servers that can store much more information than CD-ROMs, Web sites are more powerful than their CD-ROM counterparts. Because they are easy to access and use and because they are detailed and current, Web sites are now the most popular method for disseminating technical support information. As examples, you can view Novell's technical support Web site at `http://support.novell.com/`, and Microsoft's technical support Web site (TechNet, a monthly subscription) at `http://support.microsoft.com/servicedesks/technet/`.

Hardware Troubleshooting Tools

In addition to manufacturer-provided troubleshooting tools, there are a few hardware devices we can use to troubleshoot the network. These are actual devices that you can use during the troubleshooting process. Some devices have easily recognizable functions; others are more obscure. Four of the most popular hardware tools (that the Network+ exam tests you on, by the way) are:

- A crossover cable
- A hardware loopback
- A tone generator
- A tone locator

The Crossover Cable

Sometimes also called a cross cable, a *crossover cable* is typically used to connect two hubs, but it can also be used to test communications between two stations directly, bypassing the hub. A crossover cable is used only in Ethernet UTP installations. You can connect two workstation NICs (or a workstation and a server NIC) directly using a crossover cable.

A normal Ethernet (10BaseT) UTP cable uses four wires—two to transmit and two to receive. Figure 10.9 shows this wiring, with all wires going from pins on one side directly to the same pins on the other side.

FIGURE 10.9   A standard Ethernet 10BaseT cable

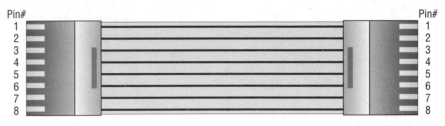

Pins 1 & 2 are transmit,
Pins 3 & 6 are receive

The standard Ethernet UTP crossover cable used in both situations has its transmit and receive wire pairs crossed so that the transmit set on one side (hooked to pins 1 and 2) is connected to the receive set (pins 3 and 6) on the other. Figure 10.10 illustrates this arrangement. Note that four of the wires are crossed as compared with the straight-through wiring of the standard 10BaseT UTP cable shown earlier in Figure 10.9.

FIGURE 10.10   A standard Ethernet 10BaseT crossover cable

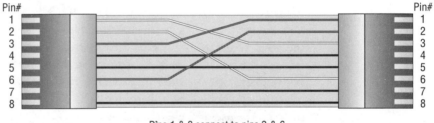

Pins 1 & 2 connect to pins 3 & 6
Pins 3 & 6 connect to pins 1 & 2

Be sure to label a crossover cable as such to ensure that no one tries to use it as a workstation patch cable. If it is used as a patch cable, the workstation won't be able to communicate with the hub and the rest of the network.

You can carry a crossover cable in the tool bag along with your laptop. If you want to ensure that a server's NIC is functioning correctly, you can connect your laptop directly to the server's NIC using the crossover cable. You should be able to log in to the server (assuming both NICs are configured correctly).

The Hardware Loopback

A *hardware loopback* is a special connector for Ethernet 10BaseT NICs. It functions similarly to a crossover cable, except that it connects the transmit pins directly to the receive pins (as shown in Figure 10.11). It is used by the NIC's software diagnostics to test transmission and reception capabilities. You cannot completely test a NIC without one of these devices.

FIGURE 10.11 A hardware loopback and its connections

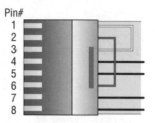

Pin#
1
2
3
4
5
6
7
8

In a loopback, pins 1 & 3 and
pins 2 & 6 are connected

Usually, the hardware loopback is no bigger than a single RJ-45 connector with a few small wires on the back. If a NIC has hardware diagnostics that can use the loopback, the hardware loopback plug will be included with the NIC. To use it, simply plug the loopback into the RJ-45 connector on the back of the NIC and start the diagnostic software. Select the option in your NIC's diagnostic software that requires the loopback, and start the diagnostic routine. You will be able to tell if the NIC can send and receive data through the use of these diagnostics.

Tone Generator and Tone Locator

This combination of devices is used most often on telephone systems to locate cables. Since telephone systems use multiple pairs of UTP, it is nearly impossible to determine which set of wires goes where. Network documentation would be extremely helpful in making this determination, but if no documentation is available, you can use a tone generator and locator.

The *tone generator* is a small electronic device that sends an electrical signal down one set of UTP wires. The *tone locator* is another device that is designed to emit a tone when it detects the signal in a particular set of wires. When you need to trace a cable, hook the generator (often called the *fox*) to the copper ends of the wire pair you want to find. Then move the locator (often called the *hound* because it chases the fox) over multiple sets of cables (you don't have to touch the copper part of the wire pairs; this tool works by induction) until you hear the tone. A soft tone indicates that you are close to the right set of wires. Keep moving the tool until the tone gets the loudest. Bingo! You have found the wire set. Figure 10.12 shows a tone generator and locator and how they are used.

FIGURE 10.12 Use of a common tone generator and locator

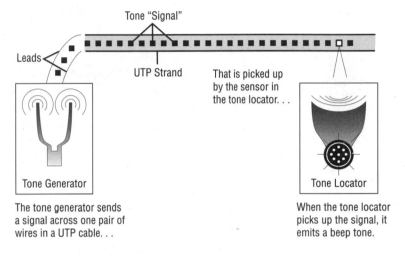

When the tone locator picks up the signal, it emits a beep tone.

That is picked up by the sensor in the tone locator. . .

Tone "Signal"

Leads

UTP Strand

Tone Generator

The tone generator sends a signal across one pair of wires in a UTP cable. . .

Tone Locator

Don't confuse these tools with a cable tester that tests cable quality. You use the tone generator and locator only to determine which UTP cable is which.

Never hook a tone generator to a cable that is hooked up to either a NIC or a hub! Because the tone generator sends electrical signals down the wire, it can blow a NIC or a hub. That is why tone generators are not usually used on networks. Cable testers are used more often. We'll discuss cable testers later in this chapter.

Software Troubleshooting Tools

In addition to these hardware troubleshooting tools, you can use software programs to gain information about the current health and state of the network. These tools fall into two main categories:

- Protocol analyzers

- Performance-monitoring tools

We use the term *network software diagnostics* to refer to these tools.

Protocol Analyzer

Any software that can analyze and display the packets it receives can be considered a *protocol analyzer*. Protocol analyzers examine packets from protocols that operate at the lower four layers of the OSI model (including Transport, Network, Data Link, and Physical) and can display any errors they detect. Additionally, most protocol analyzers can capture packets and decode their contents. Capturing packets involves copying a series of packets from the network into memory and holding the copy so that it can be analyzed.

You could, for example, capture a series of packets and decode their contents to figure out where each packet came from, where it was going, which protocol sent it, which protocol should receive it, and so on. For example, you can find out:

- The nature of the traffic on your network

- Which protocol is used most often

- If users are accessing unauthorized sites

- If a particular network card is jabbering (sending out packets when there is no data to send)

Two common examples of protocol analyzers are Sniffer, a Network General product, and Novell's LANalyzer.

Performance-Monitoring Tools

In addition to protocol analyzers, many network operating systems include tools for monitoring network performance and can display statistics such as the number of packets sent and received, server processor utilization, the amount of data going in and out of the server, and so on. NetWare comes with the MONITOR.NLM utility, and Windows NT comes with Performance Monitor. Both monitor performance statistics. You can use these utilities to determine the source of the bottleneck when users complain that the network is slow.

To start the MONITOR.NLM utility in NetWare, simply type **LOAD MONITOR** at the console prompt. To start the Performance Monitor program in Windows NT, you must first be logged in as Administrator (or a member of the Server Operators group). Once you are logged in, choose Start ➤Programs ➤ Administrative Tools ➤Performance Monitor.

Troubleshooting Tips

Now that we have covered the basics of network troubleshooting, we should go over a few troubleshooting tips. These tips will give you more "ammo" while you're hunting for network problems using the various steps of the troubleshooting model discussed earlier.

Don't Overlook the Small Stuff

If you'll remember, the first thing we discussed in this chapter was small stuff. Often a problem is caused by something simple such as a power switch in the wrong position, a card or port not functioning as indicated by a link light that's not lit, or simply operator error. Even the most experienced administrator has forgotten to turn on the power, left a cable unplugged, or mistyped a username and password.

Finally, make sure that users get training for the systems they use. That may seem like an extra bother, but an hour or two of training goes a long way toward preventing problems. The number of incidents of EEOC will decline with a little user training.

Prioritize Your Problems

It is unlikely that as a network administrator or technician you will receive problem calls one at a time. Typically, when you receive one call, you already have three people waiting for service. For this reason, you must learn to prioritize.

You start this process by asking some basic questions of the person reporting the problem so that you can determine its severity. If the current problem is minor and you have two more serious problems already facing you, your priorities are obvious.

You establish priorities to ensure that you spend your time wisely. The order in which you attempt to solve your networking problems, from highest priority to lowest, might look something like this:

- Total network failure (affects everyone)

- Partial network failure (affects small groups of users)

- Small network failure (affects a small, single group of users)

- Total workstation failure (single user can't work at all)

- Partial workstation failure (single user can't do most tasks)

- Minor issue (single user has problems that crop up now and again)

Mitigating circumstances can, of course, change the order of this list. For example, if the president of the company can't retrieve her e-mail, you'd take the express elevator to her office as soon as you hang up from the call. Also, a minor, persistent problem might move up the ladder.

Remember also that some simple problems may take more effort than larger problems. You may be able to bring up a crashed server in a matter of minutes, but a user who doesn't know how to make columns line up in Microsoft Word may take up to an hour or longer to train. The latter of these problems might get relegated toward the bottom of the list because of the time involved. It is more efficient to solve problems for a larger group of people than to fix this one user's problem immediately.

Some network administrators list all network service requests on a chalkboard or a whiteboard. They then prioritize them based on the previously discussed criteria. Some larger companies have written support-call tracking software whose only function is to track and prioritize all network and computer problems. Use whatever method makes you comfortable, but prioritize your calls.

Check the Software Configuration

Often, network problems can be traced to software configuration (as with our DNS configuration example earlier in this chapter). When you are checking for software problems, don't forget to check configuration, including the following:

- DNS configuration
- WINS configuration
- HOSTS file
- AUTOEXEC.BAT (DOS and Windows)
- CONFIG.SYS (DOS and Windows)
- STARTUP.NCF, AUTOEXEC.NCF, and server parameter settings (NetWare)
- The Registry (Windows 95/98 and NT)

Software configuration settings love to hide in places like these and can be notoriously hard to find (especially in the Registry).

Additionally, in text configuration files, look for lines that have been commented out (either intentionally or accidentally). A command such as REM or REMARK or the asterisk or semicolon characters indicate comment lines in a file.

The HOSTS file uses a # (Pound Sign) to indicate a comment line, as does NetWare's NCF files.

Don't Overlook Physical Conditions

As we discussed in Chapter 6, you want to make sure that from a network design standpoint, the physical environment for a server is optimized for placement, temperature, and humidity. When troubleshooting an obscure network problem, don't forget to check the physical conditions under which the network device is operating. Check for problems such as the following:

- Excessive heat
- Excessive humidity (condensation)

- Low humidity (leads to ESD problems)
- EMI/RFI problems
- ESD problems
- Power problems
- Unplugged cables

Don't Overlook Cable Problems

Cables, generally speaking, work fine once they are installed properly. Rarely is the cabling system the problem, unless someone has made some change to it. If you suspect that the cabling system is the problem, try replacing the patch cables at the workstation and hub first. These are easiest to get to (and replace). If that solves the problem, you know the problem was related to the patch cable. It was either faulty or the wrong type.

If the patch cable isn't the problem, use a cable tester (not a tone generator and locator) to find the source of the problem. Wires that are moved can be prone to breaking or shorting. A short can happen when the wire conductor comes in contact with another conductive surface, changing the path of the electrical signal. The signal will go someplace else instead of to the intended recipient. You can use cable testers to test for many types of problems, including:

- Broken cables
- Incorrect connections
- Interference levels
- Total cable length (for length restrictions)
- Cable shorts
- Connector problems

As a matter of fact, cable testers are so sophisticated, they can even indicate the exact location of a cable break, accurate to within 6 inches or better.

Check for Viruses

Many troubleshooters overlook virus scanning because they assume that the network virus-checking software should have picked up any viruses. We're reminded of the network virus-scanning software, such as the bio-filters in the transporter on *Star Trek: The Next Generation*. They work great as long as the computer has the latest information on what the virus is and how to eliminate it. On many occasions, though, the ship's doctor or engineer had to reprogram the bio-filters to recognize some new virus that the crew of the *Enterprise* had come across.

The same thing happens with network virus-scanning software; to be effective, it must be kept up-to-date. Updates are made available almost daily. As we discussed in Chapter 9, you must run the virus definition update utility to keep the virus definition file current.

If you are having strange, unusual, unreproducible problems with a workstation, try scanning it with an up-to-date virus scan utility. You'd be surprised how many times people have spent hours and hours troubleshooting a strange problem, only to run a virus scan utility, find and clean one or more viruses, and have the problem disappear.

Key Terms

Before you take the exam, be certain you are familiar with the following terms:

crossover cable

hardware loopback

link light

log file

network software diagnostics

protocol analyzer

README file

tone generator

tone locator

Review Questions

1. Which NetWare log file(s) always indicate the time and date at which a failure or an event occurred?

    A. SYS$LOG.ERR

    B. CONSOLE.LOG

    C. ABEND.LOG

    D. SYS$ERR.LOG

2. You have a user who cannot connect to the network. What is the first thing you could check to determine the source of the problem?

    A. Workstation configuration

    B. Station link light

    C. Patch cable

    D. Server configuration

3. A user cannot access the local intranet. Which action will not help you determine how to narrow the problem down to the intranet?

    A. Access the intranet from your workstation

    B. Access the intranet from the user's workstation as yourself

    C. Replace the patch cable on the workstation

    D. Ask another user to access the intranet from the problem user's workstation

4. Several users can't log in to the server. Which action would help you to narrow the problem down to the workstations, network, or server?

    A. Run tracert from a workstation

    B. Check the server console for user connections

    C. Run netstat on all workstations

    D. Check the network diagnostics

5. Without a _____, you may not be able to perform 100 percent of the network diagnostics for a network card.

    A. Hardware loopback

    B. Patch cable

    C. Crossover cable

    D. Protocol analyzer

6. A user can't log in to the network. She can't even connect to the Internet over the LAN. Other users in the same area aren't experiencing any problems. You attempt to log in as her from your workstation with her username and password and don't experience any problems. However, you cannot log in with either her username or yours from her workstation. What is a likely cause of the problem?

    A. Insufficient rights to access the server

    B. A bad patch cable

    C. The server is down

    D. Wrong username and password

7. A user is experiencing problems logging in to a UNIX server. He can connect to the Internet over the LAN. Other users in the same area aren't experiencing any problems. You attempt logging in as him from your workstation with his username and password and don't experience any problems. However, you cannot log in with either his username or yours from his workstation. What is a likely cause of the problem?

    A. The Caps Lock key is pressed.

    B. The network hub is malfunctioning.

    C. Downed server

    D. A jabbering NIC.

8. Which technical support resource has the most current information and up-to-date drivers and patches?

    A. README file

    B. Technical support CD-ROM

    C. Technical support Web site

    D. Technical phone support

9. You are troubleshooting your only PC at home at 11:30 PM Sunday night, but you are having trouble connecting to the Internet. You suspect that the modem needs a new driver. Which technical support resource could you possibly use to get the new driver?

    A. README file

    B. Technical support CD-ROM

    C. Technical support Web site

    D. Technical support phone support

10. Your NetWare 5 server suddenly experienced an error. It then started the shutdown procedure, and the error scrolled off the screen. You didn't have CONLOG.NLM loaded when this happened. Next to the command prompt on the console, there was a number in angle brackets, like this: <2>. Which log file could you look in to determine the source of the problem and the error message that was displayed?

    A. BOOT.LOG

    B. ABEND.LOG

    C. SYS$LOG.ERR

    D. SYS$ERR.LOG

11. A user calls you, reporting a problem logging in to the corporate intranet. You can access the Web site without problems using the user's username and password. At your request, the user has tried logging in from other workstations unsuccessfully. What is the most likely cause of the problem?

    A. The user is logging in wrong.

    B. The network is down.

    C. The intranet server is locked up.

    D. The server is not routing packets correctly to that user's workstation.

12. A user calls you reporting a problem logging in to the corporate intranet. You cannot access the Web site using the user's username and password, but you can access it when logging in with your username. At your request, the user has tried logging in from other workstations with no success. What is the most likely cause of the problem?

    A. The user is logging in wrong.

    B. The user's workstation is misconfigured.

    C. The intranet server is locked up.

    D. The user doesn't have the correct rights.

13. Which software troubleshooting tool could you use to determine which protocol is configured with the wrong address?

    A. Performance monitoring tools

    B. Protocol analyzer

    C. Antivirus checker

    D. Protocol-layer monitor

14. Which hardware troubleshooting tool(s) could you use to find out where a cable is routed?

    A. Crossover cable

    B. Hardware loopback

    C. Tone generator

    D. Tone locator

15. Which Windows NT log file keeps track of all events such as log in/log out and use of rights?

    A. Security

    B. System

    C. Application

    D. Console

16. Which Windows NT utility do you use to manage the major Windows NT log files?

    A. Log File Manager

    B. Event Viewer

    C. User Manager

    D. Server Performance Monitor

17. A user calls you, complaining that he can't access the corporate intranet Web server. You try the same address, and you receive a Host Not Found error. Several minutes later, another user reports the same problem. You can still send e-mail and transfer files to another server. What is the most likely cause of the problem?

    A. The hub is unplugged.

    B. The server is not routing protocols to your workstation.

    C. The user's workstation is not connected to the network.

    D. The Web server is down.

18. You are connecting a cubicle farm to your network. You install NICs in all the workstations and run cables to a workgroup hub. You then connect the MDI port on the workgroup hub to the main hub with a standard patch cable. Upon powering up the cubicle farm computers, none of them can see the servers on the network. What could you replace to solve this problem?

A. Hub patch cable

B. Workstation patch cables

C. Server patch cables

D. Workgroup hub

19. A user from the accounting department calls complaining that she can't see any servers on the network or log in. Her computer operates fine otherwise. No other users from the accounting department are reporting any problems. What is the first thing you could check?

A. Patch cable quality

B. Link lights

C. Power cables

D. Server status

20. Several users have complained of the server's poor performance as of late. You know that the memory installed in the server is sufficient. What could you check to determine the source of the problem?

A. Server's NIC link light

B. Protocol analyzer

C. Performance monitoring tools

D. Server's System Log file

Answers to Review Questions

1. A, C. Because both the SYS$LOGT.ERR and ABEND.LOG files both log errors that may or may not be critical, it is important that you know when these events occurred. As such, both of these NetWare log files contain date and time stamps for each event.

2. B. The link light indicates that the network card is making a basic-level connection to the rest of the network.

3. C. Replacing the patch cable is a much more difficult troubleshooting step than testing intranet access from different workstations.

4. B. Although all of these are good tests for network connectivity, checking the server console for user connections will tell you if other users are able to log into the server or not. If they can, the problem is most likely related to either those users workstation. If they can't, the problem is either the server or network connection. This helps narrow down the problem.

5. A. A hardware loopback is either a cable or plug that you attach to the network interface on a NIC. The loopback connects NIC outputs to that NIC's inputs so that you can test the transmission and reception capabilities of the NIC. Without a hardware loopback, you can't run the full batch of tests in the NIC's diagnostics program (since a transmission test is usually part of this batch of tests).

6. B. Because of all the tests given and their results, you can narrow the problem down to the network connectivity of that workstation. And because no other users in her area are having the same problem, it can't be the hub or server. You can log in as her from your workstation, so you know it isn't a rights issue or username/password issue. The only possible answer listed is a bad patch cable.

7. A. Because other users in the same area aren't having problem, it can't be a downed server, network hub, or jabbering NIC. And because both you and the user can't log in, more than likely it's a problem specific to that workstation. The only one that would affect your ability to log in from that station is the Caps Lock key being pressed. That will cause the password to be in all uppercase (which most server OSes treat as a different password) and will probably be rejected.

8. C. A vendor's technical support Web site usually has the most current information because the information can be distributed immediately.

9. B. Of those options listed, the only place to get a driver is the technical support CD-ROM or driver CD-ROM that comes with the modem.

10. B. The conditions described indicate that the NetWare server experienced an Abend. When this happens, a NetWare 5 server will write the Abend error and the conditions under which the Abend occurred to the ABEND.LOG file. So, of those listed, the best place to look would be the ABEND.LOG file.

11. A. Because the user can't log in correctly from any machine, more than likely he is using the wrong procedure to log in with.

12. D. Because you cannot log in with their password from your machine or from any other machine, the problem is most likely related to that particular username. The only answer listed that is specific to the username is that the user doesn't have the correct rights.

13. B. A protocol analyzer is a software tool that can be used to examine the details of packets as they travel across the wire. Using this kind of tool, you could examine the addresses of packets as they cross the wire and see which station is configured incorrectly.

14. C, D. A tone generator and tone locator can help you find out where cables are routed. The tone generator sends a signal down the wire. The tone locator is run along a wire to test if it contains the signal. Using this tool, you can tell where a cable (the cable that you attach the tone generator to) is running and what path it takes.

15. A. The security log file in the Event Viewer logs all security related events, including authentication, rights application, and breaches of those security methods.

16. B. The Event Viewer is the Windows NT utility used to manage the major NT log files (System, Security, and Application).

17. D. Because other people are experiencing the problem, most likely the problem is either network- or server-related. And because you can transfer files to and from another server, it can't be the network. Thus, the problem is related to the Web server.

18. A. The MDI port was designed to uplink one hub to another using a crossover cable. By putting in a standard patch cable, you prevent the hubs from communicating, thus the workgroup cannot communicate with the servers.

19. B. The link lights will tell if the computer can communicate with the rest of the network. Although you could check all of these items for this problem, trying the link light(s) on the NIC in the workstation and hub to make sure they can communicate is the first thing to do because it's the simplest.

20. C. Performance monitoring tools can give an idea of how "busy" the server and the rest of the network are. These tools use graphs to indicate how much traffic is going through that server.

Appendix A

Practice Exam

Practice Exam Questions

1. In a bus topology, how do computers receive data?

   A. A central computer sends the message directly to the intended recipient.

   B. The data is sent to all computers.

   C. The data is sent to all computers and only the intended recipient (found by reading the address on the data) reads the data into memory, all others reject it.

   D. The data is sent to all computers, one after another. Each computer, in turn, reads the address on the data. If the data is not intended for that computer, it sends it on to the next computer. If the address on the data matches that of the computer that reads it, that computer does not send it on and reads the data into memory.

2. Which network topology is the most fault tolerant?

   A. Bus

   B. Ring

   C. Mesh

   D. Star

3. Which network topology uses the least amount of network cable?

   A. Bus

   B. Ring

   C. Mesh

   D. Star

4. Which network topology responds best to moves, adds, and changes (MACs)?

   A. Bus

   B. Ring

   C. Mesh

   D. Star

5. Which network topology connects each computer directly to **only** two other computers?

   A. Bus

   B. Ring

   C. Mesh

   D. Star

6. You are the cabling installer for a small insurance company. They have asked you to install the best cabling system for their needs.

Required results:

The cabling system must be somewhat fault tolerant.

The cabling system must be easy to expand.

Optional results:

Install a cabling system that will support data, voice, and video simultaneously.

Proposed solution:

Install a 10BaseT Ethernet network.

   A. The proposed solution meets only one of the required results.

   B. The proposed solution meets both of the required results and none of the optional results.

   C. The proposed solution meets only the optional results.

   D. The proposed solution meets all of the required results and the optional results.

7. NDS is an integral part of which NOS?

    A. Unix

    B. NetWare

    C. Windows NT Server

    D. Linux

8. Windows NT Server uses which type(s) of group(s)?

    A. Remote

    B. Local

    C. Administrative

    D. Global

9. NetWare 5 servers have what additional feature that distinguishes them from earlier versions of NetWare?

    A. NDS

    B. TCP/IP support

    C. GUI

    D. IPX Support

10. Your company employs four people and each has a computer at their desk. Your company president has decided to maximize the use of the computer hardware you have by installing a network and has asked your opinion. What type of network architecture would be easiest to install and administrate at your company?

    A. Client Server

    B. Peer-to-Peer

    C. Peer-Server

    D. Client-Peer

11. You have a 250-station network that uses a combination of Windows NT, Unix, and NetWare 5 servers. For ease of administration, which protocol would you choose to standardize on for both clients and servers?

    A. IPX/SPX

    B. NetBEUI

    C. TCP/IP

    D. NWLink

12. The protocol DHCP is used with which protocol stack?

    A. TCP/IP

    B. NWLink

    C. NetBEUI

    D. IPX/SPX

13. Which protocol suite is primarily used on NetWare networks?

    A. TCP/IP

    B. NWLink

    C. NetBEUI

    D. IPX/SPX

14. Which RAID levels does Windows NT Server 4.0 support (circle all that apply)?

    A. 0

    B. 1

    C. 2

    D. 3

    E. 4

    F. 5

    G. 6

    H. 9

15. Which RAID level has no redundancy and thus provides no fault tolerance at all?

    A. RAID 0

    B. RAID 1

    C. RAID 2

    D. RAID 3

16. What technology allows you to consolidate multiple areas of free space on multiple disks into a single, named storage area?

    A. RAID 0

    B. Mirroring

    C. Striping

    D. Volumes

17. Which TCP/IP protocol is used to provide performance statistics from, as well as controls for, a specific network device.

    A. SMTP

    B. SNMP

    C. DHCP

    D. POP3

18. Put these OSI model layers in order from top to bottom.

    A. Network

    B. Transport

    C. Physical

    D. Presentation

    E. Application

    F. Session

    G. Data Link

19. At which layer of the OSI model does the IP protocol primarily operate at?

A. Physical

B. Network

C. Data Link

D. Application

20. Which layer of the OSI model is responsible for character set conversion (such as EBCDIC to ASCII and back)?

A. Application

B. Presentation

C. Session

D. Physical

21. Which OSI model layer is responsible for reliable data delivery and error control?

A. Physical

B. Data Link

C. Network

D. Transport

22. Which layer of the OSI model is responsible for routing packets and logical network addressing?

A. Physical

B. Data Link

C. Network

D. Transport

23. Which layer of the OSI model is responsible for encoding data into electrical transitions and placing the data on the wire?

    A. Physical

    B. Data Link

    C. Network

    D. Transport

24. A 10BaseT network normally has what type of connector on the patch cable(s)?

    A. BNC

    B. RJ-11

    C. Fiber Optic

    D. RJ-45

25. What is the maximum segment limit for a 10BaseT or 100BaseT network?

    A. 10 Meters

    B. 100 Meters

    C. 1,000 Meters

    D. 10,000 Meters

26. IEEE 802.3 specifies what type of network?

    A. CSMA/CD

    B. CSMA/CA

    C. Ethernet

    D. Token Ring

27. How does a router determine where a packet should be routed?

    A. It looks at the source network address.

    B. It looks at the destination network address.

    C. It looks at the source MAC address.

    D. It looks at the destination MAC address.

28. Every time you try to use your network card and sound card at the same time (like playing streaming audio from a server) they both fail. Used separately, they work well. What is the most likely cause of this problem?

    A. Bad sound card

    B. Bad network card

    C. IRQ Conflict

    D. I/O Conflict

29. The IP address 70.101.23.47 is what class of IP address?

    A. Class A

    B. Class B

    C. Class C

    D. Class D

30. Which of the following is(are) an FQDN?

    A. homer

    B. thompson.com

    C. homer.thompson.com

    D. homer.thompson.com.

31. Prior to the widespread use of WINS technology, what was used on each machine to provide NetBIOS name resolution?

    A. DNS

    B. WINS

    C. HOSTS

    D. LMHOSTS

32. What TCP/IP utility is used to verify TCP/IP communications between two entities.

    A. PING

    B. HOSTS

    C. NETSTAT

    D. NBTSTAT

33. Which TCP/IP utility is used to display the TCP/IP configuration of a Windows NT Server?

    A. PING

    B. WINIPCFG

    C. IPCONFIG

    D. IPCFG

34. Which FTP command is used to perform a remote directory listing when preparing to download files with FTP?

    A. prompt

    B. ls

    C. switch

    D. remdir

35. You are having trouble connecting to your Web site (the name just stays in the bottom left corner of the browser window) and you know the web server itself is functioning. You suspect a problem with DNS. What would check to ensure the problem is DNS-related? You know the MAC address of the server as well as the IP address (176.23.101.99).

A. PING the Web site's DNS name (www.website.com).

B. PING the Web site's IP address (176.23.101.99).

C. Use the DNSTEST utility with the MAC address.

D. Use DNSPING utility with the MAC address.

36. Which switch do you use with NETSTAT if you want to display Ethernet interface statistics and information?

A. -a

B. -b

C. -e

D. -n

37. What is the correct syntax to use with ARP command in order to manually add an IP address to the ARP cache?

A. ARP

B. ARP -a <IP ADDRESS>

C. ARP -d <IP ADDRESS>

D. ARP -e <IP ADDRESS>

38. What is the correct syntax to use with the ARP command in order to manually delete an IP address from the ARP cache?

A. ARP

B. ARP -a <IP ADDRESS>

C. ARP -d <IP ADDRESS>

D. ARP -e <IP ADDRESS>

39. If you ping 127.0.0.1 and the computer reports a "Destination host unreachable" error. What is the problem?

    A. IPX isn't configured correctly.

    B. IPX isn't installed.

    C. TCP/IP isn't configured correctly.

    D. TCP/IP isn't installed correctly.

40. Which remote access technology is installed in almost every home, business, and hotel in the U.S., and thus is the most commonly used remote access technology?

    A. POTS/PSTN

    B. ISDN

    C. DSL

    D. Satellite

41. How many "B" channels are in a standard ISDN BRI?

    A. 2

    B. 4

    C. 16

    D. 64

42. ISDN is short for _____?

    A. Instant Digital Networking

    B. Internet Standard Digital Network

    C. Internal Signaling Digital Network

    D. Integrated Services Digital Network

43. How many octets represent the network portion of a Class A TCP/IP address?

A. 1

B. 2

C. 4

D. 8

44. Which protocol could you configure to provide a secure, virtual connection over a public unsecured medium, like the Internet?

A. CHAP

B. PPTP

C. POTS

D. TCP

45. Which of the following is the most secure password?

A. john

B. smith

C. television

D. rat$f1nk

46. Which TCP/IP protocol is used for route discovery on routed TCP/IP networks?

A. TCP

B. DHCP

C. RIP

D. UDP

47. The 5-4-3 rule in networking stands for what?

   A. 5 networks, 4 routers, 3 bridges

   B. 5 segments, 4 repeaters, 3 populated segments

   C. 5 networks, 4 bridges, 3 routable protocols

   D. 5 segments, 4 repeaters, 3 different network topologies

48. Which type of cabling is the most resistant to EMI/RFI?

   A. UTP

   B. STP

   C. Fiber optic

   D. Coax

49. Which TCP/IP protocol is used to manage and receive error information from TCP/IP hosts?

   A. DHCP

   B. SNMP

   C. OSPF

   D. IPX/SPX

50. A hub operates at which layer of the OSI model?

   A. Physical

   B. Network

   C. Transport

   D. Session

51. Routers operate at which layer of the OSI model?

    A. Physical

    B. Network

    C. Transport

    D. Session

52. Which type of connector is used for 10BaseT networks?

    A. RJ-11

    B. RJ-45

    C. BNC

    D. Vampire Tap

53. Which type of connector is used for 10Base2 networks?

    A. RJ-11

    B. RJ-45

    C. BNC

    D. Vampire Tap

54. Most digital phone systems usually use what type of connector to connect a phone to the phone jack?

    A. RJ-11

    B. RJ-45

    C. BNC

    D. Vampire Tap

55. What is the maximum length of a 10Base5 segment with no repeaters?

   A. 90 meters

   B. 100 meters

   C. 500 meters

   D. 1,000 meters

56. What is the maximum distance between two nodes on a 10Base2 network?

   A. 100 meters

   B. 185 meters

   C. 500 meters

   D. 925 meters

57. Which three items must be present in the Windows Network Control Panel in order to connect to a network server?

   A. Appropriate client

   B. NIC driver

   C. File sharing

   D. Protocol

58. A user has just left your company. What should you do with their user account immediately after the user leaves?

   A. Rename the account.

   B. Delete the account.

   C. Nothing.

   D. Disable the account.

59. What two types of groups exist on a Windows NT Server?

   A. Global and Local

   B. User and Resource

   C. Global and Resource

   D. User and Global

60. If you accidentally delete a user account in User Manager, how can you get it back?

   A. Go to the user menu and select "undelete."

   B. From the command prompt type ACCOUNT <username> -undelete.

   C. You can't undelete a deleted account.

   D. Manually edit the "DELACT" file.

61. The most important procedure you must perform to keep your network protected from viruses, apart from installing anti-virus software?

   A. Patch the anti-virus software.

   B. Update the virus database frequently.

   C. Install a disk quota checking utility.

   D. Constantly run a protocol analyzer to check for suspicious packets.

62. Which of the following is an example of a global group?

   A. Domain Admins

   B. Administrators

   C. Everyone

   D. Local Users

63. Which of the following is NOT an event log for tracking errors in Windows NT Server?

A. System

B. Application

C. General

D. Security

64. What utility is used to check the Windows NT Server logs?

A. Log Viewer

B. Event Viewer

C. System Events

D. Logging Utility

65. When will you need to use a crossover cable?

A. When connecting a modem to a wall plate

B. When connecting a PC to a hub

C. When connecting two hubs together

D. When connecting a router and a bridge together

Answers to Practice Exam

1. C. In a bus topology, data is sent to all computers simultaneously and only the intended recipient takes notice of the data.

2. C. A mesh topology is the most fault tolerant of those listed because it contains multiple redundant paths to and from each computer.

3. A. Because a physical bus topology uses a single cable that runs from the first computer to the last computer in a line, it uses less cable than all of the other cabling topologies listed.

4. D. The star network topology is the most flexible and thus makes MACs much simpler. When moving or changing, you may only need to move the network device to the new location and plug it in (assuming there is a cable connection already there). If not, it's an easy matter to run a new cable run.

5. B. In a ring topology, each computer is directly connected to only two other computers. In this manner, information can flow from one computer to another, uninterrupted. If one computer goes down, the network can reconfigure itself around the problem.

6. B. Because 10BaseT uses a star topology, it is somewhat fault tolerant and relatively easy to expand. However, it does not have the bandwidth to support data, voice, and video simultaneously.

7. B. Novell Directory Services is an integral part of Novell's operating system, NetWare. It is included with all versions of NetWare after (and including) version 4.

8. B, D. Windows NT Server uses two types of groups in its domain administration model: local groups and global groups. Local groups are local to a particular server and global groups span entire domains.

9. C. NetWare 5 was the first version of NetWare that put a GUI on the server interface. Before that, NetWare was a text and menu-driven OS only.

10. B. For a network with only four users and a non-dedicated administrator, a peer-to-peer network would be the best choice because of its simplicity. Each user administrates their own machine.

11. C. Of the protocols listed, the only protocol that is ubiquitous and truly cross-platform is TCP/IP. Support for it can be found on all the operating system listed.

12. A. Although DHCP can be used with different protocol stacks, it is a subset of the TCP/IP protocol stack.

13. D. IPX/SPX was developed by Novell for use with its NetWare network operating system. Although it does see use in other environments (like Windows NT networks or heterogeneous networks), it is primarily found on NetWare networks.

14. A, B, F. Out of the box, Window NT Server 4.0 supports RAID levels 0, 1, and 5.

15. A. RAID 0 (striping) doesn't offer any redundancy; it only increases performance on a disk subsystem by writing data across multiple disks.

16. D. When combining multiple disk storage areas to form a single, named area of disk space, you are creating a volume.

17. B. The Simple Network Management Protocol (SNMP) is used to get statistics from network devices. It can also be used to control and manage a TCP/IP network device that supports SNMP.

18. E, D, F, B, A, G, C. The OSI model layers, from top to bottom, are Application, Presentation, Session, Transport, Network, Data Link, Physical.

19. B. The IP protocol (part of the TCP/IP protocol suite) operates primarily at the Network layer of the OSI model.

20. B.   The Presentation layer of the OSI model is responsible for character set conversion. And, as such, EBCDIC to ASCII conversation is done with software that operates at this layer.

21. D.   The Transport layer is responsible for ensuring the delivery of network packets. It defines functions like end-to-end error and flow control as well as data checksumming.

22. C.   The Network layer is responsible for the functions of routing and logical (network) addressing.

23. A.   As its name suggests, the Physical layer is responsible for encoding data into electrical signals and placing those signals onto the physical medium (usually a wire or cable).

24. D.   10BaseT networks typically use either STP or UTP cable. The most popular connector for this type of cable in LAN use is the RJ-45 connector.

25. B.   The maximum single segment length for a 10BaseT or 100BaseT network is 100Meters total, end-to-end.

26. A.   The IEEE 802.3 subcommittee specifies a network that uses Carrier Sense Multiple Access with Collision Detection (CSMA/CD). Although Ethernet is the name of a network that was developed using CSMA/CD technologies, it is not, in fact, what the IEEE 802.3 specified.

27. B.   A router determines how a packet should be sent by examining a packet's destination network address. The router then forwards the packet on one or more of its interfaces based on the information the router has in its routing tables.

28. C.   The nature of a problem suggests that whenever two devices try to communicate with the processor at the same time using the same IRQ, they both fail. But, when the devices are used individually, they rarely have to talk to the processor at the same time and thus function normally.

29. A.   Because the first number in the IP address falls within the Class A range of 0-127, the IP address is a Class A address.

30. C, D.   Both C and D are correct because a fully qualified domain name includes the top-level domain (such as .com, .org, .net, and so on), the domain name (thompson, in this case) and the host name (homer, in this case). The period at the end of answer D is just another way of indicating a FQDN.

31. D.   The LMHOSTS file on a Windows machine maps NetBIOS machine names to their respect IP addresses, thus performing the same function as a WINS server.

32. A.   The PING utility is used to send small test packets to a TCP/IP host. If the packets return successfully, it is possible to communicate between the two hosts on a fundamental level.

33. C.   The utility used to display the TCP/IP configuration of a Windows NT Server is the command line utility IPCONFIG. By typing "IPCONFIG /ALL" at a command prompt, you can view the detailed TCP/IP configuration of that server.

34. B.   The ls command will perform a directory listing on the remote computer during an FTP session.

35. B.   Pinging the Web site using the IP address confirms that TCP/IP is properly configured and that a session can be established between your computer and the Web site server.

36. C.   NETSTAT -e will display Ethernet interface statistics. It will display things like how many packets of different types have been sent and received.

37. B.   To add an IP address to the ARP cache, you must use the syntax ARP -a <IP ADDRESS> and replace the <IP ADDRESS> with the IP address you want to add.

38. C.   The correct syntax for deleting an entry from the ARP cache is to use ARP with the "-d" switch.

39. D.   If TCP/IP isn't installed correctly and you try to ping 127.0.0.1 (the alias for your local TCP/IP interface), you will receive the "Destination host unreachable" error.

40. A.   A POTS/PSTN line is just the technical name for the phone line installed in almost every home and business in the U.S., and thus is the most commonly used remote access technology.

41. A.   A standard ISDN BRI contains 2 "B" or "Bearer" channels and one "D" channel for out-of-band signaling.

42. D.   The correct expansion for ISDN is Integrated Services Digital Network.

43. A.   In a standard Class A TCP/IP address, the first octet represents the network portion and the last three represent the node portion.

44. B.   The point-to-point tunneling protocol (PPTP) is used to provide secure LAN-to-LAN network connections over the Internet.

45. D.   Because the password rat$f1nk contains a combination of both alphanumeric characters and symbols, it would be the most difficult to guess or crack and thus is the most secure password.

46. C.   Of the choices above, RIP (Routing Information Protocol) is the only routing protocol. It is a very basic but reliable routing protocol for use on small networks. RIP can be configured to discover routes via routing updates or via statically defined routes.

47. B.   When talking about networking bridges together, you can have a maximum of five networks connected by four bridges with only three of the segments populated with workstations.

48. C.   Because it uses light instead of electrical signals, fiber-optic transmissions are immune to EMI and RFI.

49. B.   The SNMP protocol is used to manage and receive errors from TCP/IP, SNMP-enabled hosts.

50. A.   Hubs operate at the physical layer of the OSI model.

51. B.   Routers, because the deal with Network layer information, are said to operate at the network layer of the OSI model.

52. B.   Because 10BaseT networks use twisted-pair cabling and twisted pair cables most often use RJ45 connectors to make connections, 10BaseT networks often use RJ-45 connectors for their connections.

53. C.   Because 10Base2 networks most often use coax cable and coax cable uses BNC connectors for network connections, 10Base2 network most often use BNC connectors to make the connections between networking equipment.

54. B.   The newer digital phone systems actually use an RJ-45 plug and connector (the same as data connections). Some digital phone systems may use the RJ-11 connector, but the majority of them use RJ-45 connectors at the wall plate.

55. C.   The maximum length of a 10Base5 segment without any repeaters is 500 meters.

56. B.   By definition, the maximum distance between any two nodes on a 10Base2 network is 185 meters.

57. A, B, D.   Windows Networking requires that you have a client for the server type you are using (Windows or NetWare), NIC driver for the NIC installed in your computers, and the same protocol that your server is running. File sharing will only enable your computer to share its files, but you still must have the other 3 items installed.

58. D.   To prevent an ex-employee from logging on your corporate network, but still provide maximum flexibility, you must disable that user's account once they leave the company.

59. A.   NT Server security uses two types of groups, Global and Local. Global groups span domain boundaries, whereas local groups are only valid on the machine they are created on.

60. C. In User Manager for Windows NT Server, once you delete a user, that user is gone forever. Even if you re-create the user, the new user you create will have a different ID from the old user name, even though the names are the same.

61. B. By updating the virus definition database frequently, you ensure that your antivirus software has the most current "vaccination" information.

62. A. Domain Admins is an example of one of the default global groups installed on Windows NT Server by default.

63. C. There is no such thing as a General NT Server log file.

64. B. The Event Viewer utility is used to view the three major log files on a Windows NT Server.

65. C. A crossover cable has the outputs of one set of transmission pins connected to the input on the opposite end of the cable and vice versa. When the cable is connected between two hubs, both hubs can communicate with each other.

Appendix B

Acronym and Abbreviation Expansion Guide

AC	alternating current
ACK	acknowledgment
ACL	access control list
ADSL	Asymmetric Digital Subscriber Line
ARCNet	Attached Resource Computer Network
ARP	Address Resolution Protocol
ARPA	Advanced Research Projects Agency
ASCII	American Standard Code for Information Interchange
ATM	Asynchronous Transfer Mode
AUI	Attachment Unit Interface
Bash	Bourne Again Shell
BDC	Backup Domain Controller
BGP	Border Gateway Protocol
BNC	BayoNet Connector or Bayonet Nut Connector or British Naval Connector
BSOD	Blue Screen of Death
CAD	computer-aided design
CCIE	Cisco Certified Internetworking Expert
CDM	Custom Device Module
CERT	Computer Emergency Response Team
CERT/CC	CERT Coordination Center
CIR	Committed Information Rate
CPU	central processing unit
CRC	cyclical redundancy check
CSMA/CA	Carrier Sense Multiple Access/Collision Avoidance
CSMA/CD	Carrier Sense Multiple Access/Collision Detection

CSNW	Client Services for NetWare
CTS	clear to send
DARPA	Defense Advanced Research Projects Agency
DAT	digital audiotape
DDNS	Dynamic Domain Name Services
DEC	Digital Equipment Corporation
DES	Data Encryption Standard
DHCP	Dynamic Host Configuration Protocol
DIN	Deutsches Institut für Normung e. V. (German Institute for Standardization)
DIP	dual in-line package
DIX	Digital, Intel, and Xerox
DLL	Dynamic Link Library
DLT	digital linear tape
DMA	direct memory access
DMZ	demilitarized zone
DNNS	Dynamic DNS
DNS	Domain Name Service
DOD	Department of Defense
DoS	Denial of Service
DOS	disk operating system
DQDB	Distributed Queue Dual Bus
DSL	Digital Subscriber Line
DVD	digital video disc or digital versatile disk
EBCDIC	Extended Binary Coded Decimal Interchange Code
EEPROM	Electrically Erasable Programmable Read-Only Memory

EGP	External Gateway Protocol
EISA	Extended Industry Standard Architecture
EMI	electromagnetic interference
ENS	Event Notification Services
ESD	electrostatic discharge
FDDI	Fiber Distributed Data Interface
FDM	frequency-division multiplexing
FM	frequency modulation
FPNW	File and Print Services for NetWare
FQDN	Fully Qualified Domain Name
FSMA	Field-installable SubMiniature Assembly
FTP	File Transfer Protocol
GFS	Grandfather-Father-Son
GSNW	Gateway Services for NetWare
GUI	graphical user interface
HAL	Hardware Abstraction Layer
HAM	Host Adapter Module
HCL	Hardware Compatibility List
HDSL	High-bit-rate Digital Subscriber Line
HP	Hewlett-Packard
HTML	HyperText Markup Language
HTTP	Hypertext Transfer Protocol
IBM	International Business Machines
IC	integrated circuit
ICMP	Internet Control Message Protocol
IDE	Integrated Drive Electronics

IEEE	Institute of Electrical and Electronics Engineers, Inc.
IETF	Internet Engineering Task Force
IIS	Internet Information Server
IP	Internet Protocol
IPX	Internetwork Packet eXchange
IPX/SPX	Internetwork Packet eXchange/Sequenced Packet eXchange
IRQ	interrupt request
ISA	Industry Standard Architecture
ISDN	Integrated Services Digital Network
ISO	International Organization for Standardization
ISP	Internet Service Provider
JVM	Java Virtual Machine
LAN	local area network
LCD	Liquid Crystal Display
LCP	Link Control Protocol
LDAP	Lightweight Directory Access Protocol
LED	light-emitting diode
LIP	Large Internet Packet
LLC	logical link control
LSL	Link Support Layer
LSP	Link State Packet
MAC	media access control
MAD	Microsoft Active Directory
MAN	metropolitan area network
MAP	Manufacturing Automation Protocol
MAU	Multistation Access Unit

MCA	Microchannel Architecture
MIB	Management Information Base
MIT	Massachusetts Institute of Technology
MSAU	Multistation Access Unit
NAI	Network Associates International
NAT	network address translation
NCP	NetWare Core Protocol
NCSC	National Computing Security Center
NDPS	Novell Distributed Print Services
NDS	Novell Directory Services
NetBEUI	NetBIOS Extended User Interface
NetBIOS	Network Basic Input/Output System
NFS	Network File System
NIC	network interface card
NIS	Network Information Service
NLM	NetWare Loadable Module
NLSP	NetWare Link State Protocol
NOS	network operating system
NPA	NetWare Peripheral Architecture
NSA	National Security Agency
NTDS	NT Directory Services
NWPA	NetWare Peripheral Architecture
ODI	Open Datalink Interface
OEM	original equipment manufacturer
OS	operating system
OSI	Open Systems Interconnect

OSPF	Open Shortest Path First
PARC	Palo Alto Research Center
PCI	Peripheral Component Interconnect
PCMCIA	Personal Computer Memory Card International Association
PDC	Primary Domain Controller
PGP	Pretty Good Privacy
POP	Post Office Protocol
POSIX	Portable Operating System Interface
POTS	Plain Old Telephone Service
PPP	Point-to-Point Protocol
PPTP	Point-to-Point Tunneling Protocol
PSTN	Public Switched Telephone Network
PVC	permanent virtual circuit
QIC	quarter-inch cartridge
QoS	quality of service
RAID	redundant array of independent (or inexpensive) disks
RAM	random access memory
RAS	Remote Access Server
RFC	Request for Comment
RFI	radio frequency interference
RIP	Routing Information Protocol
RISC	reduced instruction set computing
RJ	Registered Jack
RSA	Rivest, Shamir, Adleman
RTC	Real-Time Clock
RTS	Request to Send

SAM	Security Accounts Manager
SCO	Santa Cruz Operation
SCSI	Small Computer System Interface
SDLC	Synchronous Data Link Control
SDSL	Single-Line Digital Subscriber Line
SEI	Software Engineering Institute
SFM	Services for Macintosh
S-HTTP	Secure Hypertext Transfer Protocol
SID	Security Identifier
SLIP	Serial Line Internet Protocol
SMB	Server Message Block
SMS	Systems Management Server; Storage Management Services
SMTP	Simple Mail Transfer Protocol
SNDS	Scalable Novell Directory Services
SNMP	Simple Network Management Protocol
SOP	standard operating procedure
SPARC	Scalable Processor ARChitecture
SPS	Standby Power Supply
SPX	Sequenced Packet eXchange
SQL	Structured Query Language
STP	shielded twisted-pair
TCP	Transmission Control Protocol
TCP/IP	Transmission Control Protocol/Internet Protocol
TCSEC	Trusted Computer System Evaluation Criteria
TDMA	Time Division Multiple Access

TDR	time-domain reflectometer
Telnet	Terminal Emulation for Networks
TFTP	Trivial File Transfer Protocol
TNIEG	Trusted Network Interpretation Environmental Guideline
TTL	time to live
UDP	User Datagram Protocol
UID	User ID
UNC	Universal (or Uniform) Naming Convention
UPS	uninterruptible power supply
URL	Uniform Resource Locator
USB	Universal Serial Bus
UTP	unshielded twisted-pair
VAX	Virtual Address eXtension
VDM	Virtual DOS Machine
VDSL	Very High-bit-rate Digital Subscriber Line
VESA	Video Electronics Standards Association
VMS	Virtual Memory System
VPN	Virtual Private Network
WAN	wide area network
WINS	Windows Internet Naming Service
WWW	World Wide Web
XNS	Xerox Network System

Glossary

10Base2 Ethernet An implementation of Ethernet that specifies a 10Mbps signaling rate, baseband signaling, and coaxial cable with a maximum segment length of 185 meters.

10BaseFL An implementation of Ethernet that specifies a 10Mbps signaling rate, baseband signaling, and fiber-optic cabling.

10BaseT An implementation of Ethernet that specifies a 10Mbps signaling rate, baseband signaling, and twisted-pair cabling.

100BaseVG Star topology using round-robin for allowing systems to transmit data on the network.

100VG (Voice Grade) IEEE 802.12 standard for 100BaseVG networks.

100VG-AnyLAN A networking technology that runs 100 megabit Ethernet over regular (Cat 3) phone lines. It hasn't gained the industry acceptance that 100BaseT has.

access control list (ACL) List of rights an object has to resources in the network. Also a type of firewall. In this case, the lists reside on a router and determine which machines can use the router and in what direction.

ACK *See* acknowledgment.

acknowledgment (ACK) A message confirming that the data packet was received. This occurs at the Transport layer of the OSI model.

ACL *See* access control list.

active hub A hub that is powered and actively regenerates any signal that is received. *See also* hub.

active monitor Used in Token Ring networks, a process that prevents data frames from roaming the ring unchecked. If the frame passes the active monitor too many times, it is removed from the ring. Also ensures that a token is always circulating the ring.

Address Designation to allow PCs to be known by a name or number to other PCs. Addressing allows a PC to transmit data directly to another PC by using its address (IP or MAC).

alias record *See* CNAME record.

antivirus   A category of software that uses various methods to eliminate viruses in a computer. It typically also protects against future infection. *See also* virus.

Application layer   The seventh layer of the OSI model, which deals with how applications access the network and describes application functionality, such as file transfer, messaging, and so on.

ARCNet   The Attached Resource Computer Network, which was developed by Datapoint Corporation in the late 1970s as one of the first baseband networks. It can use either a physical star or bus topology.

ARP table   A table used by the ARP protocol. Contains a list of known TCP/IP addresses and their associated MAC addresses. The table is cached in memory so that ARP lookups do not have to be performed for frequently accessed TCP/IP and MAC addresses. *See also* media access control, Transmission Control Protocol/Internet Protocol.

Asymmetrical Digital Subscriber Line (ADSL)   An implementation of DSL where the upload and download speeds are different. *See* Digital Subscriber Line.

Asynchronous Transfer Mode (ATM)   A connection-oriented network architecture based on broadband ISDN technology that uses constant size 53-byte cells instead of packets. Because cells don't change size, they are switched much faster and more efficiently than packets across a network.

ATM   *See* Asynchronous Transfer Mode.

Attachment Unit Interface (AUI) port   Port on some NICs that allows connecting the NIC to different media types by using an external transceiver.

B Channel   *See* bearer channel.

backbone   The part of most networks that connects multiple segments together to form a LAN. The backbone is usually higher speed than the segments. *See* segment, local area network.

Backup Domain Controllers   Computer on a Windows NT network that has a copy of the SAM database for fault tolerance and performance enhancement purposes. *See also* Security Accounts Manager.

backup plan   Term used to describe a company's strategy to make copies of its data and be able to restore the data in case of an emergency.

backup window   The amount of time that an administrator has available to perform a complete, successful backup.

bandwidth   In network communications, the amount of data that can be sent across a wire in a given time. Each communication that passes along the wire decreases the amount of available bandwidth.

baseband   A transmission technique in which the signal uses the entire bandwidth of a transmission medium.

baseline   A category of network documentation that indicates how the network normally runs. It includes such information as network statistics, server utilization trends, and processor performance statistics.

bearer channel   The channels in an ISDN line that carry data. Each bearer channel typically has a bandwidth of 64Kbps.

blackout   *See* power blackout.

Blank   These are often referred to as slot covers. If a PC card is removed, there will be an opening in the computer case. This will allow dirt and dust to enter the computer and prevent it from being cooled properly. Some computer cases have the blanks as part of the case and they must be broken off from the case before a bus slot may be used to insert a PC card into it.

BNC connector   Tubular connectors most commonly used with coaxial cable.

bonding   A procedure where two ISDN B channels are joined together to provide greater bandwidth.

bounded media   A network medium that is used at the Physical layer where the signal travels over a cable of some kind.

bridge   A network device, operating at the Data Link layer, that logically separates a single network into segments, but lets the two segments appear to be one network to higher layer protocols.

broadband   A network transmission method in which a single transmission medium is divided so that multiple signals can travel across the same medium simultaneously.

broadcast address A special network address that refers to all users on the network. For example, the TCP/IP address 255.255.255.255 is the broadcast address. Any packets sent to that address will get sent to everyone on that LAN.

brouter A device that combines the functionality of a bridge and a router, but can't be distinctly classified as either.

brownout *See* power brownout.

bus Pathways in a PC that allow data and signals to be transmitted between the PC components. Types of buses include ISA, PCI, Vesa Local, and EIDE.

bus topology A topology where the cable and signals run in a straight line from one end of the network to the other.

cable A physical transmission medium that has a central conductor of wire or fiber surrounded by a plastic jacket.

cable map General network documentation indicating each cable's source and destination as well as where each network cable runs.

cable tester A special instrument that is used to test the integrity of LAN cables. *See also* time-domain reflectometer.

carrier Signal at a frequency that is chosen to carry data. Addition of data to the frequency is modulation and the removal of data from the frequency is demodulation. This is used on analog devices like modems.

Carrier Sense Multiple Access/Collision Avoidance (CSMA/CA) A media access method that sends a request to send (RTS) packet and waits to receive a clear to send (CTS) packet before sending. Once the CTS is received, the sender sends the packet of information.

Carrier Sense Multiple Access/Collision Detection (CSMA/CD) A media access method that first senses whether there is a signal on the wire, indicating that someone is transmitting currently. If no one else is transmitting, it attempts a transmission and listens to hear whether someone else tries to transmit at the same time. If this happens, both senders back off and don't transmit again until some random period of time has passed.

Categories Different grades of cables to offer protection against interference from outside the cable. Category 1 allows voice data only. Category 2 allows data transmissions up to 4Mbps. Category 3 allows data transmissions up to 10Mbps. Category 4 allows data transmissions up to 16Mbps. Category 5 allows data transmissions up to 100Mbps.

Central Office The office in any metropolitan or rural area that contains the telephone switching equipment for that area. The central office connects all users in that area together as well as to the rest of the PSTN. *See also* Public Switched Telephone Network.

checkpoints To save data a certain part or time to allow for a restart at the last point that the data was saved.

checksum A hexadecimal value computed from transmitted data that is used in error-checking routines.

client/server network A server-centric network in which all resources are stored on a file server; processing power is distributed among workstations and the file server.

clipper chip A hardware implementation of the skipjack encryption algorithm.

clustering A computing technology where many servers work together so they appear to be one high-powered server. If one server fails, the others in the cluster take over the services provided by the failed server.

CNAME record A DNS record type that specifies other names for existing hosts. This allows a DNS administrator to assign multiple DNS host names to a single DNS host.

coaxial cable Often referred to as coax. A type of cable used in network wiring. Typical coaxial cable types include RG-58 and RG-62. 10Base2 Ethernet networks use coaxial cable. Coaxial cable is usually shielded.

collision The error condition that occurs when two stations on a CSMA/CD network transmit data (at the Data Link layer) at the same time. *See also* Carrier Sense Multiple Access/Collision Detection.

concentrator *See* hub.

connection-oriented   Communications between two hosts that have a previous session established for synchronizing sent data. The data is acknowledged by the receiving PC. This allows for guaranteed delivery of data between PCs.

connectionless   Communications between two hosts that have no previous session established for synchronizing sent data. The data is not acknowledged at the receiving end. This can allow for data loss.

connectionless services   *See* connectionless, connectionless transport protocol.

connectionless transport protocol   A transport protocol, such as UDP, that does not create a virtual connection between sending and receiving stations. *See also* User Datagram Protocol.

connection-oriented transport protocol   A transport protocol that uses acknowledgments and responses to establish a virtual connection between sending and receiving stations. TCP is a connection-oriented protocol. *See also* Transmission Control Protocol.

control protocol   A special window inside Microsoft Windows operating systems (Windows 95 and above) that has icons for all of the configurable options for the system.

controller   Part of a PC that allows connectivity to peripheral devices. A disk controller allows the PC to be connected to a hard disk. A network controller allows a PC to be connected to a network. A keyboard controller is used to connect a keyboard to the PC.

cost   A value given to a route between PCs or subnets to determine which route may be best. The word *hop* is sometimes used to refer to the number of routers between two PCs or subnets. *See also* hop.

country codes   The two-letter abbreviations for countries; used in the DNS hierarchy. *See also* Domain Name Service.

 CRC   *See* cyclical redundancy check.

crossover cable   The troubleshooting tool used in Ethernet UTP installations to test communications between two stations, bypassing the hub. *See also* unshielded twisted-pair cable.

crosstalk   A type of interference that occurs when two LAN cables run close to each other. If one cable is carrying a signal and the other isn't, the one carrying a signal will induce a "ghost" signal (crosstalk) in the other cable.

CSMA/CA   *See* Carrier Sense Multiple Access/Collision Avoidance.

CSMA/CD   *See* Carrier Sense Multiple Access/Collision Detection.

cyclical redundancy check (CRC)   An error-checking method in data communications that runs a formula against data before transmissions. The sending station then appends the resultant value (called a checksum) to the data and sends it. The receiving station uses the same formula on the data. If the receiving station doesn't get the same checksum result for the calculation, it considers the transmission invalid, rejects the frame, and asks for a retransmission.

D Channel   *See* delta channel.

data packet   A unit of data sent over a network. A packet includes a header, addressing information, and the data itself. A packet is treated as a single unit as it is sent from device to device. Also known as a datagram.

datagram   A unit of data smaller than a packet.

Data Link layer   The second layer of the OSI model, which describes the logical topology of a network—the way that packets move throughout a network. It also describes the method of media access. *See also* Open Systems Interconnect.

default gateway   The router that all packets are sent to when the workstation doesn't know where the destination station is or when it can't find the destination station on the local segment.

delta channel   A channel on an ISDN line used for link management. *See also* Integrated Switched Digital Network.

demarc   *See* demarcation point.

demarcation point   The point on any telephone installation where the telephone lines from the central office enter the customer's premises.

Denial of Service (DoS) attack   Type of hack that prevents any users, even legitimate ones, from using the system.

destination port number   The address of the PC that data is being sent to from a sending PC. The port portion allows for demultiplexing of data to be sent to a specific application.

Digital Subscriber Line (DSL)   A digital WAN technology that brings high-speed digital networking to homes and businesses over POTS. There are many types such as HDSL (High-speed DSL) and VDSL (Very high bit-rate DSL). *See also* Plain Old Telephone Service.

DHCP   *See* Dynamic Host Configuration Protocol.

dialogs   Communications between two PCs.

directory   A network database that contains a listing of all network resources, such as users, printers, groups, and so on.

directory service   A network service that provides access to a central database of information that contains detailed information about the network resources available on a network.

disaster recovery   The procedure by which data is recovered after a disaster.

disk striping   Technology that enables writing data to multiple disks simultaneously in small portions called stripes. These stripes maximize use by having all of the read/write heads working constantly. Different data is stored on each disk and is not automatically duplicated (this means that disk striping in and of itself does not provide fault tolerance).

distance vector   A route discovery method in which each router, using broadcasts, tells every other router what networks and routes it knows about and the distance to them.

DNS   *See* Domain Name Service.

DNS server   Any server that performs DNS host name to IP address resolution. *See also* Domain Name Service, Internet Protocol.

DNS zone   An area in the DNS hierarchy that is managed as a single unit. *See also* Domain Name Service.

DOD Networking Model   A four-layer conceptual model describing how communications should take place between computer systems. The four layers are Process/Application, Host-to-Host, Internet, and Network Access.

domain   A group of networked Windows computers that share a single SAM database. *See also* Security Accounts Manager.

Domain Name Service (DNS)   The network service used in TCP/IP networks that translates host names to IP addresses. *See also* Transmission Control Protocol/Internet Protocol.

dotted decimal   Notation used by TCP/IP to designate an IP address. The notation is made up of 32 bits (4 bytes), each byte separated by a decimal. The range of numbers for each octet is 0-255. The leftmost octet is the high-order bits and the rightmost octet is the low-order bits.

DSL   *See* Digital Subscriber Line.

dumb terminal   A keyboard and monitor that send keystrokes to a central processing computer (typically a mainframe or minicomputer) that returns screen displays to the monitor. The unit has no processing power of its own; hence, the moniker *dumb*.

duplexed hard drives   Two hard drives to which identical information is written simultaneously. A dedicated controller card controls each drive. Used for fault tolerance.

duplicate server   Two servers that are identical for use in clustering.

dynamic ARP table entries   *See* dynamic entry.

dynamic entry   An entry made in the ARP table whenever an ARP request is made by the Windows TCP/IP stack and the MAC address is not found in the ARP table. The ARP request is broadcast on the local segment. When the MAC address of the requested IP address is found, that information is added to the ARP table. *See also* Internet Protocol, media access control, Transmission Control Protocol/Internet Protocol.

Dynamic Host Configuration Protocol (DHCP)   A protocol used on a TCP/IP network to send client configuration data, including TCP/IP address, default gateway, subnet mask, and DNS configuration, to clients. *See also* default gateway, Domain Name Service, subnet mask, Transmission Control Protocol/Internet Protocol.

dynamic packet filtering   A type of firewall used to accept or reject packets based on the contents of the packets.

dynamic routing   The use of route discovery protocols to talk to other routers and find out what networks they are attached to. Routers that use dynamic routing send out special packets to request updates of the other routers on the network as well as to send their own updates.

dynamic state list   *See* dynamic routing.

dynamically allocated port   TCP/IP port used by an application when needed. The port is not constantly used.

EEPROM   *See* electrically erasable programmable read-only memory.

electrically erasable programmable read-only memory (EEPROM)   A special integrated circuit on expansion cards that allows data to be stored on the chip. If necessary, the data can be erased by a special configuration program. Typically used to store hardware configuration data for expansion cards.

electromagnetic interference (EMI)   The interference that can occur during transmissions over copper cable because of electromagnetic energy outside the cable. The result is degradation of the signal.

electronic mail (e-mail)   An application that allows people to send messages via their computers on the same network or over the Internet.

electrostatic discharge (ESD)   A problem that exists when two items with dissimilar static electrical charges are brought together. The static electrical charges jump to the item with fewer electrical charges causing ESD, which can damage computer components.

e-mail   *See* electronic mail.

EMI   *See* electromagnetic interference.

encoding   The process of translating data into signals that can be transmitted on a transmission medium.

encryption key   The string of alphanumeric characters used to decrypt encrypted data.

Endpoint   The two ends of a connection for transmitting data. One would be the receiver and the other the sender.

ESD   *See* electrostatic discharge.

Ethernet   A shared-media network architecture. It operates at the Physical and Data Link layers of the OSI model. It uses baseband signaling over either a bus or a star topology with CSMA/CD as the media access method. The cabling used in Ethernet networks can be coax, twisted-pair, or fiber-optic. *See also* Carrier Sense Multiple Access/Collision Detection, Open Systems Interconnect.

Ethernet address   *See* MAC address.

expansion slot   A slot on the computer's bus. Expansion cards are plugged into these slots to expand the functionality of the computer (for example, a NIC card to be able to add the computer to a network). *See also* network interface card.

failover device   A device that comes online when another fails.

failover server   A hot site backup system in which the failover server is connected to the primary server. A heartbeat is sent from the primary server to the backup server. If the heartbeat stops, the failover system starts and takes over. Thus, the system doesn't go down, although the primary server is not running.

Fast Ethernet   The general category name given to 100Mbps Ethernet technologies.

fault-resistant network   A network that will be up and running at least 99 percent of the time or that is down less than eight hours a year.

fault-tolerant network   A network that can recover from minor errors.

FDDI   *See* Fiber Distributed Data Interface.

Fiber Channel   A type of server-to-storage system connection that uses fiber-optic connectors.

Fiber Distributed Data Interface (FDDI)   A network topology that uses fiber-optic cable as a transmission medium and dual, counter-rotating rings to provide data delivery and fault tolerance.

fiber-optic   A type of network cable that uses a central glass or plastic core surrounded by a plastic coating.

file server   A server specialized in holding and distributing files.

File Transfer Protocol (FTP)   A TCP/IP protocol and software that permit the transferring of files between computer systems. Because FTP has been implemented on numerous types of computer systems, files can be transferred between disparate computer systems (for example, a personal computer and a minicomputer). *See also* Transmission Control Protocol/Internet Protocol.

firewall   A combination of hardware and software that protects a network from attack by hackers that could gain access through public networks, including the Internet.

Frequency Division Multiplexing (FDM)   A multiplexing technique whereby the different signals are sent across multiple frequencies.

FQDN   *See* Fully Qualified Domain Name.

frame relay   A WAN technology that transmits packets over a WAN using packet switching. *See also* packet switching.

FTP   *See* File Transfer Protocol.

FTP proxy   A server that uploads and downloads files from a server on behalf of a workstation.

full backup   A backup that copies all the data to the archive medium.

Fully Qualified Domain Name (FQDN)   An address that uses both the hostname (workstation name) and the domain name.

gateway   The hardware and software needed to connect two disparate network environments so that communications can occur.

global group A type of group in Windows NT that is used network-wide. Members can be from anywhere in the network, and rights can be assigned to any resource in the network.

ground loop A condition that occurs when a signal cycles through a common ground connection between two devices, causing EMI interference. *See also* electromagnetic interference.

hardware address A Data Link layer address assigned to every NIC at the MAC sublayer. The address is in the format xx:xx:xx:xx:xx:xx; each xx is a two-digit hexadecimal number. *See also* media access control, network interface card.

hardware loopback Connects the transmission pins directly to the receiving pins, allowing diagnostic software to test if a NIC can successfully transmit and receive. *See also* network interface card.

heartbeat The data transmissions between two servers in a cluster to detect when one fails. When the standby server detects no heartbeats from the main server, it comes online and takes control of the responsibilities of the main server. This allows for all the services to stay online and accessible.

hop One pass through a router. *See also* router.

hop count As a packet travels over a network through multiple routers, each router will increment this field in the packet by one as it crosses the router. It is used to limit the number of routers a packet can cross on the way to its destination.

host Any network device with a TCP/IP network address. *See also* Transmission Control Protocol/Internet Protocol.

Host-to-Host layer A layer in the DOD model that corresponds to the Transport layer of the OSI model. *See also* DOD networking model, Open Systems Interconnect.

HTML *See* HyperText Markup Language.

HTTP *See* HyperText Transfer Protocol.

hub   A Physical layer device that serves as a central connection point for several network devices. A hub repeats the signals it receives on one port to all other ports.

HyperText Markup Language (HTML)   A set of codes used to format text and graphics that will be displayed in a browser. The codes define how data will be displayed.

HyperText Transfer Protocol (HTTP)   The protocol used for communication between a Web server and a Web browser.

ICMP   *See* Internet Control Message Protocol.

IEEE   *See* Institute of Electrical and Electronics Engineers, Inc.

IEEE 802.*x* standards   The IEEE standards for LAN and MAN networking.

IEEE 802.1 LAN/MAN Management   Standard that specifies LAN/MAN network management and internetworking.

IEEE 802.2 Logical Link Control   Standard that specifies the operation of the Logical Link Control (LLC) sublayer of the Data Link layer of the OSI model. The LLC sublayer provides an interface between the MAC sublayer and the network layer. *See also* media access control, Open Systems Interconnect.

IEEE 802.3 CSMA/CD Networking   Standard that specifies a network that uses a logical bus topology, baseband signaling, and a CSMA/CD network access method. *See also* Carrier Sense Multiple Access/Collision Detection.

IEEE 802.4 Token Bus   Standard that specifies a physical and logical bus topology that uses coaxial or fiber-optic cable and the token-passing media access method.

IEEE 802.5 Token Ring   Specifies a logical ring, physical star, and token-passing media access method based on IBM's Token Ring.

IEEE 802.6 Distributed Queue Dual Bus (DQDB) Metropolitan Area Network   Provides a definition and criteria for a DQDB Metropolitan Area Network (MAN).

IEEE 802.7 Broadband Local Area Networks Standard for broadband cabling technology.

IEEE 802.8 Fiber-Optic LANs and MANs A standard containing guidelines for the use of fiber optics on networks, which includes FDDI and Ethernet over fiber-optic cable. *See also* Ethernet, Fiber Distributed Data Interface.

IEEE 802.9 Integrated Services (IS) LAN Interface A standard containing guidelines for the integration of voice and data over the same cable.

IEEE 802.10 LAN/MAN Security A series of guidelines dealing with various aspects of network security.

IEEE 802.11 Wireless LAN Defines standards for implementing wireless technologies such as infrared and spread-spectrum radio.

IEEE 802.12 Demand Priority Access Method Defines a standard that combines the concepts of Ethernet and ATM. *See also* Asynchronous Transfer Mode, Ethernet.

IETF *See* Internet Engineering Task Force.

Institute of Electrical and Electronics Engineers, Inc. (IEEE) An international organization that sets standards for various electrical and electronics issues.

Integrated Switched Digital Network (ISDN) A telecommunications standard that is used to digitally send voice, data, and video signals over the same lines.

intelligent hub An intelligent hub is a hub that can make some intelligent decisions about network traffic flow and can provide network traffic statistics to network administrators.

internal modem A modem that is a regular PC card that is inserted into the bus slot. These modems are inside the PC.

International Organization for Standardization (ISO) The standards organization that developed the OSI model. This model provides a guideline for how communications occur between computers.

Internet   A global network made up of a large number of individual networks interconnected through the use of public telephone lines and TCP/IP protocols. *See also* Transmission Control Protocol/Internet Protocol.

Internet Architecture Board (IAB)   The committee that oversees management of the Internet. It is made up of two subcommittees: the Internet Engineering Task Force (IETF) and the Internet Research Task Force (IRTF). *See also* Internet Engineering Task Force, Internet Research Task Force.

Internet Control Message Protocol (ICMP)   A message and management protocol for TCP/IP. The Ping utility uses ICMP. *See also* Ping, Transmission Control Protocol/Internet Protocol.

Internet Engineering Task Force (IETF)   An international organization that works under the Internet Architecture Board to establish standards and protocols relating to the Internet. *See also* Internet Architecture Board.

Internet Protocol (IP)   The protocol in the TCP/IP protocol suite responsible for network addressing and routing. *See also* Transmission Control Protocol/Internet Protocol.

Internet Research Task Force (IRTF)   An international organization that works under the Internet Architecture Board to research new Internet technologies. *See also* Internet Architecture Board.

Internet Service Provider (ISP)   A company that provides direct access to the Internet for home and business computer users.

Internetwork   A network that is internal to a company and is private.

Internetwork Packet eXchange (IPX)   A connectionless, routable network protocol based on the Xerox XNS architecture. It is the default protocol for versions of NetWare before NetWare 5. It operates at the Network layer of the OSI model and is responsible for addressing and routing packets to workstations or servers on other networks. *See also* Open Systems Interconnect.

inverse multiplexing   The network technology that allows one signal to be split across multiple transmission lines at the transmission source and combined at the receiving end.

IP   *See* Internet Protocol.

IP address   An address used by the Internet Protocol that identifies the device's location on the network.

IP proxy   All communications look as if they originated from a proxy server because the IP address of the user making a request is hidden. Also known as network address translation (NAT).

IP spoofing   A hacker trying to gain access to a network by pretending his or her machine has the same network address as the internal network.

ipconfig   A Windows NT utility used to display that machine's current configuration.

IPX   *See* Internetwork Packet eXchange.

IPX network address   A number that represents an entire network. All servers on the network must use the same external network number.

ISDN   *See* Integrated Switched Digital Network.

ISDN terminal adapter   The device used on ISDN networks to connect a local network (or single machine) to an ISDN network. It provides power to the line as well as translates data from the LAN or individual computer for transmission on the ISDN line. *See also* Integrated Switched Digital Network.

ISP   *See* Internet Service Provider.

Java   A programming language, developed by Sun Microsystems, that is used to write programs that will run on any platform that has a Java Virtual Machine installed.

Java Virtual Machine (JVM)   Software, developed by Sun Microsystems, that creates a virtual Java computer on which Java programs can run. A programmer writes a program once without having to recompile or rewrite the program for all platforms.

jumper   A small connector (cap or plug) that connects pins. This creates a circuit that indicates a setting to a device.

JVM   *See* Java Virtual Machine.

kernel   The core component of any operating system that handles the functions of memory management, hardware interaction, and program execution.

key   A folder in Windows Registry that contains subkeys and values, or a value with an algorithm to encrypt and decrypt data.

LAN   *See* local area network.

LAN driver   The interface between the NetWare kernel and the NIC installed in the server. Also a general category of drivers used to enable communications between an operating system and a NIC. *See also* network interface card.

Large Internet Packet (LIP)   A technology used by the IPX protocol so that IPX can use the largest possible packet size during a transmission. *See also* Internetwork Packet eXchange.

laser printer   A printer that uses a laser to form an image on a photosensitive drum. The image is then developed with toner and transferred to paper. Finally, a heated drum fuses toner particles onto the paper.

Layer 2 switch   A switching hub that operates at the Data Link layer and builds a table of the MAC addresses of all the connected stations. *See also* media access control.

Layer 3 switch   Functioning at the Network layer, a switch that performs the multiport, virtual LAN, data pipelining functions of a standard Layer 2 switch, but it can perform basic routing functions between virtual LANs.

LCP   *See* Link Control Protocol.

line conditioner   A device used to protect against power surges and spikes. Line conditioners use several electronic methods to clean all power coming into the line conditioner.

line noise   Any extraneous signal on a power line that is not part of the power feed.

line voltage   The voltage supplied from the power company that comes out at the outlets.

Link Control Protocol (LCP)   The protocol used to establish, configure, and test the link between a client and PPP host. *See also* Point-to-Point Protocol.

link light   A small light-emitting diode (LED) that is found on both the NIC and the hub. It is usually green and labeled Link or something similar. A link light indicates that the NIC and the hub are making a Data Link layer connection. *See also* hub, network interface card.

link state route discovery   A route discovery method that transmits special packets (Link State Packets, or LSPs) that contain information about the networks to which the router is connected.

link state routing   A type of routing that broadcasts its entire routing tables only at startup and possibly at infrequently scheduled intervals. Aside from that, the router only sends messages to other routers when changes are made to the router's routing table.

Link Support Layer (LSL)   Part of the Novell client software that acts as sort of a switchboard between the Open Datalink Interface (ODI) LAN drivers and the various transport protocols.

Linux   A version of Unix, developed by Linus Torvalds. Runs on Intel-based PCs and is generally free. *See also* Unix.

LIP   *See* Large Internet Packet.

local area network (LAN)   A network that is restricted to a single building, group of buildings, or even a single room. A LAN can have one or more servers.

local groups   Groups created on individual servers. Rights can be assigned only to local resources.

local loop   The part of the PSTN that goes from the central office to the demarcation point at the customer's premises. *See also* central office, demarcation point, Public Switched Telephone Network.

log file   A file that keeps a running list of all errors and notices, the time and date they occurred, and any other pertinent information.

logical network addressing   The addressing scheme used by protocols at the Network layer.

logical parallel port   Port used by the CAPTURE command to redirect a workstation printer port to a network print queue. The logical port has no relation to the port to which the printer is actually attached, or the physical port. *See also* physical parallel port.

logical port address   A value that is used at the Transport layer to differentiate between the upper layer services.

logical bus topology   Type of topology in which the signal travels the distance of the cable and is received by all stations on the backbone. *See also* backbone.

logical link control (LLC)   A sublayer of the Data Link layer. Provides an interface between the MAC sublayer and the Network layer. *See also* media access control, topology.

logical ring topology   A network topology in which all network signals travel from one station to another, being read and forwarded by each station.

logical topology   Describes the way the information flows. The types of logical topologies are the same as the physical topologies, except that the flow of information, rather than the physical arrangement, specifies the type of topology.

LSL   *See* Link Support Layer.

MAC   *See* media access control.

MAC address   The address that is either assigned to a network card or burned into the NIC. This is how PCs keep track of one another and keep each other separate.

MAU   *See* Multistation Access Unit.

mail exchanger (MX) record   A DNS record type that specifies the DNS host name of the mail server for a particular domain name.

media access   The process of vying for transmission time on the network media.

media access control (MAC)   A sublayer of the Data Link layer that controls the way multiple devices use the same media channel. It controls which devices can transmit and when they can transmit.

media converter   A networking device that converts from one network media type to another. For example, converting from an AUI port to an RJ-45 connector for 10BaseT.

member server   A computer that has Windows NT server installed but doesn't have a copy of the SAM database. *See also* Security Accounts Manager.

modem   A communication device that converts digital computer signals into analog tones for transmission over the PSTN and converts them back to digital upon reception. The word "modem" is an acronym for "modulator/demodulator."

multiple server clustering   A system in which multiple servers run continuously, each providing backup and production services at the same time. (This way expensive servers are not sitting around as designated "backup" servers without being used unless an emergency arises.) If a server fails, another just takes over, without any interruption of service.

multiplexing   A technology that combines multiple signals into one signal for transmission over a slow medium. *See also* Frequency Division Multiplexing, inverse multiplexing.

Multistation Access Unit (MAU)   The central device in Token Ring networks that acts as the connection point for all stations and facilitates the formation of the ring.

N-series connector   Used with Thinnet and Thicknet cabling that is a male/female screw and barrel connector.

name resolution   The process of translating (resolving) logical host names to network addresses.

NAT   Abbreviation for network address translation. *See* IP proxy.

National Computing Security Center (NCSC)   The agency that developed the Trusted Computer System Evaluation Criteria (TCSEC) and the Trusted Network Interpretation Environmental Guideline (TNIEG).

National Security Agency (NSA)   The U.S. government agency responsible for protecting U.S. communications and producing foreign intelligence information. It was established by presidential directive in 1952 as a separately organized agency within the Department of Defense.

nbtstat (NetBIOS over TCP/IP statistics)   The Windows TCP/IP utility that is used to display NetBIOS over TCP/IP statistics. *See also* network basic input/output system, Transmission Control Protocol/Internet Protocol.

NCP   *See* NetWare Core Protocol.

NCSC   *See* National Computing Security Center.

NDPS   *See* Novell Distributed Print Services.

NDS   *See* Novell Directory Services.

NDS tree   A logical representation of a network's resources. Resources are represented by objects in the tree. The tree is often designed after a company's functional structure. Objects can represent organizations, departments, users, servers, printers, and other resources. *See also* Novell Directory Services.

nearline site   When two buildings can almost be seen from one another. Obstructions in between are few.

NetBEUI   Transport protocol based on the NetBIOS protocol that has datagram support and support for connectionless transmission. *See also* network basic input/output system.

NetBIOS   *See* network basic input/output system.

NetBIOS Extended User Interface   NetBEUI is a protocol that is native to Microsoft networks and is mainly for use by small businesses. NetBEUI is a non-routable protocol that cannot pass over a router, but does pass over a bridge since it operates at the Data Link layer.

netstat   A utility used to determine which TCP/IP connections, inbound and outbound, the computer has. It also allows the user to view packet statistics, such has how many have been sent and received. *See also* Transmission Control Protocol/Internet Protocol.

NetWare   The network operating system made by Novell.

NetWare 3.*x* The version series of NetWare that supported multiple, cross-platform clients with fairly minimal hardware requirements. It used a database called the bindery to keep track of users and groups and was administered with several DOS, menu-based utilities (such as SYSCON, PCONSOLE, and FILER).

NetWare 4.*x* The version series of NetWare that includes NDS. *See also* Novell Directory Services.

NetWare 5.*x* The version series of NetWare that includes a multiprocessing kernel. It also includes a five-user version of Oracle8, a relational database, and the ability to use TCP/IP in its pure form.

NetWare Administrator The utility used to administer NetWare versions 4.*x* and later by making changes to the NDS Directory. It is the only administrative utility needed to modify NDS objects and their properties. *See also* Novell Directory Services.

NetWare Core Protocol (NCP) The upper-layer NetWare protocol that functions on top of IPX and provides NetWare resource access to workstations. *See also* Internet Packet eXchange.

NetWare Link State Protocol (NLSP) Protocol that gathers routing information based on the link state routing method. Its precursor is the Routing Information Protocol (RIP). NLSP is a more efficient routing protocol than RIP. *See also* link state routing.

NetWare Loadable Module (NLM) A component used to provide a NetWare server with additional services and functionality. Unneeded services can be unloaded, thus conserving memory.

network address translation (NAT) *See* IP proxy.

network basic input/output system (NetBIOS) A Session layer protocol that opens communication sessions for applications that want to communicate on a network.

network-centric Refers to network operating systems that use directory services that maintain information about the entire network.

Network File System (NFS) A protocol that enables users to access files on remote computers as if the files were local.

network interface card (NIC)   Physical device that connects computers and other network equipment to the transmission medium.

Network layer   Layer three of the OSI model, which is responsible for logical addressing and translating logical names into physical addresses. This layer also controls the routing of data from source to destination as well as the building and dismantling of packets. *See also* Open Systems Interconnect.

network media   The physical cables that link computers in a network; also known as physical media.

network operating system (NOS)   The software that runs on a network server and offers file, print, application, and other services to clients.

Network Support Encyclopedia (NSEPro)   *See* Novell Support Connection.

NFS   *See* Network File System.

NIC   *See* network interface card.

NIC diagnostics   Software utilities that verify that the NIC is functioning correctly and that test every aspect of NIC operation. *See also* network interface card.

NIC driver   *See* LAN driver.

NLM   *See* NetWare Loadable Module.

NLSP   *See* NetWare Link State Protocol.

non-unicast packet   A packet that is not sent directly from one workstation to another.

NOS   *See* network operating system.

Novell Directory Services (NDS)   A NetWare service that provides access to a global, hierarchical directory database of network entities that can be centrally managed.

Novell Distributed Print Services (NDPS)   A printing system designed by Novell that uses NDS to install and manage printers. NDPS supports automatic network printer installation, automatic distribution of client printer drivers, and centralized printer management without the use of print queues.

Novell Support Connection   Novell's database of technical information documents, files, patches, fixes, NetWare Application Notes, Novell lab bulletins, Novell professional developer bulletins, answers to frequently asked questions, and more. The database is available from Novell and is updated quarterly.

NSA   *See* National Security Agency.

NT Directory Services (NTDS)   System of domains and trusts for a Windows NT Server network.

NTDS   *See* NT Directory Services.

object   The item that represents some network entity in NDS. *See also* Novell Directory Services.

octet   Refers to eight bits. One-fourth of an IP address.

ODI   *See* Open Datalink Interface.

Open Datalink Interface (ODI)   A driver specification, developed by Novell, that enables a single workstation to communicate transparently with several different protocol stacks, using a single NIC and a single NIC driver.

offline   The general name for the condition when some piece of electronic or computer equipment is unavailable or inoperable.

OpenLinux   A version of the Linux network operating system developed by Caldera.

Open Systems Interconnect (OSI)   A model defined by the ISO to categorize the process of communication between computers in terms of seven layers. *See also* International Organization for Standardization.

OSI   *See* Open Systems Interconnect.

overvoltage threshold   The level of over-voltage that will trip the circuit breaker in a surge protector.

oversampling   Method of synchronous bit synchronization in which the receiver samples the signal at a much faster rate than the data rate. This permits the use of an encoding method that does not add clocking transitions.

packet filtering   A firewall technology that accepts or rejects packets based on their content.

packet   The basic division of data sent over a network.

packet switching   The process of breaking messages into packets at the sending router for easier transmission over a WAN.

passive detection   A type of intruder detection that logs all network events to a file for an administrator to view later.

passive hub   A hub that simply makes physical and electrical connections between all connected stations. Generally speaking, these hubs are not powered.

password history   List of already used passwords.

patch   Software that fixes a problem with an existing program or operating system.

patch cable   A central wiring point for multiple devices on a UTP network. *See also* unshielded twisted-pair cable.

PDC   *See* Primary Domain Controller.

peer-to-peer network   Computers hooked together that have no centralized authority. Each computer is equal and can act as both a server and a workstation.

peripheral   Any device that can be attached to the computer to expand its capabilities.

permanent virtual circuit (PVC)   A technology used by frame relay that allows virtual data communications (circuits) to be set up between sender and receiver over a packet-switched network.

PGP   *See* Pretty Good Privacy.

physical address   *See* MAC Address.

physical bus topology   A network that uses one network cable that runs from one end of the network to the other. Workstations connect at various points along this cable.

Physical layer   The first layer of the OSI model that controls the functional interface. *See also* Open Systems Interconnect.

physical media   *See* network media.

physical mesh topology   A network configuration that specifies a link between each and every device in the network.

physical parallel port   A port on the back of a computer that allows a printer to be connected with a parallel cable.

physical port   An opening on a network device that allows a cable of some kind to be connected. Ports allow devices to be connected to each other with cables.

physical ring topology   A network topology that is set up in a circular fashion. Data travels around the ring in one direction, and each device on the ring acts as a repeater to keep the signal strong as it travels. Each device incorporates a receiver for the incoming signal and a transmitter to send the data on to the next device in the ring. The network is dependent on the ability of the signal to travel around the ring.

physical star topology   Describes a network in which a cable runs from each network entity to a central device called a hub. The hub allows all devices to communicate as if they were directly connected. *See also* hub.

physical topology   The physical layout of a network, such as bus, star, ring, or mesh.

Ping   A TCP/IP utility used to test whether another host is reachable. An ICMP request is sent to the host, who responds with a reply if it is reachable. The request times out if the host is not reachable.

Ping of Death   A large ICMP packet sent to overflow the remote host's buffer. This usually causes the remote host to reboot or hang.

Plain Old Telephone Service (POTS)   Another name for the Public Switched Telephone Network (PSTN). *See* Public Switched Telephone Network.

plenum-rated coating   Coaxial cable coating that does not produce toxic gas when burned.

point-to-point   Network communication in which two devices have exclusive access to a network medium. For example, a printer connected to only one workstation would be using a point-to-point connection.

Point-to Point Protocol (PPP)   The protocol used with dial-up connections to the Internet. Its functions include error control, security, dynamic IP addressing, and support for multiple protocols.

Point-to-Point Tunneling Protocol (PPTP)   A protocol that allows the creation of Virtual Private Networks (VPNs), which allow users to access a server on a corporate network over a secure, direct connection via the Internet. *See also* Virtual Private Network.

polling   A media access control method that uses a central device called a controller that polls each device, in turn, and asks if it has data to transmit.

POP3   *See* Post Office Protocol.

port   Some kind of opening that allows network data to pass through. *See also* physical port.

Post Office Protocol (POP3)   The protocol used to download e-mail from an SMTP e-mail server to a network client. *See also* Simple Mail Transfer Protocol.

POTS   *See* Plain Old Telephone Service.

power blackout   A total loss of power that may last for only a few seconds or as long as several hours.

power brownout   Power drops below normal levels for several seconds or longer.

power overage   Too much power is coming into the computer. *See also* power spike, power surge.

power sag   A lower power condition where the power drops below normal levels for a few seconds then returns to normal levels.

power spike   The power level rises above normal for less than a second and drops back to normal.

power surge   The power level rises above normal and stays there for longer than a second or two.

power underage   The power level drops below the standard level. *See also* power sag.

PPP   *See* Point-to-Point Protocol.

PPTP   *See* Point-to-Point Tunneling Protocol.

Presentation layer   Layer six of the OSI model; responsible for formatting data exchange such as graphic commands and conversion of character sets. Also responsible for data compression, data encryption, and data stream redirection. *See also* Open Systems Interconnect.

Pretty Good Privacy (PGP)   A shareware implementation of RSA encryption. *See also* RSA Data Security, Inc.

Primary Domain Controller   An NT server that contains a master copy of the SAM database. This database contains all usernames, passwords, and access control lists for a Windows NT domain. *See also* Security Accounts Manager.

print server   A centralized device that controls and manages all network printers. The print server can be hardware, software, or a combination of both. Some print servers are actually built into the network printer NICs. *See also* network interface card.

print services   The network services that manage and control printing on a network, allowing multiple and simultaneous access to printers.

private key   A technology in which both the sender and the receiver have the same key. A single key is used to encrypt and decrypt all messages. *See also* public key.

private network   The part of a network that lies behind a firewall and is not "seen" on the Internet. *See also* firewall.

protocol   A predefined set of rules that dictates how computers or devices communicate and exchange data on the network.

protocol analyzer   A software and hardware troubleshooting tool that is used to decode protocol information to try to determine the source of a network problem and to establish baselines.

proxy   A type of firewall that prevents direct communication between a client and a host by acting as an intermediary. *See also* firewall.

proxy cache server   An implementation of a Web proxy. The server receives an HTTP request from a Web browser and makes the request on behalf of the sending workstation. When the response comes, the proxy cache server caches a copy of the response locally. The next time someone makes a request for the same Web page or Internet information, the proxy cache server can fulfill the request out of the cache instead of having to retrieve the resource from the Web.

proxy server   A type of server that makes a single Internet connection and services requests on behalf of many users.

PSTN   *See* Public Switched Telephone Network.

Public   For use by everyone.

public key   A technology that uses two keys to facilitate communication, a public key and a private key. The public key is used to encrypt a message to a receiver. *See also* private key.

public network   The part of a network on the outside of a firewall that is exposed to the public. *See also* firewall.

Public Switched Telephone Network (PSTN)   This is the U.S. public telephone network. It is also called the Plain Old Telephone Service (POTS).

PVC   *See* permanent virtual circuit.

QoS   See Quality of Service.

quad decimal   Four sets of octets separated by a decimal point; an IP address.

Quality of Service (QoS)   Data prioritization at the Network layer of the OSI model. Results in guaranteed throughput rates. *See also* Open Systems Interconnect.

radio frequency interference (RFI)   Interference on copper cabling systems caused by radio frequencies.

RAID   *See* redundant array of independent (or inexpensive) disks.

README file   A file that the manufacturer includes with software to give the installer information that was too late to make it into the software manuals. It's usually a last-minute addition that includes tips on installing the software, possible incompatibilities, and any known installation problems that might have been found right before the product was shipped.

reduced instruction set computing (RISC)   Computer architecture in which the computer executes small, general-purpose instructions very rapidly.

redundant array of independent (or inexpensive) disks (RAID)   A configuration of multiple hard disks used to provide fault tolerance should a disk fail. Different levels of RAID exist, depending on the amount and type of fault tolerance provided.

regeneration process   Process in which signals are read, amplified, and repeated on the network to reduce signal degradation, which results in longer overall possible length of the network.

remote access protocol   Any networking protocol that is used to gain access to a network over public communication links.

remote access server   A computer that has one or more modems installed to enable remote connections to the network.

repeater   A physical layer device that amplifies the signals it receives on one port and resends or repeats them on another. A repeater is used to extend the maximum length of a network segment.

replication   The process of copying directory information to other servers to keep them all synchronized.

RFI   *See* radio frequency interference.

RG-58   The type designation for the coaxial cable used in thin Ethernet (10Base2). It has a 50ohm impedance rating and uses BNC connectors.

RG-62   The type designation for the coaxial cable used in ARCNet networks. It has a 93ohm impedance and uses BNC connectors.

RIP   *See* Router Information Protocol.

RISC   *See* reduced instruction set computing.

RJ-connector   A modular connection mechanism that allows for as many as eight copper wires (four pairs). Commonly found in phone (RJ-11) or 10BaseT (RJ-45) connections.

roaming profiles   Profiles downloaded from a server at each login. When a user logs out at the end of the session, changes are made and remembered for the next time the user logs in.

Route   The path to get to the destination from a source.

route cost   How many router hops there are between source and destination in an internetwork. *See also* hop, router.

router   A device that connects two networks and allows packets to be transmitted and received between them. A router determines the best path for data packets from source to destination.

Router Information Protocol (RIP)   A distance-vector route discovery protocol used by IPX. It uses hops and ticks to determine the cost for a particular route. *See also* Internet Packet eXchange.

routing   A function of the Network layer that involves moving data throughout a network. Data passes through several network segments using routers that can select the path the data takes. *See also* router.

routing table   A table that contains information about the locations of other routers on the network and their distance from the current router.

RSA Data Security, Inc. A commercial company that produces encryption software. RSA stands for Rivest, Shamir, Adleman, the founders of the company.

sag *See* power sag

SAM *See* Security Accounts Manager.

Secure HyperText Transfer Protocol (S-HTTP) A protocol used for secure communications between a Web server and a Web browser.

Security Accounts Manager (SAM) A database within Windows NT that contains information about all the users and groups and their associated rights and settings within a Windows NT domain.

Security log Log file used in Windows NT to keep track of security events specified by the domain's Audit Policy.

security policy Rules set in place by a company to ensure the security of a network. This may include how often a password must be changed or how long a password should be.

segment A unit of data smaller than a packet. Also refers to a portion of a larger network (a network can consist of multiple network segments).

self-powered A device that has its own power.

sequence number A number used to determine the order in which parts of a packet are to be reassembled after the packet has been split into sections.

Sequenced Packet eXchange (SPX) A connection-oriented protocol that is part of the IPX protocol suite. It operates at the Transport layer of the OSI model. It initiates the connection between the sender and receiver, transmits the data, and then terminates the connection. *See also* Internet Packet eXchange, Open Systems Interconnect.

Serial Line Internet Protocol (SLIP) A protocol that permits the sending of IP packets over a serial connection.

server A computer that provides resources to the clients on the network.

server and client configuation A network in which the resources are located on a server for use by the clients.

server-centric   A network design model that uses a central server to contain all data as well as control security.

service accounts   Accounts created on a server for users to perform special services, such as backup operators, account operators, and server operators.

Session layer   Layer five of the OSI model, which determines how two computers establish, use, and end a session. Security authentication and network naming functions required for applications occur here. The Session layer establishes, maintains, and breaks dialogs between two stations. *See also* Open Systems Interconnect.

share-level security   In a network that uses share-level security, instead of assigning rights to network resources to users, passwords are assigned to individual files or other network resources (such as printers). These passwords are then given to all users that need access to these resources. All resources are visible from anywhere in the network, and any user who knows the password for a particular network resource can make changes to it.

shell   Unix interfaces that are based solely upon command prompts. There is no graphical interface.

shielded   When cabling has extra protection of wrapping to protect it from stray electrical or radio signals. Shielded cabling is more expensive than unshielded.

shielded twisted-pair cable (STP)   A type of cabling that includes pairs of copper conductors, twisted around each other, inside a metal or foil shield. This type of medium can support faster speeds than nonshielded wiring.

S-HTTP   *See* Secure HyperText Transfer Protocol.

signal   Transmission from one PC to another. This could be a notification to start a session or end a session.

signal encoding   The process whereby a protocol at the Physical layer receives information from the upper layers and translates all the data into signals that can be transmitted on a transmission medium.

signaling method   The process of transmitting data across the medium. Two types of signaling are digital and analog.

Simple Mail Transfer Protocol (SMTP)   A program that looks for mail on SMTP servers and sends it along the network to its destination at another SMTP server.

Simple Network Management Protocol (SNMP)   The management protocol created for sending information about the health of the network to network management consoles.

skipjack   An encryption algorithm developed as a possible replacement for Data Encryption Standard (DES) that is classified by the National Security Agency (NSA). Not much is known about this encryption algorithm except that it uses an 80-bit key.

SLIP   *See* Serial Line Internet Protocol.

SMTP   *See* Simple Mail Transfer Protocol.

SNMP   *See* Simple Network Management Protocol.

socket   A combination of a port address and an IP address.

source address   The address of the station that sent a packet, usually found in the source area of a packet header.

source port number   The address of the PC that is sending data to a receiving PC. The port portion allows for multiplexing of data to be sent from a specific application.

splitter   Any device that electrically duplicates one signal into two.

SPS   *See* Standby Power Supply.

SPX   *See* Sequenced Packet eXchange.

Standby Power Supply (SPS)   A power backup device that has power going directly to the protected equipment. A sensor monitors the power. When a loss is detected, the computer is switched over to the battery. Thus, a loss of power might occur (typically for less than a second).

state table   A firewall security method that monitors the states of all connections through the firewall.

static ARP table entries   Entry in the ARP table that is manually added by a user when a PC will be accessed often. This will speed up the process of communicating with the PC since the IP to MAC address will not have to be resolved.

static routing   A method of routing packets where the router's routing is updated manually by the network administrator instead of automatically by a route discovery protocol.

subnet mask   A group of selected bits that identify a subnetwork within a TCP/IP network. *See also* Transmission Control Protocol/Internet Protocol.

subnetting   The process of dividing a single IP address range into multiple address ranges.

subnetwork   A network that is part of another network. The connection is made through a gateway, bridge, or router.

supernetting   The process of combining multiple IP address ranges into a single IP network.

surge protector   A device that contains a special electronic circuit that monitors the incoming voltage level and then trips a circuit breaker when an over-voltage reaches a certain level called the over-voltage threshold.

surge suppressors   *See* surge protector.

switched   A network that has multiple routes to get from a source to a destination. This allows for higher speeds.

symmetrical keys   When the same key is used to encrypt and decrypt data.

SYN flood   A Denial of Service attack in which the hacker sends a barrage of SYN packets. The receiving station tries to respond to each SYN request for a connection, thereby tying up all the resources. All incoming connections are rejected until all current connections can be established.

TCP   *See* Transmission Control Protocol.

TCP/IP   *See* Transmission Control Protocol/Internet Protocol.

TDMA   *See* Time Division Multiple Access.

TDR   *See* time-domain reflectometer.

telephony server A computer that functions as a smart answering machine for the network. It can also perform call center and call routing functions.

Telnet A protocol that functions at the Application layer of the OSI model, providing terminal emulation capabilities. *See also* Open Systems Interconnect.

template A set of guidelines that you can apply to every new user account created.

terminal emulator A program that enables a PC to act as a terminal for a mainframe or a Unix system.

terminator A device that prevents a signal from bouncing off the end of the network cable, which would cause interference with other signals.

test accounts An account set up by an administrator to confirm the basic functionality of a newly installed application, for example. The test account has equal rights to accounts that will use the new functionality. It is important to use test accounts instead of administrator accounts to test new functionality. If an administrator account is used, problems related to user rights may not manifest themselves because administrator accounts typically have full rights to all network resources.

TFTP *See* Trivial File Transfer Protocol.

Thick Ethernet A type of Ethernet that uses thick coaxial cable and supports a maximum transmissions distance of 500 meters.

Time Division Multiple Access (TDMA) A method to divide individual channels in broadband communications into separate time slots, allowing more data to be carried at the same time. It is also possible to use TDMA in baseband communications.

time-domain reflectometer (TDR) A tool, also called a cable tester, that sends out a signal and measures how much time it takes to return. It is used to find short or open circuits.

time to live (TTL) A field in IP packets that indicates how many routers the packet can still cross (hops it can still make) before it is discarded. TTL is also used in ARP tables to indicate how long an entry should remain in the table.

token   The special packet of data that is passed around the network in a Token Ring network. *See* Token Ring network.

token passing   A media access method in which a token (data packet) is passed around the ring in an orderly fashion from one device to the next. A station can transmit only when it has the token. If it doesn't have the token, it can't transmit. The token continues around the network until the original sender receives the token again. If the token has more data to send, the process repeats. If not, the original sender modifies the token to indicate that the token is free for anyone else to use.

Token Ring network   A network based on a physical star, logical ring topology, in which data is passed along the ring until it finds its intended receiver. Only one data packet can be passed along the ring at a time. If the data packet goes around the ring without being claimed, it is returned to the sender.

tone generator   A small electronic device used to test network cables for breaks and other problems that sends an electronic signal down one set of UTP wires. Used with a tone locator. *See also* tone locator, unshielded twisted-pair cable.

tone locator   A device used to test network cables for breaks and other problems; designed to sense the signal sent by the tone generator and emit a tone when the signal is detected in a particular set of wires.

topology   The physical and/or logical layout of the transmission media specified in the physical and logical layers of the OSI model. *See also* Open Systems Interconnect.

Trace Route   *See* tracert.

tracert   The TCP/IP trace route command line utility that shows the user every router interface a TCP/IP packet passes through on its way to a destination. *See also* Transmission Control Protocol/Internet Protocol.

trailer   A section of a data packet that contains error-checking information.

transceiver   The part of any network interface that transmits and receives network signals.

transient   A high-voltage burst of current.

transmission   Sending of packets from the PC to the network cable.

Transmission Control Protocol (TCP)   The protocol found at the Host-to-Host layer of the DOD model. This protocol breaks data packets into segments, numbers them, and sends them in random order. The receiving computer reassembles the data so that the information is readable for the user. In the process, the sender and the receiver confirm that all data has been received; if not, it is resent. This is a connection-oriented protocol.

Transmission Control Protocol/Internet Protocol (TCP/IP)   The protocol suite developed by the DOD in conjunction with the Internet. It was designed as an internetworking protocol suite that could route information around network failures. Today it is the de facto standard for communications on the Internet.

transmission media   Physical cables and/or wireless technology across which computers are able to communicate.

Transport layer   Layer four of the OSI model, which is responsible for checking that the data packet created in the Session layer was received error free. If necessary, it also changes the length of messages for transport up or down the remaining layers. *See also* Open Systems Interconnect.

Trivial File Transfer Protocol (TFTP)   A protocol similar to FTP that does not provide the security features of FTP. *See also* File Transfer Protocol.

trunk lines   The telephone lines that form the backbone of a telephone network for a company. These lines connect the telephone(s) to the telephone company and to the PSTN. *See also* Public Switched Telephone Network.

T-series connections   A series of digital connections leased from the telephone company. Each T-series connection is rated with a number based on speed. T-1 and T-3 are the most popular.

TTL   *See* time to live.

twisted-pair cable   A type of network transmission medium that contains pairs of color-coded, insulated copper wires that are twisted around each other. A twisted-pair cable consists of one or more twisted pairs in a common jacket.

type A DOS command that displays the contents of a file. Also, short for *data type.*

UDP *See* User Datagram Protocol.

Uniform Resource Locator (URL) A URL is one way of identifying a document on the Internet. It consists of the protocol that is used to access the document and the domain name or IP address of the host that holds the document, for example, `http://www.sybex.com`.

uninterruptible power supply (UPS) A natural line conditioner that uses a battery and power inverter to run the computer equipment that plugs into it. The battery charger continuously charges the battery. The battery charger is the only thing that runs off line voltage. During a power problem, the battery charger stops operating, and the equipment continues to run off the battery.

Unix A 32-bit, multitasking operating system developed in the 1960s for use on mainframes and minicomputers.

unshielded When cabling has little protection of wrapping to protect it from stray electrical or radio signals. Unshielded cabling is less expensive than shielded.

unshielded twisted-pair cable Twisted-pair cable consisting of a number of twisted pairs of copper wire with a simple plastic casing. Because no shielding is used in this cable, it is very susceptible to EMI, RFI, and other types of interference. *See also* electromagnetic interference, radio frequency interference.

upgrade To increase an aspect of a PC, for example, by upgrading the RAM (increasing the RAM), upgrading the CPU (changing the current CPU for a faster CPU), etc.

UPS *See* uninterruptible power supply.

uptime The amount of time a particular computer or network component has been functional.

URL *See* Uniform Resource Locator.

user The person using a computer or network.

User Datagram Protocol (UDP)   Protocol at the Host-to-Host layer of the DOD model, which corresponds to the Transport layer of the OSI model. Packets are divided into segments, given numbers, sent randomly, and put back together at the receiving end. This is a connectionless protocol. *See also* connectionless protocol, Open Systems Interconnect.

user-level security   A type of network in which user accounts can read, write, change, and take ownership of files. Rights are assigned to user accounts, and each user knows only his or her own username and password, which makes this the preferred method for securing files.

virtual COM   Serial port that is used as if it were a serial port, but the actual serial port interface does not exist.

Virtual Private Network (VPN)   Using the public Internet as a backbone for a private interconnection (network) between locations.

virus   A program intended to damage a computer system. Sophisticated viruses encrypt and hide in a computer and may not appear until the user performs a certain action or until a certain date. *See also* antivirus.

virus engine   The core program that runs the virus-scanning process.

volume   Loudness of a sound, or the portion of a hard disk that functions as if it were a separate hard disk.

VPN   *See* Virtual Private Network.

WAN   *See* wide area network.

Web proxy   A type of proxy that is used to act on behalf of a Web client or Web server.

Web server   A server that holds and delivers Web pages and other Web content using the HTTP protocol. *See also* HyperText Transfer Protocol.

wide area network (WAN)   A network that crosses local, regional, and international boundaries.

WinNuke   A Windows-based attack that affects only computers running Windows NT 3.51 or 4. It is caused by the way that the Windows NT TCP/IP stack handles bad data in the TCP header. Instead of returning an error code or rejecting the bad data, it sends NT to the Blue Screen of Death (BSOD). Figuratively speaking, the attack nukes the computer.

Windows Internet Name Service (WINS)   A Windows NT service that dynamically associates the NetBIOS name of a host with a domain name. *See also* network basic input/output system.

Windows NT   A network operating system, developed by Microsoft, that uses that same graphical interface as the desktop environment, Windows 95.

Windows NT 3.51   The version of Windows NT based on the "look and feel" of Windows 3.*x*. *See also* Windows NT.

Windows NT 4   The version of Windows NT based on the "look and feel" of Windows 95/98. *See also* Windows NT.

Windows NT Service   A type of Windows program (a file with either an EXE or a DLL extension) that is loaded automatically by the server or manually by the administrator.

winipcfg   The IP configuration utility for Windows 95/98 that allows you to view the current TCP/IP configuration of a workstation.

WINS   *See* Windows Internet Name Service.

workgroup   A specific group of users or network devices, organized by job function or proximity to shared resources.

World Wide Web (WWW)   A collection of HTTP servers running on the Internet. They support the use of documents formatted with HTML. *See also* HyperText Markup Language, HyperText Transfer Protocol.

worms   Similar to a virus. Worms, however, propagate themselves over a network. *See also* virus.

WWW   *See* World Wide Web.

X Window   A graphical user interface (GUI) developed for use with the various flavors of Unix.

Index

Note to the Reader: Throughout this index **boldfaced** page numbers indicate primary discussions of a topic. *Italicized* page numbers indicate illustrations.

E

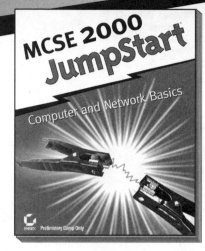
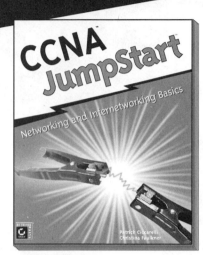

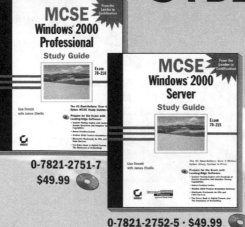
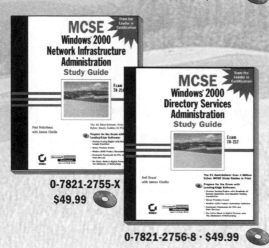

The Best Network+ Book/CD Package on the Market

Get ready for CompTIA's Network+ exam with the most comprehensive and challenging sample tests anywhere!

The Sybex EdgeTests feature:

- Chapter-by-chapter exam coverage of all the review questions from the book
- Random tests that simulate the exam format from CompTIA
- A bonus exam available only on the CD

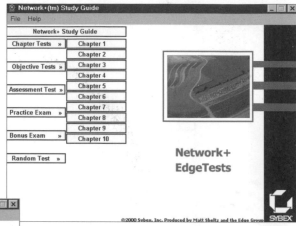

Use the Electronic Flashcards to jog your memory and prep last-minute for the exam!

- Reinforce your understanding of key Network+ exam concepts with more than 100 hardcore flashcard-style questions.

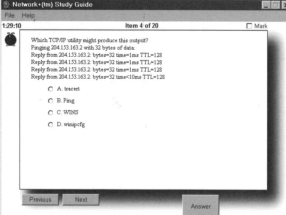

Electronic Flashcards now available for your Palm device as well!

- Download the Flashcards to your Palm device and go on the road. Now you can study for the Network+ exam anywhere, any time.

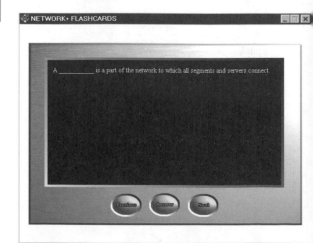